WORLD WAR II AND THE CARIBBEAN

WORLD WAR II AND THE CARIBBEAN

EDITED BY

KAREN E. ECCLES AND DEBBIE McCOLLIN

THE UNIVERSITY OF THE WEST INDIES PRESS
Jamaica • Barbados • Trinidad and Tobago

The University of the West Indies Press
7A Gibraltar Hall Road, Mona
Kingston 7, Jamaica
www.uwipress.com

© Karen E. Eccles and Debbie McCollin, 2017
All rights reserved. Published 2017

A catalogue record of this book is available
from the National Library of Jamaica.

ISBN: 978-976-640-624-0 (print)
      978-976-640-625-7 (Kindle)
      978-976-640-626-4 (ePub)

Cover photograph: Combatant units of the South Caribbean Force on parade in Port of Spain, Trinidad. Courtesy the National Archives of Trinidad and Tobago.

Set in Scala 10.25/14.5 x 24

Book and cover design by Robert Harris
Printed in the United States of America

CONTENTS

Foreword vii
BRIDGET BRERETON

Acknowledgements xi

Introduction 1
KAREN E. ECCLES AND DEBBIE McCOLLIN

PART 1. BLOCKADE AND TRADE

1. A Dance with Death: Labour Problems and the Sugar Crisis of World War II in Trinidad 17
   LOVELL FRANCIS

2. The Puerto Rico and the Caribbean Sea Frontier during the Nazi U-Boat Campaign of 1941–1943 39
   GEOFF BURROWS

3. Inversing Dependence: The Dutch Antilles, Suriname and the Desperate Netherlands during World War II 71
   ESTHER CAPTAIN AND GUNO JONES

4. War, Food and Security: Feeding Trinidad and Tobago in Wartime, 1939–1945 92
   RITA PEMBERTON

PART 2. IMPERIALISM AND INTERVENTIONISM

5. The French Caribbean in World War II: Upheavals, Repression and Resistance 125
   ERIC T. JENNINGS

6. St Lucia and the "Time of the Americans" 151
JOLIEN HARMSEN, GUY ELLIS AND ROBERT DEVAUX

7. The Exchange: Imperialism and the Impact of World War II on Trinidad and Tobago 176
RONALD WILLIAMS

8. World War II and Antigua's Sugar Industry 204
GELIEN MATTHEWS

9. Body Politics of Puerto Rican Participation in the US Military during World War II 221
DANNELLE GUTARRA

PART 3. ENGAGEMENT AND DISPLACEMENT

10. European Refugees in the Wider Caribbean in the Context of World War II 247
CHRISTIAN CWIK AND VERENA MUTH

11. Jamaica: Fixed-Term Haven and Holding Tank during World War II 273
SUZANNE FRANCIS-BROWN

12. Bodies in Conflict: Policing Sexual Liaisons in Jamaica during World War II 303
DALEA BEAN

13. Ravages and Rejuvenation: World War II and Public Health in the British Caribbean 327
DEBBIE McCOLLIN

14. Volunteerism during World War II: Trinidadian Women Mobilize in Time of War 357
KAREN E. ECCLES

Selected Bibliography 381
Index 391
Contributors 399

FOREWORD

"Humble as we in Trinidad are in the sphere of the world, we nevertheless must pray fervently that the tide of war carries the Allies to victory", wrote the editor of the *People*, a left-wing, pro-labour weekly in the British colony of Trinidad and Tobago soon after the surrender of France, when Britain stood virtually alone against the Axis powers. But a few months later, he insisted that Britain should make her war aims clear, especially in relation to India and the colonies: "a bold and clear-cut statement of war aims intended to bring about the democratisation of the Empire. . . . We cannot continue to fight for freedom and democracy while not enjoying the fullest benefits." These editorials probably reflected the general viewpoint of "progressive" men and women in the British Caribbean at the time, and in the region's French, Dutch and American colonies. But while World War II was a universal catastrophe, which caused broadly similar difficulties throughout the region, comparative analysis reveals unique and individual experiences.

These experiences are explored in this valuable collection. While nine chapters deal with the British Caribbean – four on Trinidad and Tobago (where the editors are based), two on Jamaica, one each on Antigua and St Lucia and one on public health in the subregion – there are also pieces on the Dutch colonies, the French Antilles and Puerto Rico (two), and one on German prisoners of war coming to the Caribbean. (It is especially useful to have English-language chapters on the Dutch and French Antilles, and on the German prisoners of war, particularly since they all summarize a great deal of literature and primary sources in French, Dutch and German.)

Some common themes emerge from these essays, which are mostly concerned with the unique and particular ways in which the war affected the different colonial territories (there are no chapters specifically on the three independent countries, Cuba, the Dominican Republic and Haiti). One is scarcity: the severe shortages of all imported commodities, but especially food staples, caused by the disruption of shipping and largely by the brilliantly successful German U-boat campaign in the Caribbean throughout 1942.

By coincidence, just before writing this foreword, I read the little known novel *Liana* by the American journalist, writer and war correspondent Martha Gellhorn, originally published in 1944. It emerged, she tells us in an "afterword" to the 1987 edition, from a "lunatic journey" through the Caribbean she made in 1942 with her then husband, Ernest Hemingway. It is set on a small fictional French Caribbean island, probably modelled on Marie-Galante, during 1942–43. And food shortages, the possibility of outright starvation for the people of a small island remote even from Guadeloupe, of which it was a dependency, loom large in the novel. The protagonist/villain Marc Royer, the richest man on the island, takes matters into his own hands towards the end of the book, bullying his fellow sugar planters into making over most of their cane lands to food production, organizing distribution networks, setting compulsory price limits for milk, charcoal and vegetables, and generally getting ready for a period of enforced self-sufficiency. Similar measures, though usually by the colonial authorities rather than by an individual notable, were taken throughout the colonial Caribbean during the war to deal with severe food shortages, as several of the chapters reveal; yet the hardships were real, and the poor were, as ever, especially vulnerable.

Another theme common to many of the chapters is the movement of people within and to the region caused by the war. Many thousands of British and, especially, American servicemen were stationed in the islands with major Allied bases, including Trinidad, St Lucia, Antigua and Puerto Rico. The consequences of this influx are dealt with in several of the chapters here. Civilians flocked to the base islands, especially Trinidad and Puerto Rico, in search of jobs; others went to the Dutch colonies of Aruba and Curaçao to work in the large oil refineries there. Refugees from Europe, evacuees from Gibraltar, survivors from sunken ships, and prisoners of war, especially German and Italian merchant seamen, ended up in various Caribbean colonies, some for the duration of the war. And French Antilleans, stuck in Vichy-ruled Martinique and Guadeloupe after July 1940, went in their hundreds to nearby St Lucia and Dominica, both British colonies, hoping to get to Europe to fight with the Free French forces. Again, the protagonist/hero of *Liana*,

Pierre Vauclain, makes the dangerous night-time journey from the fictional French island, in a small, rickety dinghy, to Dominica in order to fight for *la patrie* in Europe.

Though the islands did not see direct combat, unlike, say, the islands of the Mediterranean, the dangers and horrors of war were brought home to their inhabitants especially by the unrestricted German U-boat rampage of 1942. Several of the chapters discuss the human consequences for the region of this period. Despite the human costs, and the dire shortages of essential food and other commodities, the war brought some benefits to the islanders: tangibly, in improvements in the public health systems of the British colonies, intangibly, in new ideas about identity, nationalism and the right to self-determination at the war's end. War is always an essentially masculine business, but the region's women were swept into its path; some servicing the American and British troops stationed on the Allied bases in time-honoured fashion – and being policed, harassed and blamed for the prevalence of venereal diseases among their clients – while others volunteered for myriad different kinds of war-related services and activities.

This collection gives a rich picture of the ways in which the Caribbean colonies experienced World War II, a period of turmoil, hardship and opportunities – "ravages and rejuvenation", to quote one of the chapter titles – still remembered by some of the region's older inhabitants. It makes a valuable contribution to the historiography of the twentieth-century Caribbean.

Bridget Brereton
Emerita Professor of History
The University of the West Indies, St Augustine
Trinidad and Tobago

ACKNOWLEDGEMENTS

The editors would like to extend our sincerest gratitude to those who supported and facilitated the production of this text.

We are especially grateful to Emerita Professor Bridget Brereton for her guidance throughout the editing process and for the contribution of the foreword.

We are grateful to our contributors, whose outstanding research, attention to detail and deadlines have ensured the timely production of the text.

We extend our thanks, as well, to the publishers for recognizing the value of this work and the necessity for the dissemination of knowledge about the Caribbean's role in such a conflict as World War II.

We are also indebted to the National Archives of Trinidad and Tobago and the Alma Jordan Library of the University of the West Indies for their support throughout this endeavour.

We also wish to thank our colleagues at the University of the West Indies for their encouragement and useful recommendations as we developed the text, particularly Dr Rita Pemberton for her guidance.

We would further like to express our appreciation to the many Caribbean people who served, suffered and triumphed during this war (and who shared their stories with the contributors), making this period one of the most interesting in our history.

Finally, we thank God for his inspiration, and our families and friends for their unfailing support, as this book was brought from a dream into a reality.

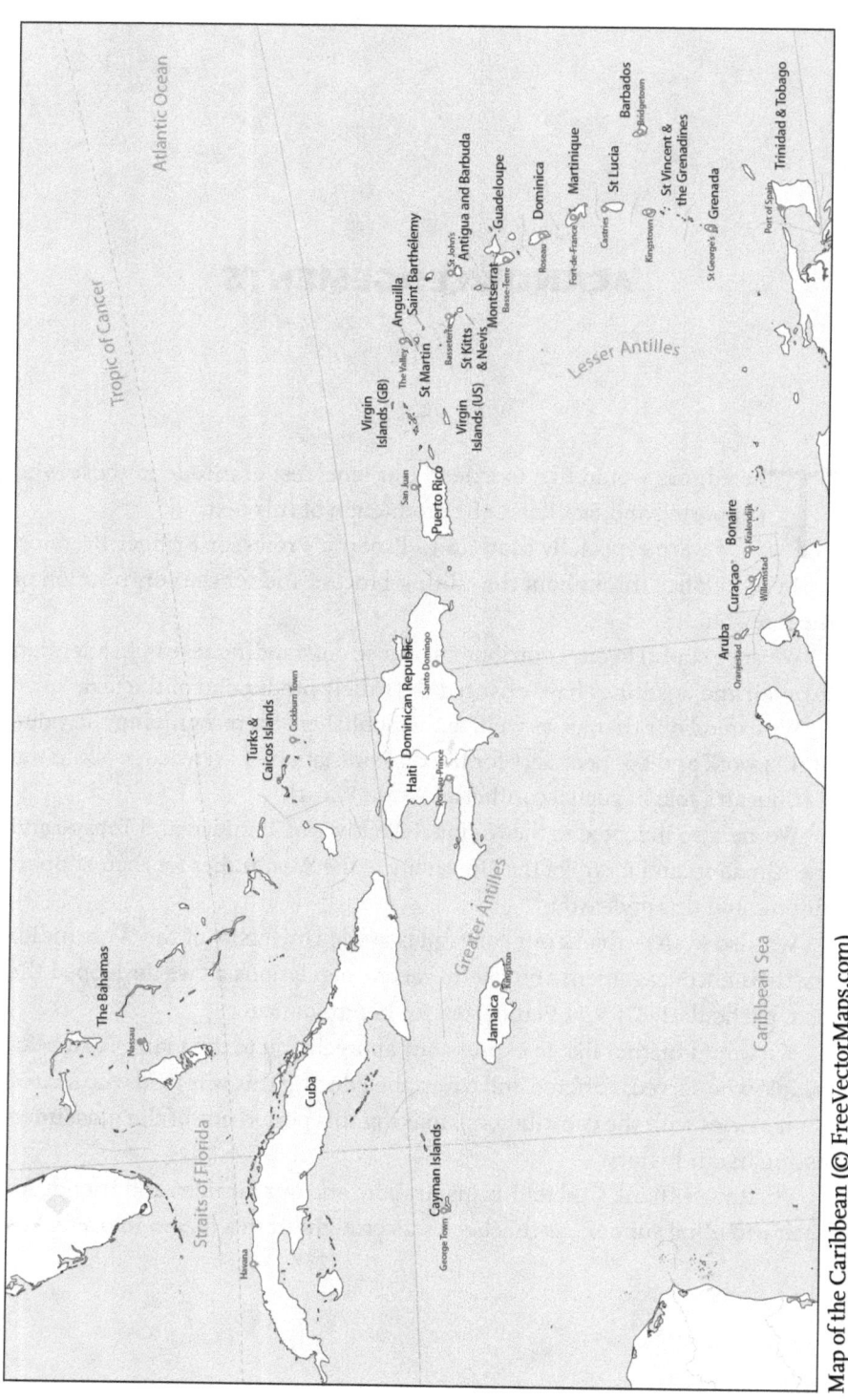

Map of the Caribbean (© FreeVectorMaps.com)

INTRODUCTION

KAREN E. ECCLES AND DEBBIE McCOLLIN

For over seventy years, the fact that World War II had a significant Caribbean dimension has been inadequately reflected in global World War II historiography. The dearth of scholarship on the topic has repeatedly stymied the development of academic programmes, publications and research and hindered the general recognition, and thus appreciation, of the role the Caribbean region played in this global conflict. During the course of other research by the editors of this book, the absence of published information on many aspects of the war and its impact on specific islands within the Caribbean region became glaring. Hence this long overdue but necessary edited work on the Caribbean during World War II was conceptualized years before the project actually began. Not only is this book an attempt to recognize the seventieth anniversary of the end of the war in 2015 and commemorate the region's soldiers and war victims, but it also attempts to highlight the contribution of many of these unique territories. Additionally, *World War II and the Caribbean* is an effort to build the body of literature on World War II studies and draw attention to the far-reaching effects of the war, adding to the global discourse on the role colonial territories played in the war. This book also pays homage to Caribbean people who remember, contributed to or had loved ones who died in the war.

It must be acknowledged, however, that over the last thirty years there have been some significant publications, foundations upon which any studies on the Caribbean in World War II must be built. Most of these treat with the Caribbean as a whole, obfuscating the uniqueness of the experiences of these very different territories, and only a few others offer specific discourses on particular islands. For the British Caribbean there has been just a handful of these publications. Fitzroy Andre Baptiste's 1988 *War, Cooperation and Conflict: The European Possessions in the Caribbean 1939–1945*[1] primarily addresses the international, political and economic environment relating to the Caribbean and measures the economic value of the region to the war effort, while Gaylord T.M. Kelshall's 1994 work, *The U-Boat War in the Caribbean*,[2] highlights the threat of submarine warfare in Caribbean waters. Both are relevant traditional approaches to history, dealing with war, politics and military tactics, but heavily neglect the social element. Claus Füllberg-Stolberg's chapter in volume 5 of the *UNESCO History of the Caribbean*,[3] edited by Bridget Brereton in 2001, again looks at the economic and strategic importance of the Caribbean. However, though he examines to an extent the social aspects of the military presence in the region, its treatment here is generally abbreviated.

Both Marika Sherwood's *Many Struggles* and Robert Murray's *Lest We Forget*, published in 1985 and 1996 respectively, explore the experiences of West Indian men while they served in Britain, while Ben Bousquet and Colin Douglas's 1991 text, *West Indian Women at War*, specifically focuses on women who served in the Auxiliary Territorial Service.[4] Though their efforts were the first to give credence to the significance of Caribbean women who served in uniform and their war-related activities, the focus is political and highlights only one aspect of Caribbean women's experiences during the war.

Produced in 2007, Harvey Neptune's *Caliban and the Yankees* is the first published text to examine specifically the economic and cultural impact of the American presence on Trinidad.[5] It, however, focuses primarily on a single territory and only one aspect of the war. In the most recent publication on the subject area, Beverly Ann Steele's *Grenada in Wartime: The Tragic Loss of the Island Queen and Other Memories of World War II* again only examines a single territory.[6]

Additionally, only a handful of publications on the French Caribbean has been published. In an autobiographical work, *Une jeunesse guadeloupéenne 1926–1946*, by Jean Belmont, who narrates his life in Guadeloupe, an account is given of his involvement in the armed forces during World War II.[7] Eric T. Jennings examines the multifaceted roles of the French Caribbean during the war, and the reaction of the Vichy government, in the article "The Best Avenue for Escape: The French Caribbean Route as Expulsion, Rescue, Trial and Encounter".[8] Additionally, Eliane Sempaire looks specifically at the resistance to the Vichy government and the term of the pro-Vichy governor Constant Sorin under such resistance in her book *La dissidence an tan Sorin (1940–1943)*.[9] In a chapter of another work on Guadeloupe, the book *Caribbean Land and Development Revisited*, Glenroy Taitt reviews the domestic food situation, including export agriculture.[10]

Admittedly, there are more works on the Spanish Caribbean than there are on the French Caribbean, although this also includes Latin American countries in South America. Additionally, quite a few articles have been published on US-Cuban relations, especially economic relations since World War II. There have also been studies on Cuban volunteers during the war, such as Denise Urcelay-Maragnès's 2008 work, *Les volontaires cubains dans la défense de la République espagnole 1936–1959: La légende rouge*, published in French, which addresses the controversial issue of the numbers of Cuban volunteers who were sent to defend the Spanish Republic, claiming that there were more Cubans sent than was previously put forth. She delves into an examination of the identity and origins of these volunteers and raises questions about their motives for entering the war to defend the Spanish Republic.[11] In a study which addresses another aspect of Spanish scholarship on World War II, Thomas D. Schoonover probes the various espionage activities of both the Allied and Axis powers. He traces Nazism in Latin America, specifically focusing on the life and activities of Heinz Lüning, who posed as a Jewish refugee in Havana, but was actually a trained spy who was eventually caught and executed.[12] With regard to Puerto Rico, Edwin Dooley assesses the role of Puerto Rico in the United States defence operations in "Wartime San Juan, Puerto Rico: The Forgotten American Home Front, 1941–1945" in the *Journal of Military History*.[13]

Regarding the Dutch colonies, there are quite a number of works. Peter Schumacher talks about the trials and successes of emigrants who had left the Netherlands earlier in the twentieth century and their strong inhibitions against fighting for the country they had long left; he highlights the experiences at Fort Zeelandia in Paramaribo, Suriname, where Dutch emigrants opposed to the exiled Dutch government's policy of conscription were imprisoned.[14] Ben Scholtens, however, specifically discusses the history, socioeconomic situation and the political developments of Suriname during World War II.[15] J.C. Bijkerk[16] looks at German threats to the Dutch colonies and specifically the fears of the planned German attacks on the refineries of both

Curaçao and Aruba, while Junnes E. Sint Jago examines the internment camps which were set up in Bonaire and Curaçao.[17] There are a few other works which address different issues involving the Dutch colonies during the war years, such as an early article on the music scene in Curaçao.[18]

These scattered efforts offer only disparate views and not a survey of the Caribbean in its entirety in one publication. Hence the need for a text which can address more of the innumerable aspects of the war in the different territories, a text that can give readers, in a single language, a survey of many Caribbean territories during the time of turbulence; *World War II and the Caribbean* is a project intended to address the paucity of published material on the Caribbean experience during the war. In addition, because it is sometimes forgotten in historical discourses on the Caribbean that the United States also possessed islands that existed under very similar conditions to the rest of the colonial Caribbean, examining this relationship during the war is essential to the story of *World War II and the Caribbean*. A thorough account of the experiences of any single territory is impossible in such a text, and as as a result the purpose of this book is to allow the reader insights into specific economic, political and social complexities engendered by the war within British, French, Spanish and Dutch Caribbean territories, and to reveal the significant role played by these territories during the conflict. Certain issues covered are revealed and published for the first time within this text.

THE CARIBBEAN CONTRIBUTION

With due recognition to the few Caribbean scholars who have focused on World War II, the importance of the Caribbean to the Allied effort in the war has been largely underestimated in wider war- and conflict-related historiography. Colonel O. C. Wenger of the US Army worked in controlling venereal disease in the region, and he explained its significance best:

> A glance at the map will show that the Caribbean islands form a natural barrier . . . which prevents an invader from entering the vulnerable, soft under-belly of the United States, reaching from the tip of Florida to the mouth of the Rio Grande, and behind which lie all of industrial America and the large agricultural areas of the United States. In addition, these islands guard the eastern entrance to the all-important Panama, the entire eastern shore of Central America and the north eastern shore of South America.[19]

Thus, as history can also attest, the Caribbean presented both a strength and weakness to the United States and Europe. It was strategically located to protect the United States, or, if not well defended, open it to attack. Additionally, as it became obvious that the intervention of the United States would be crucial to the liberation of Europe, it was equally evident that the protection of the Atlantic routes between the two major Allies – the United States and Britain – would require the support of Caribbean territories. The British West Indies, which included the Windward Islands (Grenada, St Lucia, St Vincent, the Grenadines and Dominica [from 1940]), the Leeward Islands (Antigua, Barbuda, British Virgin Islands, Montserrat, St Kitts, Nevis, Anguilla), Barbados, the Bahamas, British Guiana, British Honduras, Jamaica (with the Turks and Caicos Islands and the Cayman Islands as its dependencies), and Trinidad and Tobago, represented the vast majority of these strategic areas as compared to the French-, Dutch- and Spanish-speaking Caribbean, and therefore their role in this war and securing the area were crucial. Nonetheless, with the war also reaffirming the position of the Caribbean as supplier – its produce (staples, oil and bauxite) propping up the Allied war effort from 1939 to 1945 – the Netherland Antilles (Sint Maarten, Saba and Sint Eustatius in the eastern Caribbean; Aruba, Bonaire and Curaçao in the southern Caribbean; and Suriname in north-eastern South America) must also be recognized for their contribution as providers of oil (mainly through Aruba) as well as havens for European refugees.

After the fall of France in 1940, the importance of French Caribbean territories was indisputable as they became essential to the preservation of French autonomy. Most significantly, the fight for France played out on the shores of Martinique and Guadeloupe, territories used to secure the wealth of France and which eventually became resistance outposts, particularly after the blockade by the British and the United States from 1940 to 1943 and the subsequent collapse of the pro-Vichy government. In 1943 the Allies even occupied St Martin, and the US Army built an airfield to support their security and trade zones. So the French West Indies reflected the vulnerability and resistance of France to Nazi Fascism, as well as the growing power of the United States in global affairs.

With the region's importance recognized, Britain in 1940–41 wielded it as a tool in its ally negotiations, granting the United States the opportunity to establish itself as a major player on the Caribbean field in exchange for support against the Hitler war machine. Through the Anglo-American Destroyers for Bases Agreement, accepted on 2 September 1940 and offically signed on 27 March 1941, the United States was leased land by the British for ninety-nine years, rent free, to establish naval or air bases in various colonies throughout the West Indies in exchange for fifty old destroyers. This gave the Americans, despite conditions placed on their leases and developmental projects, open access to the Caribbean in a most critical period of transition – an intervention that irrevocably changed the trajectory of Caribbean history.

Though they are not dealt with exclusively in the text, Cuba, Haiti and the Dominican Republic, as the sole independent territories in the Caribbean, must be acknowledged for their roles in World War II. All three of these independent territories remained neutral until the bombing of Pearl Harbor in 1941, after which they declared war on Germany, Japan and Italy, strengthening their security and trade ties with the United States. Haiti, though it did not extensively provide troops to the war effort, organized projects to supply raw materials to the United States despite the rampant poverty of its largely agrarian population. The Dominican Republic as well did not contribute significantly to the number of troops involved in the Caribbean theatre. Ironically, however, this country, despite its treatment of resident Haitians (including genocide initiated by its president, Rafael Trujillo, immediately prior to the war, and continued discrimination thereafter) must be recognized for initially offering to welcome a hundred thousand Jewish refugees to its shores during the war. Unfortunately, the Sousa settlement on the northern coast ultimately only accepted a few hundred refugees.[20]

Cuba certainly was the most engaged of the three, offering both air and naval support to the Allied forces. A US naval base was established in Guantánamo Bay as a base to secure shipping throughout the Caribbean. In return, the United States strengthened the Cuban navy (eventually responsible for escorting sea-train ships between Port Everglades in Florida and Havana, Cuba) with "twelve 83 foot and five 110-foot U.S. Coast Guard cutters" between 1942 and 1943.[21] Cuba further distinguished itself in the Battle of the Caribbean, when, on 15 May 1943, Cuban warship *CS-13* sank German submarine *U-176* in the waters between Florida and Cuba. Cuba would later lose one of its vessels, the *Libertad*, off San Salvador Island.[22]

As Eric Jennings, Geoff Burrows and Debbie McCollin suggest at various points in their chapters, Cuba, Haiti and the Dominican Republic were instrumental in maintaining the convoy system and the West Indian Schooner Pool, which organized for schooners and small boats to supply food to the Eastern Caribbean territories and the Guianas. The loss of their support, particularly of Cuba, during peak periods of the U-boat crisis, as occurred in April 1942 (noted by Rita Pemberton in chapter 4), placed incredible pressure on the dependent Eastern Caribbean territories. In Cuba the war was also responsible for improving the fortunes of the sugar industry, with production increasing from 2.7 million tons to 4.2 million tons and the value of its raw sugar from $110 million to $251 million between 1940 and 1944.[23] These territories, though independent, nonetheless reinforced their already strong ties to the region during World War II and suffered, as a result, fates similar to many other Caribbean territories.

Thus was the Caribbean, just as were Europe, Africa and Asia, irrevocably altered by the war. Seen through the prisms of regionalism and imperialism and progress, these countries were in certain ways both empowered and enfeebled by the conflict, brought in specific cases to a point of economic collapse and yet also established as a critical supply base for the Allied forces. The war, therefore, allowed (or forced) Caribbean territories to redefine their national identities and economies and ensure that in the post-war era the Caribbean would challenge its pre-war status quo.

THE WORK

The contributors to *World War II and the Caribbean* have been gathered from centres of research and universities across the Caribbean, the United States, Canada and Europe to ensure a broad scope in terms of regional perspectives as well as specific knowledge. The book is divided into three parts: part 1, "Blockade and Trade", deals with the economic ramifications of war on certain islands; part 2, "Imperialism and Interventionism", looks at the political relationship of primarily three imperial powers – France, Britain and the emerging United States – in the Caribbean and their interaction with colonies during the war; and part 3, "Engagement and Displacement", chiefly addresses the ways in which groups of people engaged in war-related activities or related with each other or foreigners during the war. Included as well within this section are chapters on the impact on women and women's roles in World War II.

Part 1: Blockade and Trade

Any assessment of the impact of such a conflict on the region must first address the irony of the war: the disruption to the critical industries within colonial territories juxtaposed with their increasing pecuniary support of the war effort despite these disruptions. Lovell Francis elucidates the effects on the sugar industry in Trinidad as a result of the loss of labour to other industries, despite the high demand for West Indian sugar at that time. This was a significant force in labour relations, as the sugar industry, which had remained the major employer for Trinidad's working class just prior to the war, was able to wield unprecedented power over its employees with regard to the manipulation of wages, work hours and other remuneration benefits (or lack thereof).

Within this section of economic developments, Geoff Burrows examines the rise of the publicly owned Puerto Rico Cement Corporation as a material contributor to the war and an industry which directly facilitated the construction of Allied naval and air bases not only in Puerto Rico but throughout the Caribbean. He examines the role of this corporation, the expansion of which was facilitated by war, as a catalyst for change in the society and a symbol of Puerto Rico's evolving relationship with the United States.

Esther Captain and Guno Jones explore similar themes with regard to the Netherlands and the Dutch Antilles and Suriname. As Europe became enmeshed in war and metropolitan countries increasingly dependent on their colonies, the same occurred for the Netherlands and her colonies, as there was increasing dependence on oil, bauxite and financial contributions. This chapter examines the altered colonial relationship during the war, which, as nationalist sentiments began to prevail, led Dutch colonies to call for political autonomy; they were now in a position to make demands on a dependent mother country.

Though the resources and assistance from colonies were crucial for increasingly dependent European countries, the colonies themselves faced economic crises of their own. With trade and shipping routes blocked off and resources being pumped into the war effort, the availability of basic food supplies was a challenge. Rita Pemberton assesses this challenge for Trinidad and Tobago, both the scarcity, rationing, and inflation and the internal factors which exacerbated these wartime conditions. However, she also examines the attempts to resolve this crisis and establishes that the wartime food policies were in fact an important component of the security measures adopted.

Part 2: Imperialism and Interventionism

From the nascent stages of the war the hammer of imperialism and neocolonialism was felt on the West Indies. Eric T. Jennings explores what was in fact acknowledged as the dire economic strangulation of the French Caribbean colonies of Guadeloupe and Martinique. However, he examines this and other socioeconomic issues within the context of the changing political climate and the unravelling of events as France fell in June 1940. Within this chapter is gleaned an understanding of the diplomatic relations of not only pro-German Vichy France and the French Caribbean colonies but also the at-times untenable relations with the United States and Britain during the war.

The fall of France and the establishment of a French pro-German government with control of two Caribbean islands very close to British possessions in the Caribbean had alarming effects throughout the region. Jolien Harmsen, Guy Ellis and Robert Devaux examine the effects of this development specifically on the immediate British southern neighbour of Martinique, that is, St Lucia. With the agreement between the United States and Britain for the establishment of bases on certain British islands, the setting up of the Vieux Fort and Reduit bases began with haste, and the authors describe some of the heightened combat activity which occurred in St Lucian waters and the Free French refugees who managed to escape to the island. Throughout this chapter the impact of the Americans on the island predominates, with some of the negative social ramifications on the St Lucian people reiterated.

Despite the somewhat united front of the United States and Britain over the French colonies, Ronald Williams notes the strained diplomatic relations over the British colony of Trinidad and Tobago in his chapter. From the time of the Destroyers for Bases Agreement, internal discontent from British officials arose. Williams looks in detail at the unravelling of events and political discussions surrounding the presence of the United States on the island, including public opinion and trade-union activism.

Along similar lines, Gelien Matthews examines the disruption to the Antiguan sugar industry as a result of the presence of American forces and the consequent shift to tourism as the main industry in the post-war era. She explores the historical importance of the sugar industry to the island and the effect the injection of American capital had on the plantations, particularly with the construction of the Coolidge and Crabs bases, which created temporary alternatives for plantation workers.

Though the ambiguity of its political status is clearly acknowledged, the US Caribbean island of Puerto Rico, similar to the other Caribbean colonies, had its own strained relations with its metropolitan imperialist power during the time of war. Dannelle Gutarra elucidates the treatment of Puerto Ricans in this crucial time. Gutarra, using mostly oral sources, highlights the experiences, particularly the racial discrimination and language barriers, experienced by Puerto Ricans who served in the American military and, interestingly, how their bodies were used for experimentation to determine the efficiency of chemical-warfare weapons. She points out the nationalist sentiments which emerged towards Puerto Rico and the nostalgia experienced by those who remained in the United States.

Part 3: Engagement and Displacement

In the final part, Christian Cwik and Verena Muth examine the immigration laws in the Spanish-speaking, Dutch, French and British Caribbean which were directed towards German-speaking refugees, many of whom were fleeing certain death in Nazi Europe. They assess the role the Caribbean played as an exile space and transit hub for escaping refugees, particularly German and Austrian, and the repressive laws which sometimes even barred their entry and made it seem like further persecution. Cwik and Muth describe the European origins of these fleeing groups, how they managed their escapes and some of the obstacles they encountered en route to the Caribbean and within the Caribbean.

Elucidating on this theme, Suzanne Francis-Brown highlights the conditions in Jamaica for some of these displaced people, POWs and refugees. She explores the establishment of the various camps to house these refugees and the difference in the status and numbers of internees in each of the camps. She assesses their layout, living conditions and self-containment in order to monitor the relationship with the local Jamaican population. She analyses as well the various pieces of legislation passed in order to contain and control the movement of these groups of people, as well as the attempts to remove them after the war. The reactions of the Jamaican population to these groups of foreigners and to the camps also warrant such analysis.

With the movement of so many people into the Caribbean, relations with the local population were bound to develop, despite attempts to prevent them. In this instance, Dalea Bean explores the sexual engagements of local Jamaican women and foreign military men, particularly Americans, and the resultant consequences and controls instituted by authorities to try to minimize such relations. Stringent measures due to prevailing perceptions about black working-class women were instituted against women of lower socioeconomic classes, as they were seen as the inherent cause of the proliferation of venereal diseases and a threat to white military men. Bean also delves into the policing of prostitution and its manifestation in various forms.

While Bean focuses on the relationships which developed, Debbie McCollin, through an examination of the broader health conditions, elaborates on one negative aspect of these sexual liaisons, that is, venereal diseases. She explores the attempts made by the Americans to combat the spread of infections among their military men in Trinidad, as well as the benefits which trickled down to the larger population. She details the decline of the public health system as a result of war but its later rejuvenation with the establishment of programmes and centres to combat a wide range of diseases. Of course, the American presence was paramount to such development, though the health of their military men was the prime motivator, which had implications for the neo-imperialist thrusts catalysed by the war.

Karen Eccles explores a different aspect of women's involvement in Trinidad during the war. She looks at the ways in which mostly upper-class women voluntarily engaged in numerous activities to assist in the war effort. She identifies some of the uniformed and non-uniformed volunteer associations, groups and activities which focused on raising funds and supplies and providing services for military men stationed on the island. She highlights the publicity these women received and the headway they made in terms of mobilizing resources for their group interests.

CONCLUSION

General Eisenhower, while touring Nazi death camps in 1945, proclaimed that "the world must know what happened, and never forget".[24] Though the

West Indies cannot lay claim to the devastation within European, African and Pacific theatres, the significant contribution of these largely island territories must be acknowledged and the considerable political, social and economic upheaval within the areas recognized and never forgotten. The importance of the Caribbean territories to the preservation of European nations and empires was evidenced in World War II by their roles as spaces of refuge and providers of food, fuel and supplies. These roles, as well as their endeavours to bolster the defence of the region, were clear indications that the support of the Caribbean was fundamental to an Allied victory. As this period is reviewed and the insight of seventy years is placed on it, it is equally evident that the lives of the people of the Caribbean were forever altered by these formidable six years of war.

NOTES

1. Fitzroy André Baptiste, *War, Cooperation and Conflict: The European Possessions in the Caribbean, 1939–1945* (Westport, CT: Greenwood Press, 1988).
2. Gaylord T.M. Kelshall, *The U-Boat War in the Caribbean* (Port of Spain: Paria, 1988; repr., Annapolis: Naval Institute Press, 1994).
3. Claus Füllberg-Stolberg, "The Caribbean in the Second World War", in *UNESCO General History of the Caribbean*, vol. 5: *The Caribbean in the Twentieth Century*, ed. Bridget Brereton (Paris: UNESCO, 2004), 82–140.
4. Marika Sherwood, *Many Struggles: West Indian Workers and Service Personnel in Britain (1939–45)* (London: Karia Press, 1985); Robert N. Murray and Patrick L. Hylton, *Lest We Forget: The Experiences of World War II West Indian Ex-Service Personnel* (Nottingham: West Indian Combined Ex-Services Association, 1996); Ben Bousquet and Colin Douglas, *West Indian Women at War: British Racism in World War II* (London: Lawrence and Wishart, 1991).
5. Harvey R. Neptune, *Caliban and the Yankees: Trinidad and the United States Occupation* (Chapel Hill: University of North Carolina Press, 2007).
6. Beverly Ann Steele, *Grenada in Wartime: The Tragic Loss of the Island Queen and Other Memories of World War II* (Port of Spain: Paria, 2011).
7. Jean Belmont, *Une jeunesse guadeloupéenne: 1926–1946* (Montpellier, France: Cap Béar, 2006).
8. E. Jennings, "'The Best Avenue of Escape': The French Caribbean Route as Expulsion, Rescue, Trial and Encounter", *French Politics, Culture and Society* 30, no. 2 (Summer 2012): 33–52.

9. Eliane Sempaire, *La dissidence an tan Sorin 1940–1943: L' Opposition à Vichy en Guadeloupe* (Pointe-a-Pitre, GP: Editions Jasor, 1999).
10. J. Besson and J. Momsen, eds., *Caribbean Land and Development Revisited: Studies of the Americas* (London: Palgrave Macmillan, 2007).
11. Denise Urcelay-Maragnès, *Les volontaires cubains dans la défense de la République Espagnole 1936–1959: La légende rouge* (Paris: L'Harmattan, 2008).
12. Thomas D. Schoonover, *Hitler's Man in Havana: Heinz Luning and Nazi Espionage in Latin America* (Lexington: University Press of Kentucky, 2009).
13. Edwin Dooley, "Wartime San Juan, Puerto Rico: The Forgotten American Homefront, 1941–1945", *Journal of Military History* 63, no. 4 (October 1999): 921–38.
14. Peter Schumacher, *Voor het vaderland weg: Nederlandse dienstweigeraars in de Tweede Wereldoorlog* (Amsterdam: Van Gennep, 2007).
15. Ben Scholtens, *Suriname tijdens de Tweede Wereldoorlog* (Paramaribo: Anton de Kom Universiteit, 1985); Ben Scholtens, "Suriname en de Tweede Wereldoorlog", *Suralco* 18, no. 1 (1986): 16–25.
16. J.C. Bijkerk, *Doelwit Curaçao: Spionagethriller Wereldoorlog II* (Leersum, Netherlands: ICS-Nederland/Curaçao, 1999).
17. Junnes E. Sint Jago, *Wuiven vanaf de waranda: De interneringskampen op Bonaire en Curaçao tijdens WO-II* (Utrecht: Gopher, 2007).
18. R. Boskaljon, "Het muziekleven op Curaçao gedurende de oorlogsjaren", *Neerlandia* 5 (May–June 1945): 39–41.
19. O.C. Wenger, *Caribbean Medical Center: The Organisation, Development and Activities of the Caribbean Medical Centre at Port of Spain, Trinidad, B.W.I. From February 9, 1943 to March 1, 1945* (Washington, DC: Caribbean Commission, 1946), 1.
20. Thomas M. Leonard and John F. Bratzel, *Latin America during World War II* (Lanham, MD: Rowman and Littlefield, 2007), 76–77.
21. David Zabecki, ed., *World War II in Europe: An Encyclopaedia* (London: Garland-Taylor and Francis, 1999), 716.
22. Ibid.
23. Louis A. Pérez, *Cuba and the United States: Ties of Singular Intimacy*, 3rd ed. (Athens: University of Georgia Press, 2003), 205.
24. TIME-LIFE Books, *TIME-LIFE World War II: 1945 – The Final Victories* (New York: Time Inc. Books, 2015).

PART 1.

BLOCKADE AND TRADE

1.

A DANCE WITH DEATH
Labour Problems and the Sugar Crisis of World War II in Trinidad

LOVELL FRANCIS

"Sugar Production in the British [Caribbean] Colonies is more a political gamble than an economic proposition."[1]

The magnitude of World War II should neither be misunderstood nor historically underrepresented. Truly global in scope and impact, this conflict had resonances far beyond the theatres of fighting in Europe, Africa, Asia and the Pacific. Empires were built while others fell between 1939 and 1945, and even the small islands of the British Caribbean, though far removed from the main areas of hostility, were still very much involved in the conflict. This war affected the lives and livelihoods of Caribbean people, and in the case of one particular territory, the island of Trinidad, it had a significant impact on the sugar industry, one of the island's economic mainstays.

Where the importance of sugar was concerned, in the 1940s Trinidad was not unique in the Caribbean. In fact, few would dispute that the West Indian sugar industry was the crucible out of which a viable society and economy was birthed in the region. Before the pragmatic Dutch brought this agricultural subsector to the Caribbean, the British and French colonies of the region were little more than embryonic. Fewer still would disagree that the legacy of dehumanization and degradation aligned with its labour structures ought not to be divorced from any discussion on its legacy in the region. By the beginning of the twentieth century in the West Indies, it was still a fair assessment that "the long and intimate association of the sugar industry in the region with slavery, colonialism, coercive and exploitative production relations, glaring economic inequalities, and racial and social polarization has left a profound antipathy towards sugar cane cultivation hardly conducive to dispassionate examinations of the reasons for its existence or of its potential for progress".[2] The inheritances of this foundational industry remained multiple and resonant. It should not be surprising, then, that by the late 1930s, more than a century after the formal end of African enslavement and a full generation after that of Indian indenture, Trinidad's sugar workers still constituted a significantly disenfranchised social group on the island.

It is important to note that this casual observation was merely one facet of a larger historical trope. On one hand, these labourers were merely being afforded the same kinds of miserly comforts consistently experienced by the majority of those of their hue and ilk on the island. Conversely, as vividly delineated by the observations and recommendations of the Moyne Commission of 1938, neither the lives nor the livelihoods of their contemporaries (sugar workers or otherwise) throughout the British West Indies were significantly better, not in a region within which the commission noted that there "is abundant evidence of malnutrition among infants and young children, due in some cases to poverty, in others to ignorance or neglect on the part of the parents and in many others to the difficulty of feeding their children which is experienced by mothers who work. Fatal cases of marasmus result from these conditions".[3]

In the wake of the work of the Moyne Commission, the colonial government pledged to alleviate the concerns of the working class in the British West Indies. According to Malcolm MacDonald, the contemporary British secretary of state for the colonies:

> In the White Paper which is being published the Government accepts in principle the Commission's main recommendations for the creation of a special organisation under a comptroller to develop the social services throughout the West Indies, and for the provision by the United Kingdom Exchequer for this purpose of funds of the order of £1,000,000 a year. They also accept the recommendation for the appointment of an inspector-general of agriculture

for the West Indies. The other recommendations, which are numerous and far-reaching, are under active consideration in consultation with the Governors, and the Government express their intention to act as early as possible in the spirit of the recommendations as a whole.[4]

However, word of the government's strategy did not inspire too much confidence in the region because, according to Trinidadian pan-Africanist intellectual George Padmore,

> the Government has proposed a similar plan embracing the whole Colonial Empire. This is to be financed through the Colonial Development Fund, which is to be increased from 1,000,000 pounds to 5,000,000 pounds for a period of ten years. This works out to a penny and a half (three cents in American money) per native annually.... For this is what the imperialists understand as "colonial development". In brief, give the people less Crown Colony bureaucracy and more real democracy. The West Indian peoples are entitled to full self-determination. If they are not qualified after three hundred years of British tutelage, then it is time for Britain to get out.[5]

Neither did it change the nature of colonial sugar economics which ensured that the owners of the industry still dominated the industry's labour force. Very little, if anything, had changed in the region and on the island. This allowed the owners to artificially keep labour costs in Trinidad relatively low. According to Kusha Haraksingh, "The stranglehold which the planters were able to maintain over their workers enabled them generally to dictate the pace and extent of cultivation operations on their fields.... Their dominance was achieved partly by manipulating earnings which naturally stimulated a search by the workers for a side-line activity to supplement the income which they received from estate employment."[6]

This relationship remained unchanged despite the conflagration of 1937, when sugar workers, along with their counterparts in such other major sectors as oil and asphalt, rose up en masse in protest against the nature of the political, social and economic dominance exerted over them by the island's colonial hierarchy.[7] In the wake of this region-wide maelstrom some changes were made in the area of labour relations in Trinidad,[8] in part because the colonial hierarchy was wary of the continued "agitations"[9] of such labour leaders as Tubal Uriah "Buzz" Butler, the head of the Oilfield Workers' Trade Union, and Adrian Cola Rienzi, the leader of the All Trinidad Sugar Estates and Factory Workers Trade Union, the iconic figures of the 1937 Labour Riots in Trinidad. However, it is still critical to note that the nature of labour relations in the local sugar industry remained overwhelmingly skewed to the advantage of the owners, and in this they were overtly aided by officialdom in both Trinidad and Britain.

WORLD WAR II AND THE SUGAR INDUSTRY

In fact, as the world tottered on the cusp and then, between 1939 and 1945, plunged into a globalized conflict that killed unprecedented millions and seared the words Auschwitz, Dachau, Dresden, Hiroshima and Nagasaki forever into the human consciousness, the Trinidadian sugar industry was ideally placed for short-term economic success. Aside from stifling labour, the controllers of the industry stood to benefit from the fact that sugar was declared a "vital war commodity" by the British government, and British West Indian producers were subsequently guaranteed relatively stable and lucrative prices for their exports to the metropolis. This was an interesting historical circumstance. Since the promulgation of the Sugar Duties Equalisation Act of 1846,[10] Britain had dismantled the advantages enjoyed by West Indian sugar on the British market, including the provision of an assured terminal for sugar sales. However, the scarcity that resulted from the destruction of Western Europe's beet fields during World War I illustrated the importance of a steady supply of sugar from the colonies during times of crisis.[11] Consequently, as long as war raged in Europe, British West Indian sugar faced none of the uncertainty normal in the regional industry since the mid-nineteenth century.

Interestingly, however, these expectations of assured success were never realized, and it remains arguably one of the more underinvestigated ironies of Trinidad's wartime history. In fact, quite the opposite occurred. Trinidad's sugar industry was weakened by an impediment which manifested itself as a labour problem. Unlike the situation in the post-emancipation period of 1838–45, when many modern historians suggest that the British West Indian plantocracy's cries of a labour shortage were more "in the nature of propaganda for a cause than as description of real conditions",[12] the loss of labour during the war was mathematically verifiable. It became so severe, so very quickly, that instead of securely reaping the benefits of wartime profits, Trinidad's sugar businesses plunged into a depression that by 1944 imperilled the very survival of the industry. The root causes of this situation were internal to the local industry as well as exogenous to it. However, it is worth noting that the chain of events that led to this unexpected situation provides a good looking glass into the ways that imperial policies made at the metropolitan "centre" can have unintended effects in the "hinterlands" of an empire.

The origin of what became a sugar calamity in Trinidad resided in a wartime agreement signed between the British and American governments that was famously called Lend-Lease.[13] Britain's military performances during the early part of the war, 1939–41, were demonstrably underwhelming. The empire was outmanoeuvred and outfought by the Axis powers in the European, African, Atlantic and Pacific spheres, unable to halt the German Blitzkrieg on the continent and the advance of the Japanese in the Pacific. The very existence of the British Empire seemed endangered especially after the near-catastrophe/great escape at Dunkirk in 1940. By 1941 America had not yet formally entered the war[14] but it was willing to aid the British in return for specific territorial concessions. Trinidad featured significantly in America's hemispheric defence scheme because "strategically situated at the 'crossroads of the Atlantic,' the 1,900 square mile territory guarded paths to North and South America, the prized Panama Canal westward and to the perilous combat zone eastward. This island would be called upon to do decisive sentinel duty and indeed was worth, the tale went, forty of the fifty destroyers."[15]

In addition to troops, Trinidad was also going to operate a naval outpost for patrolling the Atlantic. It was the southernmost of eight bases that the British acquired under the Destroyers for Bases Agreement with the United States in 1940 in which they received fifty aged destroyers in exchange for the setting up of military bases in certain British colonies.[16]

Lend-Lease thus ensured that Trinidad was garrisoned by significant numbers of American army troops and naval personnel for the rest of the conflict. They began arriving in 1941. Naturally, their presence on the island necessitated the construction of military bases and naval docks in such places as Chaguaramas in north-west Trinidad and Wallerfield in the north-east, where an army base and airfield were built. To accomplish this, a sizeable local labour pool was required, and skilled and unskilled workers were recruited from the length and breadth of Trinidad. These included thousands of men who had hitherto made their living on Trinidad's sugar estates and factories. The most significant consequence of this demand for workers was that there was a flight of labour from the estates and factories that affected all of the island's sugar companies.[17] Sugar workers were literally driven away in US Army lorries to help construct the bases,[18] and the island's sugar companies were completely outmanoeuvred because they could not compete with the allure associated with,[19] and also the wages earned for, work on these facilities.[20]

The numbers involved tell their own story. Between 1939 and 1940 the local sugar industry directly employed some 25,000 individuals.[21] By 1942 the number of workers available to the industry had fallen noticeably, to 21,200,[22] and in 1943 this trend continued, as the workforce again shrank to 16,700 workers[23] and was seemingly poised to continue declining. An important side note to this worker exodus was that the number of independent cane farmers in Trinidad also fell during the war, for the same reason. Their numbers shrank from 13,058 independent proprietors in 1942 to as low as 8,305 by 1945 (see figure 1.1) It was a worrying sign for the longevity of Trinidad's sugar industry when even the local cane farmers, who had a significant stake in the industry because of the ownership of lands,[24] were enticed to abandon their relationship with it.

By 1943 the Trinidadian sugar industry did not have enough workers to

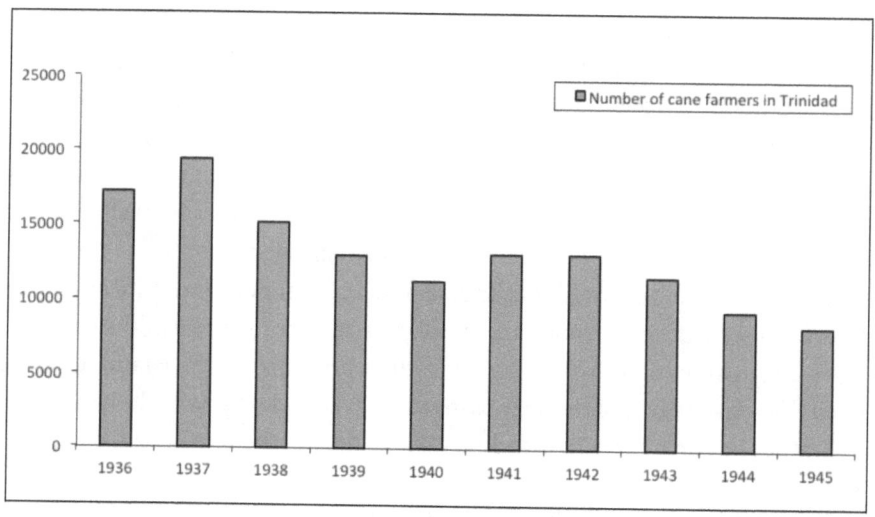

Figure 1.1. The cane-farming sector in Trinidad in numbers, 1936–1945. (Trinidad and Tobago, *Report of the Commission Appointed to Enquire into the Working of the Sugar Industry in Trinidad, 1948* [Port of Spain: Government Printing Office, 1948], 27.)

continue normal operations. The effects of their absence were observably discomforting, and the estates were severely affected. One area that suffered particularly was the replanting of canes. This was an important process, central to the continued success of the local sugar industry, as newly replanted canes helped to assure a successful crop in each coming year. Hence it was problematic for Trinidad's sugar companies that the number of acres replanted during the crisis declined significantly. In the period 1939–41, an average of 9,000 acres of land were planted with new canes annually in Trinidad.[25] This figure fell to a relatively minuscule 5,889 acres and 3,134 acres in the succeeding two years.[26] One direct consequence of this was that the total acreage under cane in Trinidad dipped from some 38,964 total acres in 1939 to 32,633 acres in 1943,[27] a fall of some 16.25 per cent.

The island's sugar factories were no more immune to the labour problem than the sugar estates. Without the requisite number of workers to man the factories, sugar manufacturing was severely hampered. In 1943 there were long delays in the processing of canes and the production of sugar throughout Trinidad. This was a major concern because canes which have been cut and burnt have to be processed with some alacrity, lest they lose too much of their sucrose content. The inability to do so directly jeopardizes the quality and the amount of sugar that can be extracted from them. In 1943 the worker situation was so acute that the five largest factories on the island, including the sugar centres at Brechin Castle, Couva, in central Trinidad and the most famous and largest at Ste Madeleine in south Trinidad, were compelled to close for long periods. The end result of a disjointed production season was a shortfall of a combined sixty-five hundred hours of factory output, which was equivalent to fifty-four days of lost manufacturing per plant.[28]

Also underscoring the direct relationship between the flight of labour and the industry's downturn was that the decline in cane and sugar production was matched by a sharp rise in the quantity of canes left unharvested in Trinidad's cane fields. This total increased exponentially from 8,489 tons in 1941 to a sizeable 207,000 tons of estate canes and 22,000 tons of farmers' canes in 1943.[29] Thus, not only were Trinidad's sugar companies producing fewer canes, but much of their output was left to rot in the fields. It was therefore predictable that sugar production plummeted during this period.

In the end, problems experienced during the cane-production phase and the sugar-manufacturing phase of the industry negatively affected the output of the estates and the sugar factories. In the period 1941–43 the local industry produced significantly less sugar cane and less sugar than in the period immediately prior to the war. For example, in 1937 Trinidad's total output of sugar cane and sugar was a respectable 1,442,239 tons and 154,218 tons respectively.[30] However, in 1943 cane output fell by almost 51 per cent, to 716,783 tons, and sugar production, even more substantially, by 54 per cent, to 70,920 tons.[31]

By the end of 1943 all of the Trinidadian sugar industry's major production and productivity indicators were displaying alarming negative growth. The dominant trends also suggested that there would be no organic reversal of its floundering fortunes. Instead, it appeared that for equilibrium to be re-established, the colonial government would have little choice but to intercede and, in doing so, prevent the complete collapse of the subsector. Despite the exigencies of waging a massive war on numerous fronts, the colonial hierarchy could not allow the sugar industry in Trinidad to implode. There were a number of justifiable reasons for doing so. One was that the industry was only Trinidadian in its geographical location but was really an overseas British enterprise. Sugar in Trinidad was dominated by British business interests. The two largest local companies, Caroni Limited (owned by Tate and Lyle) and the Ste Madeleine Sugar Company Limited, were British subsidiaries that together produced 69 per cent of Trinidad's sugar.[32]

THE THREAT OF UNREST

Predictably, however, the reasons for governmental intervention extended well beyond any concerns for the financial plight of the British estate and factory owners on the island. The spectre of 1937 and the widespread sociopolitical turbulence of that year throughout the Caribbean still resided in recent memory.[33] A still-simmering regional zeitgeist inspired the colonial hierarchy to act rather than to react in Trinidad. There was a palpable worry that there would be great disaffection if the industry collapsed and traditional sugar workers had no jobs to return to after work ceased on the American bases. Much of this concern was tied to enlarged anxieties over the sustained and strengthened influence of such labour leaders as Butler and Rienzi. Incipient war had not served to lessen this apprehension, and it was no coincidence that Butler was arrested and interned for the war's entirety on Nelson Island, a tiny islet located just off the coast of Trinidad, close to Port of Spain.[34] Pragmatic warfare mandated that the prevention of further worker unrest in a colony which produced the lifeblood of fighters, bombers, tanks and ships was of paramount importance. Though Trinidad was no more than a dot on the globe, its oil factored into Britain's military thrust in World War II because

> alongside the improvements in aerodynamics and manoeuvrability, air speed and firepower that marked out the new generation of fighter planes set to roll off British production lines in 1938–1940 went the requirement for higher performance fuel. High octane levels in petroleum spirit enhanced the capacity of aero-engines to maintain speed at high altitudes. So improvements in octane contents became part of the wider competition between rival powers to achieve competitive technological advantage in the aircraft arms race between them. Trinidad was a vital British source of this high grade fuel. Not only that, but Trinidad's oil supply, along with that from refineries in Venezuela and Dutch Curaçao, was critical to the diesel engines of Britain's Royal navy and its merchant fleet.[35]

Trinidad was thus a reliable producer and exporter of oil as delineated in figure 1.2, a situation which was not changed even in 1937, the year of the labour riots, when production and exports were fairly stable. In a war that in

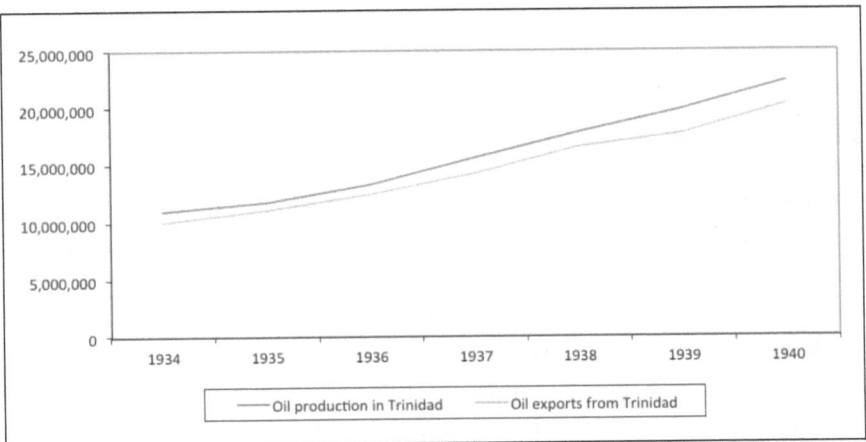

Figure 1.2. Oil production and exports from Trinidad, 1934–1940 (in barrels). (Trinidad and Tobago, *Report of the Inspector of Mines and Petroleum Technologist for the Year 1940* [Port of Spain: Government Printing Office, 1941(?)], 13.)

its earliest phase was not going to plan, Britain could ill afford any situation that threatened this vital supply of crude.

Therefore, the colonial government had a number of concrete reasons for attempting to save the Trinidadian sugar industry, and if the ones already mentioned were not important enough it certainly was not a negative that though it had been supplanted by the oil industry in monetary significance, sugar was still widely considered to be the nucleus of the Trinidadian economy. Many people of influence in Trinidad, especially among the elite, still viewed any protracted weakening of the sugar industry as an ominous portent for the economic, social and political well-being of the colony. The sentiments of one member of the local legislature, G.R. Wight, succinctly summed up this popular local perception. In a 1943 legislative debate on the sugar question, he opined that "if the oil industry disappeared (which Heaven forbid), Trinidad would still carry on although the general standard of living, and not least Government revenue, would suffer a considerable shock. On the other hand if the sugar industry went, and work on the American Bases slowed down or ceased, I do not think any of us would like to contemplate the position that would arise."[36]

Though hyperbolic and remarkably uneconomic, Wight's intriguing analysis underscored the continued psychological and cultural importance of the sugar industry in Trinidad. Additionally, with anxieties heightened after 1937 many locals were concerned that this wartime sugar crisis endangered the well-being and also the very existence of the colony.

ASSESSING THE IMPORTANCE OF SUGAR

Fortunately for Wight and those of his mindset, along with all of the factors already discussed the fact remained that while war raged in Western Europe, raw cane sugar from Trinidad helped to assure the British public of an abundant and reliable supply of the commodity. Thus, the British government made a relatively swift intercession in an effort to bolster the island's industry. Interestingly, it was aligned with Mr Wight's rather panicked appeal for assistance, which included the warning that the usual British gradualist approach to action would be economically calamitous for Trinidad's sugar manufacturers. His use of imagery in conveying this argument was especially palpable:

> The Sugar Industry is in such a state at the present time that it might well be compared with a very sick man. When you have a patient needing oxygen to assist breathing, you do not set about appointing a committee to assist breathing, you do not set about appointing a committee to decide whether or not to call a doctor. Today, cane is the oxygen needed by the sugar industry and if the mills are to have any reasonable amount of cane to grind in 1944, the time to act (Oh! blessed word, ACT) is now.[37]

He was not to be disappointed. More than that, it was indicative of the seriousness with which the matter was being treated that the colonial government quickly assembled a committee headed by noted English economist Frederic Benham to assess the status of the industry in Trinidad. This Benham Committee was dispatched across the Atlantic in 1943 at the height of the sugar crisis to make recommendations for its speedy alleviation. Paradoxically, it reported that though, theoretically, they possessed healthy long-term economic prospects, Trinidad's sugar companies existed on the verge of extinction.[38]

The Benham Committee predictably blamed the state of the industry on the workers who had abandoned it en masse. While the report made mention that this was not the only negative factor affecting the subsector in Trinidad, it stated categorically that "the shortage of labour, however, has been by far the more important reason for the fall in output. Since 1941, when work on the Bases began, the estates have not been able to get anything like the amount of labour they required for producing canes, and the total quantity of canes delivered by cane farmers has fallen heavily."[39]

Superficially the evidence seems to support this assessment. The number of workers in the industry declined between 1941 and 1944, with a direct rise in industrial disorder and dislocation. Yet this remains a facile argument that confuses symptoms with causes. Any acute assessment of the role of the Benham Committee cannot ignore that it was an instrument of the British government with a specific mandate, which was exclusively centred on making recommendations for strengthening the industry and thereby ensuring the continuation of the socioeconomic and political status quo in Trinidad. This precluded a more in-depth assessment of local circumstances, which would have unfailingly emphasized the fact that the estate owners and the sugar manufacturers in Trinidad were at fault for what seemed their apparent economic ruin.

The flight of labour from the estates and factories during the war was neither unusual nor unpredictable, and its main cause was the low wages consistently paid to sugar workers. A task system dominated the Trinidadian sugar industry. Workers were paid for the daily completion of specific jobs, which included planting, replanting and the provision of drainage, haulage, cane-cutting and sundry others. These were all allocated specific rates. However, the typical sugar worker often earned as little as forty cents a day.[40] Because of this, not even fervent industry advocates, such as the already-mentioned Mr Wight, could avoid the colloquial argument that Trinidad's sugar workers were "sweated" and then paid little more than starvation emoluments.[41] Remunerations of this level were problematic during the war, and it was puerile for anyone, especially the owners, to expect industrial loyalty from a workforce that was exploited not merely as a means to immediate profits but also as though it were a cultural and historical right.

The local manufacturers and estate owners were not unaware of the perils involved in their treatment of sugar workers. In 1939 the Manufacturers' Association presented a memorandum to the Royal Commission (the Moyne Commission), then investigating social and economic conditions in the British West Indies, in the wake of the 1937 riots. In it the association sought to justify the meagre wages paid to local sugar workers by purporting that the industry's overheads were too high and its profit margins too small, and that sugar workers had received sizeable salary increases in the previous two years.[42] The manufacturers' argument was that it was simply impossible to pay higher salaries to the workers. Unsurprisingly they placed the highest blame for this circumstance on the British public, which was unwilling to pay higher sums for British West Indian sugar.[43]

Despite this familiar and lazy argument, the manufacturers also could not avoid stating that even before the war the small salaries paid to workers made Trinidad's sugar subsector very unattractive, and consequently the estates and the factories suffered perennially from a shortage of both skilled and unskilled labour.[44] It is also important to note that the colonial government was aware of these realities. This is evidenced by the fact that it made a limited attempt to address them in 1940. The sizeable wage increase referred to in the memorandum was government-directed and totalled an extra five cents per task per day.[45] This was relatively minuscule, but it was doubled to ten cents per task per day two years later, in 1942.[46] The local manufacturers were also granted higher sugar prices on Trinidad and Tobago's internal market to make these bonuses feasible.[47]

The crux of the matter, however, was that when one considers the size of the wages offered to sugar workers, and more importantly that the average citizen in Trinidad had to contend with very sharp increases in the prices of basic foodstuffs and shortages during the war (one example, salted fish, rose exponentially by 338 per cent from nine to thirty-nine-and-a-half cents per pound[48]), as discussed in chapter 4 by Rita Pemberton, these modest pay supplements were rendered insignificant by local inflationary trends. Indeed, ironically, given the government-imposed rise in sugar prices, sugar workers would have found it difficult to purchase the commodity they worked so hard to produce. Thus, in abandoning the estates, however temporarily, these workers were making the most rational choice provided to them by the wartime circumstances in Trinidad.

The mandate of the Benham Committee, however, precluded too much concern with the socioeconomic dilemmas faced by Trinidad's sugar workers. As already mentioned, its only real objective was to fast-track the return of the local sugar industry to a position of strength and respectability. The committee, therefore, made a number of recommendations to heal the fractures in the agricultural subsector that relied heavily on the provision of subsidies and guaranteed prices to the local estate owners and manufacturers. The committee's chairman, Frederic Benham, expressed a strong personal aversion to the idea of handing out money unconditionally to industry stakeholders, stating instead a personal preference for the granting of subsidies and bonuses, which supposedly were to be earned.[49] However, ironically, the de facto situation was that quite a few of the committee's suggestions, which were rather hurriedly agreed to by the colonial government in 1944, amounted to little more than the granting of significant amounts of free money to Trinidad's sugar estates and manufacturers.[50]

Undoubtedly, the most troublesome issue facing the industry was labour relations, and to contend with this the committee preached the benefits of compromise to the owners. It proposed some changes to improve the conditions of estate and factory work in Trinidad. These included the payment of overtime rates, the granting of holidays with pay to workers and the standardization of labour tasks. Glaringly missing among the committee's labour-oriented recommendations was the question of increased wages for workers.

However, it was not an issue that this committee wished to broach. Nevertheless, most of the alterations suggested by Mr Benham's group concerning the labouring population were quickly implemented. Sugar workers were granted seven days' holiday annually with pay as long as they worked 234 days in an employment year; in addition to that, the workday was reduced to eight hours and overtime rates were to be paid as long as workers exceeded the mandatory hours of work per day. Moreover, after consultations between the manufacturers and the major sugar workers' union, a body called the Joint Consultative Committee was constituted on 4 January 1945.[51] This was a negotiating entity composed of representatives of the sugar union as well as the manufacturers.

By 1945 the only significant worker-centred recommendation made by the Benham Committee that was not fully implemented was the standardization of tasks throughout the industry.[52] However, that proposal was always going to be a difficult one to implement logically. This was largely because Trinidad's sugar industry was composed of a number of companies, including Caroni, Limited, Woodford Lodge, and the Ste Madeleine Sugar Company, which ran their affairs similarly but not identically. It was, thus, no simple undertaking to get them organized in exactly the same manner. Another hindrance to this was the reality that sugar production required a variety of tasks, which defied easy comparisons and made homogenization a daunting prospect.

Nevertheless, the British government agreed to and then implemented almost all of the Benham Committee's suggestions with a fair degree of quick success. By 1945, with the conflict in Europe coming to an end and only Japan of the Axis powers still struggling to keep alive a war of expansion which had long been lost, the sugar industry in Trinidad, which in 1944 was on the verge of collapse, was showing renewed vigour. As illustrated in figure 1.3, there were notable improvements both in terms of sugar-cane cultivation and the production of sugar, which continued for the rest of the decade. Consequently the quantity of sugar exported by Trinidad increased after 1944, as illustrated in figure 1.4, with the most significant augmentation tellingly registered in the immediate post-war year of 1945–46. By the late 1940s it was clear that the sugar industry in Trinidad had successfully survived another intense period of economic crisis.

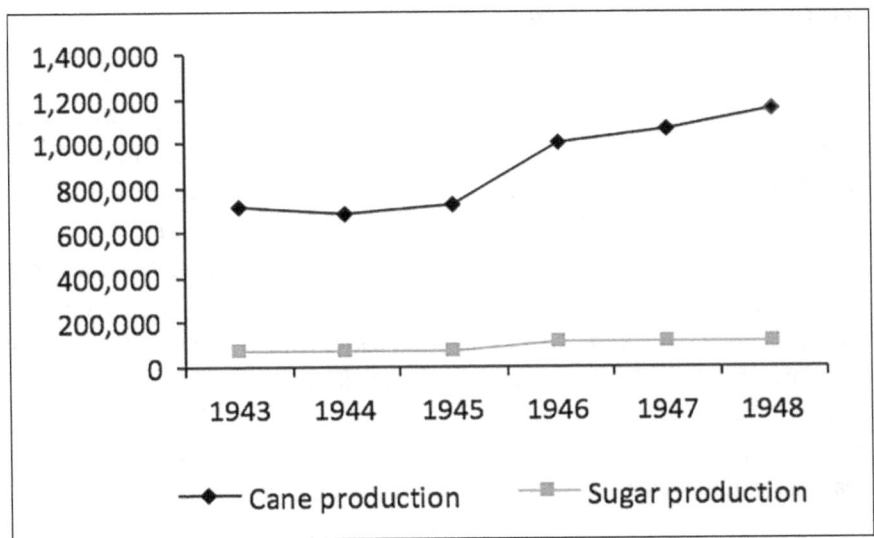

Figure 1.3. Sugar-cane and sugar production in Trinidad, 1944–1948. (Trinidad and Tobago, *Report of the Commission Appointed to Enquire into the Working of the Sugar Industry in Trinidad, 1948* [Port of Spain: Government Printing Office, 1948], 8.)

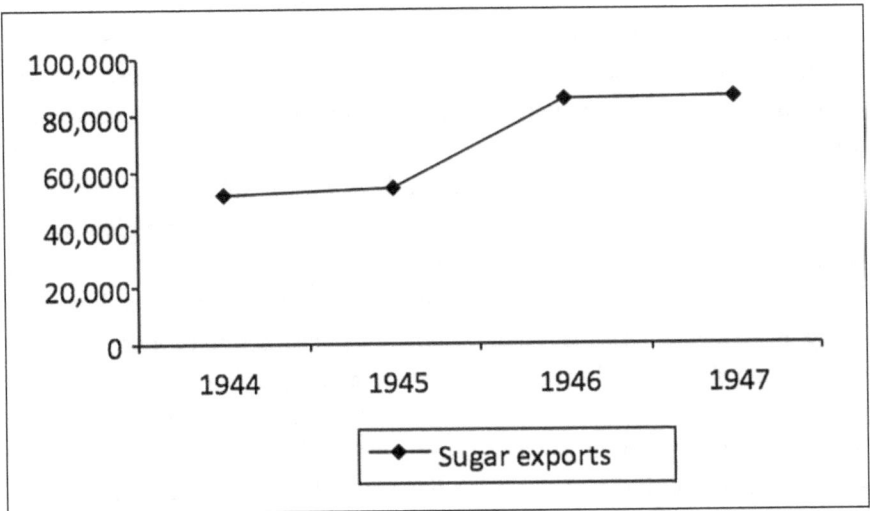

Figure 1.4. Sugar exports from Trinidad, 1944–1947 (in tons). (Trinidad and Tobago, *Report of the Commission Appointed to Enquire into the Working of the Sugar Industry in Trinidad, 1948* [Port of Spain: Government Printing Office], 4.)

POST-WAR DEVELOPMENTS

To ensure that this was the case, the colonial government dispatched a commission headed by Lord Herwald R. Soulbury to Trinidad in 1948 to make a critical appraisal of the industry's recovery. The Soulbury Commission was provided with a broader mandate than the Benham Committee which preceded it, in part because the circumstances in the subsector in 1948 were not nearly as dire as they appeared in 1943–44. Its findings concretely established that the sugar industry was in a much stronger position than was the case during the war. However, it also noted the continuation of a number of concerns and in particular a problematic labour situation on the island.[53]

The Soulbury Commission's concern over the labour situation in Trinidad at the end of the war was not misplaced. Despite what appeared to be a near-miraculous reversal of economic fortunes and the propitious support of the local legislature and the colonial government in its accomplishment, the Trinidadian sugar industry still faced a vivid labour problem. Appearances to the contrary aside, the industry had not escaped its dance with death entirely unscathed. In fact, the war years proved to be something of a watershed event for labour relations in this subsector. It was not that the industry's workers had not been concerned about their wages and living conditions before 1941; rather, it seemed that the successful if temporary abandonment of the estates had catalysed a permanent alteration in the relationship between the workers and the sugar manufacturers in Trinidad. After the war, many of the labourers who returned to the industry had altered world views and responded more antagonistically to work situations.

By the late 1940s Trinidad's sugar workers were displaying, if not a new, then definitely a strengthened level of independent thought which was in stark contrast with, and directly undermined, the age-old planter-centred ideology that life and work on the plantation were sacrosanct and that there could be no existence for them beyond it. There seemed to be a greater individual and collective willingness to stand up and fight for rights and a desire to frustrate the owners of Trinidad's sugar companies whenever opportunities were presented for them to do so. This took the form of a rising militancy among them, and in this the role of a newly freed Tubal Uriah "Buzz" Butler was critical.

With the war at an end, Butler was released from imprisonment on Nelson Island. He lived under constant surveillance and was forced to reside in Port of Spain because he was officially debarred from Trinidad's oilfields and from the counties Victoria and St Patrick in south and south-east Trinidad,[54] where Trinidad's oil interests and the majority of its oil workers resided. He shifted his focus away from the OWTU and extended some of his resolute zeal to opportunities in the sugar industry.[55] Consequently, it did not take too long for major labour disturbances to ferment in the local sugar industry; there were internal rumblings from as early as 1947. Moreover, despite the colonial culture of *divide et impera*, which supposedly precluded too much cooperation between Trinidad's largely Indo-Trinidadian sugar workers and Afro-Trinidadian oil workers, Butler's brand of fervent leadership blended well with the frustrations of the former group. He was subsequently accused by the local sugar manufacturers of intruding into an industry where he was not wanted;[56] however, in May 1947 he spearheaded a strike at one of the island's two major companies, the Tate and Lyle–owned Caroni Limited, which lasted three weeks and involved fourteen hundred workers.[57]

During February 1948, it was the turn of the island's other major company, the British-owned Ste Madeleine Sugar Company. The Butler-inspired disturbances to its operations were much more comprehensive than the 1947 strike at Caroni Limited. The work stoppage lasted two months, involved five thousand workers, the loss of seventy-six thousand man-hours of work and the destruction by fire of some twenty thousand tons of cane in the fields.[58]

Thus, by the end of the 1940s a new paradigm was seemingly established in the Trinidadian sugar industry where labour relations were concerned. It was starkly punctuated by the increased agitation of sugar workers for better wages and working conditions. This in turn pivoted on a confluence of forces, including the traditional and continued recalcitrance of Trinidad's sugar companies on the issue of better wages, ideological changes among sugar workers and collaborations between labour leaders. In lieu of a sudden volte-face on the part of the manufacturers, these circumstances portended that the labour situation in the industry would be heated throughout the 1950s.

CONCLUSION

In the end, World War II proved to be an immensely important period for the development of the sugar industry in Trinidad. This was despite the fact that for much of the conflict, instead of the expected and advertised prosperity seemingly guaranteed by high sugar prices, this agricultural subsector found itself in an economic bind that was only alleviated by the emergency intervention of the colonial government. Local sugar workers who were traditionally and habitually exploited and underpaid by Trinidad's estates and factory owners seized the unexpected work opportunities provided to them by the arrival of American troops on the island in 1941 and abandoned the industry in numbers. Its survival was not assured until the quick implementation of the measures recommended by the Benham Committee, which was hastily dispatched to Trinidad. At the end of the war equilibrium had been seemingly re-established in sugar, once again, one assumed, to the habitual economic benefit of the local estate and factory owners.

That perception, however, clearly overstated the real situation on the ground in Trinidad. After the war, the culture of the industry was not the same. No factor emphasized this more than the altered attitudes of the sugar workers who returned to the industry after their hiatus on the bases. There was a rising militancy among them, and they were no longer willing to accept the wages and working conditions still prevalent in the industry – and the role of iconic labour leader Tubal Uriah "Buzz" Butler in stoking this fire should neither be underrated nor ignored. At the end of the war sugar workers were displaying a greater sense of independence and a willingness to put their needs for recognition and rights as a labouring population above the needs of the local plantocracy. This situation augured well for the workers, who faced the collective might of the sugar businesses, which usually had the local and colonial hierarchy's support.

The war years of 1939–45 set the stage for continued conflict in the sugar industry in Trinidad, pitting the island's newly emboldened sugar workers against the owners of its sugar business and the colonial establishment. This meant that whereas in 1945 with the end of World War II the guns had gone silent around the world, in Trinidad a new battle was just beginning.

NOTES

1. C.Y. Shephard, *The Sugar Industry of the British West Indies and British Guiana with Special Reference to Trinidad*, Imperial College of Tropical Agriculture Trinidad Economic Series (St Augustine, Trinidad: Imperial College of Tropical Agriculture, 1929), 20.

2. G.B. Hagelberg, *The Caribbean Sugar Industries: Constraints and Opportunities* (New Haven: Yale University Antilles Research Program, 1974), 7.
3. Great Britain, *Report of the West India Royal Commission (1938–1939)* (London: His Majesty's Stationery Office, 1945), 139.
4. United Kingdom, *Hansard Parliamentary Debates*, West India Royal Commission Report, vol. 357 (20 February 1940).
5. George Padmore, "West Indies Needs Independence – Not Big Reports", *Labour Action* 11 (24 June 1940): 4.
6. Kusha Haraksingh, "Labour and Technology and the Sugar Estates in Trinidad", in *Crisis and Change in the International Sugar Economy 1860–1914*, ed. Bill Albert and Adrian Graves (London: ISC Press, 1984), 144.
7. It is perhaps one of the lesser-known stories of this uprising that arguably its singular resonant event, the burning of Corporal Charlie King, was instigated by a female supporter of Butler. Daniel Williams, "Voices of the Past Oral History Project" (Department of History, Faculty of Humanities and Education, University of the West Indies, St Augustine, Trinidad, 16 September 2008), 19.
8. For example, a law passed in 1939 made it illegal to employ women to work in industrial settings at night except for prescribed circumstances. Government of Trinidad and Tobago, Employment of Women (Night Work) Act, Act 3 of 1939 (Port of Spain: Government Printing Office, 1940).
9. "Agitator" and "agitation" were the bywords habitually used by the colonial hierarchy to describe, respectively, the chief protagonists and the pro-union behaviour exhibited by the labouring classes in the British West Indies in the 1930s and 1940s. National Archives of the United Kingdom (NAUK): CO 295 600/13.
10. This change made it difficult for British Caribbean sugar to compete and was the beginning of a major crisis of markets for the industry. William A. Green, *British Slave Emancipation: The Sugar Colonies and the Great Experiment 1830–1865* (Oxford: Oxford University Press, 1976), 229–35.
11. Douglas Hall, *Five of the Leewards, 1834–1870* (London: Ginn and Co., 1971), 51.
12. Kusha Haraksingh, "Sugar Estates and Labour in Trinidad 1838–1845" (paper presented at the Eleventh Association of Caribbean Historians Conference, Curaçao, 1979), 6.
13. Lend-Lease was an agreement signed between the United States and various of its allies in World War II in which the Americans were usually allowed to garrison certain territories in exchange for war aid. Negotiations with the British in 1940 led to the arrival of US troops in Trinidad in 1941. Martin Munro,

Different Drummers: Rhythm and Race in the Americas (Berkeley: University of California Press, 2010), 249.

14. This would not formally occur until the Japanese bombed Pearl Harbor in Hawaii on 7 December 1941.
15. Harvey R. Neptune, *Caliban and the Yankees: Trinidad and the United States Occupation* (Chapel Hill: University of North Carolina Press, 2007), 2.
16. Government of the United States, Bureau of Yards and Docks, *Building the Navy's Bases in World War II: History of the Bureau of Yards and Docks and the Civil Engineer Corps 1940–1946*, vol. 2 (Washington, DC: Government Printing Office, 1947), 22.
17. By the 1940s the Trinidadian sugar industry was composed of eight companies – two relatively big ones (in the local context) and six small ones. The two large ones were Caroni Limited and the Ste Madeleine Sugar Company Limited. The smaller ones were Woodford Lodge Sugar Estates Limited, Forres Park Limited, Trinidad Sugar Estates Limited, Gordon Sugar Estates Limited, William Fogarty Limited and Ramnarine Seereram Maharaj Company Limited. Trinidad and Tobago, *Report of the Committee Appointed to Enquire into the Sugar Industry*, Council Paper No. 1 of 1944 (Port of Spain: Government Printing Office, 1944), 6.
18. Ibid., 5.
19. The US army bases were alluring because they directly and indirectly provided a number of job opportunities even beyond the construction phase. A good example of this was that a number of local entertainers found steady employment at or close to the bases because of the American presence. Marjorie Boothman, "Voices of the Past Oral History Project" (Department of History, Faculty of Humanities and Education, University of the West Indies, St Augustine, Trinidad, 15 February 2009), 18–19.
20. Trinidad and Tobago, *Report of the Commission Appointed to Enquire into the Working of the Sugar Industry in Trinidad, 1948* (Port of Spain: Government Printing Office, 1948), 14.
21. Ibid., 13.
22. Ibid.
23. Ibid., 27.
24. Cane farmers owned 22 per cent of all sugar lands in Trinidad by 1943. See Trinidad and Tobago, *Report of the Committee* [1944], 27.
25. Ibid., 15.
26. Ibid.
27. Ibid.
28. Ibid., 20.

29. Ibid.
30. Trinidad and Tobago, Sugar Manufacturers' Federation, Memorandum Submitted by the Sugar Manufacturers' Association of Trinidad on the Sugar Industry to the Royal Commission Investigating the Social and Economic Conditions in the British West Indies 1939 (Port of Spain: Sugar Manufacturers' Association of Trinidad, 1939), 22.
31. Trinidad and Tobago, *Report of the Committee* [1944], 5.
32. Ibid., 9.
33. In fact, the situation had not abated. By the following decade the labour situation in Trinidad was still simmering to the extent that F.W. Dalley was dispatched by the colonial government to conduct a thorough study on labour relations on the island. Trinidad and Tobago, *General Industrial Conditions and Labour Relations in Trinidad, Report by F.W. Dalley, CBE* (Port of Spain: Government Printing Office, 1954).
34. Ivar Oxaal, *Race and Revolutionary Consciousness: A Documentary Interpretation of the 1970 Black Revolt in Trinidad* (Cambridge, MA: Schenkman, 1971), 79.
35. Martin Thomas, *Critical Perspectives on Empire: Violence and Colonial Order: Police, Workers and Protest in European Colonial Empires 1918–1940* (Cambridge: Cambridge University Press, 2012), 251.
36. Trinidad and Tobago, *Hansard*, 23 July 1943, 309.
37. Ibid.
38. Trinidad and Tobago, *Report of the Committee* [1944], 19–20.
39. Ibid., 21.
40. The jobs to be done in the Trinidadian sugar industry, like many in the region, were myriad and subdivided into individual tasks like planting, harvesting, the provision of drainage, haulage and so on. Workers were paid specific daily wages according to the tasks to which they were assigned. The pay range for most tasks in the industry prior to the war fell between forty and ninety cents per task per day. See Trinidad and Tobago, Sugar Manufacturers' Federation, Memorandum Submitted by the Sugar Manufacturers' Association, 5.
41. Trinidad and Tobago, *Hansard*, 313.
42. Trinidad and Tobago, Sugar Manufacturers' Federation, Memorandum Submitted by the Sugar Manufacturers' Association, 19.
43. Ibid.
44. Ibid.
45. Ibid., 74.
46. Ibid.
47. Ibid.
48. Ibid., 88.

49. Ibid., 23.
50. The committee suggested that the island's sugar companies should receive monetary bonuses from the British government in addition to guaranteed cane and sugar prices for the duration of the war. Trinidad and Tobago, *Report of the Committee* [1944], 23.
51. Ibid., 3.
52. Ibid.
53. Ibid., 74–88.
54. Jerome Teelucksingh, "Political Ambitions and Contributions to Trade Unionism: Tubal Uriah 'Buzz' Butler during the 1930s and 40s", *Caribbean Journal of Labour and Co-operative Studies* 1 (October 2012): 4.
55. Ibid., 7.
56. Trinidad and Tobago, *General Industrial Conditions and Labour Relations*, 8.
57. Trinidad and Tobago, *Report of the Committee* [1944], 4.
58. Ibid.

2.

PUERTO RICO AND THE CARIBBEAN SEA FRONTIER DURING THE NAZI U-BOAT CAMPAIGN OF 1941–1943

GEOFF BURROWS

Between 1941 and 1943, Nazi submarines carried out a lethal campaign against cargo ships in the Caribbean and western Atlantic, inflicting substantial loss of life and property upon ships and crews based in the United States, West Indies, Latin America and Europe. Reprising the strategy of unrestricted submarine warfare that Germany had used between 1915 and 1918 against Great Britain and its allies during World War I, Nazi U-boats operated in the Atlantic Ocean and circum-Caribbean region with almost no restrictions during the first half of 1942 – a period that German submarine commanders referred to as the "happy time" of World War II. While this macabre euphemism might speak to the universal horrors of warfare, it also illustrates the nearly complete lack of US, British, or West Indian anti-submarine defences in the region. During this time, while Nazi submariners toyed with merchant ships in either daytime or night raids, whether surfaced or submerged, Germany had twelve U-boats patrolling the western Atlantic and was building twenty more to be deployed to the Caribbean. Some, as in the 1942 submarine attack detailed below, stalked survivors in the water so closely that merchant seamen could distinctly hear the death orders being given to U-boat gun crews:

> An ominous new feature of U-boat warfare was revealed yesterday when, after the Navy announced the torpedoing of two Allied merchant ships in the Caribbean ... survivors from one of the ships told how a submarine trailed their lifeboat for five days, apparently hoping to pick off any friendly vessel that might come to their rescue.... Spokesmen for the thirty-three survivors from the vessel torpedoed March 3 declared that twice during their five-day, 540-mile trip in the lifeboats they saw friendly ships on the horizon. But they let them pass, without trying to attract their attention, because of the U-boat that was relentlessly following their course.... One man was killed when three torpedoes tore into the vessel. The ship went down in fifteen minutes and thirty-three survivors took off in two lifeboats. Later, they were hailed by the attacking submarine and the game of "shadowing" began. They saw crewmen – "young, blond and stripped to the waist" – and even saw the number painted on the U-boat which they reported to naval authorities. After the survivors were rescued, they were taken to Port of Spain, Trinidad and later brought to the United States on another ship.[1]

During 1942, with its "two-ocean" navy focused on building the Pacific fleet, the United States sank just one submarine for every 23.5 cargo ships sunk in the Caribbean or western Atlantic by German U-boats. Accounting for 80 per cent of all Caribbean casualties and 36 per cent of all global shipping losses during the entire war, direct attack on Allied cargo ships, many of which were helmed or crewed by Latin American and Caribbean merchant sailors, brought the fear, uncertainty and violence of the European war to the people of the West Indies.[2] The assault on the Caribbean, however, had dire consequences for the people and societies of the West Indies that extended beyond direct attack. In Puerto Rico, for example, the Nazi submarine campaign resulted in a dramatic decrease in food and construction supplies just as the island was beginning to recover from the decade-long turmoil caused by the global economic contraction of the Great Depression and the devastating San Felipe and San Ciprián hurricanes of 1928 and 1932 – the combined damage of which left over a million people homeless and nearly $3 billion in economic losses, mostly in infrastructure and agriculture.[3] The decline in food imports, building materials, medical supplies and other necessities of daily life during the submarine war was compounded by increased unemployment and threatened the fragile recovery under way on the island.

Puerto Rico's participation in World War II, like its recovery from the intertwined environmental, infrastructural, economic and public health crises of the hurricanes and Great Depression, reveals the island's ambiguous relationship with the rest of the Caribbean. Despite its deep and persistent bonds to the social and cultural history of Latin America and the Caribbean, Puerto Rico also developed strong legal and political bonds to the federal government of the United States. There are two primary factors for this ambiguity. On one hand is the island's "colonial" status, a subject that is actively debated throughout the world today. For example, while Puerto Rico is not included in the United Nation's list of non-self-governing territories, in 2013 the UN Special Committee on the Situation with Regard to the Implementation of the Declaration on the Granting of Independence to Colonial Countries and Peoples called for the island's complete self-determination and independence from the United States, reaffirming the "inalienable right of the people of Puerto Rico to self-determination and independence and reiterated that the Puerto Rican people constituted a Latin American and Caribbean nation with its own unequivocal national identity".[4]

Acquired by the United States in 1898 as a result of the Spanish-American War, Puerto Rico became an "unincorporated territory" according to US law, meaning that it was not placed on a path to statehood as had previously been the case for acquired territories since the 1780s. It was valued primarily for its strategic location, and US military policy towards Puerto Rico initially reflected a great deal of continuity with Spanish colonial policy. In 1917, just a month before the United States entered World War I and established mandatory conscription for men aged twenty-one to thirty-one (later changed to men aged eighteen to forty-five), President Woodrow Wilson signed the Jones-Shafroth Act (more commonly known as the Jones Act), which extended US citizenship to all Puerto Ricans.[5] Even as Puerto Ricans volunteered or were drafted by the US Army for service in World War I, other effects of this change in citizenship status were immediately felt, as Puerto Ricans had access to new legal and constitutional protections, progressive labour laws and free migration and re-migration rights. Between 1948 and 1952, following the end of World War II, Puerto Rico elected its own governor for the first time, rewrote its constitution and became the Estado Libre Asociado, or Commonwealth, of Puerto Rico, expanding its degree of self-rule but making seemingly permanent political ties to the United States. To date, the result has been more than six decades of local autonomy within what could be called the US empire, even as large parts of the British Caribbean moved towards independence between the 1960s and 1980s.[6]

On the other hand, however, the ambiguity in the relationship between Puerto Rico and other Caribbean countries rests not on a debate about Puerto Rico's colonial status but rather on its close ties to the United States *during* the twenty years of global upheaval of the Great Depression and World War II. While these transnational events created common bonds between people all over the world and are often remembered as universal catastrophes, comparative analysis exposes unique and individual local experiences.[7] Unlike its regional neighbours, nearly all aspects of Puerto Rico's recovery from the Great Depression and participation in World War II were predicated on the close political alliance with the United States during the New Deal of the Franklin D. Roosevelt administration, a time of tremendous change within the US political system. Reflecting the growth of the liberal state, the newfound powers of the federal government and the beginnings of Roosevelt's Good Neighbor Policy, the Puerto Rican New Deal operated at the crossroads of US domestic and foreign policy. Though the long-term results of changes in the colonial system, including greater self-autonomy, populist-style government and post-war industrialization, created much common ground between Puerto Rico and other areas of Latin America and the Caribbean, the shape of recovery and experience of the war were grounded in the economic modernization programmes of the Puerto Rico Reconstruction Administration (PRRA), a New Deal agency established by Roosevelt in 1935 in San Juan and administered by Puerto Rican professionals, engineers and workers.[8]

Between 1935 and 1955, PRRA (pronounced as one word, "Pra") spent over $1.36 billion in US tax dollars made available through a series of congressional emergency relief appropriations during the Great Depression.[9] The bulk of the money was spent between 1935 and 1943. After payroll, which accounted for about half of its total budget, between 75 and 80 per cent of PRRA expenditures went towards large-scale capital investments that permanently reshaped daily life in Puerto Rico and accelerated long-term economic development. On projects ranging from reforestation, soil conservation and elimination of the cattle tick to rural hydroelectrification, public housing and a new public health infrastructure (including water supply and sanitation systems) and the construction of a local cement plant, PRRA engineers made lasting contributions to personal and collective well-being in Puerto

Rico.¹⁰ Like many of the large-scale public works built by the Public Works Administration and Works Progress Administration in the United States, these federally financed projects paralleled the basic goals and accomplishments of the broader New Deal.¹¹ While PRRA came no closer than US-based New Deal agencies to completely "solving" the entrenched unemployment crisis and moribund economic outlook of the Great Depression, the $543 million spent on public works served as a kind of "holding operation" that stabilized and assuaged the worst human calamities of the era and laid the infrastructural groundwork for a period of locally planned industrialization during the post-war years.¹²

Despite the widespread consensus among historians and economists that entry into World War II, not the New Deal, ended the Great Depression in the United States, the experience of Puerto Rico exemplifies the continuity between economic relief and military fortification. Transregional public policy decisions during the New Deal allowed for the defence of the Caribbean during the greatest hemispheric crisis of the modern age. As this chapter shows, without PRRA public works projects aimed at hurricane-proof construction, rural hydroelectricity and the trained labour force employed on these projects, military defences in Puerto Rico would have been stalled by the uncertainty of maritime shipping until at least 1943. With the arrival of undetected and unencumbered U-boats in the Caribbean by the end of 1941, however, it was clear that the New Deal was vital to the island's ability to withstand the new socioeconomic crisis caused by the unrestricted submarine war against cargo shipping. It was also clear that the PRRA engineering projects completed or in progress were central to the island's ability to rapidly transform itself into one of the primary headquarters of the Caribbean Sea Frontier. As it became the largest anti-submarine command in the world, the Caribbean Sea Frontier protected thousands of miles of coastline and natural resources in North America, Central America, South America and the West Indies, and by the end of 1943 it eliminated the lethal threat of German torpedoes in the Western Hemisphere.¹³

In terms of hemispheric defence, perhaps the most significant aspect of the New Deal in Puerto Rico was the construction of the Cataño cement plant by PRRA in 1938. Originally designed to secure the island from future hurricanes by building a reinforced concrete infrastructure, protect its natural resources from private corporate control and insulate the island's local construction industry from fluctuating shipping costs, the Cataño plant became crucial to the construction of a vast new defence infrastructure on the island of military bases, docks and airfields. Increasing production during the war by over 300 per cent to meet the demand of US agencies such as PRRA, the Federal Works Agency, the War Department and the US Army Corps of Engineers, the cement plant contributed to the rapid construction of naval, air and military bases on the island and throughout the Caribbean.[14] As both a material contributor to the war against the Axis powers and a symbol of Puerto Rico's changing colonial relationship with the United States, the cement plant had a significant impact on social, economic and political life in Puerto Rico and the Caribbean during and after the war.

Less than a year after its opening, ownership of the Caribbean's second local cement plant (the first had been built in Cuba with private capital during the 1890s) was turned over to the people of Puerto Rico and controlled by a self-financed and publicly owned corporation. Part of an ongoing reinvention of the built environment in Puerto Rico, the Puerto Rican Cement Corporation (PRCC) reflected the New Deal's innovative use of public authorities and corporations to run federally financed public works projects.[15] Modelled on the Tennessee Valley Authority, which revolutionized social and economic life in parts of seven southern states by providing federally subsidized electricity, flood control and industrialization to residents who, in 1933, lived using gas or kerosene light and cooked with wood-burning or charcoal stoves, public authorities in Puerto Rico such as PRCC and the Puerto Rico Water Resources Authority contributed to the strengthening of political ties between Puerto Rico and the US federal government during the Great Depression and World War II. Whereas the colonial relationship, as it had existed since 1898, had produced fragmented and fragile bonds between Puerto Ricans and the United States, the war tempered those connections. On the battlefields, oceans and home front, Puerto Ricans and Americans shared in the innumerable sacrifices and immeasurable sufferings of the war.

To be sure, while a strong cultural and political sense of nationalism continued to be expressed and felt in Puerto Rico, the experiences of the Great Depression and World War II transformed the meaning and practice of US citizenship for Puerto Ricans on the island and facilitated dramatic changes in the colonial relationship between the United States and Puerto Rico. While these changes fostered improvements in life expectancy, physical mobility, democratic representation and economic opportunity, they failed to prevent the intense repression of dissenting voices and may have speeded up the process of rural-to-urban migration on the island and to the United States (particularly New York) that would characterize Puerto Rican life for the remainder of the twentieth century.

The submarine war in the Caribbean underscored three central components of Puerto Rican participation in World War II. First, Puerto Rico's experience in the war demonstrated some of its key differences from other countries and colonies in the region, as all aspects of Puerto Rican political life were tied to the New Deal. As Puerto Ricans served in the segregated US military as soldiers and workers on large-scale military construction projects, the racial and class-based limitations of US citizenship and Caribbean identity were revealed, as they had been in World War I. Second, as the large-scale public works projects of the New Deal years were expanded during wartime to include the construction of military and naval installations, the PRCC became vital to the defence of the Caribbean. Third, the Puerto Rican New Deal – a locally run recovery and reconstruction project centred on rural rehabilitation and hurricane-proof public works – was in fact critical to the Allied victory in World War II. Far more than a holding operation, the New Deal laid the infrastructural groundwork for the rapid mobilization for war in Puerto Rico, the United States and the West Indies.

THE NAZI SUBMARINE WAR AND THE CARIBBEAN SEA FRONTIER

To fully understand the challenges faced by Puerto Rico during World War II and the significance of Puerto Rican participation in the defence of the Caribbean, it is necessary to broaden the scope of the analysis. This section examines the Nazi submarine war and the creation of Allied defences in the region, the full extent of which Caribbean people were unaware. Indeed, as Trinidadian historian Gaylord T.M. Kelshall has written, most residents of the Caribbean were ignorant of the horrific dangers faced by merchant seamen during the U-boat war between 1941 and 1943.[16] Highly censored news coverage during the war and classified military records after it, in both the United Kingdom and United States, conspired to keep many West Indian societies oblivious to both the carnage created by submarines and the tangible dangers to their own people following the official entry of the United States into World

War II. This has led to a collective lack of appreciation of the importance of the war on the social, economic and political history of the Caribbean and a lack of analysis of the contributions of the Caribbean in destroying German submarine power and making possible the Allied victory in the Battle of the Atlantic. But as the key naval battle of the Atlantic war, the defence of the Caribbean against U-boat attack was a crucial survival link for Allied soldiers in terms of the shipment of food, arms and medical supplies from North and South America. Moreover, ridding the Atlantic of German submarine power made the D-Day landings possible and was vital to the eventual final defeat of Nazi power in 1945.

Created in the summer of 1941, six months before the attack on Pearl Harbor, the Caribbean Sea Frontier ranged over five hundred thousand square miles. Not only was it the "outer defense ring covering the soft underbelly of the United States", it would become "the lynch pin for control of the central Atlantic" as well, as U-boats began to strike private ships commissioned by the US Navy in the northern Atlantic that summer.[17] Prior to December 1941, the main priority of the submarine campaign was to halt the export of supplies to Great Britain from the United States and Canada. This phase of the Battle of the Atlantic, however, had dire consequences for Puerto Rico and other Caribbean countries; over the next two years, the scale of German submarine warfare increased as it moved southward from the Atlantic coast of the United States into the Caribbean and the Gulf of Mexico. Now ranging from the Florida Straits to the Yucatán Channel and the north-eastern coast of South America stretching from Venezuela to Brazil, the U-boat campaign shifted to the Caribbean as a result of the development of a functional convoy system during 1942 that established main lines from New York to Guantánamo Bay, Cuba, and Key West, Florida.[18]

The increased submarine warfare in the Caribbean – and the convoy system designed to defend cargo ships against attack – meant near-starvation for West Indian populations such as that of Puerto Rico, as food and other basic imports were sharply reduced. For example, total imports into Puerto Rico were reduced by 55 per cent and per capita food imports shrank by 25 per cent.[19] Much of the reduction was the direct result of a new German strategy designed to "roll out the drums" on Allied merchant ships. Beginning on 12 January 1942, the U-boat campaign *Paukenschlag* was led by Admiral Karl Doenitz, who, as commander of the German submarine fleet, was known as

"Hitler's Heir" and later became head of state of the Third Reich and supreme commander of the armed forces for twenty-three days following Adolf Hitler's suicide in 1945, during the last month of the war in Europe. Later convicted of war crimes at the International Military Tribunal at Nuremberg – specifically for his order of unrestricted warfare in the Caribbean – Doenitz unleashed his U-boats in "wolf packs", a strategy he had devised after his own capture and Germany's defeat in World War I.[20] Preying upon both armed and unarmed cargo ships with unmitigated fury, German U-boats sank 114 ships in the Caribbean between January and June 1942, making it the most deadly naval region in the world during those months.[21] The loss of property, war supplies, food and other necessities was also great. Between February and April 1942, for example, German submarines sank over 350,000 tons of cargo in the Caribbean and Gulf of Mexico.[22]

Armed with fourteen torpedoes each, the Nazi underwater fleet was no match for the three wooden "sub-chasers", two patrol craft, scores of surplus World War I–era Eagle-class boats and converted yachts that made up the US defence system at the time.[23] Merchant seamen from around the world, thousands of whom died "from the effects of torpedo explosions, of heat stroke, of thirst, of despair, or simply by drowning and by the ever present sharks", transported vital food, medical supplies, consumer goods and military equipment through the Caribbean at considerable risk.[24] Prior to the introduction of radio detection and ranging systems (radar) in 1943, submarines were virtually invisible. Further, faced with the task of fighting a naval war in both the Atlantic and Pacific oceans, the US Navy had initially concentrated on building destroyers and battleships to fight Japan following the attack on Pearl Harbor on 7 December 1941. For most of the next year, the Caribbean was left exposed.[25]

Allied with the United States against the Axis powers, many Latin American and Caribbean cargo ships faced direct attacks from German (and Italian) submarines. In other cases, Caribbean islands were used as covert refuelling stations or safe harbours, displaying the vulnerability of West Indian coastlines to potential Nazi occupation and Caribbean natural resources to Axis control. A sampling of newspaper accounts conveys the menacing impact of the submarine war on Puerto Rico, the Dominican Republic, Aruba, Curaçao, Uruguay, Chile and Brazil.[26] As Samuel Morison wrote, during the first half of 1942 U-boats waged war on Allied natural resources in the Caribbean with grim efficiency. Between January and June 1942, German submarines operated with "devilish economy [as] Admiral Doenitz concentrated on two particularly soft spots – the Dutch islands of Curaçao and Aruba, where over half a million barrels of gasoline and oil derivatives were produced daily; and Trinidad, through or by which most of our shipping to and from South America and all of the bauxite trade, had to pass".[27] Like oil, bauxite was one of the most important commodities to the Allied war effort; a common source of aluminium, it was heavily used in weapons manufacture during World War II. But even while German U-boats targeted Allied natural resources with calculated efficiency, Doenitz's men, at times, also relished in toying with their victims. Often "denied any opportunity to abandon ship", many merchant seamen "were slaughtered by machine-gun fire" from the decks of surfaced submarines as they frantically clung to life by treading water in the swirling currents of the Caribbean Sea or western Atlantic Ocean.[28]

Assaults on oil tankers, the uppermost prize of German war strategy in the region, produced the most gruesome carnage of the entire Battle of the Atlantic. Unarmed crew members who somehow survived the initial torpedo blast and managed to stay afloat in the acrid water suffered a fate worse than death, as frantic chaos reigned amid burning "oil scum ignited by signal flares on life preservers, men attempting to swim in a heavy viscous layer of fuel oil, [and] men trying to swim underwater to avoid flames".[29] According to Admiral John Hoover, the commander of the Caribbean Sea Frontier from 1942 until August 1943, the US Navy was able to do little more than rescue survivors from the water, and Allied cargo ships were "easy meat" for undetectable and undeterred German submarines.[30]

As horrific as these attacks were, the loss of civilian sailors and precious natural resources did not immediately alter Allied defence objectives in the region. Prior to Pearl Harbor, the primary US defence strategy in the Caribbean and southern United States was to protect the Panama Canal from air attack.[31] The canal had opened in 1914, eleven years after the United States officially recognized and negotiated an agreement with the newly independent state of Panama to construct a water passageway through what had been part of the northern frontier of Colombia. It was a vital link in the free movement of commercial and military vessels from the Atlantic to Pacific oceans. Since the end of World War I, defence strategists in the United States had concluded that the canal was most vulnerable from the air.

Puerto Rico was crucial to the defence of the canal. Focused on defending it from either Japanese or Luftwaffe attack, from the Pacific or Atlantic, the United States concentrated defence resources to insulate the Canal Zone from aerial assault. Over a year before Pearl Harbor, the United States had entered negotiations with Pan American Airways to construct landing fields, hydroplane bases, radio and weather stations and fuel deposit depots in the Caribbean and South America.[32] For US military planners, Puerto Rico was not only part of the plan to protect the canal but "effectively became the centre of the Hemispheric Defense strategy and the first American line of defence against German aggression" as well.[33] As the defence of the Caribbean against U-boat attacks and the protection of the Panama Canal became synonymous to US political and military planners, Puerto Rico once again assumed heightened strategic importance to the United States. This is a position it has occupied historically and geographically for over four hundred years.[34]

Franklin Roosevelt personally articulated the belief that defending the canal was of vital importance. Referring to the submarines as the "rattlesnakes of the Atlantic", Roosevelt declared that the Nazi objective was to ultimately "acquire absolute control and domination of the seas", through which Hitler would terrorize the Western Hemisphere by creating a "permanent world system based on force, terror and murder".[35] Three months before officially entering the war, Roosevelt warned that Hitler would attempt to isolate the United States from Latin America, seize control of the Panama Canal and begin an assault on the United States. Addressing the public directly in a radio broadcast, Roosevelt claimed that the "Nazi attempt to seize control of the oceans is but a counterpart of all of the Nazi plots now being carried on throughout the western hemisphere", including intrigues in Uruguay, plots in Argentina, sabotage in Bolivia and machinations in Colombia – where "secret air-landing fields ... within easy range of the Panama Canal" had recently been discovered.[36]

Roosevelt articulated Puerto Rico's role in the defence of the canal during a message to Congress about self-government for Puerto Rico in 1943. He declared that during the Nazi submarine war the islands of the West Indies had been transformed from "something of a backwater in the broad current of world affairs" into "a vast natural shield for the Panama Canal". It was obvious, he continued, that "of this island shield, Puerto Rico is the center. Its possession or control by any foreign power – or even the remote threat of such possession – would be repugnant to the most elementary principles of national defense."[37]

While the defence of the canal was a primary concern for Roosevelt and military planners, the United States had already entered agreements with Great Britain and other nations regarding the defence of the Western Hemisphere prior to the attack on Pearl Harbor. These included the American-British-Canadian agreement in March 1941 that, upon entry into the war, US military strategy would be to prevent German, Italian or Japanese incursion into the hemisphere. Second, the US objective would be to defeat Nazi Germany.[38] As for US defence of the Caribbean, war planners developed a broad strategy of interlocking sea frontiers defended by US ground and naval forces. While the exact plans changed from five to three interconnected zones (called alternately "base areas", "coastal frontiers" and "sea frontiers"), the primary three bases of the Caribbean Sea Frontier were originally Puerto Rico, Panama and Trinidad (later Puerto Rico, Trinidad and Guantánamo, Cuba).[39] Due to its strategic geographic location, San Juan, Puerto Rico was not only the headquarters of the Tenth Naval District but also central to the movement and storage of supplies, ships and personnel throughout the circum-Caribbean during the war.[40]

PUERTO RICAN MOBILIZATION FOR WORLD WAR II

Puerto Rico's formal participation in World War II began with an official declaration of war on Japan, which was voted on just hours after Roosevelt's "Day of Infamy" speech before both houses of the US Congress on 8 December 1941. As Andrew Lefebvre has written, as a US colonial possession, Puerto Rico "did not have a choice about joining the Allied cause", and was "required to assist the United States in its Caribbean defense strategies".[41] Even before the Japanese attacks on Pearl Harbor, Hong Kong, Malaya and the Philippines on 7 and 8 December 1941, however, Puerto Rico – like the United States itself – had already been involved in the war in Europe for some time, and the island was subject to various political and military agreements between the United States and other nations signed during 1940 and 1941.

Since the end of World War I, the United States had maintained an official position of neutrality in European affairs, and during the Great Depression, isolationism deepened, as most US citizens wanted the federal government to concentrate on providing relief and recovery from the growing unemployment crisis. Reacting to the public demand, the US Congress passed a series of neutrality acts between 1935 and 1937 that bound President Roosevelt and the United States to a position of neutrality by law. Seeking to move around this legally mandated neutrality, Franklin Roosevelt signed a series of agreements, particularly with the United Kingdom, which brought the United States and its territories up to the edges of the war without technically violating the terms of the neutrality laws. These agreements included the Destroyers for Bases Agreement of 2 September 1940, which authorized the United States to construct military and naval bases in the British colonies of Antigua, the Bahamas, Bermuda, British Guiana, Jamaica, Newfoundland, St Lucia and Trinidad; the Lend-Lease Act of 11 March 1941, which facilitated the export of "defense articles" such as weapons, munitions, aircraft, vessels, boats, machinery, tools and other material supplies from the United States to Great Britain; the Brazil–United States Joint Planning Agreement of 24 July 1941, which allowed for the construction of US airbases in north-eastern Brazil, and the Atlantic Charter of 14 August 1941, in which Franklin Roosevelt and Winston Churchill articulated several common principles, including the "final destruction of the Nazi tyranny" and a future peace that would allow all nations to "traverse the high seas and oceans without hindrance".[42]

Beyond these diplomatic and defence agreements, Puerto Rico was intimately involved in the mobilization for war in other ways as well.[43] As in the United States, Puerto Ricans were preparing for war through training and active participation in the military and through their service as administrators and workers on New Deal public works projects. In terms of military service, Puerto Ricans in the 295th and 296th regiments of the Puerto Rico National Guard and the 65th US Infantry regiment had been readying for the potential of US entry into the European war since the late 1930s.[44] After 1938, members of the national guard were trained by Adjutant General Luis Raúl Esteves Volkers, a World War I veteran and the first Puerto Rican to graduate from West Point. He was also the brother of the highest-ranking Puerto Rican in the Puerto Rico Reconstruction Administration, Assistant Administrator Guillermo Esteves.

After Pearl Harbor, tens of thousands of Puerto Rican men joined the US military, most of whom volunteered for military service with enthusiasm. During the war, Puerto Rican women also served in the military, in the Women's Auxiliary Army Corps, the Army Nurses Corps and the Naval Women's Reserve. For Puerto Rican soldiers, enthusiasm for joining the Allied cause against German and Japanese totalitarianism was mitigated by the reality of racial segregation in the military. As in the case of World War I, Puerto Rican soldiers served in the "Jim Crow" army, in which African Americans and Afro-Puerto Ricans were segregated from white soldiers, had limited possibilities for promotion, were kept mostly out of combat positions and relegated to menial, service, garrison or highly dangerous positions (such as loading live explosives onto ships, as at Port Chicago, California).[45]

For Puerto Ricans, however, racial segregation was also mediated by other factors, resulting in official discrimination based on a complex calculus of race, class, fluency in English and even location at the time of induction into the military. While longstanding historical racial prejudice in the United States was a large part of its military's segregationist policies, the island's colonial status and relationship with other European countries and their Caribbean possessions affected both *how* segregation operated for Puerto Rican troops and *where* Puerto Rican soldiers served. As Harry Franqui-Rivera has demonstrated, US officials believed that Puerto Ricans inducted in Puerto Rico (as opposed to Puerto Ricans who had migrated to the continental United States) had inherent intellectual deficiencies that, according to official military policy, made them less fluent in English, less educated and in all measures "drastically inferior to Continental troops".[46]

To further complicate matters, racial concerns about Puerto Rican soldiers mixing with Afro-Caribbean populations in other West Indian societies affected where they served. Colonial administrators in the British, Free French and Dutch Caribbean opposed the presence of both African American and Afro–Puerto Rican troops. As Governor Bede Edmund Hugh Clifford claimed, elite blacks from Trinidad and Tobago "rejected" the idea that African Americans would serve in the British colonies and requested Puerto Rican troops to replace them. Stating that "prominent" Trinidadians protested the arrival of lowly educated, ill-mannered and sexually promiscuous black soldiers, Clifford posited that US-born African Americans posed a danger to elite black family life in Trinidad.[47] As in Trinidad, colonial administrations in the Free French and Dutch Caribbean rejected not only the presence of African Americans but also Afro-Puerto Ricans, and they requested that only "white" Puerto Ricans serve in the region.[48] To facilitate such requests and subdue resentment from Puerto Ricans in the military who resisted the racialized label of "non-white", the US military created the category of "Portorican white", or "Puerto Rican white", during World War II.[49]

Throughout the war, the regular Army 65th and the 295th and 296th regiments of the Puerto Rico National Guard were primarily deployed in non-combat missions, including garrison duty and protecting the Panama Canal and Allied territories of the Caribbean. By 1943 nearly 60 per cent of all US military troops in the Caribbean Defense Command were Puerto Rican whites.[50] As Humberto García Muñiz and Rebeca Campo argue, there is an ambiguous duality to Puerto Rican service in World War II. Segregated from both US-born white troops and from Afro–Puerto Ricans and restricted to guard and menial duties, Puerto Rican white troops were garrisoned in the Caribbean at the request of colonial authorities precisely because of their non-black status.[51]

Beyond their service in the military, Puerto Ricans were deeply involved in the mobilization for war through their labour as administrators and workers on New Deal public works projects as well. The construction of public works and a new public health infrastructure by PRRA were designed to relieve the greatest problems of the Great Depression. They also had a substantial impact on the ability of the island to assist the infrastructural mobilization for war. While others have pointed to the decline of New Deal spending in Puerto Rico, the war in fact generated an increase in federal spending, and wartime public works should be seen as a continuation of PRRA programmes despite the ever-changing political rationale from work relief to economic reconstruction to hemispheric defence.[52] According to monthly civilian personnel reports, the War Department's Engineer Office in San Juan employed over eighteen thousand men and women workers by November 1943.[53] Ranging from highly skilled engineers and administrators to unskilled labourers, Puerto Rican men and women were employed in civil and military construction across the island during the early years of the war.[54]

As Jason Scott Smith has argued, the coming of World War II did not signal the "end" of the New Deal. Rather, in terms of public works, war mobilization led to an expansion of federally funded infrastructural development, including airports, roads and housing that aided military defence during the war and accelerated industrialization in the post-war era. As in the United States, the wartime state in Puerto Rico "was constructed on the deep and vital foundations that had been laid down by the New Deal and the public works programmes created state capacities essential to the preparedness effort".[55] From the local availability of concrete and cement-based products and cheap hydroelectric power to the skilled labour force that worked on these projects, PRRA engineering projects enhanced and strengthened the island's ability to serve as one of the three headquarters of the Caribbean Sea Frontier. Perhaps none of the PRRA projects was as vital as the construction of the Cataño cement plant.

THE PUERTO RICAN CEMENT CORPORATION AND WAR MOBILIZATION

Although it was originally designed as the centrepiece of a new public health infrastructure that would provide permanent security from future natural disasters through the construction of hurricane-proof roads, houses, schools and hospitals, the Cataño cement plant directly aided the construction of Allied naval and air bases in Puerto Rico and the West Indies.[56] Built between 1935 and 1938 by Puerto Rican engineers working for PRRA, the Cataño cement plant crushed magnesium-rich Puerto Rican limestone and mixed it into high-quality "Portland"-style cement. Within six months of opening, the plant was turned over to a newly created public authority called the Puerto Rican Cement Corporation (PRCC).[57] Located about ten miles south of San Juan, the Cataño plant was funded through the Emergency Relief Appropriation Act in a series of federal allocations totalling about $24 million today.[58] Viewed in the broader context of the Great Depression, the plant was built to address local environmental, infrastructural and public health concerns amid the global economic collapse. Locally produced cement was seen as protection against hurricanes, a bulwark against the spread of disease and a tool in long-term industrial modernization and economic development.[59]

Designed by Manuel Font Jiménez, the head of the engineering division, the construction of the plant was overseen by Guillermo Esteves Volkers, assistant administrator of PRRA. To the benefit of labour relations, the plant's workers were supervised by a Puerto Rican head foreman, Arturo Cordova Infante.[60] Benefiting from pre-existing local studies of the geological availability of raw materials and economic viability of markets and transportation, PRRA engineers believed cement to be vital to constructing a permanent socioeconomic recovery on the island and that any other construction material would prove to be a bad investment of local finances and labour, as "under

Figure 2.1. Puerto Rican cement workers at the Puerto Rican Cement Corporation. (NARA-NYC: Photographs folder, Box 2, General Records Relating to the Cement Plant Project, RG 323.)

our exacting climatic conditions, concrete is the only durable and hence socially economical construction material".[61] Although a local cement plant had been a long-standing goal of such civil engineers as Font and Esteves, its construction had been impossible before the influx of new federal financing for public works during the New Deal. In 1939 the legal transfer of the Cataño plant from PRRA to PRCC marked a turning point towards the construction of publicly owned infrastructure in Puerto Rico.[62] While the cement plant represented the Second New Deal's shift towards permanent reconstruction through the construction of public works built to last, or *para permanencia*, its opening in 1938 and transfer to Puerto Rican control in 1939 occurred against a backdrop of increasing US preparations for war. Within months, PRCC began contributing discounted cement products to federal agencies in charge of the construction of Allied naval and air bases in Puerto Rico and the West Indies. From the Destroyers for Bases Agreement of 1940 to the end of the submarine war in 1943, PRCC assisted the rapid construction of naval, air and military bases on the island and throughout the region.

This wartime construction – which began before Pearl Harbor and continued throughout the end of the war – had a huge impact on Puerto Rican society. As José Bolívar has argued, military construction in Puerto Rico should be viewed in context of New Deal public works programmes such as the Works Progress Administration and PRRA. Financed for strategic purposes, wartime construction in Puerto Rico had the ancillary effect of promoting local economic development during and after the war.[63] These constructions, comprising mostly military infrastructure such as docks and roads, also included such large projects as the construction or expansion of Fort Buchanan, Fort Bundy, Camp Tortuguero, Borinquen Army Air Field in Aguadilla (later called Ramey Air Force Base), Roosevelt Roads Naval Station in Ceiba, San Juan Naval Air Station, US Army National Guard and naval training facilities on the islands of Vieques and Culebra. If wartime federal investment turned US cities such as Birmingham, Detroit, Oakland and Seattle into the vanguard of the "Arsenal of Democracy", wartime public works projects on the island helped transform Puerto Rico into the "bulwark" or "Gibraltar" of the Caribbean.[64] While Fort Buchanan served as the army headquarters and primary induction centre, the newly built Isla Grande naval station on San Juan Bay was the headquarters of the Tenth Naval District and the Caribbean Sea Frontier.[65]

Like the public works built during the Great Depression, wartime construction contributed to the industrialization of the island through both infrastructural improvements and jobs. By 1943, while PRRA continued its work in public housing and rural rehabilitation, nearly 60 per cent of the Works Progress Administration's 14,500 employees in Puerto Rico were working on military projects.[66] Additionally, the engineer's office of the US War Department employed over 18,000 employees to work on a wide variety of internal improvements related to military construction, including work on public utilities, flood control on the island's rivers (and tributaries) such as the Buncana, Chico, Guamani, Lapa, Maunabo, Portuguez, Quebrada, Susua and work on the large harbours in San Juan and Mayagüez and smaller harbours in Aguadilla, Arecibo, Fajardo, Guanica, Guayanes, Humacao and Ponce.[67] By 1940 over 32,000 New Deal employees were directly working on defence projects.[68] Ranging from professional and clerical work to skilled and unskilled labour, the vast majority of these jobs went to men – except in clerical and office work, where nearly 50 per cent of those employed were women.[69] Reflecting

Puerto Rico's ambiguous relationship with other areas of the Caribbean, these federal jobs were in contrast to how US military defences were built in such other areas as Cuba, where the expansion of the Guantánamo Bay naval base in eastern Cuba was a largely private and federal enterprise of the Frederick Snare Corporation and the US Navy.[70]

CONCLUSION

As the other essays in this volume attest, the experiences of the people, territories and nations of the West Indies in World War II were as diverse as life in the region itself. Throughout Latin America and the Caribbean, in fact, it was initially unclear how the people of individual countries and territories would respond to the war, given the long history of US imperialism in the region since 1898, when, following the Spanish-American War, the United States fashioned itself as a regional "police force" capable of exerting direct and indirect influence over large parts of Latin America, the Caribbean and the South Pacific through the use of military force and economic leverage. As John F. Bratzel has argued, however, the immediacy of World War II created a new "urgency" in the relationship between Latin America and the United States that lessened several points of disagreement; in fact, by 1 January 1942 much of the Western Hemisphere had declared war on the Axis powers.[71] This included Canada, Cuba, the Dominican Republic, El Salvador, Guatemala, Haiti, Panama, Honduras, Nicaragua and the United States. By 1943 Bolivia, Brazil and Colombia had joined the Allies, and by 1945 so had Peru, Chile, Paraguay, Venezuela, Uruguay, Ecuador and Argentina. Nonindependent islands of the West Indies and North Atlantic, including Antigua, the Bahamas, Bermuda, British Guiana (Guyana), British Honduras (Belize), Jamaica, Newfoundland, Puerto Rico, St Lucia, and Trinidad and Tobago also contributed to the Allied war effort.

Although the Cataño cement plant was built to assist Puerto Rico's economic recovery from the Great Depression, roll back the increase of deadly diseases through the construction of a new public health infrastructure and provide permanent security from future natural disasters, perhaps its most significant contribution to daily life on the island followed Puerto Rico's entry into World War II. The plant contributed to Puerto Rico's ability both to withstand the socioeconomic crisis caused by the submarine war and to the rapid construction of naval, air and military bases on the island. During World War II, however, the primary reason for PRCC's success was the dramatic increase in federal spending between 1941 and 1943 during the building of military defences in Puerto Rico. Centred on military construction, this work was largely carried out by a combination of federal agencies, including the Federal Works Agency, the War Department and PRRA. During the two years of the U-boat crisis, federal spending in Puerto Rico expanded over 275 per cent, from $40.2 million to $110 million.[72] As in the United States, wartime construction projects in Puerto Rico were a continuation of PRRA public works programmes and had lasting effects during and after World War II.

The defence of the Caribbean was not a peripheral event to the history of Puerto Rico. Nor was it peripheral to the broader course of World War II. Rather, defending the region against submarine attack was central to the Battle of the Atlantic, for control of the ocean commerce between North and South America and Africa, Europe and the United Kingdom proved to be both a survival link for Allied soldiers and a key aspect of Allied war strategy. Not only did control of the Atlantic result in the unencumbered transport of food, medical supplies and arms, but it was also vital to the planning and timing of the Allied European invasion of June 1944 and the eventual defeat of Nazi Germany.[73]

Highlighting three central components of Puerto Rican participation in World War II, the U-boat campaign in the Caribbean demonstrated the ambiguity between Puerto Rico and its regional neighbours. Serving as soldiers and workers on large-scale military construction projects, Puerto Ricans were nonetheless bound by limits of racial and class-based segregation in the US military and society and racial prejudice within the intra-Caribbean world. At the same time, however, through the transformation and expansion of New Deal public works projects during wartime to include the construction of military and naval installations, Puerto Rican-owned public authorities such as PRCC became vital to the broader defence of the Caribbean and Western Hemisphere. Long understood to be of geographic and strategic value, Puerto Rico took on a critical importance during the Battle of the Atlantic. Furthermore, like the New Deal in the United States, the New Deal in Puerto Rico established infrastructural groundwork for rapid mobilization during the war and set the stage for the future post-war industrialization programmes that were, above all else, contingent on Allied victory in World War II.

ACKNOWLEDGEMENTS

The author would like to thank the CUNY Graduate Center and Franklin and Eleanor Roosevelt Institute for institutional support as well as the archivists of the National Archives and Records Administration of New York City, the Fundación Luis Muñoz Marín, the Archivo General de Puerto Rico, the Ponce History Museum and the Franklin D. Roosevelt Presidential Library for their helpful and knowledgeable assistance on this project. Special thanks should also go to Debbie McCollin and Karen Eccles of the University of the West Indies. In addition, the author would like to thank Laird Bergad, David Nasaw, Herman Bennett, Gerald Markowitz, Teresita Levy, Anne Macpherson, Antonio Gaztambide-Géigel, Anna Alexander, Mike Bess, Mark Healey, Harry Franqui-Rivera, Aldo Lauria-Santiago, Ismael García-Colón and Vanessa Burrows for reading earlier drafts of this chapter and/or related research on Puerto Rico during the 1930s and 1940s.

NOTES

1. "Victims of U-Boat Trailed as Lure: Raider Followed Lifeboat Five Days but Men Refused to Hail Passing Ships", *New York Times*, 4 April 1942.
2. José L. Bolívar, *Guerra (banca) y desarrollo: El Banco de Fomento y la industrialización de Puerto Rico* (San Juan: Fundación Luis Muñoz Marín/Instituto de Cultura Puertorriqueña, 2011), 22, 31. See also César J. Ayala and José L. Bolívar, *Battleship Vieques: Puerto Rico from World War II to the Korean War* (Princeton, NJ: Markus Weiner, 2011), 9–28; Gaylord T.M. Kelshall, *The U-Boat War in the Caribbean* (Port of Spain: Paria, 1988; repr., Annapolis: Naval Institute Press, 1994), xiv and 7.
3. Although Puerto Rico is an archipelago consisting of the inhabited islands of Puerto Rico, Vieques and Culebra and the natural preserve Isla de Mona, this chapter will refer to Puerto Rico and the colloquial phrase "the island" interchangeably. For more on the impact of the San Felipe and San Ciprián hurricanes on local social, economic and political life, see Geoff Burrows, "The New Deal in Puerto Rico: Public Works, Public Health and the Puerto Rico Reconstruction Administration, 1935–1955" (PhD diss., CUNY Graduate Center, 2014).
4. United Nations, "Non-Self-Governing Territories", http://www.un.org/en/decolonization/nonselfgovterritories.shtml (accessed 10 January 2015); United Nations, "Special Committee on Decolonization Approves Text Calling upon United States to Initiate Self-determination Process for Puerto Rico", https://www.un.org/press/en/2013/gacol3255.doc.htm (accessed 10 January 2015). On

how Puerto Rico's status as a "neither independent nor wholly colonial" territory alienates it from the rest of the Caribbean, see Humberto García Muñiz, "The Colonial Persuasion: Puerto Rico and the Dutch and French Antilles", in *The Caribbean: A History of the Region and Its Peoples*, ed. Stephan Palmié and Francisco Scarano (Chicago: University of Chicago Press, 2011), 538.

5. The Jones Act was signed on 4 March 1917, just one month before President Woodrow Wilson made the case for entry into the Great War by arguing that the United States must "make the world safe for democracy". During World War I and World War II, Puerto Ricans served the US military in segregated units under an all-white officer corps. See "Making the World 'Safe for Democracy': Woodrow Wilson Asks for War, April 2, 1917", http://historymatters.gmu.edu/d/4943/ (accessed 8 March 2014), Text of the Jones Act can be found at the International Foundation for Electoral Systems website, http://www.ifes.org/election-materials/jones-act-1917 (accessed 22 January 2015). For analytical work on the legacy of the Jones Act, see the upcoming special issue of the *CENTRO Journal* based on the two-day symposium "One Hundred Years of the Jones Act and Puerto Rican US Citizenship", which took place on 15–16 October 2015 at the Center for Puerto Rican Studies, Hunter College CUNY.

6. For more on Puerto Rican migration to New York, see Félix V. Matos-Rodríguez and Pedro Juan Hernandez, *Pioneros: Puerto Ricans in New York City, 1896–1948* (Charleston: Arcadia Publishing, 2001); Carmen Teresa Whalen and Victor Vásquez-Hernández, eds., *The Puerto Rican Diaspora: Historical Perspectives* (Philadelphia: Temple University Press, 2005); Lorrin Thomas, *Puerto Rican Citizen: History and Political Identity in the Twentieth Century* (Chicago: University of Chicago Press, 2010).

7. The Great Depression and World War II were global events that require historical study at the local level. As Lizabeth Cohen has written, the reduction of the Great Depression to a series of external and "impersonal events – the stock market crash, unemployment, mortgage foreclosures, bank failures – obscures the reality of these disasters as people experienced them". Lizbeth Cohen, *Making a New Deal: Industrial Workers in Chicago* (Cambridge: Cambridge University Press, 1995), 214.

8. Roughly 98 per cent of the entire PRRA payroll was Puerto Rican, including more than 90 per cent of all administrative, supervisory and clerical personnel and 99.9 per cent of all other workers. See "Federal Agencies Operating in Puerto Rico", *Investigation of Political, Economic and Social Conditions in Puerto Rico: Hearings before the Subcommittee of the House Committee of Insular Affairs, Part 19, Pursuant to HR 159, 78th Cong., 2nd sess., 1944* (Washington DC: Government Printing Office, 1944), 1756 and 1760.

9. All figures have been adjusted for inflation. Adjusting dollar values from the 1930s and 1940s, however, can be difficult due to the extremely volatile economy during the Great Depression and World War II. For consistency, all values pertaining to PRRA expenditures in this essay are adjusted from 1938 to 2014 dollars. See Bureau of Labour Statistics Consumer Price Index Inflation Calculator, http://data.bls.gov/cgi-bin/cpicalc.pl (accessed March 5, 2014).
10. Miles H. Fairbank, *The Chardón Plan and the Puerto Rico Reconstruction Administration, 1934–1954* (San Juan: Fairbank Corporation, 1978), 53, 55–56.
11. Together, the Public Works Administration or Works Progress Administration transformed the built infrastructure of the United States and put millions of people back to work during the darkest period of the Great Depression. As Jason Scott Smith has argued, the large-scale public works projects of these agencies were "the New Deal's central enterprise" and should be regarded as one of the most significant and long-term modernization projects of the New Deal era. See Jason Scott Smith, *Building New Deal Liberalism: The Political Economy of Public Works, 1933–1956* (Cambridge University Press, 2006), 19, 84, 88, 118. See also Robert Leighninger, *Long-Range Public Investment: The Forgotten Legacy of the New Deal* (Charleston: University of South Carolina Press, 2007).
12. On the New Deal as a "holding operation", see Anthony Badger, *The New Deal: The Depression Years, 1933–1940* (1989; repr. Chicago: Ivan R. Dee, 2002), 10, 67. For more on Puerto Rico's post-war development programmes, see A.W. Maldonado, *Teodoro Moscoso and Puerto Rico's Operation Bootstrap* (Gainesville: University Press of Florida, 1997); Emilio Pantojas García, "End-of-the-Century Studies of Puerto Rico's Economy, Politics and Culture: What Lies Ahead?", *Latin American Research Review* 35, no. 3 (2000): 227–40; Emilio Pantojas García, "The Puerto Rican Paradox: Colonialism Revisited", *Latin American Research Review* 40, no. 3 (2005): 163–76.
13. Kelshall, *U-Boat War in the Caribbean*, 8; Fitzroy André Baptiste, *War, Cooperation and Conflict: The European Possessions in the Caribbean, 1939–1945* (Westport, CT: Greenwood Press, 1988), 79–81, 160. See also the charts located between pages 129, 130.
14. Bolívar, *Guerra (banca) y desarrollo*, 26, 31–35, 39.
15. "Public works" are identified by their quasi-independent status as state-owned but autonomously run agencies. In the most widely accepted definition, Ellis Armstrong wrote that they are "the physical structures and facilities developed or acquired by public agencies to house government functions and provide water, waste disposal, power, transportation and similar services to facilitate the

achievement of common social and economic objectives". Ellis L. Armstrong, ed., *History of Public Works in the United States, 1776–1976* (Chicago: American Public Works Association, 1976), 1. On the use of "public authorities" during the New Deal, see Robert Caro, *The Power Broker: Robert Moses and the Fall of New York* (New York: Vintage Books, 1975), 615–36. As Gail Radford has recently warned, however, the over-reliance on public authorities in the twentieth century contributed to the growth of a fragmented, semi-secretive bureaucracy that is largely unaccountable to the electorate. See Gail Radford, *The Rise of the Public Authority: Statebuilding and Economic Development in Twentieth-Century America* (Chicago: University of Chicago Press, 2013), 14–15.

16. Kelshall, *U-Boat War in the Caribbean*, xvi.
17. Ibid., xiii, 8 and 16; Baptiste, *War, Cooperation and Conflict*, 141–42.
18. Humberto García Muñiz and Rebeca Campo, "French and American Imperial Accommodation in the Caribbean During World War II: The Experience of the Guyane and the Subaltern Roles of Puerto Rico", in *Colonial Crucible: Empire and the Making of the Modern American State*, ed. Alfred W. McCoy and Francisco A. Scarano (Madison: University of Wisconsin Press, 2009), 443–44; Kelshall, *U-Boat War in the Caribbean*, 8; Samuel Morison, *The Two-Ocean War: A Short History of the United States Navy in the Second World War* (Boston: Little, Brown., 1963), 113–14.
19. Bolívar, *Guerra (banca) y desarrollo*, 26, 31–35, 39.
20. John Vinocur, "War Veterans Come to Bury, and to Praise, Doenitz", *New York Times*, 7 January 1981; Morison, *Two-Ocean War*, 108–9. Karl Doenitz was convicted at Nuremberg largely for his orders to attack unarmed ships, including those sunk in the Caribbean Sea Frontier. He served ten years at Spandau prison, was released in 1956 and died in 1980. For more on his conviction, see "Judgement: Doenitz", Avalon Project: Documents in Law, History and Diplomacy, Yale Law School, http://avalon.law.yale.edu/imt/juddoeni.asp (accessed 11 October 2014).
21. Morison, *Two-Ocean War*, 118.
22. Baptiste, *War, Cooperation and Conflict*, 144.
23. Samuel Morison, *Two-Ocean War*, 109–10. Ernest Hemingway was among the private citizens who armed privately owned fishing boats with rifles and machine guns during civilian "patrols" of the Caribbean searching for U-boats. See Hilary Hemingway and Carlene Brennen, eds., *Hemingway in Cuba* (New York: Rugged Land, 2003).
24. Kelshall, *U-Boat War in the Caribbean*, xiv.
25. García Muñiz and Campo, "French and American Imperial Accommodation", 443–44; Kelshall, *U-Boat War in the Caribbean*, 8.

26. For example, see "Submarines off Our Coast", *New York Times*, 23 September 1939; "Dominican Cutter Seen a War Victim", *New York Times*, 3 October 1939; "Nazi Fueling Bases for U-Boats and Raiders Set Up in Caribbean", *New York Times*, 21 August 1940; "Nazi Threat to Puerto Rico Recalled By Raid on Aruba", *New York Times*, 17 February 1942; "U-Boat Lair Hunted in Caribbean Area", *New York Times*, 18 February 1942; "39 Die on Tanker Fired off Curaçao", *New York Times*, 22 February 1942; "U-Boat Raids Used for Axis Propaganda", *New York Times*, 22 February 1942; "Puerto Rican Isle Is Shelled by Enemy", *New York Times*, 4 March 1942; "Escapes 4 U-Boats, Is Sunk by a 5th", *New York Times*, 6 April 1942; "Sinking Hints Italy Has U-Boats: Brazilian Freighter Is Sent to Bottom off Virginia", *New York Times*, 30 May 1942; "Axis Mines off Atlantic Coast New Menace to Our Shipping", *New York Times*, 21 June 1942; "2 More Ships Sunk by U-Boat Raiders", *New York Times*, 27 June 1942; "Submarines Plague Caribbean Coast", *New York Times*, 12 July 1942; "Uruguayan Taken Captive by U-Boat", *New York Times*, 8 August 1942.
27. Morison, *Two-Ocean War*, 116.
28. Ibid., 113.
29. Ibid.
30. Baptiste, *War, Cooperation and Conflict*, 143.
31. Orlando J. Pérez, "Panama: Nationalism and the Challenge to Canal Security", in *Latin America during World War II*, ed. Thomas M. Leonard and John F. Bratzel (Lanham, MD: Rowman and Littlefield, 2006), 65; Kelshall, *U-Boat War in the Caribbean*, 7. On Puerto Rico's strategic value in securing the canal prior to Pearl Harbor, see Stetson Conn, Rose C. Engelman and Byron Fairchild, *Guarding the United States and Its Outposts* (Washington, DC: Center for Military History/US Army, 1964), 322–26.
32. García Muñiz and Campo, "French and American Imperial Accommodation", 445.
33. Harry Franqui-Rivera, "Fighting for the Nation: Military Service, Popular Political Mobilization and the Creation of Modern Puerto Rican National Identities: 1868–1952" (PhD diss., University of Massachusetts Amherst, 2010), 220.
34. García Muñiz, "Colonial Persuasion", 538–40.
35. Robert A. Divine, *Roosevelt and World War II* (Baltimore: Johns Hopkins University Press, 1969; repr. New York: Penguin, 1977), 44.
36. Franklin D. Roosevelt, "Fireside Chat (on German Submarine Attacks)", Washington, DC, 11 September 1941, in *Franklin Delano Roosevelt: Great Speeches*, ed. John Graft (Mineola, NY: Dover, 1999), 108.

37. Franklin D. Roosevelt, "Message to Congress on Self-Government for Puerto Rico", 28 September 1943, in Gerhard Peters and John T. Woolley, *The American Presidency Project*, http://www.presidency.ucsb.edu/ws/?pid=16318 (accessed 22 October 2015). Part of this message has also been quoted in Ronald Fernandez, *The Disenchanted Island: Puerto Rico and the United States in the Twentieth Century* (Westport, CT: Praeger, 1996), 137.
38. Baptiste, *War, Cooperation and Conflict*, 75–76.
39. Ibid., 79–81, 160. See also charts 3 and 4 (located between pp. 129, 130).
40. NARA-NYC: Record Group (RG) 181, *Plans, Projects and Policies*, folder A1, Classified General Correspondence, Naval Districts and Shore Establishments, Records of the Tenth Naval District, Confidential memo, Lieutenant Commander Conrad to President Roosevelt, 26 December 1940; NARA-NYC: RG 181, Records of the Tenth Naval District, *Plans, Projects and Policies*, folder A1, Classified General Correspondence, Naval Districts and Shore Establishments, Confidential memo, Navy Department Office of Chief of Naval Operations to All Bureaus and Offices, Navy Department, 5 January 1941; NARA- NYC: RG 181, Records of the Tenth Naval District, *Plans, Projects and Policies*, folder A1, Classified General Correspondence, Naval Districts and Shore Establishments, Confidential memo, 26 February 1941.
41. Andrew Lefebvre, "Puerto Rico: Quiet Participant", in *Latin America during World War II*, ed. Thomas M. Leonard and John F. Bratzel (Lanham, MD: Rowman and Littlefield, 2007), 95. Unlike the rest of Latin America, most of the Caribbean was under colonial or "territorial" control during World War II.
42. Baptiste, *War, Cooperation and Conflict*, 51–52, 75–76; Naval Historical Center, "Destroyers for Bases Agreement", https://www.history.navy.mil/research/library/online-reading-room/title-list-alphabetically/d/destroyers-for-bases-agreement-1941.html (accessed 14 October 2014); "Lend-Lease Act", Our Documents, http://www.ourdocuments.gov/doc.php?doc=71&page=transcript; "Atlantic Charter", *Avalon Project: Documents in Law, History and Diplomacy*, Yale Law School, http://avalon.law.yale.edu/wwii/atlantic.asp (accessed 11 October 2014).
43. For a personal account of Puerto Rico during war mobilization, see Edwin Dooley, "Wartime San Juan: The Forgotten American Home Front, 1941–1946", *Journal of Military History* 63, no. 4 (October 1999): 921–38. For a pointed critique of war mobilization in Puerto Rico, see Ronald Fernández, "Prisoners of War", in Ronald Fernández, *The Disenchanted Island: Puerto Rico and the United States in the Twentieth Century* (Westport, CT: Greenwood Press, 1996), 137–64.

44. José L. Bolívar Fresneda, "Las Inversiones y los Programmeas Militares: Construyendo la Infrastructura y los Recursos Humanos de la Posguerra", in Jorge Rodríguez Beruff and José L. Bolívar Fresneda, eds., *Puerto Rico en la Segunda Guerra Mundial: Baluarte del Caribe* (San Juan: Ediciones Callejón, 2012), 154; Barry M. Stentiford, *The American Home Guard: The State Militia in the Twentieth Century* (College Station: Texas A&M University Press, 2002), 160–61. For more on Esteves, see Ramón Bosque Pérez and José Javier Colón Morera, *Puerto Rico under Colonial Rule: Political Persecution and the Quest for Human Rights* (Albany, NY: SUNY Press, 2006). As with many other important Puerto Rican political, military and public figures, critical biographies of Luis Raul Esteves and Guillermo Esteves are needed.

45. On 17 July 1944, 320 mostly African American sailors were instantly killed and nearly 400 more injured when live ammunition exploded at the Port Chicago Naval Magazine in Contra Costa County, California. In the aftermath, 50 sailors were court-martialled for refusing to return to work, while the most dangerous labour was assigned to segregated all-black units. The court-martialled sailors' appeal was argued by Thurgood Marshall of the National Association of Colored People Legal Defense Fund. Today, the National Parks Service runs the Port Chicago National Memorial, http://www.nps.gov/poch/index.htm (accessed 14 January 2015). For a broader discussion of the long-term consequences of African American service in the Jim Crow military of World War II, see Ira Katznelson, *When Affirmative Action Was White: An Untold History of Racial Inequality in Twentieth-Century America* (New York: Norton, 2005). There are very few studies on Puerto Rican participation in World War II or the effects of segregation on Puerto Rican soldiers. For an excellent analysis of Puerto Rican participation in World War II in the context of the island's colonial status and political and economic development programmes after the war, see Harry Franqui-Rivera, "Education, Industrialization and Decolonization: The Battlefields of the Puerto Rican Soldier During the Second World War", in Franqui-Rivera, "Fighting for the Nation", 213–71. See also Héctor Marín Roman, *Llego la Gringada! El Contexto Social-Militar Estadounidense en Puerto Rico y otros lugares del Caribe hasta 1919* (San Juan: Academia Puertorriqueña de la Lengua Española, 2009); Silvia Alvarez Curbelo, "The Color of War: Puerto Rican Soldiers and Discrimination during World War II", in Maggie Rivas-Rodríguez and Emilio Zamora, eds., *Beyond the Latino World War II Hero: The Social and Political Legacy of a Generation* (Austin: University of Texas Press, 2009), 110–24. The lack of analysis of segregation in Puerto Rico is compounded by the relative historiographic "silence" on issues of race in Puerto Rico. For the best book on this subject, see Ileana M. Rodríguez-Silva,

Silencing Race: Disentangling Blackness, Colonialism and National Identities in Puerto Rico (New York: Palgrave Macmillan, 2012).

46. War Department, Bureau of the Budget, *Puerto Rican Induction Programme*, 15 April 1945, 1, quoted in Franqui-Rivera, "Fighting for the Nation", 238. Despite the problems and complications of segregation, mobilization in Puerto Rico occurred rapidly. Between 1940 and 1941 the Selective Service registered over 500,000 men, who were then inducted at Fort Buchanan in San Juan, went through basic training station at Camp O'Reilly in Gurabo and advanced training at Camp Tortuguero in Vega Baja. See Franqui-Rivera, "Fighting for the Nation", 237–38.
47. Clifford is quoted in García Muñiz and Campo, "French and American Imperial Accommodation", 445. Previously the governor of the Bahamas and Mauritius, the New Zealand–born Clifford was governor of Trinidad and Tobago from 1942 to 1947.
48. Franqui-Rivera, "Fighting for the Nation", 239.
49. García Muñiz and Campo, "French and American Imperial Accommodation", 446. Tangibly demonstrating how racial categories are socially and politically constructed, the term "Puerto Rican white" is a discursive precursor to the contemporary status of "Hispanic white" and "Hispanic non-white" on US census forms and official documents today.
50. Franqui-Rivera, "Fighting for the Nation" 238–39, 238; García Muñiz and Campo, "French and American Imperial Accommodation", 446.
51. García Muñiz and Campo, "French and American Imperial Accommodation", 446.
52. As in the United States, part of the shift from a depression to war economy included a discursive rationalization for federal appropriations. Whereas a rhetorical focus on jobs was necessary to extract money from Congress during the Depression, a rhetorical focus on war defense was essential to obtain money during World War II.
53. NARA-NYC: Records of the Office of the Chief of Engineers, RG 77, Correspondence Relating to Civil and Military Construction Projects, 1941–1950, folder 1, Strength Reports – District Engineer, 1940–1943, box 5, Buenventura J. Jane, Chief Administrative Assistant, War Department, US Engineer Office, Puerto Rico District, San Juan Monthly Civilian Personnel Reports, 1 November 1943 and 30 November 1943. About one-quarter of these workers were employed on civil engineering projects, such as utilities work and river navigation projects. The remaining three-quarters were employed on military projects. See Major Gus A. Draper, Corps of Engineers, Executive Officer to the Chief of Engineers, US Army, 31 March 1943. The vast majority

of civil and military construction–related jobs were held by men, with women employed in mostly clerical positions in the district office. For example, as of July 1943, of the 1,339 employees in the district office there were 268 women: one sub-professional grade, one craft grade, and 266 clerical grade. Among non-office workers, 16 of the 11,391 skilled, semi-skilled or unskilled labourers were women. See NARA-NYC: Records of the Office of the Chief of Engineers, RG 77, Correspondence Relating to Civil and Military Construction Projects, 1941–1950, folder 1, Strength Reports – District Engineer, 1940–1943, box 5, Buenventura J. Jane to Chief of Engineers, US Army, Washington DC, 3 July 1943.

54. The work on civil and military engineering projects varied widely and offered Puerto Ricans access to on-the-job training and skill development across a spectrum of job activities. These included: inspector, surveyor, leverman, rodman, chauffeur, guard, janitor, construction supervisor, subinspector, subsurveyman, recorder, chainman, gage reader, watchman, lineman, packer, gardener, packmaster, caretaker, waiter, deckhand, boatman, sailor, dredge hand, scowman, axeman, drill man, driver, subforeman, foreman, engineman, carpenter, electrician, plumber, mechanic, mate, oiler, handyman, leadsman, labourer (skilled and unskilled), operator of mechanical equipment, helper, pilot, engineer (steam, gasoline, motor), engraver, lithographer, transferer, shader, lockmaster, assistant lockmaster, brakeman, cable splicer, bridge tender, boatswain, car repairer, cement tester, cement worker, concrete finisher, cranesman, dam tender, diesel engineer, fish-counter, fireman (marine and stationary), drag tender, pipe setter, powderman, quartermaster, steerman, rigger, shipkeeper, steward, switchman, transformer tender, truck driver (heavy and light duty), tool sharpener, valve tender, welder (steel, oxyacetylene, electric), winchman. Also derrick hand, lamplighter, laundress, stevedore, teamster, cook, spotter, draftsmen, typist, stenographer, bookkeeper, photographer, and radio operator. See NARA-NYC, RG 77, Records of the Office of the Chief of Engineers, Correspondence Relating to Civil and Military Construction Projects, 1941–1950, folder 2, Strength Reports – District Engineer,1940–1943, box 5, W.D. Tomlin to Post Utilities Officer, US Engineers Office, Ponce, Puerto Rico, 10 March 1942.

55. Smith, *Building New Deal Liberalism*, 192–93.

56. The construction of cement-based houses that would provide a permanent bulwark against both hurricanes and the spread of disease; according to J.C. Hitchman, head of the engineering division, PRRA's primary aim was to "provide a hurricane-proof house and for that reason our construction work has gone largely to the building of concrete houses". See NARA-NYC: RG

323, Records Relating to Construction Projects Directed by the Engineering Division, Farmers Houses – General Memoranda folder, J.C. Hitchman to Miles Fairbank, 19 August 1938.

57. NARA-NYC: RG 323, box 2, Records Relating to the Cement Plant Project, Accounting and Cost folder, Memorandum on the Cement Plant, 16 January 1939; NARA-NYC: RG 323, box 2, Records Relating to the Cement Plant Project, Accounting and Cost folder, Accounting Report, July 1944; NARA-NYC: RG 323, General Records Relating to the Cement Plant Project.

58. NARA-NYC: RG 323, General Records Relating to the Cement Plant Project, Puerto Rico Cement Corporation folder, Manuel Font to Arturo Cordova Infante, 18 March 1938; NARA-NYC: RG 323, Records Relating to the Cement Plant Project, box 2, Accounting and Cost folder, "Outline of the History of the Cement Plant Project". In December 1935 President Franklin Roosevelt allocated $850,000 from the Emergency Relief Appropriation Act of 1935 for the Cataño plant, which was augmented by additional allotments totalling $616,500 in 1936, 1937 and 1938. The total construction cost of the cement plant was $1,444,831.14 (just below the $1,466,500 allocated). See Fairbank, *Chardón Plan*, 8–9.

59. NARA-NYC: RG 323, Records of the Finance Division, PRRA History Report folder, box 1, Miles Fairbank, "PRRA Organization, Financial Policies and Functions Prepared Pursuant to the Requirements of Senate Resolution 150, 75th Congress, First Session". Cement construction proved to be the most effective at tackling the multiple vectors of disease and poverty that were increasing on the island. Not only were hundreds of thousands of Puerto Rican men and women made homeless by the 1928 and 1932 hurricanes, but strategies for recovery before PRRA had actually *increased* the three deadliest public health crises confronting the island in the 1930s: malaria, hookworm and malnutrition – which included dietary-related gastrointestinal disorders such as chronic diarrhoea and enteritis. NARA-NYC: RG 323, Records Relating to Construction Projects Directed by the Engineering Division, Progress Reports, box 3, Engineering Division Construction Projects, "Swamp Land Filling and Draining for Malaria Control" folder; NARA-NYC: RG 323, General Records Relating to the Cement Plant Project. See also Burrows, "New Deal in Puerto Rico".

60. NARA-NYC: RG 323, PRCC folder, box 1, General Records Relating to the Cement Plant Project, Manuel Font to Arturo Cordova Infante, 18 March 1938.

61. NARA-NYC: Records Relating to the Cement Plant Corporation, Accounting and Cost folder, box 2, "Memorandum on the Cement Plant", 16 January 1939; NARA-NYC: RG 323, Records Relating to Construction Projects Directed by

the Engineering Division, Progress Reports, box 3, Engineering Division Construction Projects, "Swamp Land Filling and Draining for Malaria Control" folder; NARA-NYC: RG 323, General Records Relating to the Cement Plant Project.

62. Prior to the 1930s, nearly all "public" works and utilities in Latin America and the Caribbean were constructed by private local and international capital.
63. Bolívar, "Las Inversiones y los Programmeas Militares", 137.
64. Gerardo M. Piñero Cádiz, "La Base Aeronaval Roosevelt Roads: El Pearl Harbor del Caribe", in Beruff and Bolívar, *Puerto Rico en la Segunda Guerra Mundial*, 293; Carlos M. González Morales, "Borinquen Field y Aguadilla: Un Municipio en la Guerra", in Beruff and Bolívar, *Puerto Rico en la Segunda Guerra Mundial*, 261.
65. Franqui-Rivera, "Fighting for the Nation", 221.
66. Bolívar, "Las Inversiones y los Programmeas Militares", 151.
67. NARA-NYC: RG 77, Records of the Office of the Chief of Engineers, Puerto Rico District, Correspondence Relating to Civil and Military Construction Projects, Strength Reports – District Engineer, 1940–1943, 1941–1950, Buenaventura J. Jane, Chief Administrative Assistant, War Department, US Engineer's Office, Puerto Rico District, San Juan, Monthly Civilian Personnel Report, 1 November 1943; NARA-NYC: RG 77, Records of the Office of the Chief of Engineers, Puerto Rico District, Civil Works – Miscellaneous Administrative Matters, Strength Reports – District Engineer, 1940–1943, Correspondence Relating to Civil and Military Construction Projects, 1941–1950, "Report Upon the Improvement of Rivers and Harbors in the Panama District".
68. Jorge Rodríguez Beruff, *Strategy as Politics: Puerto Rico on the Eve of the Second World War* (San Juan: La Editorial Universidad de Puerto Rico, 2007), ix.
69. NARA-NYC: RG 77, Records of the Office of the Chief of Engineers, Puerto Rico District, Strength Reports – District Engineer, 1940–1943, Correspondence Relating to Civil and Military Construction Projects, 1941–1950, Buenaventura J. Jane, Chief Administrative Assistant, War Department, US Engineer's Office, Puerto Rico District, San Juan, Monthly Civilian Personnel Report, 1 November 1943; NARA-NYC: RG 77, Records of the Office of the Chief of Engineers, Puerto Rico District, Correspondence Relating to Civil and Military Construction Projects, 1941–1950, Major Gus A. Draper, Corps of Engineers, to Chief of Engineers, US Army, Civil Works – Miscellaneous Administrative Matters, Strength Reports – District Engineer, 1940–1943, 31 March 1943; NARA-NYC: RG 77, Records of the Office of the Chief of Engineers, Puerto Rico District, Correspondence Relating to Civil and Military Construction Projects, 1941–1950, W.D. Tomlin, Chief Administrative Assistant, to Post

Utilities Officer, US Engineer's Office, Ponce, Puerto Rico, Civil Works – Miscellaneous Administrative Matters, Strength Reports – District Engineer, 1940–1943, 10 March 1942.
70. Jana K. Lipman, "Guantánamo and the Case of Kid Chicle: Private Contract Labor and the Development of the US Military", in *Colonial Crucible: Empire and the Making of the Modern American State*, ed. Alfred W. McCoy and Francisco A. Scarano (Madison: University of Wisconsin Press, 2009), 454–55.
71. John F. Bratzel, introduction, in *Latin America during World War II*, ed. Thomas M. Leonard and John F. Bratzel (Lanham, MD: Rowman and Littlefield, 2007), 5.
72. Bolívar, *Guerra (banca) y desarrollo*, 22, 31.
73. Kelshall, *U-Boat War in the Caribbean*, xiii, 8, 16.

3.

INVERSING DEPENDENCE
The Dutch Antilles, Suriname and the Desperate Netherlands during World War II

ESTHER CAPTAIN AND GUNO JONES

The overriding perception of relationships between European motherlands and overseas colonies is that the former occupy the position of omnipotent power and possess political, economic and military independence from the latter, which are considered "the dependents".[1] In the case of the Dutch empire, this concept was fundamentally altered by World War II. This chapter discusses the ways in which World War II signified a reversion of the relation between the Netherlands and the Dutch Antilles and Suriname and the impact of this on the development of war heritage and on increased political consciousness in the latter.

After the German occupation of the Netherlands in May 1940 and the Japanese occupation of the Dutch East Indies in 1942, the motherland became dependent on the Dutch Antilles and Suriname, the only unoccupied territories of the Kingdom of the Netherlands. That being so, this chapter opens with a brief sketch of the colonial relations that existed within the Dutch Empire from the late 1930s to the nascent stages of World War II. Attention is then drawn to the occupation of the Netherlands and Indonesia (then known as the Dutch East Indies in colonial discourse) and the consequences for Dutch colonial policies in the remaining parts of the Dutch Empire in the Caribbean. The chapter further analyses the extent to which Dutch sovereign power was contested by American troops deployed in Suriname and the Dutch Antilles to protect the strategically important oil and bauxite industries and how the Dutch government responded to this development by (among other things) the recruitment of local troops and personnel for a variety of military and non-military purposes (to defend the essential oil and bauxite industries, to serve as health-care workers or colonial seamen or to fight the Japanese army in Indonesia). The chapter also explores the varied meanings of military and personnel support among Dutch colonial authorities and local actors. To the latter, these contributions signified the need to dismantle colonial relationships, to the former they were a symbol of a unified Dutch kingdom, as the chapter demonstrates. Additionally, an analysis is made of the ways in which the population in Suriname and the Dutch Antilles, via relief funds and support committees, collected money and goods for the needy population in the Netherlands on a relatively substantial scale and the manner in which people in the colonies gave meaning to these efforts. While the material, military and personnel contributions became connected with a new sense of pride and political awareness in the Dutch Antilles and Suriname, as is demonstrated throughout this chapter, they have been largely neglected in post–World War II scholarship and historiography, as well as in the heritage of the war in the Netherlands. This chapter concludes with some final reflections on these discrepancies.

THE DUTCH EMPIRE BEFORE WORLD WAR II

To better understand why the situation during World War II was one of, as it is argued, "inversed dependence", it is instructive to take a brief look at colonial relations that existed within the Dutch Empire immediately prior to and at the commencement of the war. Because of the significance of Indonesia to Dutch colonial prestige and national identity, a brief sketch of the situation in the Dutch East Indies (today Indonesia) is also included in this description. The sovereignty of the Dutch over Suriname, the Dutch Antilles and the huge, now Indonesian archipelago (the size of Western Europe, stretching from Ireland to Moscow) was naturalized in Dutch political discourse and public opinion. The possession of these overseas territories, legitimized by the

Dutch version of a civilizing discourse, was one of the elements in dominant constructions of Dutch national identity.[2]

The prevalence of imperial mentality among the Dutch political class was clearly visible in the ways in which the Dutch government and parliament dealt with pleas for autonomy immediately before the war. The Dutch colonial authorities consistently rejected claims of moderate nationalists in Indonesia for internal self-rule in the decades after 1900 and even immediately after the German occupation of the Netherlands in May 1940.[3] The local representative bodies both in the Dutch East Indies and the West Indies (Suriname and the Dutch Caribbean islands) at the time did not represent the majority of the colonized population, as they were dominated by members of the male European colonial elite. In the Dutch East Indies the political representation of the colonized Indonesians, the overwhelming majority of the population classified as "native Dutch subjects", was formally kept limited (and in effect non-existent) in De Volksraad (the People's Council) to the advantage of those classified as Dutch citizens and the Dutch governor general.[4] This racialized hierarchy of political citizenship was paralleled by socioeconomic hierarchies of citizenship between "subjects" and "citizens": senior positions in the colonial bureaucracy and the colonial army were reserved for citizens, while the subjects were excluded from these positions).[5] In Suriname and Curaçao (the main island and as such the political centre of the Dutch Caribbean islands), while the entire settled population was classified as Dutch citizens, until the introduction of general suffrage in 1949 only a small percentage (the affluent and educated) held voting rights in local representative bodies, De Staten van Suriname and De Staten van Curaçao (the People's Council of Suriname and the People's Council of Curaçao).[6] As in the Dutch East Indies, socioeconomic stratification in Suriname and Curaçao was strongly racialized. Moreover, it should be remembered that the constitutional rights (and hence the political influence regarding the rule of the colonies) of De Volksraad, De Staten van Suriname and De Staten van Curaçao were limited. Before the beginning of World War II (and even thereafter), the local colonial authorities held extensive powers vis-à-vis these representative bodies and sovereignty was still firmly held by the Dutch government and the Dutch parliament.[7]

RUPTURE IN THE DUTCH EMPIRE: THE MOTHERLAND OCCUPIED

The outbreak of World War II signified a rupture in colonial relationships within the Dutch Empire. Germany occupied the Netherlands on 10 May 1940, forcing the Dutch Queen Wilhelmina and the government into exile in London. This was followed by the territorial takeover of Indonesian territory by the Japanese Army on 9 March 1942, leading to a "reversed colonial hierarchy" after the internment of the European part of the population.[8] While the Japanese presented their territorial control over the archipelago as liberation of the Indonesian people from European conquerors, Dutch politicians – implicitly naturalizing and legitimizing colonial rule by the Dutch before the Japanese takeover – characterized this redistribution of power as occupation of their most cherished colonial territory, their "emerald belt".[9] As the Netherlands and Indonesia were controlled by Germany and Japan, the remaining parts of the Dutch kingdom instantly gained in symbolic significance as Suriname and the Dutch Antilles were the only parts of the Dutch Empire not controlled by the Axis powers, and people in these colonies were well aware of this. As a member of the local voluntary Surinamese military force (Korps Stads-en Landwachten) recalled,

> Of great importance is that Suriname and the Dutch Antilles remained the only territories [within the Dutch kingdom] on which the Dutch flag still waved freely when the Netherlands was invaded [by Germany]. Suriname and the Dutch Antilles held full responsibility. The Netherlands had fallen out. This territory [Suriname] and the Dutch Antilles were free and we were holding aloft the Dutch flag. For this reason there was a lively awareness that "we need to join the fight".[10]

Notwithstanding being "in exile" in London, the Dutch government firmly held a grip on internal affairs in Suriname and the Dutch Antilles via the local Dutch colonial authorities. The Dutch government did everything in its power to continue ruling the remaining parts of the empire. Martial law entered into force after the German occupation of the Netherlands, enabling the Dutch governors to extend their powers over local political affairs.

Of great significance in this regard were the internment policies of the Dutch governors Gielliam J.J. Wouters in Curaçao and J.C. Kielstra in Suriname. Both governors used special powers granted to them by martial law to intern those groups and individuals classified as enemies of the state. In

Curaçao, where 65,231 people were living in 1939, Governor Wouters ordered the internment of a total of 461 individuals into special camps on 10 May 1940, most of them with German or Austrian nationality.[11] Strikingly, some of the interned were people of Jewish background. The internment policies of Governor Kielstra in Suriname in particular were heavily contested by local opposition parties and the local population. Of a population of 142,225[12] people living in Suriname at the time (in 1940), Kielstra ordered the internment of 138 Germans, mostly members of the Moravian Church, which had a long history in the country.[13] Furthermore, deliberation between the Dutch government, Governor General Tjarda van Starkenborgh Stachouwer of the Dutch East Indies and Governor Kielstra of Suriname resulted in the relocation of 146 individuals classified as members of the National Socialist movement (Nationaal-Socialistische Beweging) from the Dutch East Indies to Suriname, where they – after arriving in Suriname on 1 March 1942 – were separately interned.[14] This intense consultation between the Dutch government and the governors of the Dutch East Indies and Suriname once again underscores the strong efforts by the Dutch government to keep control over its overseas empire.

These internments were not uncontested among the local population. Most interned Germans were missionaries and their family members. They were in the service of the Protestant Moravian church, which had a large following among the creoles, who were a substantial part of the population. Because of a variety of historical reasons, the missionaries enjoyed much more authority and credit among this part of the population than did the colonial authorities and colonial elite; for this reason, they were known as "other whites".[15] While they were interned, local guards tried to soften the fate of the German missionaries and their family members since, unlike the situation in Europe, many Surinamese did not perceive them as Nazis because they were known as people who dedicated their lives to the service of the Surinamese population. When the Dutch colonial authorities expelled the German missionaries and their families on 19 February 1947, a large crowd gathered to wave them goodbye and call for their return to Suriname.[16] As for the interned "Dutch-East Indisch" members of the National Socialist movement,[17] their ill treatment by the colonial authorities, and especially the execution of two of them on order of the commander of the Dutch colonial troops, led to fierce political debates (in 1949 and 1950) in the local representative body, De Staten, after the war had ended.[18]

More significantly, the fact that Governor Kielstra used the state of emergency to intern his political opponents (from 1940 onwards) made him very unpopular in Surinamese society and gave a strong impulse to the plea for internal self-rule. Moderate nationalists, including prominent and popular member of De Staten Wim Bos Verschuur, gained in strength because of the Dutch governor's authoritarian rule before and during World War II. The Surinamese and Dutch Antillean population loved the Dutch royal family, as was demonstrated during the war by the very enthusiastic responses of locals to the very first visits of Princess Juliana and Prince Bernhard to these remaining unoccupied parts of the Dutch kingdom. This was to a large extent also true for the moderate nationalists in Suriname. In contrast to their positive perceptions of the Dutch royal family, moderate nationalists in Suriname strongly criticized the policies of the Dutch colonial authorities.[19] Indeed, it may be argued that for a long time the soft face of Dutch imperial power (the Dutch royal family) was instrumental in the acceptance and continuation of the "hard side" of Dutch imperial rule: the use of sovereign power by the Dutch government and Dutch colonial authorities to control the overseas territories, in this case by unpopular internment policies. Moderate nationalism, of particular prominence in Suriname, embraced the kingdom as symbolized by the queen but strongly rejected the continued interference of the Dutch government in local internal affairs.

DUTCH SOVEREIGN POWER CONTESTED: OIL, BAUXITE AND AMERICAN TROOPS

The geopolitical importance of Suriname and the Dutch Antilles to the Allied war efforts during World War II led to the deployment of American troops in both territories, which seriously contested Dutch sovereignty over these territories. As has been argued, while Suriname provided a significant part of the raw material for the production of Allied combat aircraft, the islands of Curaçao and Aruba provided a substantial part of the fuel needed for the operation of these aircraft, as well as other war material.[20] Suriname was the largest supplier of bauxite to the United States by 1941. Bauxite was refined to alumina for the production of combat aircraft that were vital to the Allied victory. Approximately 82 per cent of the bauxite used by the United States during World War II was supplied by Suriname. Similarly, oil refined in

Curaçao and Aruba made up 80 per cent of the Western Allied stock in 1941; Allied efforts in northern Africa "completely depended on Antillean oil".[21]

US president Roosevelt, unconvinced that the "Dutch territories" – of crucial importance for the US war efforts – were properly defended against potential German attacks, firmly expressed his wish to send troops to Suriname. The Dutch government, which had requested the supply of air-defence weapons and coastal patrol, not the deployment of US troops in Suriname, was troubled by this expanded request. Because of the fear of the loss of Dutch sovereignty over Suriname, the Dutch government firmly requested that it wield supreme control over the US troops that were to be deployed in Suriname and the funding of the operation, and it demanded as well the guarantee that the United States not interfere in internal affairs.[22] Furthermore, to add to the contentions, proposals by Roosevelt to include Brazil and Venezuela in the defence of Suriname and the Dutch Antilles respectively were not followed through after being rejected by the Netherlands.[23]

Along with the military importance of the bauxite and oil industry of Suriname and the Dutch Antilles to the Allied war efforts, the energetic US proposals may also have been inspired by the Monroe Doctrine, which assumed a US responsibility towards the liberation of countries on the American continent from European colonization and interference.[24] As a result, the United States did not succumb to the Dutch demands and maintained the supreme command over its troops and also responsibility for funding. As a compromise, the US mission was formally represented as being requested by the Dutch government.[25]

Completely to the surprise and anger of Governor Kielstra of Suriname – who had requested postponement of the arrival of the US troops – the American troops arrived in Suriname on the same day a Dutch-American statement announced their deployment, underscoring the determination of the United States to send in the troops and revealing a certain disregard for Dutch colonial authorities.[26] In Suriname, some two thousand American troops began arriving on 24 November 1941. From 11 February 1942 fourteen hundred US troops arrived on the island of Curaçao while Aruba received an estimated eleven hundred.[27]

PRESERVING THE UNITY OF THE KINGDOM: DUTCH SYMBOLISM AND THE RECRUITMENT OF LOCAL TROOPS

In response to the huge influx of US military into the Dutch Antilles and Suriname, the Dutch government in London attempted to assert Dutch sovereignty by implementing policies geared towards promoting Dutch imperial symbolism. The Dutch government instructed public institutions and offices (district offices, police offices, military encampments and schools) to perform flag instructions (the Dutch flag had to be raised and lowered every day) and students were required to show respect for the Dutch anthem. The loyalty of newly recruited public officials towards the Dutch was tested.[28]

Furthermore, the Dutch colonial authorities significantly increased the militarization of Suriname and the Dutch Antilles after the arrival of US troops. In addition to the need to defend the bauxite and oil industries of Suriname and the Dutch Antilles respectively from German military attacks, this measure was meant to counterbalance the American military presence.[29] The relatively small number of Dutch colonial forces (consisting in Suriname of the Dutch East Indies Army, the marines and the elite Princess Irene Brigade) was substantially supplemented by the conscription and recruitment of local people.[30] From 1942 onwards the Dutch government introduced compulsory military service for the male population of Suriname and the Dutch Antilles. All males aged eighteen and older were conscripted for military service in the local armed forces, called De Schutterij.[31] On Curaçao the number of males conscripted was three thousand, while the Surinamese Schutterij counted five thousand men at full strength.[32] As well as compulsory military service, the Dutch governors set up voluntary armed forces, known as the Korps Stads- en Landwachten in Suriname (some thousand during World War II) and the Burgerwacht in the Dutch Antilles in 1942. In Suriname, Governor Kielstra also established the Female Home Guard, consisting of some three hundred women.[33] The Dutch government recruited people from Suriname and the Dutch Antilles as gunners (to defend the merchant ships, some two hundred Surinamese men) and less than a hundred marines. Surinamese men fought in the ranks of the Dutch army in Europe throughout World War II (and some, such as Hugo Desire Rijhiner, were even decorated for their bravery during the war with the highest Dutch military order). Antillean and Surinamese women, as well, served as health-care workers in Belgium and the Netherlands.[34] Antillean and Surinamese Dutch in the Netherlands also served in the Dutch resistance against the German occupation. For example, men such as George Maduro from Curaçao, Boy Ecury from Aruba and Anton de Kom from Suriname were active in the Dutch resistance movement, as they were living in the Netherlands during World War II, and they died as a consequence of their involvement. Their public recognition after the end of World War II was varied, complex and sometimes ambiguous.[35]

The recruitment of West Indian troops involved the deployment of Surinamese and Dutch Antilleans in the Dutch East Indies to fight the Japanese army. For this purpose, some 300 men from the Dutch Antilles volunteered (they mostly served in non-combatant roles) while 450 men from Suriname volunteered (mostly for combatant roles). In addition, some 32 Surinamese and Antillean women served in the Red Cross in Indonesia/Dutch East Indies.[36] The Surinamese (together with volunteers from the Dutch Antilles) were deployed to recapture the important oil port cities of Tarakan and Balikpapan in Indonesia from the Japanese army and to carry out mopping-up operations in New Guinea against remaining Japanese soldiers.[37] One of the Surinamese-Dutch soldiers in the service of the Dutch East Indies Army, Harry Voss, gained heroic status after the war in Suriname because of his bravery and loyalty to the Dutch queen.[38]

MILITARY AND PERSONNEL SUPPORT: DIFFERENT MEANINGS

The meaning of the recruitment and deployment of people from the Dutch Antilles and Suriname (to the different theatres of war) varied according to political orientation and position.

For the Dutch authorities, the deployment of people from the Dutch Antilles and Suriname was meant to symbolize and enhance the unity of the Dutch kingdom. While the Dutch Queen Wilhelmina, in a radio speech broadcast from London on 7 December 1942, had promised the overseas territories internal self-rule, this was certainly not intended to herald their independence; quite the contrary, these constitutional promises were meant to "safeguard" the Dutch Empire against the background of rising nationalism in Indonesia and Suriname.[39] The idea of a unified Dutch kingdom was, for instance, exemplified by a telegraphed message from Dutch secretary of colonies Hubertus Johannes Van Mook to Dutch governor Johannes Cornelis Brons of Suriname on 28 July 1944 regarding the deployment of Surinamese

Dutch soldiers against the Japanese army in Indonesia: "I want to express my deep appreciation for the exceptional personnel contribution [of the Surinamese] to the liberation and building up of Indonesia."[40]

However, the meanings of war contributions escaped, to a certain extent, the influence of the Dutch colonial authorities, as welcome ceremonies, newspaper reports, personal memories, written memories and secondary literature demonstrate. Almost everyone praised the colonial troops – especially those deployed against the Japanese in Indonesia – as heroes. But the preferred meaning the Dutch colonial authorities attached to these heroic deeds – as symbolizing the unity of the Dutch Kingdom – was complemented and sometimes even contested in these settings. Shortly after the end of World War II, welcome ceremonies and memory initiatives in Suriname, of which local politician and fierce proponent of autonomy Wim Bos Verschuur was an important instigator, were scenes where a strong sense of national pride was articulated.[41] For Percy Wijngaarde, chair of the committee that was erected to celebrate and honour the homecoming of troops deployed in Indonesia, the men of different ethnic backgrounds symbolized the unity of the Surinamese people. Wijngaarde praised the "deeds, attitude and courage" of the men in a welcome ceremony and added, "You held up the honour of Suriname. You have demonstrated that this small country can produce fighters which are on equal footing with others."[42] A report in one of Suriname's main newspapers on 17 February 1947, *De West*, more explicitly made the connection between war contributions and constitutional changes in the kingdom. After commemorating the wide-ranging contributions the "sons and daughters of this country" made to "the liberation of the [Dutch] empire in Europe and Asia", the report continued, "Have our war volunteers with their glorious achievements in the name of democracy, succeeded so that this country will be considered and treated equally by the Netherlands"?[43] To some others, the war contributions explicitly necessitated the granting of internal self-rule. Consistent with the ideology of moderate nationalism, they argued that the "war contributions of our fighters" paved the way for "demanding internal self-rule without timidity".[44] The connection between war contributions and internal self-rule was also made by veterans themselves. Some, such as gunner August Hermelijn, were motivated by the prospect of internal self-rule when signing for service, believing that "the sooner the Netherlands was liberated, the sooner we would get some sort of internal self-rule".[45] The veterans, as their personal memories testify, were well aware of their ambiguous positions as soldiers in the service of the Allied forces *and* as (racialized) colonized. They had experienced authoritarian colonial rule (in their case by Governor Kielstra in Suriname) and US segregation laws during training in the United States before travelling to Indonesia. After being deployed to fight the Japanese army in Indonesia, the troops from the West Indies were reluctant to fight Indonesian nationalists, as ordered by the Dutch authorities. They did not want to become involved in a Dutch colonial war against the Indonesian nationalists, as they understood their wish to free themselves from Dutch colonial rule. Moreover, they recognized Indonesians as fellow colonized people, subjected to European rule.[46]

Even deeds of war heroes who seemed to symbolize unequivocal loyalty to the Dutch queen could be signified in multiple ways after the war. The iconic figure of Harry Voss, born in 1912 in Suriname's capital Paramaribo, is telling in this regard. As a sergeant in service of the Dutch East Indies army, he was sent to fight in the Dutch East Indies, where he was captured as a prisoner of war by the Japanese army. After Voss refused to cooperate with the Japanese army (who among other things wanted to utilize his skills as a trainer), he was executed in Kotatjane (Indonesia) on 29 May 1943. His reputation as a hero was established by his last deeds and words. After being granted a last wish by a Japanese officer, he requested a Dutch flag, in which he covered himself. He refused to be blindfolded, uttering, "I am a Dutchman, I am not afraid to die." After the first shots Voss was still alive, and shortly before he was finally killed, he cried out, "Long live the Queen!"[47]

The Dutch queen posthumously granted Harry Voss the highest Dutch military order for his bravery (the Militaire Willems-orde, to be compared with the British Victoria Cross or American Medal of Honor).[48] To the Dutch civil and military authorities, Voss was an excellent soldier and a good Dutchman. However, after the war he also became *the* symbol of bravery of Surinamese troops during the war. Within circles of the Surinamese war veterans and moderate nationalists, he became a Surinamese hero. To attest to this, Pieter Polanen, chair of the League of Surinamese War Veterans, stated, "Harry Voss has shown himself to be a completely brave and strong Surinamer."[49] This two-sided appropriation of Harry Voss, in which he was constructed as a symbol of unity within the kingdom by Dutch authorities and as "true Surinamer" by moderate nationalist and others, was characteristic of the varied meanings attached to war efforts by "colonials" after the war.

NURTURING THE MOTHERLAND: THE COLLECTION OF MONEY AND GOODS

The relief efforts the population of the Dutch Antilles and Suriname intended for the Dutch population are probably the most imaginative expression of inversed dependence during World War II. These efforts must be understood against the backdrop of the transformation of the motherland from a "leading country to a suffering country".[50] As a conspicuous sign of the loss of omnipotent imperial power, the Dutch government in London officially sent a request to the overseas territories in the West Indies to collect relief funds in September 1944.[51] While the Netherlands still held formal sovereignty over Suriname and the Dutch Antilles, the Dutch authorities were well aware of the factual inversion of power relations between the motherland and the colonies. As Governor Isaac Wagemaker of Aruba stated, "No one knows the Netherlands as a suffering country, it is rather known as a wealthy country."[52]

In response, the population of the Dutch Antilles and Suriname became involved in substantial relief efforts for the population of the Netherlands. The first relief fund, Steun aan Nederlandse Oorlogsslachtoffers Curaçao (Support to Dutch War Victims Curaçao), was established at Willemstad, the capital of Curaçao. From Willemstad, the governor asked his colleagues in the other Antillean islands to unite forces in order to work efficiently. Their partner organization, Steun aan Nederlandse Oorlogsslachtoffers Aruba (SANOA, Support to Dutch War Victims Aruba), is well documented in the archives, thus providing excellent insight into its efforts.

SANOA was established by Governor Isaac Wagemaker on 28 May 1940. The committee consisted of twenty-eight associations, boards, church denominations, schools, trade and oil companies and military and civilian institutions. In total, SANOA collected 290,428.17 Dutch guilders. Converted to a 2009 price rate, this would be approximately €3.1 million.[53] When the south of the Netherlands was liberated from the German occupier in mid-September 1944 and it became effectively possible to send relief goods, the Aruba Relief Fund for the Netherlands was established. The Aruba Relief Fund turned out to be very active in collecting money by using direct mail to all Aruban residents in three languages (Dutch, Papiamentu and English). In total, 126,000 guilders were collected.

On 19 November 1945 the first batch of relief goods was shipped to the Netherlands by the MS *Cadila*. This shipment consisted of forty-nine boxes of blankets, clothing and shoes for women, men and children, goods bought at the American Buying Service in New York. The invoice shows flannel shirts, trousers, coats and woollen socks for men, navy coats, and woollen and cotton underwear and trousers for children, woollen sweaters, underwear and knitted vests for women, as well as hats. Besides SANOA, employees of Lago Oil and Transport Company, an American enterprise based at San Nicolas at the southern tip of Aruba, were committed to supporting the war as well. The employees not only produced oil for the Allied war industry but also collected money for the Dutch within the Aruba War Association. Moreover, twenty-one employees were killed while working at the Lago refinery. An orbituary in the Antillean newspaper *Amigoe di Curaçao* read, "1940–1945: In grateful remembrance and homage to those who gave their lives in the struggle for freedom and justice. Lago Oil & Transport Company".[54]

Like Curaçao and Aruba, the population of Suriname mobilized to support the population of the Netherlands. The material support from the Surinamese population served both military and civilian purposes. With regard to the former, the Spitfire Fund (named after the famous British fighter jet) collected a total sum of 135,000 guilders during the war. Money for military vehicles, vessels and planes was collected for the Submarine Fund and the Prince Bernhard Fund, the latter receiving 128,506 guilders between 1940 and 1943. The Surinamese population also collected money for a torpedo boat, while the Surinamese-Dutch military collected 50,000 guilders in 1944 for their captured Dutch comrades overseas. Moreover, the Surinamese population also supported the Dutch citizens via the War Relief Fund Suriname (which had succeeded in collecting 50,000 guilders within two months), the Red Cross Suriname and the National Support Committee for support to the Netherlands.[55] The latter committee even had plans to give shelter to malnourished Dutch children in Suriname and the Dutch Antilles after the German capitulation, an idea which would have been unimaginable in the pre-war relationships between the Netherlands and Dutch Caribbean.[56] The Surinamese Red Cross, in particular, played an important role in supplying goods to the Netherlands. As Johan Ferrier, who was to become the last

Dutch governor and first president of the independent republic of Suriname, remembered, "A stream of goods, organized by The Red Cross, was sent to the hungry Netherlands" after the liberation of the Netherlands on 5 May 1945.[57] During relief campaigns, as Ferrier's daughter Cynthia McLeod, historian and author, remembers, a variety of goods were collected such as "clothes, sheets, towels . . . peanut and coconut cookies . . . and don't forget our nutritious, self-made cocoa which the anaemic children in Holland needed in order to recover. But will the Dutch people still remember? Alas, I think they have long [since] forgotten about this."[58]

The political meaning of the elaborate relief efforts by the population of the Dutch Antilles and Suriname is paradoxical. These efforts may be viewed as both a sign of unity and of rupture in the Dutch Kingdom. By enthusiastically supporting the relief funds, the population of the Dutch Antilles and Suriname demonstrated that they deeply cared about the predicaments of their fellow Dutch citizens in the Netherlands. However, by nurturing the motherland these relief efforts also nourished the political self-consciousness and moderate nationalist ideology (aimed at internal self-rule) in the Dutch Antilles and Suriname as well. In Curaçao and Aruba, old assumptions about the Netherlands were shattered by the poverty and famine that Dutchmen experienced during the war. The power and wealth of the Netherlands were not as obvious and strong as people had assumed. The dominant role of the motherland within the Kingdom of the Netherlands turned out not to be self-evident, and a revision of the roles between the Caribbean islands and the Netherlands was inevitable in the end. The intense connection between the Dutch Caribbean islands and the Netherlands experienced during World War II ran parallel to the wish for more autonomy of these colonies. After all, during the war they had proven to be able to maintain themselves without the direct influence of the Netherlands. From 1954 on, the Statute of the Kingdom of the Netherlands would be the leading document for the relationship between the Netherlands and the Dutch Antilles. Via this statute, the Antillean islands were granted the status of autonomous and equal parts of the kingdom.

In Suriname the "double-sidedness" of the relief efforts is exemplified by the fact that moderate nationalists such as Wim Bos Verschuur and Johan Wijngaarde were both active supporters of these efforts as well as fierce proponents of internal self-rule.[59] As Johan Ferrier, at the time a prominent moderate nationalist, remembered, being "boss in our own home" was consistent with the promises of more autonomy made by the Dutch queen.[60] Against the backdrop of material, military, personnel and relief efforts made by the population of the Dutch Antilles and Suriname for the Netherlands and Allies, the political ideal of internal self-rule was much more feasible after the end of World War II than ever before. In that sense, World War II enhanced and legitimized the plea for internal self-rule that was particularly strong in Suriname. After tough negotiations with the Netherlands, the Dutch Antilles and Suriname were granted internal self-rule in 1954, while remaining part of the Kingdom of the Netherlands. In 1975 Suriname became an independent nation-state, while the islands formerly known as the Dutch Antilles are at present still part of the Dutch kingdom.

CONCLUSION: FORGOTTEN GRATITUDE

The relief efforts that were made by the population of the Dutch Antilles and Suriname were remembered, generously, by the two Monuments of Gratitude that the Netherlands erected in 1953 in Willemstad, the capital of Curaçao, and in 1955 in Paramaribo, the capital of Suriname.[61] Via these monuments, the Netherlands "thankfully remembered" the relief efforts made by the population of the Dutch Antilles and Suriname. The unveilings of these monuments were solemn moments, both in the Dutch Antilles as well as in Suriname. In the Dutch Antilles, Prince Bernhard was present at the inaugural ceremony of the monument *Lady of Plenty*, which was placed at the entrance of Fortress Amsterdam in Willemstad, where the governor was residing. *Lady of Plenty* was a monumental statue by artist Albert Termote, a well-known Dutch sculptor. The bronze statue on a pedestal of stone shows a female figure almost five metres tall, dressed in a long robe, carrying the horn of plenty in her left hand and a rose in her right hand. The inscription at the pedestal reads, "The Netherlands gratefully remembers the relief provided for during and after the war 1940–1945 by the Antilles out of feelings of solidarity."[62]

In Suriname, a large crowd had gathered to celebrate Queen Juliana's unveiling of the Monument of Gratitude on 6 November 1955. The monument, situated in Siva Square in the centre of Paramaribo, was designed by artist Mari Andriessen. Three standing figures of girls on a pedestal and

Figure 3.1. *Lady of Plenty*, by sculptor Albert Termote, in Willemstad, Curaçao, established August 1953. (Photograph by Claartje Wesselink.)

three girls' heads on the side of the pedestal represent the ethnic diversity of Suriname. Just like the *Lady of Plenty* in Willemstad, the inscription on the pedestal of the Monument of Gratitude in Paramaribo reads, "The Netherlands gratefully remembers the relief provided during and after the war 1940–1945 by Suriname out of feelings of solidarity."[63]

Keeping in mind the place of the war, contributions of people from the Dutch Antilles and Suriname in the Dutch *lieu de mémoire* (site of memory), as well as the heritage and historiography of World War II, the gratitude which had once been bestowed on the population of both territories by the Netherlands may be characterized as a forgotten gratitude. The fact that the monuments were erected on Antillean Dutch and Surinamese soil, not in the Netherlands, exemplifies the symbolic position of the war contributions of people from Suriname and the Dutch Antilles in the Netherlands. While being remembered in these countries, they are silenced in the Dutch culture and historiography of World War II. However, the war contributions by the colonized population in the Dutch Caribbean did result in greater political self-awareness and assertiveness among the people and political elites of the Dutch Antilles and Suriname and thus paved the way for political autonomy and even independence in the case of Suriname. While being almost silenced in the Dutch historiography and memory landscape, the war contributions of the colonized in Suriname and the Dutch Antilles clearly accelerated decolonization in the Dutch Empire.

ACKNOWLEDGEMENTS

The material for this chapter is based on our monograph *Oorlogserfgoed overzee: De erfenis van de Tweede Wereldoorlog in Aruba, Curaçao, Indonesië en Suriname* (Amsterdam: Bert Bakker, 2010).

NOTES

1. Esther Captain and Guno Jones, "The Netherlands: A Small Country with Imperial Ambitions" in Robert Aldridge, ed., *The Age of Empires: Overseas Empires in the Early Modern and Modern World* (London: Thames and Hudson, 2007), 92–111.
2. Esther Captain and Guno Jones, *Oorlogserfgoed overzee: De erfenis van de Tweede*

Wereldoorlog in Aruba, Curaçao, Indonesië en Suriname (Amsterdam: Bert Bakker, 2010), 36.

3. Elsbeth Locher-Scholten, "Interraciale ontmoetingen naar sekse in Nederlands-Indië: De onmacht van het getal", in Esther Captain, Marieke Hellevoort and Marian ven der Klein, eds., *Vertrouwd en vreemd: Ontmoetingen tussen Nederland, Indië en Indonesië* (Hilversum, Netherlands: Verloren, 2000), 16; Hans Meijer, *In Indië geworteld. De twintigste eeuw* (Amsterdam: Bert Bakker, 2004), 169–73; J.A. Somers, *Nederlansch-Indië: staatkundige ontwikkelingen binnen een koloniale relatie* (Zutphen, Netherlands: Walburg Pers, 2005), 181–97.

4. Somers, *Nederlansch-Indië*, 150–56.

5. Guno Jones, *Tussen onderdanen, rijksgenoten en Nederlanders: Nederlandse politici over burgers uit Oost & West en Nederland 1945–2005* (Amsterdam: Rozenberg, 2007), 59–60.

6. Loosely translated by the authors. Hugo Fernandes Mendes, "Parliamentary Structures Reconsidered: The Constitutional System of Suriname", in Rosemarijn Hoefte and Peter Meel, eds., *Twentieth-Century Suriname: Continuities and Discontinuities in a New World Society* (Leiden: KITLV Press, 2001), 114; Gert Oostindie and Inge Klinkers, *Het Koninkrijk in de Caraïben: Een korte geschiedenis van het Nederlandse dekolonisatiebeleid, 1940–2000* (Amsterdam: Amsterdam University Press, 2001), 19–20.

7. Somers, *Nederlansch-Indië*, 181–97; Fernandes Mendes, "Parliamentary Structures Reconsidered", 114; Captain and Jones, *Oorlogserfgoed overzee*, 37–40.

8. The attack of the Japanese army on the Dutch colonial troops in the Indonesian archipelago started in January 1942. See also Esther Captain, *Achter het kawat was Nederland: Indische oorlogservaringen en -herinneringen 1942–1995* (Kampen, Netherlands: Kok, 2002), 51–52, 75–91.

9. Captain, *Achter het kawat was Nederland*, 52–54; Jones, *Tussen onderdanen, rijksgenoten en Nederlanders*, 77–78.

10. Cited in Captain and Jones, *Oorlogserfgoed overzee*, 246. Translation by the authors.

11. Ibid., 39, 56.

12. Michiel van Kempen, *Een geschiedenis van de Surinaamse literatuur, Deel 4* (2002), http://www.dbnl.org/tekst/kemp009gesc04_01/kemp009gesc04_01_0002.php (accessed 13 February 2015). This figure does not include the indigenous population and the Maroons.

13. C. Lamur and H.E. Lamur, *Duitse zendelingen in interneringskamp Copieweg, Suriname, 1940–1947: Vrijlating en uitwijzing* (Paramaribo: Herrnhutter Archieven Suriname, 2008), 78–85; Johan Frits Jones, "Kwakoe en Christus.

Een beschouwing over de ontmoeting van de Afro-Amerikaanse cultuur en religie met de Herrnhutter zending in Suriname" (PhD diss., Brussels University, 1981), 32–40; Captain and Jones, *Oorlogserfgoed overzee*, 58–59.

14. Twan Van den Brand, *De Strafkolonie; Een Nederlands concentratiekamp in Suriname 1942–1946* (Amsterdam: Uitgeverij Balans, 2006), 53–60; Captain and Jones, *Oorlogserfgoed overzee*, 58–59.
15. Jones, "Kwakoe en Christus", 32–40; Captain and Jones, *Oorlogserfgoed overzee*, 58–60.
16. Lamur and Lamur, *Duitse zendelingen*, 40–44 and 52–55.
17. This classification is contested by journalist Twan van den Brand because at least 25 per cent of the members were not affiliated with this movement and because the Dutch East Indies NSB (Nationaal Socialistische Beweging/ National Socialist Movement), unlike the mother party in the Netherlands, was not anti-Semitic and did not support the ideology of racial purity of the mother party.
18. Captain and Jones, *Oorlogserfgoed oversee*, 60.
19. Ibid., 96–102, 272–76.
20. Ibid., 47.
21. Ibid.
22. Ibid., 51; Pieter-Jan van Eyk, "Oorlogsjaren in Suriname: Nederlands Koloniaal beleid binnen Amerikaanse marges", *OSO, Tijdschrift voor Surinaamse taalkunde, letterkunde, cultuur en geschiedenis* 14, no. 2 (1995): 148–58 and 150–51; Liesbeth van der Horst, *Wereldoorlog in de West: Suriname, de Nederlandse Antillen en Aruba 1940–1945* (Hilversum, Netherlands: Verloren, 2004), 20–22.
23. Captain and Jones, *Oorlogserfgoed oversee*, 51–52; van Eyk, "Oorlogsjaren in Suriname", 152–53.
24. Captain and Jones, *Oorlogserfgoed oversee*, 47–48; van Eyk, "Oorlogsjaren in Suriname", 150.
25. Captain and Jones, *Oorlogserfgoed oversee*, 51–52; van Eyk, "Oorlogsjaren in Suriname", 152–52; van der Horst, *Wereldoorlog in de West*, 21.
26. Ben Scholtens, *Suriname tijdens de Tweede Wereldoorlog* (Paramaribo, Suriname: Anton de Kom Universiteit, 1988), 10; van der Horst, *Wereldoorlog in de West*, 21; Captain and Jones, *Oorlogserfgoed oversee*, 47.
27. Van der Horst, *Wereldoorlog in de West*, 21–23.
28. Hans Ramsoedh, "Rumcola en Yankee-dollars", *OSO, Tijdschrift voor Surinaamse taalkunde, letterkunde, cultuur en geschiedenis* 14, no. 2 (1995): 144; Captain and Jones, *Oorlogserfgoed oversee*, 52.
29. Scholtens, *Suriname tijdens de Tweede Wereldoorlog*, 10–11; Van der Horst, *Wereldoorlog in de West*, 59.

30. Scholtens, *Suriname tijdens de Tweede Wereldoorlog*, 10–12.
31. Jules Rijssen, "Suriname tijdens de Tweede Wereldoorlog", in Ad van den Oord, Jules Rijssen and Ted Schouten, *Een gemeenschappelijke strijd: Tilburg, Suriname, Aruba en de Antillen in de Tweede Wereldoorlog* (Tilburg: Commissie Wereldoorlog II in de West te Tilburg, 2007), 53–101; Van der Horst, *Wereldoorlog in de West*, 53–54; Captain and Jones, *Oorlogserfgoed oversee*, 52–56.
32. Johan Hartog, "West-Indië in de oorlog", in *Onderdrukking en verzet*, ed. J.J. van Bolhuis, C.D.J. Brand, H.M. van Randwijk and B.C. Slotemaker (Amsterdam: J.M. Meulenhoff, 1954), 588–602; Van der Horst, *Wereldoorlog in de West*, 55.
33. Pearl J. Pengel, "Female Soldiers in Suriname 1942–1946", in *Engagement en distantie: Wetenschap in vele facetten: Liber Amicorum voor Prof. dr. Humphrey E. Lamur*, ed. Edwin Marshall (Amsterdam: NiNsee, 2006); Rijssen, "Suriname tijdens de Tweede Wereldoorlog", 94; Van der Horst, *Wereldoorlog in de West*, 62.
34. Captain and Jones, *Oorlogserfgoed oversee*, 55.
35. Ibid., 66–82, 285–90.
36. Van der Horst, *Wereldoorlog in de West*, 65–66; Rijssen, "Suriname tijdens de Tweede Wereldoorlog", 89–94; Captain and Jones, *Oorlogserfgoed oversee*, 55.
37. Rijssen, "Suriname tijdens de Tweede Wereldoorlog", 93; Van der Horst, *Wereldoorlog in de West*, 67; Captain and Jones, *Oorlogserfgoed oversee*, 55.
38. Captain and Jones, *Oorlogserfgoed oversee*, 256–72.
39. Ibid., 100; Jones, *Tussen onderdanen, rijksgenoten en Nederlanders*, 186.
40. Captain and Jones, *Oorlogserfgoed oversee*, 246 (translated by the authors).
41. Hans Breeveld, *Baas in eigen huis: Wim Bos Verschuur, heraut van Surinames onafhankelijkheid 1904–1985* (Paramaribo: Uitgeverij Djinipi, 2004).
42. Captain and Jones, *Oorlogserfgoed oversee*, 251 (translated by the authors).
43. Ibid.
44. Ibid., 248.
45. Ibid., 251.
46. Ibid., 253–56; Jules Rijssen, *Teken en zie de Wereld! Oorlogsveteranen van Suriname* (Amsterdam: KIT, 2012); Paul Scheer, "Voor Koningin en Moederland: De uitzending van Surinaamse vrijwilligers naar Nederlands-Indie", *OSO, Tijdschrift voor Surinaamse taalkunde, letterkunde, cultuur en geschiedenis* 14, no. 2 (1995): 188–94.
47. Captain and Jones, *Oorlogserfgoed oversee*, 256–59.
48. Ibid., 262.
49. Ibid., 259–60.
50. Ibid., 93.
51. Ibid., 86.

52. Ibid.
53. Ibid., 85.
54. Ibid., 92.
55. Ibid., 276–78; Rijssen, "Suriname tijdens de Tweede Wereldoorlog", 71–75; Van der Horst, *Wereldoorlog in de West*, 95–106; Percy Wijngaarde, "Een Spitfire voor het Moederland", in *Oso, tijdschrift voor Surinaamse taalkunde, letterkunde, cultuur en geschiedenis* 14, no. 2 (1995): 185–87.
56. Van der Horst, *Wereldoorlog in de West*, 99.
57. Johan Ferrier, "De Unie Suriname", in *OSO, Tijdschrift voor Surinaamse taalkunde, letterkunde, cultuur en geschiedenis* 14, no. 2 (1995): 164
58. Captain and Jones, *Oorlogserfgoed oversee*, 278.
59. Ibid., 276–79.
60. Ferrier, "De Unie Suriname", 159–62.
61. Captain and Jones, *Oorlogserfgoed oversee*, 102–6 and 279–85.
62. Ibid., 105.
63. Ibid., 279.

4.

WAR, FOOD AND SECURITY
Feeding Trinidad and Tobago in Wartime, 1939–1945

RITA PEMBERTON

World War II is considered a watershed in the history of the Caribbean, and its consequences for the region have been the focus of many studies. These have primarily discussed the overall political, social, cultural and economic impact, which, save for the health and some aspects of the cultural consequences, have been largely positive. Some underscore the implications for labour, with particular reference to the construction of US bases and activity within their precincts. However, the interrelationships of these variables have not been examined. While there is generally passing reference to the difficulties citizens encountered during the war, lack of detail tends to minimize the visibility of the trauma the war brought to the average citizen. Where food is mentioned in the discourse, it is also dismissed as "shortages" of imported items and usually to commend the increase in local food production, suggesting that this had made up the shortfall.

Because of its oil resources, Trinidad was central to the defence system of the Allied powers. It was the site of two military bases and was, therefore, well enmeshed in the war defence network, which, it is argued here, helped to sharpen the paradox of the people's experiences during the war years, creating and aggravating social issues which worsened and reflected the food problem. The wartime food experience can, therefore, only be properly understood if it is placed in the context of the social stresses on the society before and during the war. The study begins with an outline of the relevant works on Trinidad and Tobago in wartime and their approach in addressing the food issue.

THE HISTORIOGRAPHY

The existing literature on World War II in Trinidad and Tobago reflects the varied interests of writers who have focused on different aspects of the war. Eric Williams, with a nationalist agenda, discusses the Leased Bases Agreement of 1941 and the grounds for the local resistance to the American demands, which was led by the governor, Sir Hubert Young. These included opposition to Chaguaramas as the base site, to the length of the lease, to the fiscal and customs privileges and extraterritorial rights afforded to the American forces and the continuation of US control of the area after the war.[1] To Williams, these issues had bearing on the colony's movement for independence; however, he makes no direct reference to food-related issues, although their connection with his areas of focus is clear.

In her general history of Trinidad, Bridget Brereton summarizes the impact of World War II as having, through base construction, "a tremendous socio-economic impact", citing higher wages, rising living costs and the creation of a "boom-time atmosphere"[2] without directly mentioning how food was affected. Michael Anthony's more detailed account raises the food issue, stating that by the second half of 1942 the country was gripped by "the most critical food shortages".[3] He identifies scarcity of flour, which created desperate unruly crowds, price increases and profiteering, which in turn stimulated "critical attention to food",[4] including the introduction of the not-so-popular wholewheat flour[5] on the local market. Anthony does provide a window into the complexity of the food issue as he describes the scenario in the midst of a boom atmosphere, where gangs of violent unemployed youths roamed the streets of Port of Spain, robbing and terrorizing the population, while there was depression in the countryside, where agricultural production slumped.[6] Residents of Chaguaramas were relocated, some tearfully, to make way for the bases, while the pace of life quickened in the adjoining areas.[7] There was a shortage of tyres and vehicular spare parts, which caused rail traffic to become the dominant form of wartime travel.[8] Thus, Anthony points to the social dislocation of the war, which also had serious implications for the food supply.

Fitzroy Baptiste, in a regional, military and strategic study, notes that Trinidad experienced a war economy as a result of the United States' base-construction programme, and "inflation became the major economic problem, linked to the interplay of relatively high employment, high liquidity, declining agriculture, scarcity of imported food and other supply items for the civilian sector of the population".[9] These, he asserts, provided the need for "some rationing" in 1942. Baptiste also details local objections to several parts of the lease-bases agreement,[10] food-quality problems and the contest between British, Americans and Canadians to supply the region with imported items.[11] He argues that shortage was not on the supply side, as reorganized shipping arrangements by July and August 1942 allowed Trinidad and Guyana to build up a two-month reserve of basic food items,[12] but details of the wartime food experience are not accorded pride of place in his discussion.

In his assessment of the impact of the war, Kelvin Singh states that the imperial and colonial authorities were both concerned about buttressing the plantation sector, favouring imperial more than colonial interest.[13] Singh notes the exaggerated planter claims of labour shortage, which they ascribed to the labour diversion to the bases and the Grow More Food campaign. However, he suggests that the authorities had food matters fully in hand with the Grow More Food strategy. He asserts:

> War conditions, especially after the German U-boat attacks on the Caribbean in 1942, forced the colonial government to initiate a "Grow More Food" campaign, to start irrigation projects in Caroni in order to facilitate rice growing, to organize marketing depots at strategic points in the colony and to give guaranteed prices to farmers and fishermen. These measures resulted in a rapid rise in local food production. By April 1943 rice growers were producing record harvests. Large quantities of sweet potatoes, eddoes, yams and Indian corn were being produced. This rapid local production of food helped not only to meet the problems arising from a shortage of shipping, which forced a reduction in the import of foodstuffs, but enabled the local population to cope with wartime price inflation.[14]

Claus Füllberg-Stolberg's regional study explores the issue of shortages and the establishment of food-generation schemes during the war. He details the efforts to implement a schooner system to supply the islands of the Caribbean and stimulate the exchange of food during the worst years of the war. He also examines the issue of labour, noting, "In Antigua, as in Trinidad, the construction works of the American bases absorbed the bulk of the labour force."[15] Therefore, in his analysis it is to be presumed that in wartime Trinidad labour was no longer a problem. Also focusing on labour, Harvey Neptune describes the "island's hopeful majority" who "relished the opportunity to take advantage of the new market created by Americans' demands" and expected "more remunerative U.S. employers".[16] Neptune never fully addresses the food issue, however.

In a recent work Bridget Brereton[17] discusses the pro-labour left-wing press, which continued to be active during the war and served as the voice of the working class. These newspapers, while remaining loyal to the imperial cause, were concerned with the right to carry on union and political activities in wartime and the objectionable prohibitions of the Colonial Defence Regulations. She does not discuss food, which was an important concern of the working class.

While the existing literature does raise some aspects of the food question, it is deficient in examining the very important links between food issues and other critical areas. It is centred on specific aspects of World War II, and while it provides indices of the importance of the food question in wartime, there is no detailed discussion of the food experiences of the population and the relationship between these and other war themes. This study seeks to reverse this trend by according food centrality of focus in the colony's wartime experience.

Based on the premise that the antinomies of the wartime era demonstrate how the pre-existing social conflicts, as well as those stimulated by the war, are of relevance to the wartime food question, this study seeks to provide a people-oriented perspective of the war experience of Trinidad and Tobago. It aims to show the difficulties faced by the mass of the population in producing, purchasing, preparing and preserving food during the war and establish the relationship between food issues and the social dislocation that was evident in the colony during the period. It argues that while food was central to the wartime survival strategy, despite increased local food production, the war food strategy did not satisfy the food needs of the population, and that even without the physical devastation normally associated with war conditions, the food experiences of the working and unemployed classes during the war years constitute a particularly traumatic period in the history of the colony.

METHODOLOGY

This chapter is a study of the sociology of food during wartime. It is food-centric, with a focus on the most difficult years, 1942 and 1943, and on developments in Trinidad, the epicentre of the colony's wartime activities. In this study the theory of social disorganization,[18] with its characteristic traits, is applied to developments in the society at that time. The food issue is examined against the matrix of these traits – disputes, distress, displacement and dispossession and the war food strategies – to illustrate how, despite the security measures, war conditions created disequilibrium in the society and aggravated the existing unhappy social divisions. It will demonstrate that these traits also affected and were affected by food matters, indicating the symbiosis between food concerns and the aggravated social tensions of the period.

In this chapter newspaper accounts, calypsoes and literature, representative of the people's voice as well as official sources, are used to direct and support the discussion. Reliance is placed on one of the main daily newspapers, the *Trinidad Guardian*. Though it is pro-establishment, its detailed coverage of war and food-related matters allows an important window, perhaps unwittingly, on developments on the ground.

HISTORICAL BACKGROUND

War conditions were imposed on a society that was already in contest in 1939. This was well demonstrated by the social turbidity that characterized the first four decades of twentieth-century Trinidad and Tobago. The century dawned with ruling-class furore over the imperial imposition of a union of Trinidad and Tobago, a raging smallpox epidemic (1902–1903), social upheaval expressed in the Water Riots (1903), a disastrous fire and the articulations of groups such as the Trinidad Workingmen's Association and the Rate Payers Association demanding political change as the avenue for social change. While the development of an oil industry strengthened the colony's economy, its benefits did not filter down to the mass of the population. As Brinsley Samaroo has argued, during the period 1917–37 there was "an eruption of a festering sore which was covered over by a plaster of repression and concession that did nothing to heal the wound" which emanated from "a longer process of struggle by a colonial people against a hated metropolitan order".[19] The agricultural sector was the main employer but the wages of its workers lagged behind the escalating cost of living, despite increased sugar prices during World War I. The reality was that despite an aura of wealth, the mass of the population was poor, sick, unemployed and unable to feed themselves and their families.

Post–World War I developments brought further social aggravation. Worldwide depression caused prices to rise while wages remained unresponsive. The Trinidad cocoa industry crashed, leaving many families without a source of income. For the masses, food was a major problem. There were hunger marches and protests for increased wages in the face of severe price increases, but to no avail. Returning soldiers and sailors, who faced discrimination in the war zone and with respect to post-war compensation, found it unbearable on the home front. Their protest provided the nucleus of a new militancy, which infused the advocates for political and social change. Censorship and attempts to ban cultural expression caused calypsonians to sing in protest, as Tiger did in 1934:

> We can't fight physically cause we won't prevail
> On account of ammunition, cruel laws and jail
> But every man was born to be free
> From this oppression and tyrannic slavery.[20]

Beginning in 1935 and culminating in the 1937 labour rebellion, the protests represented "the concentrated essence"[21] of a longer period of distress stimulated by exploitation. Implementation of the recommendations of the Moyne Commission was pre-empted by the outbreak of the war in 1939. Hence, at the outbreak of World War II the battle lines were drawn between the rulers and the ruled, reflecting the existing divisions based on racial and ethnic lines, since race, colour and class were used as the defining identities of the Trinidadian population. For the masses, life in pre–World War II Trinidad and Tobago was centred on contestation for economic, political, social, cultural and physical space. At the base of it all was the overwhelming number of people who were unable to feed themselves.

A CONTESTED TERRAIN: WARTIME TENSIONS AND PARADOXES

One of the first concerns of the imperial authorities in 1939 was to stem the tide of protest, provide some alleviatory measures and court the loyalty and support of the struggling population for the wartime venture. Food was an important avenue in this process.

Between 1939 and 1945 Trinidad can be seen as facing two wars, the external, which, according to the calypsonians, "was not their business", and the internal contested terrain. In addition to the ingrained pre-war tensions in the society, war requirements brought tensions of their own. In the first place, the significant and visible foreign presence in the colony caused many to become dispossessed. The land areas occupied by the United States displaced residents. All residents of Chaguaramas were given notice to vacate their properties, as the military took over the entire peninsula, leaving many permanently dispossessed. This was a contest the residents lost, for although the Resettlement Committee assisted in relocation of the displaced, there were disgruntled families whose descendants are, to this day, seeking restitutive justice.

For the general population, the occupied areas, both land and marine, were out of bounds. The population was deprived of access to the popular beaches in the north-western peninsula, which spawned local resentment against the military takeover. This resentment intensified because the occupation had serious implications for the colony's food supply. Fishermen as well as farmers were among the aggrieved who were displaced from the area. This was a popular fishing area, and in addition to the move's affecting the livelihood of the fishermen and their ability to support their families, the supply of fish during the war was dramatically curtailed, causing severe shortages on the market and stimulating escalating prices and conflict to obtain food. For a people who had encountered decades of social distress, wartime dislocation was unbearable. It contributed to food shortages, higher prices and unemployment and added to their distress.

The Colonial Defence Regulations provided wide powers for the governor, who prohibited public meetings and was allowed to hold people without trial and impose censorship on the population. The working-class struggle was contained and the voices of protesters of the 1930s were silenced, but the spirit of resistance remained, as the issues which stimulated the protests continued to gnaw at the population, in addition to those stimulated by the war itself. A paradox of the war years is how the distressed population remained loyal while they continued to nurse the ills associated with the inequities of colonial rule and those imposed by the war.

The defence regulations established military personnel as a separate and privileged group who were not subject to the laws of the land. In a society where the mass of the population was underprivileged, this was an infuriating imposition, to which the excesses of the soldiers and sailors added insult to injury. The food and other demands of the military displaced the supply to residents and resulted in serious food shortages and accompanying price increases, as the military had first call on what was available, particularly chicken and eggs, which were destined to be in short supply for the duration of the war.[22] In addition to these difficulties, the negative behaviour of some members of the military placed additional burdens on the population, stirring up disputes and causing distress.

On 16 April 1942 a riot occurred in Laventille in north-west Trinidad. A band of helmet-wearing soldiers, armed with sticks and boulders, swept through the Laventille area, after a conflict involving them and local men over local women, with "homicidal fury", beating men, destroying furniture and damaging property, terrorizing and infuriating the residents of the area. The aggrieved residents called for swift punishment from the local courts for the offending Americans, similar to that recently given to locals for acts of hooliganism.[23] Their insistence resulted in ten soldiers being charged. Five were found guilty and given five years' imprisonment with hard labour and dishonourable discharge from the army. The other five were acquitted.[24]

Drunken soldiers and sailors habitually terrorized residents within the precincts of the army camp. Residents of St Vincent Street in the capital, Port of Spain, complained of disturbances created by the US military, who invaded their yards at night, breaking and smashing articles of furniture and terrorizing residents.[25] Woodbrook residents, on the outskirts of the main urban centre, also complained about soldiers disturbing the neighbourhood with noise and foul language, harassing residents and passers-by.[26] Not only was this behaviour unexpected and unacceptable from the security forces but it also added an element of hostility to the military, as they were perceived as the cause of the food shortages and other burdens people were forced to bear.

Tensions also developed as the Americans, there to defend the colony, were seen in a negative light, as aggressive invaders with whom residents had to contest for control of their own space. The novel *Rum and Coca-Cola* captures local disgust expressed in the complaints of residents to the authorities about the disturbances caused by US Air Force training exercises. Failing to get a response, their conclusion, arrived at with resignation, was that "the US army had the right to do as it pleases".[27] There was, at the very least, resentment of the military, whose actions resulted in further inflictions on a society that was already severely stressed. There were also clashes between locals and Barbadian immigrants, which culminated in the Good Friday Riots in Arima, which involved twenty-eight people.[28] These signs of social dislocation put the government on an anti-hooliganism drive, with a measure that sought to deal with the gangs of unemployed youth on the streets of Port of Spain, imposing stiff penalties for acts of hooliganism, and increased those for violence, disorder and keeping disorderly houses.[29] This, of course, did not solve the root problem of social, political and economic dispossession which afflicted the masses and heightened tensions in the society. This was the social context of the food dimension of wartime security in Trinidad and Tobago during World War II.

THE DISSONANCE OF WAR

Shortages of food and essential items have characterized Trinidad from the earliest periods of colonization. The early Spanish settlers depended on illegal trade to provide them with the basic necessities. The situation did not change when plantations were established, for, as in other plantation colonies, it was considered more profitable to produce the export crop and import food.

Concerns about the dependence on food imports by an agricultural colony were heightened during the twentieth century. The magnitude of the colony's food bill alarmed administrators, particularly when war conditions revealed how vulnerable this made the colony. In 1918 Governor John Robert Chancellor observed, "It seems paradoxical that an essentially agricultural colony does not feed its people; but has paid better in the past to employ the limited supply of labour in growing the staples of sugar and cocoa in order to buy imported flour, rice and fish to feed its labourers."[30] Tobago produced a significant proportion of its food and sold substantial quantities to Trinidad, which also depended on food supplies from Grenada, St Vincent and Venezuela. These were cut off owing to prohibitions of the supply from these territories during World War I, forcing Trinidad and Tobago to develop its own food resources.[31]

World War I had stimulated a programme of increased local food production which involved sensitization of the population to the gravity of the situation and the need to grow more food, the formation of committees to oversee the food-production programme and making land available to food producers.[32] There was a propaganda campaign which urged the population to eat ground provisions rather than bread, distributed recipes on the use of flour substitutes and gave demonstrations on innovative uses of locally produced items. District meetings, information pamphlets on cultivation and food preparation and preservation, and competitions brought schools, the press, clergy, planters, wardens and district agricultural societies, as well as the general public, into the campaign.[33] At the end of the war the authorities were satisfied that the crisis had been averted, and the secretary of state expressed his pleasure with the outcomes of the food campaign in Trinidad and Tobago.[34]

While the quantities of some items – notably corn, edible oils, peas, beans, cheese, fish, condensed milk and canned and salted meats – were reduced during World War I, there were increases in the imports of dhal (split peas) and rice. However, the cost of imports was not reduced: "The overall picture for food imports in the colony over the period 1891 to 1918 was one of increasing value of imports."[35] Concern about the colony's food bill was justifiable. However, with the war crisis removed there was a discontinuation of the wartime food-production measures and a return to pre-war food importation patterns. After the war, despite price fluctuations and quantity reductions in some items, the food bill – particularly the prices of canned meats, fish, cheese, condensed milk and edible oils – climbed steadily, beginning in 1924.[36] Local food production, branded by post-war disuse as a temporary emergency measure, stalled as the food bill escalated. For the masses, the situation was intensified in the 1930s, when earnings could not keep pace with food prices and unemployment levels soared. The turmoil of the 1930s was crisis enough, but there were imperial and colonial fears that worse would come with the aggravations of war. The food-production issue would therefore feature more dramatically during World War II.

To the Allied powers, the question of survival of the Caribbean populations was critical to the war strategy, as it was important to prevent any social distress which might facilitate enemy incursions into the region. The government sought to curtail these and at the same time save money and shipping space for the war effort. The response to the 1930s disturbances targeted, inter alia, increased employment opportunities to put food on the tables of the masses. War presented an opportunity to effect this policy, but while the various schemes that operated during the war created new employment and earning opportunities, these were not universal. Some people lost their jobs and the ability to feed their families as a result of the strictures of war. These included those whose trades had to be curtailed because of defence-regulation mandates. Shortages of supplies caused some businesses to reduce their staff and in some instances to close down permanently.[37] These included hardware and dry-goods stores and bakeries. Even the largest city commercial operators threatened to shut down in protest against the price regulations, which they found "unjust and unworkable".[38] While some people enjoyed increased incomes and were better off, there were those whose situation worsened. In the reports and the existing literature, the unemployed and the dispossessed of the war era are invisible.

In his address to the Legislative Council in 1941, Governor Hubert Young urged members "to reduce the consumption of non-essential goods . . . and, as regards really essential goods, to consume goods of sterling origin in preference to other goods".[39] The intent was to avoid deflection of revenue, particularly to the enemy, so that more funds would be available for the war effort. But very early in the war, Governor Young noted that increased earnings from the US bases increased the purchasing power of the labouring classes, and as a result "there has been a marked increase in our importations resulting in a very appreciable increase in revenue".[40] This would reflect one contradictory impact of World War II on the people of Trinidad and Tobago. Just when more money was available to some of the people, there was so much less available for sale, and the escalating food prices put those items that were available out of the reach of many, posing challenges to the large number of unemployed people in the colony. This was the food legacy of World War I, which clearly influenced developments during World War II.

FEEDING TRINIDAD AND TOBAGO DURING WORLD WAR II

The World War II food effort was a replay of that used for World War I. A Grow More Food campaign was relaunched in 1939 under the direction of the food controller and his department with the aim of increasing self-sufficiency in each locality, decreasing dependency on imports and ensuring distribution of essential imported items.[41] Land was released for food cultivation at low prices, and emergency war gardens were established to facilitate increased local food production. To increase productivity, demonstration gardens were laid out across the country. Subcommittees of the food control department focused on specific areas such as marketing, poultry, ground provisions and tyres. Imported items were handled through a bulk-purchasing facility[42] and the supporting West Indian Schooner Pool organized by the Anglo-American Caribbean Commission.

The population was urged to grow food in every available land space, and the Short Term Crop Regulations mandated estates to devote 40 per cent of estate land to food cultivation, with sanctions for breaches of this law; to estates $2,400 and to cane farmers $480.[43] Estates were to make land available to workers for food cultivation and the Control Board acquired land to be subdivided for allocation to producers. In a society where the number of landless was disproportionally high, this might have been a golden opportunity for land acquisition, but some of those who might have benefited were either employed on the bases or were among the thousands of hopefuls who had migrated from rural areas and were hovering around the base recruitment office in St James, in western Port of Spain, waiting and hoping (some in vain) for the call to work.

The food strategy also included price controls of food and essential items, which were published regularly, and by 1943 included green coconuts (scheduled to be retailed at four cents).[44] This measure was intended to protect consumers from high prices, especially in light of the distress signals of the pre-war era. There was strict policing to ensure compliance with the scheduled prices, but this restriction did not embrace the importing firms.

After the first year, the director of agriculture noted that, in addition to lands given out by private owners, government had allocated over 600 acres as war gardens, "a larger than usual" crop of corn had been harvested and imports had been reduced by nearly a thousand tons. He cited a reduction in the imports of corn by 62.2 per cent; rice, 20.2 per cent; peas and beans, 8.2 per cent, and potatoes, 9.5 per cent, as well as beef, pork, pickled and salted meat and fish, canned meats and condensed milk, and he indicated that demonstrations of drying, bottling, canning and preserving excess food had been undertaken across the country.[45]

The food strategy did not record the anticipated successes in the early years of the war. In his report for 1941, the director of agriculture noted that there was a decline in the production of root crops, corn and pulses, due, in Tobago, to recruitment of workers for the American bases in Trinidad,[46] but he did acknowledge that "a substantial increase" in rice cultivation had been achieved. Noting that since the war began the volume of cargo at the Port of Spain wharf had increased, in his 1942 message Governor Sir Bede Clifford urged the population to reduce its consumption of imported goods, if only to save on shipping space, and announced that 10,000 acres more land than the previous year had been put under food cultivation. He advocated the use of cassava as a substitute for wheat flour and encouraged rice cultivation in the Nariva swamp.[47]

While the rice crop was larger than in any previous year, corn cultivation consumed 1,600 acres; ground provisions, 20,000 acres and pulses and vegetables, 4,000 acres each; the wholesale value of food produced was $9 million.[48] The Caribbean Commission commended increases in local food production, progress of the inter-island trade and development of fisheries, while noting problems associated with maintaining the levels of imported food.[49]

In his report for 1944, the director of agriculture announced "a substantial all round increase in food crop production in 1944". There were 54,000 acres under annual food crops with over 7,000 acres of plantain and bananas, which "was equivalent to more than 2 times the estimated prewar acreage".[50] Thus, for the officials, the situation had improved and the Grow More Food campaign had averted a food crisis in Trinidad and Tobago. But was this the reality on the ground for the masses?

Official reports on the Grow More Food campaign do not reveal the difficulties the population encountered in the production effort, which prevented maximum returns from being achieved, and the distribution-related complications which caused shortages of basic items in many parts of the country and added stress to the population. These are related to some longstanding inadequacies of the colony's infrastructure.

The first problem was water. Trinidad had been plagued by an inadequate water supply right up to the war years, and lock-offs were common features of life, especially during the dry season. If the colony's water supply was inadequate to the needs of its population in peacetime, wartime conditions would only aggravate the situation. The colony's limited water resources had to serve the needs of the US bases and a population swelled by migrants seeking jobs on the bases. The army camp alone consumed 30,000 gallons of water daily.[51]

During the war, the water supply to Port of Spain was locked off daily between two o'clock and five o'clock in the afternoon, and the explanation given was that the pumps were inadequate.[52] The pumps had to be imported at a time when there were restrictions on imports. A special committee, which included Mayor Achong of Port of Spain and Adrian Cola Rienzi, a member of the Legislative Council, was established to deal with the matter. This committee held frequent meetings but never seemed able to provide a resolution during the war period.

The situation was no better in San Fernando in the south of the island, where the water supply was unpredictable, and it experienced its fourth cut for the year in April 1942. The town's normally inadequate supply of 850,000 gallons was reduced to 600,000 gallons, and the cut-off times for supply were increased from three to four, then later to six hours per day and even longer on some days.[53] In spite of an increased supply to 900,000 gallons in May,[54] San Fernando was still short 200,000 gallons of water,[55] and in June the water supply continued to be deficient.[56]

While the authorities spoke through the newspaper to encourage self-sufficiency in food,[57] water shortage and its hindrance to food cultivation across the colony echoed in the press. In a letter to the newspaper, Councillor Fitt,[58] while accepting the need to be more aggressive in the food campaign, indicated that water shortage complicated cultivation.[59] Ranjit Kumar also asserted that water was already short in Trinidad.[60] Distressed residents of St Joseph/Tunapuna presented a petition to the visiting representative of the secretary of state, Sir Cosmo Parkinson, for an improved water supply.[61] Arima residents were made worse off when, after Cumuto-based contractors started operations at the Verdant Vale Quarry on the Blanchisseuse Road[62] in north-east Trinidad, they lost their water supply.

Letters to the editor provide further evidence of the colony's water woes. Taxpayers of Flanagin Town complained that the community had received no water for five days, and from the agricultural village of St John's in Tunapuna there was a plea for water.[63] Alidath Khan of Bejucal lamented the water situation in his agricultural district. He said that residents had to join crowds at a standpipe located two miles away and cart it to their homes; those without carts, of course, endured untold difficulty. Residents of Carenage in the west, especially those in the resettlement area, echoed a similar cry.[64] "R.S.K.", writing from Tobago, commented that the colony's food problem was caused by scarcity of reliable labour and shortage of water and tools.[65]

A major deficiency of the Grow More Food campaign was the colony's lack of a satisfactory system of water supply to the population that could serve both domestic and agricultural purposes. The inverse relationship between demand and supply was a contradiction of wartime. There was pressure for water for production when the society was pressured by the unreliability of the supply, and the shortage of water frustrated the food-production effort. But there were other complications.

In a letter to the editor, "Sweet Cassava" explained the "deadlock" in the Grow More Food campaign. He (or she) asserts that some who planted found it difficult to transport the food over bad roads or no roads at all or because of lack of transportation.[66] The writer also lamented the distribution system, which allowed

> groceries in Port of Spain, St. Clair, Belmont and Woodbrook to carry carrots, cabbage, potato, onions and beets. Why not make it compulsory for all from captain to cook to carry locally grown produce so that all the people and not only a certain class, can be served? This is the only way to induce people to eat more homegrown vegetables and avoid importation and the use of much needed shipping space.[67]

"Ex-Convict 999", arguing that there was no time for complacency on the food question, expressed the view that the Grow More Food campaign was still-born owing to a definite shortage of labour. By way of a solution he referred to the seven hundred men in prison who could be utilized. There were three hundred inmates at the Carrera Island prison, he asserted, who could easily be transported to work the land, for "we are closer to starvation than many imagine".[68]

Thus, labour, transportation and road infrastructure posed impediments to both everyday living as well as the local food-production effort. The distributive arm of the strategy, which seemed to favour particular sections of the society, reflected existing class biases. This experience is captured in the novel *Rum and Coca-Cola*, where, while a crowd is pushing for rice outside a Chinese shop, "privileged people" are seen exiting from the side door with their purchases, prompting one character to observe, "Like white people too great to stand in line like we chile."[69]

The food strategy also involved food preservation, but the colony's domestic energy supply was severely challenged in wartime. At best, the supply of electricity was fickle. In response to rumours, householders complained about a proposed scheme to ration electricity,[70] and towards the end of April the Electricity Company did put city consumers on a 90 per cent consumption quota for the five-month period April to August 1941, as part of the Defence Regulations.[71]

Rationing of electricity started with the issuing of ration cards showing the amount to be allocated to each household. Those who exceeded their quotas by more than 10 per cent were liable to a fine of up to $480 on conviction or for a second offence.[72] As the war progressed, war demands on the electricity supply caused the electricity company to maintain the restrictions.[73] The Electricity Board admitted that it was overwhelmed by the increased demand for electricity and that it also faced a shortage of wooden poles, as the British government was given preferential access to supplies of wallaba wood from Guyana. In addition, the company had to service all the military sites and the lighting of sheds for the new deep-water harbour.[74] Obviously local consumers were at the end of the priority line for supply, and since those in the city were least able to produce food, their ability to preserve food would have been important to their survival. However, the unpredictable supply of electricity reduced this ability.

At the same time, charcoal, which was imported from Guyana, was scarce. City housewives were forced to line up to obtain charcoal,[75] which was scarce across the colony and was totally unavailable in La Brea.[76] The electricity quota sparked a rush for kerosene[77] and candles, which were also in short supply.[78] Food preparation and some forms of preservation were made extremely difficult, putting additional stresses on the population.

Land was also not readily accessible to farmers in all parts of the colony. Timothy Roodal appealed to the government to force sugar estates to rent small plots around San Fernando to small farmers because he claimed that there was not enough land available around San Fernando for food production.[79] The People's Party of Trinidad and Tobago urged greater attention to food production, as the party was "not satisfied that the food production programme of the government had effected any material change from dependence on imported food to consumption of foods grown on our own soil". This party advocated land-settlement programmes rather than war gardens.[80]

The question of food supply was indeed problematic and was particularly harrowing for women of the colony. Such were the shortages that people virtually had to fight to be able to purchase scarce supplies of food items. Critically short during the entire war period were meat supplies. The *Trinidad Guardian* reported the continuation of the "acute meat shortage", as only 6,141 pounds of beef and 316 pounds of pork were supplied to the Eastern Market in Port of Spain, where chicken and egg vendors were noticeably absent.[81] Meat vendors, it asserted, exploited the opportunity to "marry the articles making it a condition not to serve customers who are not prepared to accept at least a quite disheartening proportion of bone along with their beef and pork purchases".[82] As the market clerk explained, "If you want a pound of pork you must be prepared to accept at least a quarter pound of bones otherwise you get no pork."[83] This meant a significant price increase, as bone and pork that used to be sold for twelve cents per pound were now being sold at twenty-four cents. In addition, consumers faced a shortage of frozen meat, cold-storage fish, butter, eggs and chicken.[84] The irony was that while there were official reports of increased food production, there were also reports of food scarcity across the colony.

So intense was the scarcity that food acquisition fuelled serious contentions between desperate and angry women. For instance, the *Trinidad Guardian* reported a fracas outside the Eastern Market in Port of Spain on Sunday, 1 March 1942, when three thousand women crashed the gate in a "frenzied attempt to purchase beef and pork",[85] stimulated by rumours of a shortage of meat. The crowd buildup began at both the George Street and Charlotte Street entrances to the market long before opening hours. At about 5:00 a.m. the crowd on the George Street side was about "10 people deep" when the women crashed the gate, injuring ten and causing four women to faint. The police had to be called to restore order. There had been a severe shortage of beef for the previous two weeks, with the regular supply being thirty thousand pounds, but on Saturday, 30 April, only eight thousand pounds of beef were available. By 7:30 a.m. all stalls were empty. One older vendor felt the situation was "much worse than it [had been] in World War I".[86] A similar situation occurred at the market in Woodbrook, where one woman was cut on the head and police had to be called.[87]

Mixed signals from the government contributed to the buying rush. A government advisory recommended that homeowners should keep an emergency reserve food stock, causing people to buy groceries in hoarding quantities. Shopkeepers applied their own "rationing" in an attempt "to be fair to all and to save buyers from themselves" and also "to conserve their stock as long as possible".[88] The disruptions of war upset normal market relations, leading to mob behaviour, a trait of social disorganization.

In a failed bid to provide some relief, the Market Committee promised the city a bigger meat supply, but the seventy-five hundred pounds of beef in the market on that day was short of the amount demanded.[89] One solution was the formation of the Trinidad Goat Society to educate the population about the benefits of goat milk[90] and goat meat.[91] "Agricola" advised readers "to keep meat buy a goat and keep a goat", and in the following week the first Goat Show was held on 29 March 1942 at the Trinidad Turf Club paddock.[92]

The situation was the same with fish. The shortage, which existed for months, worsened to the point where there was no fish in the Eastern Market. This was partly as a result of closure of some fishing areas, which led to protests by fishermen, who were temporarily appeased when they were allowed to go back to sea.[93] But fish, particularly the more popular varieties (redfish, carite and kingfish), as well as shrimp, continued to be in short supply during 1942 and 1943. Consumers' choices were restricted to herring and shark.[94]

Fishermen in the southern town of San Fernando, who were in protest mode, refused to go to sea. The Defence Regulations closed their traditional fishing grounds and required them to move to new fishing areas on the east coast, specifically Moruga and Erin. They were protesting what they considered the unfavourable scheduled prices of six cents per pound, for popular species of fish, which was uneconomical to them, particularly in light of their relocation to distant fishing grounds.[95] The fishermen too had to fight for survival. The schedule, which was intended to buffer the consumer from high prices, did not protect the interests of the fishermen, who felt they had no choice but to withdraw their services.

Fred Grant, a member of the Legislative Council and head of the merchant firm T. Geddes Grant Limited, was appointed food controller amid many complaints about food distribution. In particular, profiteering in the market was heavily criticized for aggravating the food situation. City councillors in Town Hall criticized wholesalers in the Eastern Market, who, they claimed, preferred to sell the best grades of fish, shrimp, fowls and other items to "Chinese restaurants and other large buyers because they got more than the scheduled prices for their goods".[96] Profiteering is an axiom in business, and it also reflected resistance of the small businessmen to the limited profit margins offered by the controls. In a boom atmosphere, restrictions on profits were unacceptable to the small businessmen, who wanted to grasp opportunities they did not normally enjoy.

As food problems persisted, consumers were urged to prepare for a long struggle and work the land.[97] Popular perception of the Food Committee was reflected in letters to the editor. In one such, H.E. Fahey dubbed the Food Production Committee Report as the "We Will Plant When We Start to Starve Report" and indicated that in Arima milk was scarce and the beef stalls were empty. He observed that while many items were not available for sale to the public, some classes of people were able to buy fowls and eggs, which could not be obtained at market prices.[98] To underscore the class issue in the supply chain, "Democrat" complained of the shortage of condensed milk to regular customers in the country areas, and "A.B" about the inability to obtain poultry feed.[99]

By mid-April 1942, the food controller, lamenting that "Trinidad is a large, and I would say too large, importer of food" declared that "the food situation is serious and is getting more serious".[100] The calypsonian Tiger summed up the situation as:

> Time so hard you cannot deny
> That even saltfish and rice I can hardly buy
> Things so hard you cannot deny
> That even saltfish and rice I could hardly buy
> As the war declare with England and Germany
> Ah can't drink a little bit of milk in me tea
> But I would plant provision and fix my affairs
> And let the war continue fighting ten thousand years.[101]

As a result, the Grow More Food campaign was intensified. Lectures and demonstrations to teach householders how to plant were conducted at the Horticultural Club.[102] Fred Grant announced that the sugar manufacturers had agreed to devote three thousand acres to the planting of short-term crops (sweet potatoes, black-eyed peas and eddoes), and as their contribution to the campaign, oil companies were also making land available to their staff. The lectures and demonstrations continued to be conducted by the Department of Agriculture and the Horticultural Society. The Cocoa Subsidy Board offered landowners ten dollars per acre for cutting down uneconomical cocoa trees to make land available for food production.[103]

Grant explained that his department was collaborating with the Land Settlements section for the purpose of acquiring more lands to increase food production. The 150-acre Las Mercedes Estate in Talparo was the first property to be purchased for that purpose, and plans were afoot to acquire the El Recuerdo Estate, Manzanilla, in east Trinidad, which was to be allocated in blocks of 1.5 to 2 acres under the controller's scheme. Over 200 acres of land were allocated in the Buenos Ayres settlement and 200 acres at Allandale in Toco, and settlements in Guaico, Tamana and Sangre Grande were almost complete. These, Grant anticipated, would contribute significantly to food production.[104]

When Eastern Caribbean food exports to Trinidad ceased, the Food Production Department acquired 300 acres of land for cultivation. Orange Grove Estate rented 200 acres to the Food Production Department, which also acquired a 200-acre property adjoining the old Agricultural Bank and distributed sixty 1-acre lots at Bonaire.[105]

Despite these efforts, food shortages remained acute. There was no pork available in the city during the first week of May,[106] and the severe milk shortage continued. Of pre-war milk imports valued at $860,132 came from Europe, the United States and Canada and that which were valued at $768,000 came from Nazi-influenced countries – Holland, Denmark, Norway, Switzerland and Sweden. U-boat activity made it difficult to obtain supplies from American sources, so scarcity reigned.[107]

The meat situation was compounded by the cessation of supplies of cattle from Cuba and Guyana and of frozen meat from Argentina, which left the colony dependent on supplies from Venezuela.[108] Wartime scarcity made it necessary for vendors to create their own systems to manage limited supplies, which were criticized as "profiteering". In an article entitled "Too Much Bone in the Meat", a special correspondent complained that pork vendors added trotters to snout, ears and other parts that were usually sold separately.[109]

But in the face of shortages, there was wastage. Between August and December 1942, nine hundred barrels of potatoes, a scarce item, deteriorated in the warehouse and were condemned by the Board of Health, as was a later consignment. The deterioration was blamed on blight rot disease, which raged in Halifax, Prince Edward Island, Nova Scotia and New Brunswick in Canada.[110] Fitzroy Andre Baptiste also refers to food-quality problems citing the example of a shipment of five thousand cases of milk which arrived in Trinidad "old and mostly dried up".[111] There appeared to have been no satisfactory quality controls on imports by the Control Board.

The next case is also instructive. MI Bakery in Port of Spain went out of business and was bought out by Coelho. The owner of MI had a stock of milk, which had been on his hands since the prohibition order on the preparation and sale of cakes and pastries. Having been stockpiled for a lengthy period, the forty cases of milk were declared unfit for human consumption and confiscated. Such was the desperation of some people that when the stock was dumped a crowd of people scrambled for the hard, dried milk.[112] In a separate case, 1,248 tins of milk were destroyed in May 1943 because they had been in storage for too long.[113] These episodes reveal flaws in the distribution system. As will be indicated below, the Control Board required those with excess flour to provide returns to the board. It is noteworthy that this was not done in the case of milk when the board prohibited cake- and pastry-making.

By June 1942 the crisis had worsened. Trinidad's quota of supplies from overseas was cut by 25 per cent, and a number of prohibitions were announced. The preparation of fancy cakes and pastries and the serving of meals in hotels (except for transients) and public places were prohibited between the hours of 9:15 p.m. and 5:00 a.m.[114] Bakers were permitted to sell only one pound of flour per day per person. Wholesalers and retailers were restricted to 75 per cent of their previous requirements and were also required to provide a return of existing stocks of flour. The population was asked to eat less bread and cakes, to buy only just what was needed and to desist from asking their shopkeeper or baker for special favours. Consumers were put on a quarter-pound-per-day flour ration.[115] The flour shortage triggered the closing of a number of bakeries in Port of Spain in June 1942.[116]

Rice also became critically short towards the end of 1942. It was announced at the end of October that Trinidad possessed only a few days' supply, as the Indian government had banned all rice exports. Consumers were asked to substitute rice with cornmeal and local vegetables.[117] The Food Production Department had acquired 200 acres of land at Brothers Road in southern

Trinidad for the cultivation of hill rice and corn,[118] but real benefits from this measure had not yet materialized and shortages became more acute across the colony. In November 1943 there were complaints of severe food shortages in Tunapuna, in north Trinidad, and one resident grumbled that "in the shops there have been no salt fish for weeks. A little rice now and then. No salt meat of any kind and lately no flour. No onions, tea or lard and just two cents' cooking oil at a time. No fish. Truly a sorry state of affairs."[119]

The shortage was compounded by price increases, which affected consumers in two ways. First, the food controller revised prices on the schedule list periodically, prescribing prices for wholesaling and retailing, which operated at the end of the supply line, excluding the importers. Throughout the war period there were increases in the retail price of rice, pork heads, beef, edible oils, salmon, tomato sauce, live cattle, condensed milk, charcoal, codfish, potatoes, onions, evaporated milk, smoked salmon, linseed meal (animal feed), pigtails, fresh corn and fresh fish.[120] At the beginning of 1943 the cost of living had moved three points up the index, as there were increases in the cost of all items, and an 85 per cent increase in food costs, especially fish, beef, butter and lard.[121]

Consumers also faced increases associated with the dilution and/or marriage of products. One consumer complained about the addition of corn to coffee which was being sold in San Fernando as pure coffee.[122] For the consumers some items were overpriced by vendors, as they were offered for sale above the scheduled price and therefore considered onerous. While for many it was a welcome opportunity to access scarce items, to the control department the law had to be upheld. As a result harsh punishments were inflicted on noncompliant vendors and their customers. A fish vendor in the Eastern Market was fined $300 or three months' hard labour for selling a pound and a half of cavalli for eighteen rather than fourteen cents per pound and a Belmont peas vendor was fined $480 (an exorbitant sum) or six months' incarceration for selling a pound of peas two cents above the scheduled price.[123] Two vendors were charged $15 each for selling corn a half-cent above the scheduled price.[124] Two others were each fined $25 or six months' imprisonment for selling less than one imperial pint of coconut oil for eight cents, exceeding the scheduled price of six cents per pint.[125] A city restaurateur was fined $150 for instructing an employee to sell a tin of grapefruit juice above the scheduled price of ten cents and the employee was fined $15 for selling the item at fourteen cents.[126]

Beef vendors at the Eastern Market were fined $170 for profiteering by adding stew to a pound and a half of steak and selling it at the price of steak – fifty-three cents per pound, another was fined $25 for the same offence[127] and a St James meat vendor was charged $200 for selling "lights and liver" for the price of liver.[128]

The Control Board was rigid in its policing of vendors, and the charges inflicted were certainly not equivalent to the value of the items sold. It is perhaps easy to see these individuals who were charged as exploiters, but they should be seen as resisters against a system of price scheduling that they felt was unfair to them. It was a boom period, general prices were on the increase, and they had to increase their earnings to be able to afford to purchase the other essential items. Scarcity was also a reality for them, so they had to manage their supplies to keep business afloat, and as with everyone else, they desired to take advantage of boom conditions to increase their profits. But at the end of the line, consumers, particularly those with limited resources, could not afford basic food items.

Similarly, the fishermen resisted the low prices on the scheduled list for fresh fish, and their refusal to go to sea ultimately resulted in the posting of new scheduled prices for fresh fish, which brought price increases for the more popular species.[129] Fishermen in San Fernando, Icacos, Point Fortin, La Brea, Erin and Moruga, seeking better prices for their fish, refused to go to sea in protest against the food controllers' orders that the catch be sold only wholesale in the city markets.[130] Also in protest, port vendors boycotted the Eastern Market over low prices and sold meat clandestinely to restaurants above the scheduled prices.[131] Several restaurateurs were fined $50 for hoarding condensed milk, corned beef, butter, coconut oil and rice, and the items were confiscated.[132] Edward Sandy of Tobago was the first person to be jailed for profiteering, as he sold chickens for sixty-eight cents per pound when the scheduled price was twenty-eight cents, and Cornelius George was fined $120 for buying the item above the scheduled price.[133]

Shopkeepers of Dow Village, in the south, were fined $50 for hoarding rice, which was forfeited, and two others in central and south Trinidad, who each owned two businesses, were charged $50 for diverting flour supplies from one to the other and their stocks forfeited.[134] Small traders were up in arms against the system of scheduling. They asked for a review of the markup, since they felt that they were in danger of being forced out of business. They found the profit margins too meagre, and they had concerns about stock depletion and inability to restock.[135] South butchers and meat vendors resumed trading under strong protest and promised to take further action if their matter was not attended to.[136]

Tobago was in a favourable situation and was said to be able to supply Trinidad with three months' of food, but the island also faced problems. Anne Juliani wrote to the newspaper that the restrictions on coconut oil permitted its sale only by official manufacturers, and this, as one can imagine, negatively affected peasants in Tobago, who traditionally made and sold coconut oil. Furthermore, they used the residual meal from the coconuts to feed pigs, so the pork supply was also jeopardized. Some pig farmers and oil makers bought coconuts from other small proprietors, whose business was similarly threatened. The writer lamented, "Trinidad seems quite satisfied to drain Tobago of all her foodstuffs, regardless of how little is returned."[137]

By the end of June 1943 the situation began to ease,[138] as imports were permitted and more items became available. With the "smell of victory" further slacking off was evident,[139] signalling the denouement of the food campaign. Prices remained high but a level of normality in the supply of basic items returned to the colony. As the war came to an end the official reports sanitized the experience, praising the administrative achievements and engaging in obscurantism regarding the negative experiences of the poorer classes. This is well exemplified by the former governor, Sir Hubert Young, in an address to the Royal Empire Society in London. Despite the pressures on the public, the distress that was evident in the society, the displacement and dispossession of individuals and communities and the disputes between rowdy soldiers, migrants and locals, former Governor Young proudly lauded the war effort in Trinidad and Tobago, stating that

> the solidarity of the whole community is remarkable, and there is nothing more solid than their loyalty to the crown and the Empire. Income tax has been stepped up until it is higher than in any colony in the empire . . . we were remarkably successful in price control . . . there was spontaneous prohibition of luxuries. . . . We lent the Americans sites to put up camps . . . and the behaviour of all ranks was beyond all praise.[140]

CONCLUSION

Although local food production increased significantly, this discussion has shown that the food campaign, which was a central part of the defence strategy, did not achieve maximum returns and failed to avert a crisis of food scarcity. It has shown how wartime Trinidad and Tobago epitomized contradictions. This period was both liberating and oppressive. The war stimulated increased liquidity, but in the midst of a boom there was poverty. Some enjoyed new employment opportunities at the US bases, but others lost their jobs and/or faced reduced capacity to earn a living and feed their families, and many remained unemployed and underemployed. The social problems of the previous era continued to be manifested, causing the authorities to implement new regulations to deal with "hooliganism". Many of these "hooligans" were desperate, unemployed people. The call to grow and eat more local food was hampered by the inadequacies of water and fuel supplies and variable access to land in different localities. The presence of the foreign military, their privileges and their excesses aggravated the locals, whose basic needs had to be sacrificed in the interest of security.

Despite the Grow More Food campaign, the colony's food bill increased during the war. The Control Department offered protection to consumers from high prices, yet the cost of living skyrocketed as controlled prices were constantly adjusted, leaving the big importers unrestricted while subjecting the small operators to tight controls, strangling some out of existence in the process. Vendors and small business operators resisted price controls, which threatened their businesses, and faced stiff penalties for breaches of the control laws. The bulk-buying mechanism was intended to ensure supplies to all, but the distribution system was not equitable, for some communities and classes were more favoured than others. The war scarcity put intense pressure on women, who in the struggle to obtain food found themselves enmeshed in brawls of desperation; the vendors and fishermen fought to save their livelihood; and residents opposed the incursions of the military.

The years 1939 to 1945, particularly 1942 and 1943, constitute a period of distress, dislocation, dispossession and disputes, with the food question at the centre. This trauma-filled period was characterized by social disorganization, as the poorer section of the population struggled for survival in a contest for a place in its own terrain and for the ability to feed itself. It was a period of "contradictory omens", when the colony was faced with both an internal and external war and an "imposed imperium" that kept the society together.[141]

NOTES

1. Eric Williams, *History of the People of Trinidad and Tobago* (London: Andre Deutsch, 1964), 268–72.
2. Bridget Brereton, *A History of Modern Trinidad, 1783–1962* (Oxford: Heinemann, 1981), 192.
3. Michael Anthony, *The Making of Port-of-Spain*, vol. 2: *Port-of-Spain in a World at War, 1939–1945* (Port of Spain: Ministry of Sport, Culture and Youth Affairs, 1983), 113.
4. Ibid., 114–16.
5. Ibid., 116.
6. Ibid., 118.
7. Ibid., 61–65.
8. Ibid., 121.
9. Fitzroy Baptiste, *War, Cooperation and Conflict: The European Possessions in the Caribbean, 1939–1945* (Westport, CT: Greenwood Press, 1988), 146–47.
10. Ibid., 87–100.
11. Ibid., 156.
12. Ibid., 157.
13. Kelvin Singh, *Race and Class Struggles in a Colonial State: Trinidad 1917–1945* (Kingston: University of the West Indies Press, 1994), 195–96.
14. Ibid., 197.
15. Claus Füllberg-Stolberg, "The Caribbean in the Second World War", in *UNESCO General History of the Caribbean*, vol. 5: *The Caribbean in the Twentieth Century*, ed. Bridget Brereton (Paris: UNESCO, 2004), 115.
16. Harvey R. Neptune, *Caliban and the Yankees: Trinidad and the United States Occupation* (Chapel Hill: University of North Carolina Press, 2007), 79.
17. Bridget Brereton, "A Loyal Opposition? Trinidad's Left Wing Press and World War II" (paper presented at Staff Seminar Series 2015, Department of History, University of the West Indies, St Augustine, 10 April 2015).
18. Robert Lee Faris extended the concept of social disequilibrium to explain social problems in general, including crime and mob violence. He defined social disorganization as the weakening or destruction of the relationships which hold a social organization together. See Robert Lee Faris, *Social Disorganization* (New York: Ronald Press, 1955).

19. Brinsley Samaroo, "The Trinidad Disturbances of 1917–20: Precursor to 1937", in *The Trinidad Labour Riots of 1937: Perspectives 50 Years Later*, ed. Roy Thomas (St Augustine, Trinidad: Extra Mural Studies Unit, University of the West Indies, 1987), 21.
20. Hollis "Chalkdust" Liverpool, *Rituals of Power and Rebellion: The Carnival Tradition in Trinidad and Tobago, 1763–1962* (Chicago: Frontline Research Associates School Times Publications/Frontline Distribution Int'l, 2001), 455.
21. Lloyd Braithwaite, "Introduction: The Trinidad Labour Riots of 1937", in Thomas, *Trinidad Labour Riots of 1937*, 1.
22. Rita Pemberton, "The Evolution of Agricultural Policy in Trinidad and Tobago 1890–1945" (PhD diss., University of the West Indies, St Augustine, 1997), 291.
23. *Trinidad Guardian*, 23 April 1943, 2.
24. *Trinidad Guardian*, 16 June 1943, 1.
25. George Mitchell, letter to the editor, *Sunday Guardian*, 31 October 1943, 4.
26. Alfred de Silva, letter to the editor, *Trinidad Guardian*, 4 December 1943, 4.
27. Ralph de Boissière, *Rum and Coca-Cola* (London: Allison and Busby, 1984), 122.
28. *Trinidad Guardian*, 13 May 1942, 8.
29. *Trinidad Guardian*, 14 November 1942, 1, 5.
30. National Archives of the United Kingdom (NAUK): CO 295/518 59968, The Empire and War in Trinidad, Dispatch 382 Enclosure H. Hancock, "Activities of the Colony During the War", Governor Chancellor to Secretary of State Long, 8 November 1918.
31. *Bulletin of the Department of Agriculture* 13, no. 83 (August–October 1914): 250.
32. Pemberton, "Evolution of Agricultural Policy", 203–4.
33. Ibid., 206–8.
34. NAUK: CO 295/520 34469/19, Dispatch No. 226, Trinidad 522, Milner to Governor Gordon.
35. Ibid., 199.
36. Ibid., 271.
37. *Trinidad Guardian*, 5 January 1942, 1.
38. *Trinidad Guardian*, 9 February 1942, 1.
39. National Archives of Trinidad and Tobago (NATT): Council Paper (CP) No. 17 of 1941, Address of the Governor to the Legislative Council, 5.
40. NATT: CP. No. 60 of 1941, Address of the Governor to the Legislative Council, November 1941, 7.
41. Pemberton, "Evolution of Agricultural Policy", 277–88.

42. *Trinidad Guardian*, 4 June 1942, 1.
43. *Trinidad Guardian*, 24 May 1942.
44. *Sunday Guardian*, 7 February 1943, 5.
45. NATT: CP No. 71 of 1941, Administrative Report of the Director of Agriculture for 1940, 5.
46. NATT: CP No. 31 of 1942, 3.
47. NATT: CP No. 1 of 1943, 4, 6 , 7.
48. *Sunday Guardian*, 29 March 1942, 2.
49. Ibid., 1.
50. NATT: CP No. 47 of 1945, Administrative Report of the Director of Agriculture for the Year 1944, 2.
51. *Trinidad Guardian*, 14 May 1942, 2.
52. *Trinidad Guardian* 1 January 1942, 2.
53. *Sunday Guardian*, 12 April 1942, 1.
54. *Sunday Guardian*, 19 April 1942, 1.
55. *Sunday Guardian*, 17 May 1942, 2.
56. *Trinidad Guardian*, 8 June 1942.
57. *Sunday Guardian*, 22 February 1942, 4.
58. The commentator's first name was not provided in the newspaper.
59. *Sunday Guardian*, 22 February 1942, 2.
60. *Trinidad Guardian*, 7 March 1942, 4.
61. *Trinidad Guardian*, 12 November 1942, 7.
62. *Trinidad Guardian*, 9 February 1943, 1.
63. *Trinidad Guardian*, 11 April 1942, 4.
64. *Trinidad Guardian*, 10 April 1942, 4, 3.
65. *Trinidad Guardian*, 18 June 1942, 4.
66. *Trinidad Guardian*, 7 March 1942, 4.
67. Ibid.
68. Ibid.
69. de Boissière, *Rum and Coca-Cola*, 124.
70. *Trinidad Guardian*, 11 April 1942, 8.
71. *Trinidad Guardian*, 25 April 1942, 1.
72. *Trinidad Guardian*, 13 May 1942, 1.
73. *Trinidad Guardian*, 7 November 1942, 1.
74. NATT: CP No. 19 of 1941, Trinidad Electricity Board, Electricity Supply and Transportation Department, Annual Report for the Year Ending 31 December 1940, 3.
75. *Trinidad Guardian*, 7 May 1942, 3.
76. *Trinidad Guardian*, 23 June 1942, 4.

77. *Trinidad Guardian*, 27 June 1942, 3.
78. *Trinidad Guardian*, 5 February 1943, 1.
79. *Trinidad Guardian*, 19 February 1943, 4.
80. *Trinidad Guardian*, 24 January 1942, 2.
81. *Trinidad Guardian*, 24 April 1942, 5.
82. Ibid.
83. Ibid.
84. Ibid.
85. *Trinidad Guardian*, 3 March 1942, 2.
86. Ibid.
87. Ibid.
88. Ibid., 1.
89. *Sunday Guardian*, 8 March 1942, 8.
90. *Trinidad Guardian*, 2 April 1942, 8.
91. *Sunday Guardian*, 22 March 1942, 4.
92. *Trinidad Guardian*, 31 March 1942, 3.
93. *Trinidad Guardian*, 23 April 1942, 4.
94. *Trinidad Guardian*, 12 March 1942, 2.
95. *Trinidad Guardian*, 2 April 1942, 2.
96. *Trinidad Guardian*, 18 March 1942, 2.
97. Ibid., 15.
98. H.E. Fahey, "We Will Plant When We Start to Starve Report", *Trinidad Guardian*, 10 March 1942, 4.
99. *Trinidad Guardian*, 11 April 1942, letters to the editor, 4.
100. *Trinidad Guardian*, 17 April 1942, 7.
101. Gordon Rohlehr, *Calypso and Society in Pre-Independence Trinidad* (Port of Spain: Gordon Rohlehr, 1990), 343.
102. *Trinidad Guardian*, 10 April 1942, 1.
103. Ibid.
104. *Trinidad Guardian*, 24 April 1942, 4.
105. *Trinidad Guardian*, 23 May 1942, 2.
106. *Trinidad Guardian*, 6 May 1942, 1.
107. Ibid., "Comment by Agricola", 15.
108. *Trinidad Guardian*, 16 May 1942, 1.
109. Special Correspondent, "Too Much Bone in the Meat", *Sunday Guardian*, 17 May 1942, 15.
110. *Sunday Guardian*, 8 March 1942, 2.
111. Baptiste, *War, Cooperation and Conflict*, 155.
112. *Trinidad Guardian*, 9 October 1942, 1.

113. *Trinidad Guardian*, 18 June 1943, 2.
114. *Trinidad Guardian*, 4 June 1942, 1.
115. *Sunday Guardian*, 7 June 1942, 1.
116. *Trinidad Guardian*, 9 June 1942, 7.
117. *Trinidad Guardian*, 28 October 1942, 1.
118. *Trinidad Guardian*, 7 October 1942, 2.
119. Resident of Tunapuna, letter to the editor, *Trinidad Guardian*, 20 November 1943, 4.
120. See issues of: *Sunday Guardian*, 8 March 1942, 2; *Trinidad Guardian*, 10 March 1942, 1; *Trinidad Guardian*, 19 March 1942, 4; *Trinidad Guardian*, 8 April 1942, 1: *Sunday Guardian*, 12 April 1942, 5; *Sunday Guardian*, 26 April 1942, 5; *Trinidad Guardian*, 23 April 1942, 4.
121. *Trinidad Guardian*, 16 January 1943, 4.
122. "Letter by Pro Bono Publico", *Trinidad Guardian*, 3 November 1943, 4.
123. *Trinidad Guardian*, 26 March 1942, 4.
124. *Trinidad Guardian*, 13 March 1942, 8.
125. *Trinidad Guardian*, 10 April 1942, 8.
126. *Trinidad Guardian*, 22 April 1942, 3.
127. *Trinidad Guardian*, 21 May 1942, 8.
128. *Sunday Guardian*, 11 April 1943, 2.
129. *Trinidad Guardian*, 23 April 1942, 4.
130. *Trinidad Guardian*, 14 October 1942, 1.
131. *Trinidad Guardian*, 19 May 1942, 3.
132. *Trinidad Guardian*, 14 November 1943, 1.
133. *Sunday Guardian*, 25 April 1943, 2.
134. *Trinidad Guardian*, 9 June 1943, 1.
135. *Trinidad Guardian*, 16 January 1943, 2.
136. *Trinidad Guardian*, 17 April 1943, 1.
137. Anne Guiliiany, letter to the editor, *Trinidad Guardian*, 2 November 1943, 4.
138. *Sunday Guardian*, 30 June 1943, 5.
139. *Trinidad Guardian*, 19 November 1943, 3.
140. Address of Sir Hubert Young to the Royal Empire Society entitled "Trinidad and Tobago in Wartime", *Sunday Guardian*, 31 January 1943, 2.
141. This is the title of a book by Edward Brathwaite which deals with paradoxes of colonial identity, language and culture and in which he notes that the contradictory developments were traumatic. It is argued here that this description is applicable to Trinidad and Tobago during World War II. See Edward Brathwaite, *Contradictory Omens: Cultural Diversity and Integration in the Caribbean* (Kingston: Savacou Publications, 1974).

PART 2.

IMPERIALISM AND INTERVENTIONISM

5.

THE FRENCH CARIBBEAN IN WORLD WAR II
Upheavals, Repression and Resistance

ERIC T. JENNINGS

This chapter analyses the experience of World War II in the French West Indies from multiple vantage points. It begins by considering the socioeconomic impact of Martinique and Guadeloupe remaining in the orbit of Vichy France from the summer of 1940 until June 1943. The consequences included a series of restrictions that virtual autarky implied. The chapter then explores the political ramifications of Vichy measures in Martinique and Guadeloupe and a wide range of popular reactions to them.

As France fell to Nazi Germany in May and June 1940, French colonies, the gold of the Bank of France and the French fleet became major international stakes. Over the summer of 1940, the new government that was granted full powers in July 1940 in the resort town of Vichy vied for control over these three bargaining chips with General Charles de Gaulle in London. De Gaulle and his Free French movement would only win over a few overseas territories over the coming months, in French Equatorial Africa, in Cameroon, in the South Pacific and in the Indian subcontinent.[1] The vast majority of French colonies, including the French West Indies, remained "loyal" to Philippe Pétain's authoritarian government, which initially held the edge in credibility. In reality, local populations had little choice. To be sure, Martinique and Guadeloupe's elected officials boldly attempted to join de Gaulle's Free French. However, French naval authorities reined them in. In Guadeloupe, on 1 July 1940 Councillor Paul Valentino delivered an impassioned plea for liberty at an extraordinary session of the island's general council: "Let us work to liberate France from its invader.... It is not by supplying the enemy that we will manage to give our nation the strength it needs to rise up from under the German boot." Valentino continued, "I belong to a race that is loathed by Nazism and Hitler is now in France. He had announced that he would place France under tutelage and wipe non-aryans from its soil. A misery greater than that we experienced prior to 1789 awaits us."[2] Valentino clearly implied that the advent of Vichy would signal a return to authoritarian racism and, consequently, slavery.

However eloquent, Valentino's voice failed to carry the day. Ultimately, Admiral Georges Robert and his clique of sailors orchestrated what I have termed "a quiet naval coup",[3] stripping civil authorities of their powers.[4] Indeed, the navy and gold alluded to above entered into play in June 1940. As Fitzroy Baptiste has shown, French warships faithful to the authorities in France converged on Martinique and Guadeloupe in late June 1940.[5] Among them was the rapid cruiser *Emile Bertin*, capable of sailing at a remarkable forty knots. The *Emile Bertin* carried on board a substantial portion of the gold of the Bank of France. Off Fort-de-France, it joined the aircraft carrier *Béarn*. The *Jeanne d'Arc* and its crew dropped anchor in nearby Guadeloupe. This assembly of warships served not only to dissuade foreign powers from challenging Vichy head-on in the French Caribbean but also as a powerful instrument of intimidation over French West Indians. Nevertheless, warships and gold could not in themselves render the regime more palatable. Nor could they serve to break what rapidly became a situation of economic isolation. Indeed, after the Netherlands fell, first French and British, then later US troops landed in the Dutch West Indies. Martinique, Guadeloupe and their possessions thereby became the only satellites of the Axis in the Western Hemisphere and the growing fixation of British and American attention. From 1940 through 1943, inhabitants of the French Caribbean would pay the price of this gradually mounting isolation and would grapple with the Vichy regime as it stretched its tentacles across the French West Indies.

INTERNATIONAL TENSIONS, AUTARKY AND THEIR CONSEQUENCES

World War II brought both penury and a degree of economic autonomy to the French Caribbean. Chiefly sugar-producing islands, Martinique and Guadeloupe had long relied upon metropolitan France for finished goods, as well as for flour and a host of other foodstuffs. Cod, meanwhile, had historically reached the French West Indies via triangular trade with Saint-Pierre and Miquelon, the tiny French isles off the coast of Newfoundland. All of this would change between 1940 and 1943, a period that, for all of its hardships, is still sometimes remembered locally as an era of economic emancipation of sorts, emblematized on one island by the phrase "the Guadeloupean effort".

The issue, a chronologically sensitive one, requires a zoom outwards to consider global tensions surrounding the French Caribbean. From November 1940 to December 1941, a modus vivendi between US and Vichy officials meant that the French Caribbean was still relatively well supplied. After France fell in June 1940, the United States demanded that the naval vessels in Martinique and Guadeloupe be immobilized, along with the gold of the Bank of France. Admiral Georges Robert, Vichy's high commissioner to the Caribbean, acceded to these demands in November 1940, in what became known as the Robert-Greenslade Accord. Public opinion in the United States remained nevertheless riveted on Martinique and the potential Axis pocket that the French Caribbean represented. Indeed, Vichy's presence in the Western Hemisphere seemed to constitute an especially brazen flouting of the Monroe doctrine. For its part, the United Kingdom adopted in principle a much harsher line towards Vichy in the Caribbean and enforced an admittedly rather porous blockade on Vichy colonies in general. Or rather, the British regretted that the United States allowed a "Martinique Leak" to flout their blockade of Vichy colonies.[6]

Indeed, at this juncture, despite pressure from the United Kingdom, trade continued, including along the Marseille-Casablanca-Fort-de-France route and local ones from Pointe-à-Pitre and Fort-de-France to destinations that included New York, the Dominican Republic and Brazil. This period of accommodation between Vichy and the United States in the Caribbean can be interpreted in different ways. Most obviously, it coincided with relatively cordial relations between Washington and Vichy France; it bears repeating that Vichy broke off diplomatic relations with Washington on 8 November 1942, rather than vice versa. Washington was also eager to ensure that the Vichy war vessels at dock in the French West Indies remained there and deemed this possible via negotiation. One source at the British Foreign Office offered a different explanation for the seemingly lenient US position on Martinique and Guadeloupe. W.H.B. Mack, the France specialist at the Foreign Office, wrote in January 1942, "The State Department have surely made it clear for over a year that it is their policy to keep these islands going economically in order to prevent trouble with the coloured population which the US would probably have to help to put down."[7] Fears of racially charged unrest, rather than the threat posed by an aircraft carrier and three cruisers, or maintaining Vichy neutrality, allegedly constituted Washington's driving force on this matter.

This was no isolated case of US-British divergence on the Vichy Caribbean. Indeed, London and Washington rarely saw eye to eye on how to grapple with the Vichy-controlled isles of the Western Hemisphere.[8] In 1942 the British Foreign Office again attempted to persuade Washington to adopt a harsher line, drawing on the testimony of Félix Eboué, the black former governor of Guadeloupe and now leading Free Frenchman. Eboué estimated that a plebiscite would show 97 per cent of French West Indians in favour of Charles de Gaulle's Free French. He added that Britain and the United States must intervene, for Admiral Robert had implemented a police state in Martinique and Guadeloupe that had systematically jailed opponents. On this last score, British notes reveal tellingly that the "State Department have been informed of the substance of [Félix Eboué's] remarks. They were not much impressed and observed that the majority of the islanders were illiterate negroes without political views." Eboué's addendum featuring a list of internees at Fort Napoléon in les Saintes and at the Balata internment camp in Martinique seems not to have swayed the State Department either.[9]

Yet it would be an error to suggest that the United States merely appeased Admiral Robert. In effect, the screws on the Vichy Caribbean were tightened incrementally. In April and May 1941 the United States brought an abrupt end to the Marseille–Casablanca–Fort-de-France shipping line, which had theretofore transported passengers, mail and goods from France to the Caribbean. Initially the United States simply cut off oil shipments. The allies then proceeded to seize two French commercial vessels bound for Martinique on the high seas, the *Winnipeg* on 26 May and the *Arica* on 1 June.[10] Also in 1941, the United Kingdom convinced Dutch authorities to suspend service to Martinique and Guadeloupe.[11] Vichy's Rear Admiral Pierre Rouyer interpreted this turn of events as a reaction to Admiral François Darlan's visit to Hitler at Berchtesgaden. Much more was at stake in point of fact, but clearly Vichy rule over the French West Indies was tributary to tectonic forces well beyond the control of its henchmen on location in the Caribbean.[12]

On 18 August 1941 a deal was reached to allow the resumption of the Morocco-to-Martinique line (but not the connection to Marseille), with accrued surveillance and oversight by the Allies. The line only actually reopened on 30 September.[13] Subsequently, the entry of the United States into the war further heightened tensions, especially after an incident that occurred on the evening of 20 February 1942, when a German U-boat disembarked a wounded officer in Martinique. The United States got wind of the incident and issued severe reprimands. Given Vichy's putative neutrality and its lenient treatment of the German U-boat officer, it is interesting to note that Admiral Robert refused to free British seamen who managed to reach Martinique after the same German submarine sank the merchant steamship *Norman Prince* on 29 May 1942: the British sailors languished for many months in the Balata internment camp above Fort-de-France.[14]

In May 1942 renewed US-Vichy friction brought a complete halt to commercial relations between the French Caribbean on the one hand and Europe and Africa on the other. Meanwhile, for a time Germany refused to guarantee the safety of commercial shipping between the French Caribbean and the continental Americas. It demanded assurances that Vichy vessels bound for the United States would return to the French Caribbean.[15] Finally, when presented with guarantees that a test vessel would return to the French West Indies and that it would be used only to supply the islands, the German Armistice Commission relented, on 20 June 1942, and roughly a week later it reversed its decision or, rather, it identified a no-sail zone. The Germans explicitly placed any ships that headed towards the eastern seaboard of the United States at risk of sinking by U-boats.[16] The Vichy Caribbean was increasingly caught between a rock and a hard place.[17] By April 1943 all official dialogue ceased between Vichy officials in the Caribbean and their US interlocutors, and a "complete blockade" of the French West Indies was put in place.[18] One could compellingly argue that this was the nail in Vichy's coffin in the French West Indies.

As multilateral negotiations dragged on, penury set in. One Vichy report remarked that in Martinique "storage facilities are completely empty: there is no oil, and nearly no flour left". It added, "Guadeloupe is without petrol." This state of affairs was all the more vexing, noted the official, given that thirteen thousand tons of merchandise bound for the French Caribbean were stranded in New York, and another three thousand tons in Brazil.[19] Meanwhile, on 24 December 1941 a small Free French expedition seized Saint-Pierre and Miquelon, effectively stopping cod shipments that had previously reached Martinique and Guadeloupe, and in early February 1942 the governor of Martinique, Yves Nicol, telegrammed that "for several days now there has been neither cod nor flour, which are the staples of the local diet".[20] Indeed, the two make up the basis most notably for the traditional accras, or cod fritters.

On May Day 1942 Nicol made a public pronouncement in which he readily acknowledged the economic strangulation of the French Caribbean. He stated bluntly, "Supply is going badly. Oil, cod and meat are arriving in insufficient quantities. We are doing everything we can to obtain supplies from abroad, but difficulties are constantly mounting. Boats have become scarce and foreign currencies harder to come by." He added, "You know that the British blockade, as well as a crisis in production resulting from the war, has caused cruel restrictions that we are feeling in many domains. I know well that you are suffering from a shortage of food and of clothing articles, from shortages of fertilizer for your land, and the absence of various commercial products."[21] Furthermore, Nicol mentioned, the sugar-cane harvest had been poor. He neglected to add that this was due in large part to the exodus of young harvesters to such neighbouring islands as St Lucia and Dominica. Indeed, as we shall see, some roughly four thousand mostly young Antillais absconded for these neighbouring British isles in hope of joining the Fighting French; they did so at a trickle in 1940, which would soon turn into a steady stream by 1942 and 1943. The forthrightness with which Nicol broached the question of penury seems striking.

No doubt Nicol had little choice but to face the truth: Guadeloupe and Martinique were tightening their belts. By 1942 the administration had imposed serious restrictions on food consumption. Ration cards, closely resembling those utilized in metropolitan France under German occupation, served to both impose and enforce restrictions, most notably on bread. The latter had grown scarce as early as November 1940, when the government issued a statement asking citizens for their patience and adding that privations were "nothing next to what our brethren in France are experiencing"; flour did arrive on board the *Eastern Sword* a few days later, but this supply lasted only a few months.[22] Indeed, in mid-January 1941 Fort-de-France was once again without bread.[23] By late 1941 meat could only be consumed three days a week, and even then it was limited first to 360, then to 310 grams a day.[24] By 1943 many inhabitants of Fort-de-France went weeks on end without access to meat or fish.

Certainly, efforts were undertaken to produce locally, thereby diminishing reliance on imported goods. As soon as France fell, Martinique and Guadeloupe looked towards new food sources. On 24 August 1940, the pro-Vichy Martiniquais mouthpiece *La Paix* evoked a very Vichyite "return to the soil", exhorting islanders to "abandon an artificial economy" and to find food locally (literally, "ask for our bread from the fertile earth"). That same month, the head of Martinique's agricultural services, Henri Stehlé, broadcast over the radio a rather academic presentation on fruits, vegetables and the island's cultivation potential.[25] According to an official report, from July 1940 to January 1941 alone in Martinique, four thousand additional hectares of land were devoted to manioc, sweet potato and soy cultivation, marking a doubling of the crops in question. The figures may have been exaggerated, but there is no doubt that local crops were intensely privileged.[26] By February 1941 *La Paix* was reporting on positive experiments on manioc flour in Guadeloupe.[27] The Vichy administration made clear to farmers that henceforth "imports would only complement local production",[28] which constituted a complete reversal of the situation prior to the war. Fishing and cattle raising were promoted in Guadeloupe, with excess production sent to Martinique. This about-face occurred rapidly, as Vichy authorities grasped the isolation they suddenly faced in the summer of 1940. However, the shift towards autarky met with some difficulties. Dominique Chathuant terms the famed "Guadeloupean effort" at self-sufficiency largely "mythic", pointing to the ill will of sugar magnates who refused to support the administration's call to diversify crops. The planters, as was typical, wished to stick to sugar cane.[29]

In addition to stepping up local production, authorities resorted to new strategies and partners. Beef, for example, was imported from the Dominican Republic,[30] and other, more unexpected avenues were also explored. High Commissioner Robert even made overtures to French Indochina, asking authorities there to dispatch rice to the French West Indies, in vain.[31] And in his 1 March 1941 instructions to Guadeloupe's mayors, Governor Yves Nicol demanded that every school on the island feature a teaching garden of sufficient importance to feed students at lunchtime. This reform was in keeping with both the imperatives of autarky and a second goal of making school less "bookish" and more "virile", to borrow Nicol's phrasing.[32] Here Vichy's ideological and economic imperatives coalesced. The gymnasium and the garden mattered more than the classroom to Vichy officials, both in France and in the French West Indies. Producing locally became such an imperative that the regime organized an exhibition of ersatz materials, held in June 1942 in Martinique.[33] Desperate, Admiral Robert even assigned 350 much-needed soldiers to agricultural production in May 1943.[34]

On May 4, 1943, with food shortages having reached chronic levels in Martinique, authorities purchased a hundred head of cattle from the Dutch half of St Martin, for immediate expedition to Martinique.[35] The situation being dire, privately owned livestock was requisitioned for public distribution in Martinique. Martiniquan farmers fought back, arguing that the beasts were vital for farm work and, in many cases, requisition attempts got bogged down in "interminable negotiations".[36]

Over the long term, the lasting impact of Vichy-era privations can leave no doubt. David Macey has aptly written of French West Indian literature's obsession with the era's ersatz products and the lack of bread and cod: "The dominant memory of the war years [in the French West Indies] is that of hunger, and it has become part of a collective memory that can be shared even by those who are too young to have lived through the war." He proceeds to give the example of Martiniquan novelist Raphaël Confiant, who, although born in 1951, was told by his grandmother that any child having lived under Admiral Robert would have dutifully finished his soup without wasting any.[37]

Over the shorter term, there can be no doubt that food shortages played an important role in fuelling the popular rage that led to the protests at Fort-de-France and Captain Henri Tourtet's infantry uprising at Balata that finally dislodged Vichy from the French Caribbean in June and July 1943. None other than Vichy's henchman in Guadeloupe, Rear Admiral Rouyer, recognized that discriminatory food distribution had fostered the growing discontent. In particular, Rouyer explained, the largely black infantry in Martinique deeply resented the far more generous food rations dispensed to the mostly white navy. The long-standing French-colonial double standard in rations between white and black troops, he explained, "fanned rumours that spread like wildfire, and proved impossible to extinguish. These rumours suggested that the navy was hoarding food, leaving both the black infantry and the black population of the islands to die of famine."[38] As Eliane Sempaire has argued, it was not so much hunger in itself as it was the uneven distribution of foodstuffs in a time of shortages that led to revolt in June 1943.[39]

REPRESSION AND RUMOUR

The Vichy years in the French Caribbean can usefully be viewed through three prisms: as a civil war, a regional war and part of a global war. Vichy was clearly waging a battle against Free France across the French empire and, as such, desperately tried to maintain Martinique and Guadeloupe within its own orbit. Regionally, the Caribbean was riddled with tensions as US claims clashed with other sovereignties, and as the United States itself grappled with whether or not to throw its support behind General de Gaulle's Free French movement. From a global standpoint, the Gaullist sympathizers who left Martinique and Guadeloupe for St Lucia and Dominica were soon on their way to Trinidad, then on to Fort Dix or to Canada, and from there to a series of fronts in North Africa and Europe.

The repression that Vichy exerted in Martinique and Guadeloupe actually relates to all three of these layers of conflict. Vichy enacted laws of exception and authorized courts martial as part of its civil war against Gaullists, it bid for time in its endless negotiations with the United States and it desperately sought to stem the tide of dissidents wanting to join the fight against the Axis. Vichy agents generally undertook these tasks not so much out of overt pro-Nazi sentiment but most often out of loyalty to Marshal Philippe Pétain, ultra-conservative conviction, Anglophobia, inertia and legalism. On this last point, it is easy to lose track of the fact that Vichy passed as official France in many quarters at least until 1942.

At the helm of the entire Vichy state in the French West Indies was the high commissioner, Admiral Georges Robert, who had been named to head the region under the Third Republic. An "ultraconservative" with convictions close to the monarchist Action Française,[40] Robert was first and foremost an admiral, part of a clique of admirals that exerted considerable sway within the halls of Vichy, and Robert quite naturally relied upon the naval hierarchy to carry out Vichy's instructions. Repression in Guadeloupe was organized and coordinated by the far more zealous Rear Admiral Rouyer. Rouyer's archives suggest that he tilted the local situation in Vichy's favour over the summer of 1940. In a remarkable letter to Admiral François Darlan at Vichy in the fall of 1940, he boasted of having personally brought the French West Indies back into line and of wielding real control in Guadeloupe: the governor, Constant Sorin, was now under his "tutelage", he asserted boldly. He added, "I have taken all of the following under my hand: radio broadcasts, the press, censorship, police control. I also regularly intervene in matters of law, economy, education and commerce."[41] Rouyer's motivations included a vicious Anglophobic streak, which surfaced for instance in his letter to the editor of the newspaper *L'Action* dated 31 May 1941. After drawing up an inventory of British "crimes", he concluded: "To be a good Frenchman, one must hate England ... and have at least as much resentment against Britain as against Germany."[42]

The new regime went about jailing vocal French West Indian opponents swiftly and systematically. As I have shown elsewhere, justice was reduced to a sham.[43] Among those whom Vichy interned in such camps as Balata in Martinique or Fort Napoléon on les Saintes, one counts Augereau Lara, jailed for being an outspoken journalist; Sully Lacoma, interned in May 1941 for listening to US radio, and Jean Toulouse, suspected of sharing information with a US journalist. Leading Guadeloupean dissident Paul Valentino was likewise jailed, as were men like Léoville Pacard, Robert Chartol and Charles Catherine. The last three had fallen into the same trap. Vichy sailors had persuaded them that they wanted to desert and asked the men to shuttle them to Dominica. When the three men agreed to help, the trap closed. Others were jailed for Gaullist sympathies, and one individual, Ides Coudoux, for having slandered the head of state, Marshal Philippe Pétain.[44]

From 1940 to 1943 Vichy's police, gendarmerie and navy kept close watch on dissenting opinion. Thus, in March 1942 Vichy's police chief in the French Caribbean, Rear Admiral Robert Battet, made note of the suspicious political convictions of one Théodore Bellonie, vice-president of Fort-de-France's chamber of commerce. His purported misdeeds included having a sister-in-law who was married to a Barbadian man serving in the British army. More damning still, Bellonie had allegedly received a telegram from London in September 1940 that held the following pledge: "Martinique and Guadeloupe would ... be given extensive facilities if they decided to join Free France."[45]

The battle for public opinion hinged on information control. An 11 August 1941 report signed by Vichy's colonial inspector, Emile Devouton, revealed mixed results. On the one hand, it noted, local authorities had passed and enforced decrees banning British radio from public places (a Vichy law dated 28 October 1940 outlawed listening in public to British radio and other "anti-French" outlets). On the other hand, it noted with regret, French West Indians continued to listen to British radio within their homes and then proceeded to pass along whatever news they gleaned by way of mouth. Devouton observed that "it has only been possible up to now to scramble the British post of Antigua".[46] Blocking Antiguan wavelengths was akin to clogging but one hole in a watering spout: inhabitants of Martinique and Guadeloupe could still tune in to Boston and Miami radio, to the BBC and to Radio Colombia.[47] Word of mouth, foreign radios and popular grumbling proved difficult to match, Devouton conceded.[48] The Caribbean's multi-imperial and multinational configuration rendered Vichy's propaganda mission especially challenging. Yet Vichy did its utmost to wage this losing battle. As early as 25 November 1940, Rear Admiral Rouyer had Radio Martinique broadcast Anglophobic invective. Some was reheated, such as the anti-English rant by the Marquise de Pompadour from 1753. Other broadcasts involved incantations to Joan of Arc and Napoleon. Rouyer also composed and aired a series of rebuttals against General de Gaulle's famous appeals from London.[49]

With freedom of opinion muzzled, those sympathetic to the allies often decamped. From exile in Roseau, Dominica, Jean Augereau-Lara wrote touchingly to Félix Eboué, the former governor of Guadeloupe and now right-hand man to de Gaulle in Brazzaville: "The current leadership in Guadeloupe is taking advantage of the power inherent in its official positions to exert reprisals against those who do not share their politics and against those who refuse to commit acts of brigandry."[50] Another dissident, named Frédéric Bouvil, left for St Lucia. From Castries he reported to British colonial authorities on 26 November 1940 that "the people at Sainte Luce [in southern Martinique] are all de Gaulle sympathizers, also it is the wish of the people to serve under de Gaulle for the liberty and freedom of their mother country. At present all the districts are governed by mayors but it is rumoured that at any time they will be ejected from their office and administrators will be appointed by the admiral to replace them."[51] The allies were manifestly well informed of Vichy's authoritarian actions and even its future intentions. Most importantly, both writers suggested that Vichy had failed to win hearts and minds, and that the population of the French West Indies remained overwhelmingly and defiantly Gaullist.

In Martinique and Guadeloupe, a once thriving democratic culture was reduced to a sham. A perusal of the *journaux officiels*, or registers of laws and decrees from this era, reveals removal after removal of democratically elected officials. To replace them, Vichy nominated notables who shared the new regime's values. Indeed, in 1941 Vichy inspector Emile Devouton wrote, "Political men who occupied the position of mayor have mostly been replaced by notables, who are being asked to run municipalities as good family fathers might."[52] This needs to be situated within the context of a heavily stratified colonial society in Martinique and Guadeloupe, where sugar magnates and the white so-called *béké* class in particular already held disproportionate sway before 1940. To take only a small sample, the *journal officiel de la Guadeloupe* of 15 March 1941 announced the nomination of an entirely new municipal council at Lamentin, another one at Terre-de-Haut (Ile des Saintes), another still at Saint-Claude. A new mayor, a lawyer named Gaston Feuillard, was named in the capital, Basse-Terre (interestingly, even he would resign of his own volition on 3 May 1941). The town of Petit Bourg saw both its mayor and its municipal council replaced, as did the municipality of Port-Louis and that of Grand-Bourg on Marie-Galante island. Many of the new mayors were white "industrialists", as were Roger Damoiseau, the newly named mayor of Port-Louis, and another "industrialist", Pierre Langlois, the new mayor of Le Gosier.[53] A veritable purge was under way.

Dominique Chathuant has shown persuasively that in Guadeloupe legally elected black mayors were replaced by designated white ones in thirteen of the twenty-four municipalities on the two butterfly-shaped halves of Guadeloupe, known as Basse-Terre and Grande-Terre (excluding the isles of La Désirade, Les Saintes and Marie-Galante). On the sugar-producing island of Marie-Galante, interestingly, the three new mayors named in 1941 were black. To explain this exception, Chathuant hypothesizes that Vichy might have been seeking to avoid offending the local population or might simply not have found ideologically suitable non-black candidates.[54] The former theory seems validated by internal Vichy discussions of the situation in Martinique. There, in February 1941, Devouton wrote, "Given the touchiness of the coloured population, and particularly the métis element, the Admiral [Robert] and myself have endeavoured to limit to a strict minimum the designation of white creoles as mayors. Some excellent candidates had to be ruled out as a result."⁵⁵ Devouton's balancing act yielded the following results. Of the twelve newly named mayors in Martinique, four were white creoles; of the nine existing mayors whom Vichy deigned to keep, three were white creoles. Paternalism, authoritarianism and racism were all undergoing careful calibrations in the halls of power at Fort-de-France. The regime was conscious, in other words, that its nominations were being watched closely and that a purge that could be perceived as both racist and powerfully undemocratic was likely to create a backlash. Under the circumstances, Robert, Devouton and consort were willing to ease up on the racism in their nomination process in order to achieve their authoritarian agenda.

Mayors and municipal councils were not the only offices to be targeted. Vichy banned unions at home and in overseas territories, replacing them with chimerical and vaguely Salazarist or Mussolinian "corporations" intended to bring workers and managers in specific sectors into dialogue. In the French Caribbean, the regime took aim at other organizations as well. The case of Bellonie, evoked above, was the tip of a much larger iceberg. Indeed, Vichy targeted chambers of commerce and chambers of agriculture, which it suspected of orchestrating sedition. On 10 April 1942 Robert wrote to Vichy recommending the abolition and dissolution of "these organizations that have ruined the [islands] with their verbose parliamentarianism". A police file on one member of a chamber of commerce, Albert Bocle, squarely accused the man of leading an anti-Vichy plot. He had written, in an 11 September 1940 article entirely censored by the new regime, "We want to believe against the odds that the France of 1789, 1848 and 1914 will spare us the shame of looking elsewhere to find the liberalism that had been its hallmark for centuries." The ominous implication was not lost on Vichy's police, which suspected Bocle of "contemplating a possible rapprochement between Martinique and the USA".⁵⁶

Vichy also exported some of its domestic fixtures to the French Caribbean. These included the Legion of Combatants and Volunteers of the National Revolution, an ideological vanguard of the regime that doubled as a veterans' organization. By 1943 the Chantiers de la jeunesse, a youth-camp network and Vichyite indoctrination organization, was introduced to both Martinique and Guadeloupe.⁵⁷ Both the Legion and the Chantiers were intended as instruments of social control and of ideological propagation. Vichy also introduced its witch-hunts to the French Caribbean, including the persecution of the islands' few Jews and its far more numerous Freemasons. The persecutions were admittedly not murderous in nature, but they did involve firings and property confiscation, not to mention enumeration by census and numerous vexations and humiliations.[58]

Freemasons, Jews and elected officials were certainly not Vichy's only victims in the French West Indies. The regime also targeted gainfully employed women, by way of Marshal Philippe Pétain's new laws removing women from the workforce so as to increase the birth rate and return to ultra-traditionalist gender norms. The Vichy law of 11 October 1940, intended for mainland France, had stipulated that all recruitment of women in the administration would be halted; that any woman under twenty-eight who voluntarily resigned so as to marry would be granted a stipend; that for families earning a certain income in which the husband worked and the wife had fewer than three children, the wife could legally be placed on indefinite leave without pay; lastly, any female public employee over the age of fifty could be immediately retired.[59] The measures were applied to the French Caribbean in November 1940, merely a month after their promulgation in mainland France. In both Martinique and Guadeloupe, women were gradually removed from a wide range of professions, including postal and teaching positions, tax offices and so on. Sixty-nine primary schoolteachers were dismissed from office in Martinique alone, another sixty-four in Guadeloupe.[60] In Guadeloupe, the head of youth affairs, Jacques Grandjouan, courageously and strenuously opposed the firings, noting that they were not only sexist but also racist. Indeed, he observed that some white female teachers in Pointe-à-Pitre had been kept on, while their black peers had not.[61] The purge of female schoolteachers proved particularly intense. Here Inspector Devouton revealed an ulterior motive, in addition to the regime's paternalism. He wrote of needing to bring in "teachers from the motherland" trained in Vichy's pedagogical methods and implicated in the Scout movement, so as to undertake a moral cleanse of the French Caribbean.[62] Whatever their motivations, the impact of these firings was felt acutely in a time of shortages and privations. From Brazzaville in December 1943, Félix Eboué wrote to now Free French Martinique to recommend that a primary schoolteacher by the name of Mrs Altorn be immediately rehired, given how "harmed her family had been by Vichy's [revocation] measure".[63]

With democracy and civil society under attack between 1940 and 1943, the French Caribbean witnessed a rash of denunciations, reminiscent of those sent to French and German officials in occupied mainland France. Denunciations tended to target purported secret political enemies of the regime, real or imagined, and often betrayed other kinds of antagonisms and rivalries. One of these letters, preserved at the gendarmerie archives, was signed "a supporter of Pétain". It originated from Le Diamant, Martinique, on 27 October 1941. The terse note alleged that a Gaullist ring in that town was conspiring to subvert Vichy rule. An administrator named Emile Defort supposedly led the ring along with several co-conspirators, including an "English priest" (actually Canadian), Abbot Plante, the parish priest of Le Robert, Martinique.[64]

The major steps backwards undertaken by the Vichy regime fostered a tense atmosphere in which all rights acquired under the French Republic seemed jeopardized. A report from Martinique on 9 March 1942 bluntly conveyed popular opinion, relaying in particular "rumours in Gros Morne announcing the return of slavery".[65] In 1848 the Second Republic had definitively abolished slavery in French colonies. The advent of an unabashedly authoritarian regime evidently conjured up the legacy of Napoleonic and pre-revolutionary slavery. Indeed, departure to St Lucia and Dominica between 1940 and 1943 was often coded and experienced as a form of modern-day *marronnage*.[66] Slavery had been definitively abolished in 1848, yet its memory remained powerful; in the second half of the nineteenth century, for instance, the introduction of a worker pass in Martinique and Guadeloupe under Napoleon III had likewise fanned fears of re-enslavement (the fact that slavery had initially been abolished in French colonies in 1794 only to be reintroduced under Napoleon I also lent credence to the possibility of a terrible step backwards).

These fears of a return to slavery were also the product of economic circumstance and of Vichy's ways of dealing with this circumstance. The new regime passed laws severely punishing the destruction of crops. Productivity became an official priority, indeed the key to the survival of a besieged Vichy regime in an otherwise hostile Caribbean sea. In a particularly candid set of instructions dated 30 May 1941, the head of the gendarmerie in Martinique, a Captain Delpech, outlined ways of returning agricultural workers to the fields. "Alas," he said regretfully, "no law requires cane workers to work." However, he outlined to his staff a series of measures they could adopt to achieve precisely such an end: "Use vagabondage laws as scarecrows," he urged. He then added, "This, along with the verification of people's identification . . . usually suffices to achieve the results that the government so keenly desires at present."[67] Here is precisely where fears of a return of slavery and new Vichy imperatives met. Vichy's police and gendarmerie utilised intimidation and vagabondage laws to foster a climate of fear in which any person of colour could be brought in for questioning. Little wonder that, as a Guadeloupean agricultural worker named Jean-Charles Timoléon would recall,

> rumours circulated that plantation owners were growing prickly aloe with which to whip blacks. After the war, slavery would be re-established . . . [next thing I knew] gendarmes showed up on the plantation and began noting our names, ages and addresses. They had us sign a register and gave us each a work document. . . . They told us that we could only leave the plantation after having informed the gendarmerie. . . . This confirmed my fears and my companions and I decided that things had been the same under slavery.[68]

RESISTANCE

Inhabitants of the French West Indies mastered or recast "forms of insubordination" that James Scott has termed "weapons of the weak",[69] and in Martinique the administration registered numerous acts of non-violent resistance over the course of 1942. Workers tended to vote with their feet. As one report signalled, "On 6 March, in the Lamentin area, a majority of cane cutters left work without any apparent motive. At Seudon, at Lareinty, we are noticing a shortage of workers on the order of 50 per cent. At the Mahaut distillery, no employee has come to work for the past two days. On 27 February, 240 cane cutters absconded from the Terrier sugar plantation."[70]

Football matches provided ideal opportunities for oppositional practices. On 2 May 1943 in Basse-Terre, Guadeloupe, a crowd poured through the streets alternating cries of *"Vive le goal"* (Long live the goalkeeper) with *"Vive de Gaulle"* (Long live de Gaulle). The gendarmerie opened fire and killed a seventeen-year-old fan of the Cygne Noir football club named Serge Balguy, an incident that triggered the resignation of Basse-Terre's mayor and its municipal council and contributed to the unrest that would bring about the toppling of Vichy in the Caribbean a month later.[71] Football had provided the cover for a mass grouping, large gatherings having otherwise been banned by Vichy. The incident was not unique. On 30 May 1943 several thousand fans at the Bellevue stadium in Martinique cheered deliriously as an American aircraft flew over the stadium: hats, handkerchiefs and caps flew to the chant, "Long live America."[72]

Other venues propitious to oppositional voices included movie theatres. In early June 1943, for instance, the 1938 Hollywood film *Her Jungle Love* was shown at Fort-de-France's Gaumont cinema. Upon hearing a Pacific Islander exclaim on screen, "I hate whites," some black members of the audience applauded.[73] Anonymous nocturnal singing offered the same opportunity of expression under the cover of darkness. On the evening of 14 June 1943, the following defiant verses rang through the streets of Martinique's capital: "We don't have anything to eat, but we aren't afraid of you."[74]

The most radical course of action involved leaving Martinique and Guadeloupe altogether to join General de Gaulle's Fighting French. Inter-insular connections played an important role in shaping escape routes. Some of the earliest to assist those wanting to leave Vichy-controlled Martinique and Guadeloupe in late 1940 were British nationals from Dominica with French West Indian kinship connections. In December 1940 Vichy authorities arrested one Strasfort Didnoit, hailing from Dominica, on charges of vagabondage and soon discovered that he had assisted French sailors escaping to neighbouring British isles. Vichy police rightly suspected another man from Dominica, Herman François Gachette, known under the pseudonym Amant, of leading a ring of human smugglers.[75] Indeed, a document dated 2 November 1940 preserved in the St Lucian police archives confirms that Gachette was "pro-de Gaulle" and was "a Dominican who is married to a native of Martinique". It also features lengthy reports by Gachette on conditions in Martinique, including low food stocks, the distribution of Gaullist pamphlets, the state of public opinion, gun-battery locations and the cost of living.[76] Evidently, inter-island information gathering, passages and ties proved essential for resistance activities in the French Caribbean.

After the war, one Guadeloupe newspaper would write, "In our eyes, Dominica represents more than a leisure excursion. It served as the refuge for our threatened freedoms . . . In a very recent past, it was the hospitable land where the best French West Indian sons regrouped before leaving for battle."[77] Here we see a potent demonstration of Matthew J. Smith's argument about the Caribbean's profound interconnectedness through exile.[78]

A former socialist municipal councillor named Maurice des Etages also proved instrumental in organizing passages from Martinique to St Lucia. He travelled personally to St Lucia to liaise with British military authorities and rationalize the largely nocturnal departures by boat. In February 1941 he further provided British authorities in St Lucia with a wealth of information about conditions in Martinique. His detailed report included estimates of support for Pétain and de Gaulle among different segments of society. Des Etages even considered the profile of new arrivals in Martinique from Marseille on board the vessels that at that juncture were still undertaking the transatlantic crossing to Fort-de-France. He noted, "There are . . . some German Jews in Martinique who appear to be harmless. They came on troop ships arriving from Casablanca."[79] He discussed plans to use fishermen to bring more volunteers from Martinique to Castries. He detailed which Gaullist leaflets he had been able to distribute. However, a month later des Etages was denounced after returning to Martinique. He attempted suicide aboard the Vichy vessel where he was interrogated, before being condemned to fifteen years' hard labour in French Guiana, on charges of treason. At his trial, des Etages spoke of his ardent patriotism and his desire to defeat Nazism.[80]

Notwithstanding such setbacks as the arrest of des Etages, the flow of exiles and volunteers from Martinique and Guadeloupe to St Lucia and Dominica increased steadily between 1940 and 1943. On 20 February 1941, Captain Noël coordinated coastal defences for Admiral Robert; rather than focusing on the possibility of US or UK landings, he mainly sought to prevent departures. Noël organized two watch posts in Martinique. He raised the possibility of seeking "the voluntary collaboration of a certain number of people along the coast, especially along vulnerable and unsupervised stretches of coastline".[81] While Vichy's police, navy, and gendarmerie succeeded in foiling many departures by arresting such men as Didnoit and des Etages, it could not stem the growing tide. Dissidents, as they called themselves, managed to reach Dominica from much of Guadeloupe's southern coast, as well as from several locations in Martinique, including Grand-Rivière, where a plaque in their memory now stands. Several sites in southern Martinique lent themselves to departure to St Lucia.[82]

The crossings were risky, conditions challenging. Jean Massip, the Free

Frenchman responsible for coordinating escapes and then the voyage onward to the United Kingdom or the United States, recalls that passage from Martinique and Guadeloupe to St Lucia or Dominica cost somewhere between two and three thousand francs.[83] Volunteers rightly worried about the trustworthiness of boat owners offering the service, especially in the wake of the spectacular arrests of Léoville Pacard, Robert Chartol and Charles Catherine. Indeed, a deserter from Vichy's navy who reached St Lucia in 1941 explained to the British authorities that two hundred of his comrades likewise wished to join Free France. He depicted the obstacles in their way as follows: "The only difficulties are (1) money – the men have not the funds to pay for transport, (2) they do not know with whom to make contact in Martinique to arrange their escape as they are afraid to approach persons there for fear they will be betrayed to the authorities."[84] Other perils lurked at sea. Indeed, the roughly twenty kilometres separating French from British isles were treacherous themselves, especially by night, as they featured both dangerous currents and sharks. A variety of small vessels was utilized to undertake the clandestine crossings. Sailboats were on average only between five and seven metres (between sixteen and twenty-three feet) long.[85] Many arrived by canoe.[86] Czechoslovakian soldiers, whose incredible wartime odyssey took them from Marseille to Martinique and then illegally on to St Lucia, provide an intriguing testimony. They describe the boat that took them from Martinique to St Lucia as follows: "a native dugout . . . propelled by rough hewn oars and sails made of handkerchiefs. It took them ten hours to reach St. Lucia."[87]

An archival file from the St Lucian police services, a copy of which is held at the French military archives, allows us to reconstruct part of the wave of departures from Martinique to St Lucia between 1940 and 1943. Although the file features some major gaps for the year 1942, it nonetheless identifies some one thousand individuals having undertaken the crossing. Total estimates from both Martinique and Guadeloupe to St Lucia and Dominica vary, some reaching five thousand (Jean Massip, who helped send on the volunteers from Dominica and St Lucia, cites the figure of four thousand).[88] The file mostly reveals an incredible sociological diversity among the exiles. They included the cast of characters we have already encountered – Czechoslovak soldiers stranded in the French West Indies and wishing to resume the fight against Nazi Germany, sailors from Vichy's navy, European refugees who had managed to reach Fort-de-France between 1939 and 1942 and, of course, a great many French West Indians from diverse social backgrounds – all wanting to fight in the ranks of de Gaulle's Free French.[89] On location in Castries, Free French officials made these volunteers pass medical and military exams, before incorporating them into Free French ranks.

Some cases are quite touching, such as the 15 September 1941 report indicating that Albert Lahely and René Gagnepain were deemed medically fit to join the Free French forces. It specifies that St Lucian authorities had to clothe the two men "for neither of these volunteers have any clothes other than those which they are wearing". Many dissidents evidently did undertake the dangerous crossing with a bare minimum of belongings. A report dated 20 April 1943 draws up the list of dissidents having arrived from Martinique since September, adding the name of their hotel or host. Most of them were subsequently directed towards Trinidad en route to joining the Fighting French. Other documents consist of lists of dissidents who had not yet undertaken military service. Still others feature numerous complaints from hotel managers claiming that the French West Indians never paid for their lodgings in St Lucia, and demanding compensation.[90]

CONCLUSION

In December 1943, five months after Vichy had been dislodged from the French West Indies, the cruiser *Emile Bertin* returned to haunt Fort-de-France. This vessel had served as one of the main instruments of power of Admiral Robert and his Vichy cabal. It now returned, for a short visit nominally under Fighting French command. Yet its sailors seemed bent on exacting revenge on Martinique's black population. The new governor of Martinique complained that during the ship's five-day stay in port, "part of the crew came to shore and made hostile political pronouncements, molesting and hitting isolated civilians in the streets. We counted eight wounded civilians, one seriously." The new governor acidly evoked the "unspeakable actions of sailors who had supposedly rallied to the Free French side". He demanded that no other vessel previously posted in the French Caribbean under Vichy be allowed to return there. He added that

> conversely, it would be desirable for a Free French vessel with the Cross of Lorraine flag to be sent here with a propaganda mission as soon as possible.

We need to show another side of the navy than the one that for three years maintained the population in forced neutrality by means of violence and police terror. We must demonstrate this to a population that is Gaullist in its heart.[91]

Vichy's afterlives were many in the French Caribbean. In June 1944, some inhabitants of the French West Indies remained frustrated at the limited purges that had occurred since Vichy was dethroned. The press joined the chorus demanding that justice be served. Articles often identified high-ranking supporters of the former regime. Thus, the 10 June 1944 edition of the Martiniquan newspaper *Justice* published a list of volunteers for Vichy's vanguard legion of volunteers for the National Revolution. Like lists of resisters, it betrays remarkable social diversity: schoolteachers, a mechanic, a hairdresser, a cobbler, a woodworker, "industrialists" and a purveyor of bras were all listed as leading legionaries. In keeping with the discourses of the dissident movement, they were now all deemed undifferentiated "henchmen . . . of Nazi supporters of slavery".[92]

In the final analysis, the Vichy years in the French Caribbean betray the significance of memory and insular interconnectedness. The memory of slavery emerged as a spectre as soon as France fell in 1940 and was rekindled with each passing Vichy measure aimed at stoking production or marking an authoritarian step backwards. Similarly, the memory of *An tan Wobè*, or of the Robert years, as they are known on Martinique (*An tan Sorin* in Guadeloupe), has itself been subject to countless resurfacings and meanderings. This reminds us of the remarkable ties that bound the Lesser Antilles and the ways in which these connections facilitated resistance to Vichy rule.

ACKNOWLEDGEMENTS

The author would like to thank the Social Science and Humanities Research Council of Canada for its generous support of his project on exile and encounter in the French Caribbean (1940–1942) that made possible the research for this chapter.

NOTES

1. See Eric Jennings, *Free French Africa in World War II: The African Resistance* (Cambridge: Cambridge University Press, 2015).

2. Guadeloupe et dépendances, "Délibérations du Conseil général, session extraordinaire du 1er juillet 1940", 8, 17.
3. Eric Jennings, *Vichy in the Tropics* (Stanford: Stanford University Press, 2001), 86.
4. On the constitutional contortions made to orchestrate this coup, see Jacques Dumont, *L'amère patrie: Histoire des Antilles françaises au xxème siècle* (Paris: Fayard, 2010), 91.
5. Fitzroy Baptiste, *War, Cooperation and Conflict: the European Possessions in the Caribbean, 1939–1945* (Westport, CT: Greenwood Press, 1988), 64.
6. Ibid., 174–75.
7. National Archives of the United Kingdom (NAUK): FO 371-32017.
8. US-British relations deteriorated after Free France took control of Saint Pierre and Miquelon in December 1941, for instance.
9. NAUK: FO 371-32058, May 1942.
10. French Naval Archives, Vincennes (SHDMV): TTE 33, historique et description de la crise de mai 1942 aux Antilles.
11. On this British-Dutch decision, see NAUK: FO 371-32058, Ministry of Economic Warfare, 26 November 1942.
12. French Naval Archives, Toulon (SHDMT): 18S 14, Rouyer green notebook, 23.
13. SHDMV: TTE 33, historique et description de la crise de mai 1942 aux Antilles.
14. On Robert's refusal to release the British sailors, see French Colonial Archives, Aix-en-Provence (ANOM): 1Affpol 768, telegram from Robert to the French admiralty, 6 August 1942. On the survivors of the *Norman Prince*, see http://uboat.net/allies/merchants/1720.html.
15. SHDMV: TTE 33, historique et description de la crise de mai 1942 aux Antilles.
16. ANOM: 1Affpol 767, document on commercial relations, dated 21 June 1942. The reverse decision can be found in ANOM: 1Affpol 768, which places the new German threats on 30 June. Rear Admiral Rouyer places the new German threats on 27 June. SHDMT: 18S 14, Rouyer green notebook, 35.
17. See Léo Elisabeth, "Vichy aux Antilles et en Guyane, 1940–1943", *Outre-mers, revue d'histoire* 342 (2004): 155.
18. SHDMT: 18S 14, Rouyer green notebook, 39, 47.
19. SHDMV: TTE 33, historique et description de la crise de mai 1942 aux Antilles.
20. ANOM: 1Affpol 769, Nicol to Vichy, 9 February 1942.
21. "Un appel du gouverneur de la Martinique", Service central d'information des Antilles françaises, *Bulletin hebdomadaire* (7 May 1942): 581.
22. "Notre pain", *La Paix*, 20 November 1940, 2; "Arrivage de farine", *La Paix*, 23 November 1940, 1.

23. "Farines", *La Paix*, 15 January 1941, 1. When flour did arrive on 22 January 1941, *La Paix* renewed its comparative formula, noting: "2,800 bags of flour arrived this morning on board the *Eastern Sword*. May this small penury here allow us to reflect on the larger one that is being experienced in France" ("Notre pain", *La Paix*, 21 January 1941, 1).
24. SHDMV: TTE 32, Order from Robert on meat consumption, 24 December 1941.
25. "En vue d'un retour à la terre", *La Paix*, 24 August 1940, 1.
26. The figure of 4,000 hectares comes from SHDMV, TTE 32, affaires économiques, rapport mensuel d'activité, 10 February 1941. In 1946 Eugène Revert came up with lower figures. He discerned an increase from 3,500 hectares to 4,167 hectares of land in Martinique devoted to potato, cabbage, manioc, vegetable and bean cultivation between 1939 and 1942. Eugène Revert, "L'économie martiniquaise pendant la guerre" (1946 text reprinted in *Les Cahiers du CERAG*, 33 [1977]: 4–11.
27. "La farine de manioc, un précieux cadeau de la Nature", *La Paix*, 19 February 1941, 1.
28. SHDMV: TTE 32, Affaires économiques, rapport mensuel d'activité.
29. Dominique Chathuant, "La Guadeloupe dans l'obédience de Vichy", *Bulletin de la Société d'Histoire de la Guadeloupe* 91 (1992): 15–17. On the breakdown of the dialogue between Vichy officials and the leading planters in Guadeloupe, see Marine-Christine Touchelay, "Les enterprises en Guadeloupe, vecteurs du changement politique de 1946?", in Hubert Bonin, Christophe Bourneau and Hervé Joly, eds., *Les entreprises et l'outre-mer français pendant la Seconde guerre mondiale* (Bordeaux: MSHA, 2010), 296.
30. SHDMT: 18S 14, Rouyer green notebook, 48.
31. SHDMV: TTE 32, Affaires économiques, rapport mensuel d'activité.
32. ANOM: 1Affpol 768, Nicol 1 March 1941.
33. See Dumont, *L'amère patrie*, 114–15.
34. SHDMV: TTE 32, Robert, 10 May 1943.
35. SHDMV: TTE 32, Rocques to Nicol, May 1943.
36. SHDMT: 18S 14, Rouyer green notebook. 48.
37. David Macey, *Frantz Fanon* (New York: Picador, 2001), 85.
38. SHDMT: 18S 14, Rouyer green notebook, 48.
39. Eliane Sempaire, *La Guadeloupe an tan Sorin* (Matoury, GF: Ibis Rouge, 2004), 130.
40. Laurent Jalabert, "Les Antilles de l'Amiral Robert", in *L'Empire Colonial sous Vichy*, ed. Eric Jennings and Jacques Cantier (Paris: Odile Jacob, 2004), 52–53.
41. ANOM: 1Affpol 768, Rouyer 9 September 1940.

42. Archives of the de Gaulle Foundation (FCDG): Eboué carton F22 18, Rouyer to *L'Action*, 31 May 1941.
43. Jennings, *Vichy in the Tropics*, 92–94.
44. FCDG: Eboué carton F22 18.
45. ANOM: 1Affpol 767, Battet report, 2 March 1942.
46. ANOM: 2APOM 7, Fort-de-France, 11 August 1941. On the 28 October law, see SHMT Rouyer, 18S 14.
47. FCDG: Eboué carton F22 18, Rouyer to *L'Action*, 31 May 1941.
48. ANOM: 2APOM 7, Fort-de-France, 11 August 1941.
49. ANOM: 1Affpol 768, Rouyer file, text broadcast on 25 November 1940.
50. FCDG: Eboué carton F22 18, Augereau-Lara to Eboué.
51. SHDMV: 1K518 Fonds Steiner, Bouvil report, 26 November 1940.
52. ANOM: 1Affpol 767, Devouton, 11 April 1941.
53. *Journal officiel de la Guadeloupe*, 15 March 1941, 276–77. On the resignation of Feuillard, Archives départementales de la Guadeloupe (ADG): 4Mi 411.
54. Chathuant, "La Guadeloupe dans l'obédience de Vichy", 22–25.
55. ANOM: 24 APOM 7, Devouton 14 February 1941.
56. ANOM: 1Affpol 766, d. 2, Bocle file, 2 March 1942.
57. Archives de la Martinique (ADM): 1R1085, Robert to Nicol, 5 May 1943.
58. On Vichy's anti-Masonic measures in the French West Indies, see ADM 12155. On Vichy's anti-Semitic measures in Guadeloupe, see Jennings, *Vichy in the Tropics*, 95–96. On Martinique, see Eric Jennings and Sébastien Verney, "Vichy aux Colonies. L'exportation des statuts des Juifs dans l'Empire" *Archives juives*, 41 (2008), 111–13; and William Miles, "Caribbean Hybridity in Martinique" in *The Jewish Diaspora in Latin America and the Caribbean*, ed. Kristin Ruggiero (Eastborne: Sussex Academic Press, 2005), 140–43.
59. *Journal Officiel de l'Etat Français*, 27 October 1940, law on Travail Féminin, dated 11 October 1940.
60. ADM: 2M1616, Travail féminin.
61. Jennings, *Vichy in the Tropics*, 98–99.
62. ANOM: 1Affpol 769, Devouton to the Ministry of Colonies Vichy, 28 May [year illegible].
63. National Archives of the Republic of Congo, Brazzaville: GGAEF 82, Eboué to the Governor of Martinique, 16 December 1943.
64. French gendarmerie archives, Vincennes (SHDG): 972E43, Diamant, 27 October 1941.
65. SHDG: 972^{F}33, report signed Delpech.
66. Eric Jennings, "La dissidence aux Antilles, 1940–1943", *Vingtième Siècle, Revue d'histoire* 68 (October–December 2000), 60; Richard Burton, "Vichysme et

Vichystes à la Martinique", *Les Cahiers du CERAG* 34 (February 1978), 1–101.
67. SHDG: 972E33, Delpech, 30 May 1941.
68. Jean-Charles Timoléon, *Chronique du temps passé* (Basse-Terre, GP: OMCS, 1987), 26.
69. James Scott, *Weapons of the Weak: Everyday forms of Peasant Resistance* (New Haven, CT: Yale University Press, 1985); James Scott, *Domination and the Arts of Resistance* (New Haven, CT: Yale University Press, 1990), xiii.
70. SHDG: 972E33, report signed Delpech.
71. Eric Jennings, *Vichy in the Tropics*, 125; Jacques Dumont, *Sport et assimilation à la Guadeloupe* (Paris: L'Harmattan, 2002), 205. On the politics of football and the French Caribbean more broadly, see Laurent Dubois, *Soccer Empire: The World Cup and the Future of France* (Berkeley: University of California Press, 2010), 47–71. The Cygne Noir events including Balguy's murder are discussed on p. 60.
72. SHDG: 972E35, 31 May, 1943, report signed Delpech
73. SHDG: 972E35, 15 June 1943, report signed Delpech.
74. Ibid.
75. SHDG: 972E42, report signed Eychenne, dated 18 December 1940, featuring a photo of Didnoit.
76. SHDMV: 1K518 Fonds Steiner, "Martinique, Conditions There", Police headquarters, St Lucia, 2 November 1940.
77. ADG: 4mi411, excerpt from *Le Dimanche sportif*, dated 31 August 1947.
78. Matthew J. Smith, *Liberty, Fraternity, Exile: Haiti and Jamaica after Emancipation* (Chapel Hill: University of North Carolina Press, 2014).
79. SHDMV: 1K518 Fonds Steiner, des Etages report.
80. ANOM: 173 APOM 1, multiple reports on des Etages.
81. SHDG: 972 E32 Capitaine Noël à la Gendarmerie, 20 February 1941.
82. Lucien Abenon and Henry Joseph, *Les Dissidents des Antilles dans les Forces françaises libres combattantes, 1940–1945* (Fort-de-France: Désormeaux, 1999), 37–38.
83. Jean Massip, "La Résistance aux Antilles", *Revue de Paris*, May 1945, 65.
84. SHDMV: 1K518 Fonds Steiner, René Essen [spelling uncertain] testimony, 3 February 1941.
85. Jean Massip, "La Résistance aux Antilles", *Revue de Paris*, May 1945, 65.
86. SHDMV: 1K518 Fonds Steiner, Joseph Paquemar file.
87. "Conditions in Martinique: Czechs Tell of Escapades", *Port of Spain Gazette*, 26 January 1941, 1.
88. Abenon et Joseph, *Les Dissidents des Antilles dans les Forces françaises libres*, 35.
89. SHDMV: 1K518 Fonds Steiner.

90. Ibid.
91. ANOM: 173 APOM 1, Ponton to the Ministry of the Colonies in Algiers, 30 December 1943.
92. "Légionnaires et volontaires", *Justice* (Fort-de-France), 10 June 1944, 2. Lucien-René Abenon noted a similar social diversity among friends of the Legion in Guadeloupe. See his *Petite histoire de la Guadeloupe* (Paris: L'Harmattan, 1992), 181–82.

6.

ST LUCIA AND THE "TIME OF THE AMERICANS"

JOLIEN HARMSEN, GUY ELLIS AND
ROBERT DEVAUX

In St Lucia, the "Time of the Americans" is still collectively remembered as a period when the island – and especially the southern town of Vieux Fort – flourished. The American army put seemingly limitless amounts of money into circulation, most of which was spent on living high without a thought for tomorrow. Tales of almost mythical proportions show Yankee soldiers and local workmen chasing down shots of whisky by swigging from freshly opened bottles of beer and, arm outstretched, pouring the remainder into the gutter. Others portray men wiping the sweat off their brows with dollar bills. Dance halls and rum shops flourished *an tan Méwitjen* – as the Kwéyòl term has it. An elderly woman from Castries related how, as a little girl visiting Vieux Fort, she was awestruck by the sight of dozens of beautiful local women, dressed Hollywood style in pleated slacks, wearing bright red lipstick and smoking cigarettes with dramatic hand gestures. "All I could think was: Lord, I want to be like that when I grow up! Hah! Little did I realize that these were women of the night."

In the long run, World War II resulted in Vieux Fortians being commonly stigmatized as suffering from a dependency syndrome: that they are "waiting for the Americans to come back and give them a hand-out". Up until the turn of the millennium, tales of Vieux Fortians' alleged unreliability, obstinacy, untrustworthiness and general carelessness abounded among local employers. In turn, Vieux Fortians themselves often expressed sentiments of having been hard done by the government, employers, the establishment, or simply "dem". Undeniably, a long history of extreme powerlessness in the face of externally induced vicissitudes has helped to shape the response of Vieux Fortians to challenges and opportunities in life. Equally undeniable is that outsiders and authorities have often run roughshod over Vieux Fort and Vieux Fortians – a habit, some argue, that continues up to this very day.[1]

For almost two centuries (from the 1760s until the 1950s), St Lucia's economy was dominated by the sugar industry and, increasingly, by just a handful of large sugar companies. There are only four sizeable flat areas tucked away amid the island's hills and mountains: Roseau, Cul-de-Sac and Mabouya in the north-east, and Vieux Fort in the deep south. In all four areas, households were highly dependent on wages from agricultural occupations. In the north and east, during the decades leading up to World War II, sugar workers became increasingly militant, and on more than one occasion, they joined the coal carriers from Castries in strike action. Being more isolated geographically and politically, sugar workers in Vieux Fort laboured on while their grumbles went unheeded. They had been paid below-minimum wages since the Depression, but their only alternatives to earning a starvation wage in the factory or cane fields were migration, fishing or charcoal making. All four thousand acres of flat, fertile land around the town were owned by the Vieux Fort Sugar Company, leaving no room whatsoever for the development of a peasantry. It may be argued that Vieux Fortians formed the truest and most powerless proletariat in St Lucia at the time. When, in 1936, the Vieux Fort Sugar Company decided to close its operations, about one thousand wage labourers and their six thousand dependents were left staring starvation squarely in the eye. The government attempted to set up a land-settlement scheme but, lacking funds, had to turn to Barbados for help. The upshot was that several thousand Barbadians were given the opportunity to become independent, landowning peasants in Vieux Fort, while Vieux Fortians themselves were once again relegated to being wage labourers – this time in a Barbadian-owned sugar factory. The Barbados settlement scheme was still getting off the ground when World War II intervened and Vieux Fort was selected for a US military base.

The "Time of the Americans" only confirmed and more deeply ingrained Vieux Fortians' sense of vulnerability in the face of externally induced change. The American army had a job to do and dollars to spend, and Vieux Fortians took as much as they could, for as long as it lasted – in much the same way that they knew to do without whenever work was scarce. The pay was better, the work different, the equipment modern and the town temporarily thriving with rum shops and nightclubs: but on a fundamental level, Vieux Fortians did not perceive the time of the Americans as a discontinuity in the ways of the world. The almost-overnight change the Americans brought to Vieux Fort is part of a continuing story as far as Vieux Fortians are concerned: a story of never-ending exploitation and passive resistance interspersed with brief episodes of "boom and bust". This sense of historical continuity is reflected in the way Vieux Fortians recollect the war. The time of the Americans is remembered only in stereotypes: dollar bills burning in people's pockets, prolific drinking and "girls cheap as water". Vieux Fortians' historical narratives tend to centre on personal life events: the birth of a child, migration, some event of good or bad luck, and theirs are "histories of the self", not narratives of "the self in history".[2] Therefore, when interviewing people in the mid-1990s, it was difficult to ascertain a complete picture of war events. Gold-rush memories and allegations of post-war dependency syndrome aside, Vieux Fortians' recollections about the time of the Americans are characterized by a deafening silence,[3] which means that to discover how World War II played out in St Lucia, one must largely turn to written records.

WAR SPREADS TO MARTINIQUE AND THE AMERICAS

After a decade of mounting aggression, on 1 September 1939, Germany invaded Poland. This initiated the Nazis' alarming march across Europe: invading Denmark, Norway, the Netherlands and Belgium in rapid succession. By May 1940 France was next in line, and the British gravely foresaw that soon they would be facing the Nazi scourge alone in Europe. During a secret meeting on 15 May 1940, Prime Minister Winston Churchill urged US President Roosevelt to provide help, asking for escort destroyers to protect the vital Atlantic supply line from German U-boat aggression around the British Isles and the Canadian Maritimes. Roosevelt, while sympathetic to Churchill's plight, was faced with an American public that regarded the war as a strictly European affair. Having publicly pledged neutrality, Roosevelt needed to find a way to help Britain without appearing to do so.

On 29 May 1940, Hitler's army forced 350,000 British soldiers at Dunkirk to retreat. The French government, seeing that German invasion was imminent, secretly loaded all the gold reserves of the Bank of France into the cruiser *Emile Bertin*: eight hundred tons of gold, packaged in fourteen thousand sacks. Accompanied by her sister ship *Jeanne d'Arc* and protected by the aircraft carrier *Béarn*, heavy destroyer *Le Terrible*, armed auxiliary vessel *Barfleur* and several other ships (carrying a total of two thousand French troops), the *Emile Bertin* headed across the Atlantic Ocean, first to Canada and then on to Martinique.

On 10 June 1940 Italy joined forces with Germany, and four days later France surrendered. The French government was replaced with a puppet German-affiliated government, the Vichy regime. As Martinique's southerly neighbour, this catapulted St Lucia into a position of vital importance. Now that it occupied France, Germany had potentially also gained access to the French Caribbean territories of Martinique, Guadeloupe and Cayenne. In particular, the Nazis were after the mainstay of the French fleet, which had escaped with all of France's gold reserves hidden in its bowels. This gold was now stored underground in the ancient Fort Desaix near Fort-de-France, guarded by two thousand French troops. As Jennings notes in chapter 5, to prevent the gold, the warships and troops from leaving Martinique and joining the German navy, from 5 July 1940 onwards, British naval vessels blockaded Martinique, checking every vessel entering and leaving the island. Although this greatly annoyed Martinique's senior officials and inconvenienced the civilian population (as lamented in St Lucia's *Voice* newspaper throughout July and August),[4] the British deemed this action to be absolutely necessary in order to curb Nazi aggression.

On 21 July 1940 the governments of Canada and the United States met in Ogdensburg, New York, to discuss the defence of North America. A second meeting on the protection of the Western Hemisphere, attended by twenty-seven nations, was held on 17 August in Cuba. Two concerns ranked top of the list: defence of the Panama Canal and containment of the French navy and gold deposits in Martinique, out of reach of the Nazis. On 2 September the United States and Great Britain signed the Destroyers for Bases Agreement. The United States would give Britain fifty obsolete destroyer ships along with twenty torpedo motor boats and a certain number of aircraft and rifles, in return for ninety-nine-year leases on seven selected base sites in the British West Indies (Bermuda, the Bahamas, Jamaica, Antigua, St Lucia, Trinidad and British Guiana) and one in Newfoundland, Canada. A week later the Greenslade Board was appointed to select the sites, and because of the urgent situation in Martinique, St Lucia was the first island identified for naval and army airbases.

The St Lucian populace closely monitored negotiations between the United States and Britain. Local enthusiasm for the war effort was high right from the start, and by November 1940 excitement about the advent of an American base was mounting. St Lucia's main newspaper at the time, the *Voice*, wrote: "The general feeling in Vieux Fort, and even at the village of Laborie three miles away, is one of jubilant expectancy. 'Work will be increased and we will be well paid' a labourer at Vieux Fort told me, while one woman to whom I spoke . . . said 'I am sure I will get a good price for my yams and other provision, and my husband and my children will all get work'."[5] On 22 August 1941 the *Voice* reported that parish priest Charles Jesse and headmaster Henry Smith had organized a scrap-iron collection, which saw teachers and students of the Vieux Fort Boys' School going door to door, ringing handbells and carrying placards. "On reaching Laborie Street an old woman of 76 years of age brought up a piece of iron, saying, 'This is the only piece of iron I have. Take it, for it is this piece that will be converted into a weapon to pluck out Hitler's eyes'." On 5 September the paper further reported that the "man on the street . . . looks forward to a new era of prosperity although remaining loyal to Britain. Americans are popular here, and American influence is strong".[6]

On 17 October 1940 members of the Greenslade Board arrived in Port Castries on board the USS *St Louis*. They investigated Gros Islet (in the north) and Vieux Fort (in the south) by sea, air and motor car. A week later, a team of engineers arrived from Puerto Rico to survey the proposed sites in detail. It was decided that Vieux Fort would receive an airbase as part of an arc of bases to protect the Panama Canal, while Reduit Bay near Gros Islet would get a naval base to help monitor the urgent situation in Martinique. Naturally, priority was given to the Reduit base.

START OF THE REDUIT BASE

On 1 November 1940 the USS *Goldsborough* anchored off Reduit Bay to serve as a base for American personnel in St Lucia.⁷ The US navy also took over the blockade of Martinique, releasing British vessels for deployment back in Europe. One aim was to prevent the French warships and gold reserves from being smuggled out to the Germans. The other was to prevent German U-boats from entering Martinique for refuelling. By mid-November the United States had bought Reduit Estate from Charles Devaux for the purpose of constructing a seaplane base. St Lucians welcomed the news: one Gros Islet resident, "her face wreathed in smiles", told the *Voice*'s reporter on 12 November, "'Monsieur, it is a god send. The sailors come ashore and we get a good price for our eggs'."

On 8 December 1940 President Roosevelt anchored at Reduit Bay aboard the cruiser USS *Tuscaloosa* to discuss progress. On Boxing Day US engineers set up an office at 5 Mongiraud Street in Castries. Part of the northern wharf was fenced off for the Aluminum Company of America steamship company, which was the official carrier for the US navy. In January 1941 a large landing-ship arrived at Reduit and deposited heavy construction equipment directly onto the beach,⁸ and by early February over two hundred coconut trees were being uprooted and foundation work started. On 5 March President Roosevelt finally signed the Lend-Lease Act, which detailed the Destroyers for Bases deal. Later, on 22 March, sixty marines arrived aboard the USS *Curtis* and set up camp near the base headquarters at the Reduit Estate house. A flag-raising ceremony was conducted at Reduit on 31 March 1941, accompanied by gun salutes from the USS *Goff* and speeches by the St Lucian administrator, the American consul and the senior commanding officer. With that, the naval base in Reduit was officially under way.

START OF THE VIEUX FORT BASE

Meanwhile, construction on the Vieux Fort airbase was advancing as well. On 27 March 1941, the day the lease was signed, US engineers began uprooting hundreds of coconut trees at Pointe Sable Estate. By April, work was in full swing with forty Americans and 390 local employees. First priority was given to drainage of the swamps and housing for the American engineers.

From the outset, the Americans were faced with a huge job, as first lieutenant in the Corps of Engineers, Thomas Bentley, explained in a secret report. Vieux Fort was a remote corner of St Lucia, he wrote, lacking "any semblance of modern civilization and facilities". It was connected to Castries "only by a narrow, winding, hilly road. There were no railway systems, no water, sewage or power facilities. . . . All materials except stone and sand had to be imported and unloaded in a harbor devoid of any docking facilities save a few small lighters."

The Americans' first goal was to build a dock with a long jetty and good access – still known today as New Dock Road. "Another great obstacle to normal production was the type of local labor available", Bentley continued. "Although not wanting in numbers, they were deficient in competence and endurance. It was often necessary to recruit labor completely unfamiliar with modern tools and methods of construction. These men had to be trained before beginning work and close supervision was necessary." Added to this, he wrote that "there was a great deal of stealing of all types of equipment and material. It became necessary to set up an auxiliary police system which at one time numbered close to 100 men."[9]

Nevertheless, by the middle of April 1941 ships were offloading equipment and supplies in Vieux Fort for use by the contractor (Minder Construction Company), and on 16 June a temporary runway permitted the first US bomber to land. The base's radio station (WVDQ) came into operation as well. On 4 August 1941 fourteen more American officers plus 296 enlisted men arrived in Vieux Fort, followed in October by a medical staff of three doctors and five nurses. The former Barbados Settlement headquarters at Beausejour was turned into an interim hospital, while a brand-new hospital was constructed at Cantonement. On 28 October 1941, the American flag was raised for the first time near base headquarters, which was located at Ralph Giraudy's former estate house at Pointe Sable. In November, twenty-four officers and 177 enlisted men arrived at the base to be trained as a bombardment squadron.

America's role in the war changed dramatically on 7 December 1941, when a Japanese attack on Pearl Harbor in Hawaii killed two thousand US army personnel on home territory and dealt a devastating blow to the US Pacific fleet. America joined the war the next day, and US bases worldwide were placed on alert. Shortly thereafter, Vichy France became completely allied with the Rome/Berlin axis, and Germany and Italy declared war on the United States. After two years of ostrich policies about "the distant European war", Americans suddenly found themselves in the thick of things. In St Lucia Lieutenant-Colonel Ronald Ring assumed command of all military forces, including the local defence force.[10] In the north of the island, the US military was granted permission to build a coastal defence base at Cap Estate to keep watch over Martinique and to protect the base at Reduit. The US defence secretary publicly announced America's determination to seize control of Martinique, should the Germans attempt to occupy that island.

THE REDUIT BASE IN ACTION

The base at Reduit was completed in December 1941. By then it occupied 221 acres of Reduit Estate and 17 acres of land at Morne Pimant, along with the southern flank of Pigeon Island, which was used as a communication station (code-named "Peter Item"). All the buildings had prefabricated steel frames, poured concrete foundations and stucco exteriors. There were barracks for three hundred men, quarters for twenty-five officers, a ten-bed dispensary, a mess hall and kitchen, power plant, cold-storage plant, two industrial buildings, three magazines, a concrete parking apron, two timber ramps, two timber piers, a huge concrete catchment area for rainwater with two storage tanks and ten steel tanks for gasoline. Additionally, three magazines were built on the hill to the south of the base. Reduit Swamp was partially filled in with half a million cubic yards of sand dredged from the bay, and a public road to Gros Islet village was built over this reclaimed land, just outside the chain-link fence that surrounded the base. Strict security measures were enforced, and the public was obliged to use this new road, rather than take shortcuts across the base.

On 1 February 1942 the Reduit base formally became a naval air station. It functioned as a substation of the Trinidad sector and was capable of handling a squadron of twelve VP aeroplanes, although it never handled more than four or five amphibious planes at any one time. There was a navy complement of six officers and forty-six enlisted men, plus a marine corps of three officers and forty-nine men. They undertook patrols, convoy and rescue missions in the Windward Islands and were responsible for the surveillance of Martinique, using Catalina (flying boat) PBY-5s and Grumman (Goose) PBMs. In addition, seventy-four St Lucians were employed at the Reduit base in various jobs, varying from powerhouse foreman (Lionel Ellis) to truck driver (Walter Alleyne), cook (Joseph Louis) and mess-hall officer (Altenor Joseph).

WAR ACTION AT PORT CASTRIES

War came frighteningly close to St Lucia on 9 March 1942, when the German submarine *U-161* entered Port Castries under cover of darkness. At 10:50 p.m. she fired two torpedoes at ships berthed alongside the wharf: the CNS *Lady Nelson*, principal carrier of the Caribbean Fruit Trade Company and the SS *Umtata* from Calcutta. Twenty people died in the attack – sixteen West Indians and four Indian nationals – and nineteen others were hospitalized. Both ships had been under floodlights, handling passengers and cargo, when the torpedoes were released. In the ensuing confusion, the German U-boat escaped unscathed, still on the surface line. Eyewitnesses from the Pavée area dimly recalled seeing the submarine leave the harbour. They also heard rifle fire, which was later discovered to have emanated from a policeman, on duty in Vigie, who fired at the departing submarine with his .303 rifle.[11]

According to some accounts,[12] a third torpedo was fired at the ALCOA ship *Evangeline*, which lay anchored in the northern part of the harbour, but missed, ending up buried in the soft ground of the cove. This story was embellished by reports that the *Evangeline* contained a full cargo of TNT explosives for the Vieux Fort base, so that a direct hit would likely have destroyed the entire town of Castries. The rumour was persistent enough to eventually warrant an investigation, but it was concluded that a third torpedo was never actually fired. Captain Albrecht Achilles of the *U-161* had been under clear orders to disrupt shipping at Port Castries, and the best way to accomplish this was by blocking the northern wharf with two sunken ships.[13]

Marvelling at the fact that the *Evangeline* was left unmolested, another popular explanation has been forwarded. Shortly before the commencement of World War II, in May of 1939, the German naval-training tall ship *Gorch Fock* visited St Lucia. The two hundred sailors and officers on board were warmly welcomed and shown around the island by eager, self-proclaimed tour guides. The *Voice* reported on 19 and 23 May 1939 that "during her stay of six days in St. Lucia, some of the [Germans] visited the Sulphur Springs, and the landslides. They spoke very highly of St. Lucia and its magnificent scenery, saying that it was not only the prettiest island they had visited on their cruise, but that it was the "key position" of the British West Indies.[14] H.A. Clement Welch, in an exasperated letter to the editor, showed far more common sense:

> From all such friends, Good Lord deliver St. Lucia.... These men are Nazi naval Students in their last year's training and will be officers in 1940 in the various branches of the German Navy. In spite of all this, these men went all over the Island, the majority of them with cameras; I saw them myself at Vigie, the Morne, la Toc, and Rat Island taking photographs.... There were always a few Wharf Rats piloting them and readily answering their questions. I am sure I will never get 1st prize for politeness from the one who asked me to show him the road to Meadow's Battery. Are our authorities blind?... A man in jail is no use to his country; otherwise I would have knocked down a few Huns last week.[15]

Welch was quite perceptive, as Captain Achilles of *U-161* had been one of the Nazi naval officers on board the *Gorch Fock* and so knew his way around Castries Harbour exactly. Whether he spared Castries out of gratitude for his enjoyable stay in 1939, as popular account has it, or for strategic reasons, remains debatable.[16]

Public response to the submarine attack in Port Castries was mixed. Some people began to resent the American presence, feeling it made St Lucia an enemy target. Ships in Caribbean waters were regularly attacked by German submarines (including a tanker, just twenty-six miles west of St Lucia), and occasionally survivors washed up on the island's shores.[17] Others took a more opportunistic approach and joined in the looting of cargo from the torpedoed vessels. In fact, it was in the aftermath of this that St Lucia saw its first "war victims" on home soil: one man (Arnold Maynard) died from a ricocheting bullet after a US marine fired shots at the legs of a fleeing looter; another died from eating spoilt ice cream stolen from one of the shipwrecks. The damaged vessels eventually became health hazards in themselves, as flies and vermin were attracted to their decaying cargo.[18] After the attack in Castries, a steel anti-submarine net (made with the help of students of St Mary's College, a male secondary school located in the capital) was laid across the harbour's mouth, and the US army offered increased coastal infantry protection to the naval air station at Reduit.[19]

German aggression in the region peaked in early and mid-1942. Initially unbeknown to the Allied forces, from 20 April onwards German U-tankers capable of refuelling and rearming twelve submarines were deployed in the mid-Atlantic region. Meanwhile, the American destroyers USS *Blakeley* and USS *Ellis* continued to patrol Fort-de-France to prevent exactly that. They, however, were unaware that the German submarines *U-69* and *U-156* were also watching Fort-de-France, in case French warships tried to slip out and join the US navy.

On 26 May 1942, at two o'clock in the afternoon, four miles off the coast of Martinique, the USS *Blakeley* was struck by one of two torpedoes fired from *U-156*. The missile ripped thirty feet of steel out of the ship's bow but Captain Mitchell Matthews managed to manoeuvre the damaged ship into Fort-de-France Harbour, where he berthed next to the carrier *Béarn*. Meanwhile, dozens of US ships and aircraft converged on the area to provide cover and search for the submarine. Captain Matthews was given twenty-four hours for emergency repairs at what was, formally, a neutral port. As the damaged USS *Blakeley* limped towards Port Castries two days later, under heavy escort, an alarm was raised that another U-boat (probably *U-69*) was lurking outside the harbour, intending to sink the *Blakeley* for good. Grumman Helldivers were scrambled from the Vieux Fort airbase, and along with escort destroyers from Reduit, attacked an area a mile outside Castries Harbour.[20] Watched by amazed onlookers in Castries, the little planes vertically dive-bombed the suspected target with depth charges, which exploded with a terrific noise and huge plumes of water.[21] The U-boat escaped but was unable to fire its torpedoes while under attack. The *Blakeley* arrived safely at the western wharf, where she obtained assistance from the USS *Killerig* (already in port to repair the *Lady Nelson* and *Umtata*). Eleven days later, with a timber bulkhead installed across her shattered bow and all loose metal plates cut away, the *Blakeley* sailed to Puerto Rico for further repairs.

St Lucia was shaken by war activity once more on the evening of 20 July 1942, when another one of the *Gorch Fock*'s Nazi naval students, a Captain Friedrich Markworth, brought his submarine, *U-66*, right up to the steel net across Castries Harbour and laid six mines along the outer channel. The next day, a huge explosion alerted St Lucia to the grim reality that the Caribbean Sea had been mined. First a US Coast Guard cutter struck one, then a US Army launch. Both ships were towed back to port, and minesweeping operations were put in place. At least four different minesweepers operated off Port Castries during 1942–43.

As a result of the increased war activity, blackouts were implemented islandwide, and the United States stepped up its vigilance around Martinique. Six destroyers were ready at Gros Islet to intervene at short notice, and US naval bombers from Puerto Rico checked in at St Lucia daily.[22]

THE FREE FRENCH REFUGEES

By June 1943 the United States was planning to turn the tables on Germany by invading Martinique and ending the standoff by force. While the US navy was rehearsing its invasion plans in Trinidad, openly publicizing its intention, it simultaneously tightened its blockade of Martinique, limiting food supplies in an effort to force Admiral Georges Robert to the bargaining table. This had more than the desired effect, and more high-ranking naval officers under Robert began to desert the Vichy regime and join the so-called Free French overseas. By the middle of July 1943, without need for an invasion, Admiral Robert surrendered his fleet to the Allied forces and left Martinique.

Between September 1940 and July 1943, hundreds of Free French had already fled Vichy-led Martinique and arrived in St Lucia by whatever means they could, including wooden rafts. Many hired local fishermen to drop them off at night. Some were robbed and dumped overboard mid-sea, and several men never made it to St Lucia alive. The first escapee was a man by the name of Pujol, who landed at Cap Estate on 19 September 1940. More followed, at an average of ten or fifteen per month. Eighteen Czechs arrived in November and December 1940, along with two Poles, and they were instrumental in saving Castries from fire on 14 January 1941. On 22 September 1942, a group of men from the French cruiser *Emile Bertin* escaped and made it to St Lucia. They were in bad shape, having spent several days at sea without water or food. Some weeks later the commander of the Martinique garrison made his escape, and on 15 March 1943 the son of Governor Yves Nicol, along with two other young men, escaped to St Lucia as well. Once in St Lucia, they were formed into the Free French Fighting Force. Several moved on to Trinidad or the United States and ended up fighting the Nazis in North Africa and Europe. After Admiral Georges Robert surrendered, the remainder of the refugees returned to Martinique.[23]

The surrender of Martinique in July 1943 rendered the Cap Estate encampment obsolete, and by 1 September 1943 it had been deactivated, along with the naval air station at Reduit, although in 1945 public access to the base area was reopened after the bypass road had begun to sink. Thanks to the extensive efforts of the West Indian governments, and in particular the Government of Trinidad and Tobago, all the leased territories in the British Caribbean were handed back before their ninety-nine-year leases were up, and Reduit was returned to the government in a simple ceremony on 11 March 1959.[24]

IMPACTS OF THE VIEUX FORT BASE

Whereas the Reduit base had existed for the specific purpose of containing enemy activity in Martinique, the Vieux Fort air force base was part of an arc of protection for the crucially important Panama Canal. The base in Vieux Fort was much larger and so, concomitantly, was its impact on the local community. At first the effects of the base were mostly positive. Drainage of the remaining swamps, a larger market for local produce, increased employment and higher wages led to better standards of living. A young reporter for the *Voice*, Clendon Mason, witnessed these changes first hand on 23 May 1941. What had been "a town of lifeless sandy streets lined on either side with a parade of closed and battered houses standing at drooping attention" was transforming before his eyes. "The capital of yesterday, the busy town of today, and the metropolis of tomorrow is now seething with activity. On groggy legs, the town of the Old Fort struggles to shake off its senility and to raise its proud head once more atop rejuvenated limbs." At eight o'clock on a Monday morning, Mason strolled from Vieux Fort town to the site of the new base.

> Cars and trucks passed up and down in steady streams, some driven by Americans, some by local chauffeurs.... Every other face almost was one from Castries, and nearly every other one was from Barbados or somewhere. And things were humming! There was the ... sight of a giant motor shovel cutting through earth like paper, and lifting several hundred-weight to dump it onto the huge waiting truck.... Americans in khaki pants and helmets, broad bare backs baked to a brown tan beneath the blazing sun.

Mason walked as far as the newly named Beane Field area,[25] where the Pointe Sable estate house had been converted into modern offices for the contractors and army officials. He described it: "Several ... desks, each with one or two or more persons seated at it, were scattered over the floor. Around the room were safes and lockers of every description. . . . On the desks were streamlined typewriters, the latest models. Electric lights were burning all the while from the roof. . . . In the inner office some lady stenographers were rattling the keys of their typewriters." At the time, the base was occupied by 115 Americans and over 600 West Indian workers (St Lucians and others) who were paid twenty-five hundred pounds weekly in local salaries. Between April 1941 and June 1942, the local workforce expanded until it peaked at 4,615 local employees, directed by 600 Americans.

NEGATIVE IMPACTS OF THE VIEUX FORT BASE: OVERCROWDING

However, by 1942 the military base was beginning to have some clearly negative impacts as well. Within a year, Vieux Fort's population had quadrupled from two thousand to between eight and nine thousand (mid-1942). The government neglected the increasing demands for improved infrastructure to support this expanded population, particularly in relation to water supplies, garbage disposal, housing and policing, and Vieux Fort thus became a breeding ground for pulmonary tuberculosis, venereal disease and gastroenteric diseases. "Vieux Fort burns while government fiddles away", the *Voice* exclaimed on 9 December 1941. House rents had become "excessive, exorbitant, cruel".[26] By 1942, 296 residential buildings in Vieux Fort town were serving a population of eight thousand, making for an average of twenty-seven occupants per house. People slept under balconies and trees, on the pavement and in fishing boats. Renting a small house cost five dollars a week, and the *Voice* reported on 12 November 1942 that

> about ten and twenty and often more persons live[d] in one of these houses. They ha[d] to squeeze together on the bare floor at night. In the smaller houses, sleeping [was] done by relays. The first relay would snatch as much rest as possible during the earlier part of the night. Later, another relay would come in, and the first relay [went] out to accommodate them. [Areas] under houses, balconies, kitchens and outhouses [were] used as dormitories.[27]

For drinking water, all these thousands of people depended on the muddy and increasingly polluted Vieux Fort River, whose water was, reportedly, dark blue in colour.

THE TYPHOID EPIDEMIC

An area adjacent to the place where drinking water was stored in old tanks was used as a bush latrine, and, unsurprisingly, the last three months of 1942 saw St Lucia's severest epidemic of typhoid, affecting 233 and killing 47 in Vieux Fort town. There was no doubt about the cause: "This epidemic was the result of unsatisfactory housing and sanitary conditions due to overcrowding of the labourers on construction work at the United States Base and also to a grossly inadequate and polluted water supply."[28]

The government did make an attempt to bring the situation under control. It repaired and enclosed the storage-tank area, administered inoculations and issued an advisory to boil all drinking water. Furthermore, in the course of 1943 a supply of filtered and chlorinated water was extended from the US base to the town of Vieux Fort, new communal latrines were constructed and fifty homes were supplied with fly-proof latrines. While this helped to prevent further outbreaks of typhoid, protests over the lack of government attention to general infrastructure and facilities in Vieux Fort continued. "Every stranger who came to work in this part of the island had revolting remarks to make about the conditions that existed, and visitors turned their noses and never came back", a delegation from Vieux Fort told the island's administrator in May 1943.[29] They lamented the still-insufficient water system, the disrepair of the jetty, a failing telephone system and lack of personnel at the government offices (where two clerks, one copyist and a bailiff were supposed to run the post office, the registry, the savings bank, the treasury, the customs department and the judiciary office). Clearly, the advent of the Yankee dollar had done nothing to change the government's historical lack of interest in the welfare or development of this southern town.[30]

PROSTITUTION AND VENEREAL DISEASE

High rates of prostitution and venereal disease are historically linked with the presence of military troops and immigrant workers (see chapters 12 and 13, this volume). The American bases at Reduit and Vieux Fort were no exception. In January 1943, according to a military report, 283 out of 1,000 military men in St Lucia were affected by venereal disease and STDs were "the rule rather than the exception among the natives" as well. The report went on to say:

Local government physicians could not obtain sulpha drugs, arsenicals or bismuth for the treatment of prostitutes even if they sought treatment. There was an almost total absence of white women in the area and the monotony of wartime disposition for combat in an essentially peacetime situation, led men to visit native shacks, drink a local rum called 'Smack' and have sexual intercourse with black native women practically all of whom were infected. The fact that native huts were dispersed throughout the Army area on private land increased control problems greatly. The Base Surgeon also considered the high rate due to the character of personnel of the worst offending unit which had an average I.Q. of 89.7 % (Grade 4, below average) and the long periods the troops had served in the tropics.

In March of 1943, after consultation with the British government physician at Vieux Fort, it was decided to open a clinic for prostitutes. On 3 April, sixty-two women of the "on-limits" village of Beausejour had been examined and forty-two cases of syphilis, five cases of gonorrhoea, one case of chanchroid and three cases of lymphogranuloma venereum were found. Every effort was made to get these women out of the infectious stages as rapidly as possible, and no woman refused treatment. Extensive education programs were started among the troops and additional prophylaxis stations constructed. Athletic and recreation activities received increased attention, particularly between the hours of 5:30 p.m. and 11:00 p.m. Overnight passes were issued only to those individuals whose past records of good conduct entitled them to reward, and all intoxicated soldiers found in civilian areas were taken into custody and returned to the post. Venereal disease rates were lowered but remained unduly high and far above the goal of 20 per 1,000 per annum. The base surgeon considered the rates "theoretically" inexcusable, when in November 1943, after ten months of extensive control measures, the rate was 174 per 1,000 per annum.[31]

To help lower rates of STD, military authorities recommended that men who had been in the Caribbean for two years or longer and "who felt they were 'forgotten men'" be reassigned as soon as possible. "Many men ceased to have an interest in themselves or their unit." At the same time, out of four hundred "supposedly healthy working men" applying for jobs on the Vieux Fort base, one in five showed up positive on blood tests for syphilis, while "other types of venereal disease were seen in their usual large numbers". Oral-history accounts dwell extensively on STDs and soldiers engaging in sexual encounters with the local "belles".³² By 1945 the introduction of sulpha drugs and penicillin greatly helped the fight. But until then, local men, women and American military personnel shared these venereal afflictions alike.

LAW AND ORDER

The maintenance of law and order was another problem, with just eight local policemen trying to keep control over an increasingly agitated population. The cocktail of a fast-growing population (including many men from other islands), ready availability of cash, alcohol and sex and a lack of the most basic amenities created an easily flammable atmosphere in Vieux Fort.

The Americans had a police force of their own, but in some ways this only aggravated matters. In November 1941, for instance, a conflict between an American policeman and a St Lucian quickly got out of control, and the crowd started pelting stones at the four local police officers who rushed in to try to restore order. In the ensuing confusion, a young girl was hit in the leg by a stray bullet, allegedly fired by an American policeman.

It must be kept in mind that, as far as can be ascertained through documentation, the Americans in St Lucia were all white men. It is inconceivable that their native tradition of segregation and racial discrimination would not have come into play in their approach and dealings with St Lucian and other West Indian workers, the vast majority of whom were black. Particularly in potential conflict situations, it is only fair to assume that these white American soldiers and police officers often felt threatened and sometimes responded with unnecessarily high levels of aggression.

Shooting incidents involving the American military police occurred more than once, to the point where in April 1942 military authorities saw fit to make a public apology to the St Lucian people. Most cases did not incur loss of life, but one did turn lethal. In August 1943 Joseph Wilson, a worker on the Vieux Fort base, was shot by an American guard after Wilson's dog had repeatedly attempted to follow him onto the base. The guard, a Private Cook, threatened to shoot the dog, after which Wilson told the American he needed shooting more than the dog. Private Cook tried to strike Wilson, who responded, successfully, in kind. Cook stepped back and shot Wilson in the abdomen. He died two days later. Cook was eventually court-martialled and found guilty.³³

Another headache for lawkeepers was recurring incidents of theft and larceny, particularly in the face of shortages. The *Voice* reported in July 1943: "The shortage of tyres for motor vehicles . . . resulted in wholesale larceny of tyres from the United States bases. . . . The larceny of gasoline from the bases gave rise to further complications and the disappearance of cigarettes in bulk showed that the incidence of robbery was on the increase. Up to last Saturday, a number of chits was stolen from the American Service Club in Castries."[34] In St Lucia, suspicion typically fell on local and West Indian workers, not American staff, though evidence from other Caribbean territories supported the fact that Americans engaged in larceny to resell the goods to the local population.[35] Local workmen were also occasionally accused of sabotaging their tasks with a view to prolonging their employment.[36] But if the army authorities sometimes felt robbed, St Lucian workers had good reason to share the sentiment. While it is often said that workers in Vieux Fort were flush with money during the war, and it is true that wages paid by the American army were about four times higher than those paid in the sugar industry, they were not nearly as high as the Americans had originally intended. Just as had happened in 1895–96 (when a British naval station was constructed in Castries), St Lucia's sugar barons had put pressure on the American authorities to keep wage levels low so as not to compete too much with the wages they paid to their workers in Cul-de-Sac, Roseau and Mabouya. This knowledge and perceived blatant disregard for their welfare created much resentment among the St Lucian working class, all the more so in light of the significantly risen cost of living.[37]

COMPLETION AND DECLINE OF THE BASE

Despite these challenges, work on the Vieux Fort base progressed smoothly. With the exception of one or two buildings, construction was completed on 15 November 1942, and in March 1943 the engineering department handed over the completed Beane Field airbase to the post engineer. By then, the base occupied over 3,000 acres of land and had cost over $10 million. The main base was divided into two sections: 1,289 acres at Beane Field (just north of the town of Vieux Fort) and another 671 acres at Cantonment (north-west of the town). Thomas Bentley reported:

As originally built the base consisted of 352 buildings, two 5,000 ft concrete runways, with taxiways, hard stands, revetments, two nose hangars and other Air Corps maintenance buildings. There are housing facilities for 4,673 Enlisted Men and 649 Officers on the base, making a total troop capacity of 5,332 men. There is 96,951 sq ft of warehouse area, a 1,000 man Laundry and a completely equipped 150 bed Hospital.[38]

The Americans installed systems for generating electricity, distribution of drinking water and sewage disposal and built a fire station, radio station, fuel depots, incinerator, garage, barber shop, general store, movie theatre, stockade, fifty-line telephone exchange, cold storage and ice plant, docks and warehousing and an officers' club with a day room and library.

At nearby Mankoté mangrove, they created an intricate network of dirt roads in an attempt to make spying German aircraft believe that this was where their planes were hidden. In reality, low bunkers covered with soil and vegetation located on flat terrain just north of Vieux Fort town acted as hangars to keep the aircraft safe. St Lucians nicknamed these mounds in the landscape *kai plane* and for many years after the war used them as pig pens.

Military staff were trained at the Vieux Fort base in navigation flying, instrument flying, transition flying, cross-country flying, formation flying (day and night) and all types of bombing. In addition, ground training involved armament, bombardment, communications, engineering, link training, medical training, intelligence, navigation, photography and radar. Also included were submarine-warfare training, tactics, sheet-metal work and instruction on engines and aircraft structure.[39]

Although Vieux Fort was essentially a training base, a certain number of casualties occurred. On 23 April 1942 a B-18 bomber and a P-39 fighter plane of the Fifth Bomber Squadron failed to return to Vieux Fort from a patrol over open water. The bodies of the seven victims were never found.[40] Shortly before that, on 24 February, two planes had collided on take-off from the runway, causing one pilot to sustain a fractured skull. A year later, two men were killed when their US Marine Corps OS2N aircraft crashed at sea while on its way from Castries to Beane Field. The plane was never recovered.[41]

World War II ended in August 1945. To celebrate the victory over Japan and the new peace in Europe, flares were fired at the American base, reportedly much to the delight and awe of spectators in Vieux Fort. They were also treated to some radical air manoeuvres by three Lockheed P-38 fighters.

IMMEDIATE POST-WAR PERIOD IN THE SOUTH

As soon as construction of the base was completed, in mid-1943, the employment boom collapsed. In 1944, a government report stated that "labour conditions generally reverted further to normal. There was little or no demand for labour on the United States Bases and, as a result, there was a noticeable increase in peasant agriculture as compared with previous years; most estates were able to obtain their labour requirements without difficulty." Once again, unemployment and underemployment were business as usual.[42]

Vieux Fort quickly ceased to be a hub of activity, and, with no access to agricultural land and no sugar factory, the townspeople became dependent on fishing, charcoal making, trades and small shopkeeping. Despite a sharply increased demand for fish during the war, Vieux Fort's fishermen had hardly benefited, partly because technological and ecological ceilings curtailed their catches.[43] Farmers in the surrounding countryside, on the other hand, had generally fared well during the boom, and when the base closed they simply returned to growing food for themselves and a small surplus for the local market. The town of Vieux Fort, meanwhile, slumped into a state of desolation. Those who could, left.

On 29 August 1949 the US Army offered its remaining facilities for sale to the government of St Lucia.[44] For two hundred thousand dollars the government purchased 150 buildings, two 150-kilowatt generators, a cold storage plant, a water-filtration plant, gasoline storage and pipelines, sand-washing tanks and miscellaneous other items. At the same time, seven hundred acres of land were returned to the government.[45] For a short while, dismantling of the base triggered hopes for new development in the south, including tourism – but none of these plans materialized. Instead, the disposal of surplus material from the base created a climate for graft and corruption, and many items eventually changed hands at rock-bottom prices.[46] In 1947 a land-settlement scheme was proposed for the landless workers of the south, but the attempt was half-hearted and failed.[47]

And so Vieux Fort entered the 1950s as a town dazed by its recent roller-coaster ride through economic and social upheaval. While the older town folk attempted to pick up the threads of their pre-war lives, a rising generation desperately aspired to leave this boring, poverty-stricken and once-again neglected town in search of brighter horizons.

CONCLUSION

Objectively speaking, the "Time of the Americans" completely changed the physical, social and economic landscape of Vieux Fort. The Reduit area was less drastically affected, and apart from a few U-boat incidents, the north of St Lucia escaped World War II relatively unscathed.

Today, seventy years after the war, Vieux Fort continues to bear testimony to the massive amounts of infrastructural work undertaken in 1941–42. Although many of the original buildings have since been demolished or removed, the presence of two airport runways and a long concrete taxiway (now used as a highway), the commercial docks and a hospital all bear silent witness to the time of the Americans.

And yet this time was not a fundamental break from St Lucia's past as a sugar-plantation economy and colonial military stronghold. To Vieux Fortians it reinforced the exploitation that they had experienced in centuries past and the impression that their value was only ever measured in terms of their temporary usefulness to others. Also strengthened by this brief, intoxicating spell in St Lucia's history was a new generation's aspiration for a better life, which often led them elsewhere.

NOTES

1. Anderson Reynolds, "Who Runs Vieux Fort?", *Voice*, 26 March 2015; Anderson Reynolds, "The Exploitation of Vieux Fort", *Voice*, 31 March 2015; Anderson Reynolds, "The Problem with Vieux Fort", *Voice*, 2 April 2015 and Anderson Reynolds, "Vieux Fort: A Freak of Nature?", *Voice*, 7 April 2015.
2. Virginia Yans-McLaughlin, "Metaphors of Self in History: Subjectivity, Oral Narrative, and Imigration Studies", in *Immigration Reconsidered: History, Sociology, and Politics*, ed. Virginia Yans-McLaughlin (New York: Oxford University Press, 1990), 254–90.
3. This subject is further explored in Jolien Harmsen, "Down the Line: Four Generations in a Caribbean Town, 1910–1998" (PhD diss., Erasmus University, Rotterdam, 1999), chapter 2.
4. The *Voice* is St Lucia's oldest running newspaper. Although generally reflecting upper- and middle-class interests, the paper also regularly published opinions critical of the status quo.

5. *Voice*, 13 November 1940.
6. *Voice*, 5 September 1941.
7. This and the following based in large part on Robert Devaux, "History of the US Naval Air Station Reduit, St Lucia, 1939–1947" (research paper, St Lucia Research Centre, Castries, 2003); Robert Devaux, "Recollections of the US Naval Base at Reduit" (research paper, St Lucia Research Centre, Castries, 1995); Robert Devaux, "History of the US Army Air Force Base Beane Field, St Lucia" (research paper, St Lucia Research Centre, Castries, 2000).
8. The Arundel Corporation was the contractor, with Consolidated Engineering Company carrying out the engineering works. All work was supervised from Puerto Rico.
9. Thomas Bentley, "Acquisition of Territory for US Air Base. Historical report" (declassified secret report, United States Military, 1945), Archaeological and Historical Society, Castries, St Lucia.
10. At this time, the Vieux Fort base was protected by three 30-millimetre guns and two machine guns placed on both sides of the runway. Later, heavier guns were installed in strategic locations around the base, including small rapid-fire anti-aircraft guns and a mobile 155-millimetre gun on the Moule à Chique peninsula. There was also a mobile cannon on a hill south of Laborie, at Anse Noir.
11. A Barbadian sergeant by the name of Armstrong.
12. For variations on this event and hundreds of other St Lucian war memories, see Gregor Williams, *Unsung War Heroes of Saint Lucia* (Castries: St Lucia Ex-Service Legion, 2008).
13. Indeed, it took the USS *Killerig* six months to salvage the two struck ships and restore normality to the port. Sinking the *Evangeline* would have also involved complicated manoeuvring, adding unwarranted risk without contributing to Captain Achilles's primary goal. In any case, the *Evangeline* was not loaded with TNT: she carried a small amount of (explosive) magnesium but for the most part general supplies.
14. *Voice*, 19 and 23 May 1939. The first article speaks of "one hundred sailors", the second of "a compliment [sic] of 200 sailors and officers".
15. *Voice*, 25 May 1939.
16. Achilles and his crew were sunk and killed in a 1944 air attack, during their third posting to the Western Atlantic.
17. Claudia Francis, "A Brief History of the United States Base in St Lucia during the Second World War" (BA thesis, University of the West Indies, Faculty of Arts and General Studies, 1979), 21. *Voice*, 24 March 1942, reported the arrival in St Lucia of a rescue boat carrying survivors of a ship bound for Rio

de Janeiro which had been torpedoed on 28 February 1942. Throughout May, shipwreck survivors landed in St Lucia and Martinique, some after as many as forty-six days at sea.

18. St Lucia, *Annual Report, Health Department 1942* (Castries: Government Printing Office, 1943).
19. A public notice announced that any vessel approaching the shore inside an imaginary line between Labrelotte Point, Pigeon Island and Gros Islet cemetery would be challenged by the US Coast Guard, and if it failed to respond, it was liable to come under fire.
20. Francis, "A Brief History", 21, provides an alternative version of this event. She states that the ship came under attack for a second time while entering Castries Harbour, "but this time she returned fire, and a short battle ensued right in the Castries harbour where thousands of townsfolk gathered to witness the spectacle. The submarine got away but it is believed that she suffered some damage."
21. Robert Devaux, "Military Face of Castries, U-Boat Attacks: WWII" (research paper, St Lucia Research Centre, Castries, 1995). At age nine, Robert Devaux witnessed this attack firsthand from the third-floor balcony of his family home on 11 High Street, Castries. A similar attack on a suspected U-boat occurred on 16 September 1942 and involved both US Navy and Air Force weaponry. Again, the enemy vessel escaped.
22. According to Francis, "A Brief History", 21–22, this occurred after the United States learned that the German cargo boat *Heligoland* was trying to slip through US naval patrol to put German pilots into the cockpits of 110 dive-bombers and pursuit planes stored in Martinique. This seems unlikely, though, since those planes were tightly packed away under canvas with no runway at hand. They were regularly maintained but never flown, and some remained there until the 1960s, when they were eventually used for spraying banana fields.
23. Robert Devaux, "Military Face of Castries: The Free French" (research paper, St Lucia Research Centre, Castries, 1995). In this, Devaux draws on the Police Daily Occurrence Registers for Castries, 1940–44 (St Lucia National Archives) and articles in the *Voice* (1940–1944).
24. Devaux, "History of Reduit" contains a list with names of all US personnel (Marines, Navy, Coast Guard and staff of the Arundel Corporation) who were based at Reduit.
25. *Voice*, 18 September 1941. The area was named after First Lieutenant James S. Beane of New York City, who was twice recommended for extraordinary heroism in battle during World War I. Beane shot down five German planes before his own death in action on 30 October 1918. See also Maxwell Air Force

Base, "Historical Report Beane Air Force Base, 1941–1949" (Montgomery, AL: US Air Force, 1949).
26. *Voice*, 9 December 1941.
27. Joyce Auguste, *Oral and Folk Traditions of Saint Lucia*, Cultural Heritage Series No. 1 (Castries: Lithographic Press, 1986), 10.
28. National Archives of the United Kingdom (NAUK): CO 256/41, Annual Report, Medical Department, 1943.
29. They were Eldridge Eudoxie, Antoine Theodore, Charles Moffat, Ralph Giraudy, Everton Williams and Oddie Leslin. *Voice*, 22 June 1943.
30. Another backlash from the American presence was more indirect. The huge demand for local produce resulted in a rapid increase in the stock of pigs, which in turn led to an epidemic of swine fever. Between July and September 1941, 90 per cent of all pigs in St. Lucia were wiped out by the disease, and it was evident that the disease had emanated from the Reduit base.
31. This and subsequent quotes in Maxwell Air Force Base, "Historical Report", 21.
32. Harmsen, "Down the Line", 35–48.
33. *Voice*, 21 September 1943; Harmsen, "Down the Line", 43–44.
34. Also *Voice*, 26 September 1944. On the night of 2 October 1944, the officers' mess at Cantonment was robbed and an attempt on the officers' club was prevented.
35. "$250 for Having a Revolver", *Trinidad Guardian*, 7 June 1942.
36. *Voice*, 1 May 1952, 2.
37. See: Francis, "A Brief History", 24; *Voice*, 10 December 1940 and 9 December 1941.
38. Bentley, "Acquisition of Territory for US Air Base".
39. As far as we know, St Lucians were excluded from these types of training.
40. They were First Lieutenant William E. Johnson Jr., Second Lieutenant Ralph W. Mauch, Second Lieutenant Roy Mcnutt Jr., Second Lieutenant Frank P. Rott Jr., Corporal Arthur J. Lupo, Corporal Porter B. Armstrong and Corporal Ashbury H. Dayton.
41. This happened on 28 September 1943. The plane's occupants were Second Lieutenant Edward S. Frantz, USMC rescue, and Corporal John H. Dearborn, AC.
42. NAUK: CO 256/41, Annual Report, Labour Department, 1944.
43. Fishermen had been complaining about diminishing catches close to shore since the 1930s. NAUK: CO 256/41, Annual Report, Department of Agriculture, 1941.
44. The base was partially reactivated in 1955 as part of the US Space Program

Long Range Proving Ground for Guided Missiles. Tracking facilities were constructed on Moule à Chique and on 2.51 acres of land at Morne le Blanc (north of Laborie) and remained in operation for about a decade. In early 1961 Beane Field (excluding the dock, two runways and the missile-tracking stations) was handed back to the St Lucia government. On 1 September 1964, St Lucia received the remaining lands and assets. The missile-tracking stations followed shortly thereafter.
45. *Voice*, 3 May 1952, 4.
46. Ibid.
47. *Voice*, 17 and 18 July 1952, 2.

7.

THE EXCHANGE

Imperialism and the Impact of World War II on Trinidad and Tobago

RONALD WILLIAMS

This chapter examines primarily the political ramifications of World War II on the British territory of Trinidad and Tobago. The financial challenges which confronted Britain during this period had several implications for the Caribbean region. Owing to these financial woes this metropolitan power sought several accommodations with its ally the United States, even though such undertakings would have injured British prestige and stature as an imperial power. On the other hand, such manoeuvrings served to facilitate the aims of the Monroe Doctrine and Manifest Destiny with direct consequences for the colony of Trinidad. The political negotiations were an indicator of the diminishing influence of Britain, while they signalled the continued rise of the United States. An obvious feature of US influence was the diffusion of its culture, which became more visible in Trinidad during the period. Unequivocally, the accommodations between Britain and the United States served to impress upon the inhabitants of Trinidad the manner and extent to which the forces of imperialism affected their development as well as that of the territory. While such machinations had diverse and resonant implications for the socioeconomic circumstances of the inhabitants of the colony, the political ramifications form the main focus of the study. Therefore, several issues are examined, namely the Anglo-American Lend-Lease Act signed in March 1941 (also known as the Destroyers for Bases Agreement), the defensive measures which were employed in the colony and the impact on the trade-union movement, as well as the perceived encroachment on the civil liberties of the colony's inhabitants.

Irrefutably, the Destroyers for Bases Agreement was a defining one for Britain and the inhabitants of the territories, all of whom were affected by the influx of Americans. Negotiations which paved the path for the Destroyers for Bases Agreement had commenced even before the Havana Conference[1] had concluded. Essentially, in a bid to counter the Axis transatlantic menace, the Destroyers for Bases Agreement gave the United States the right to construct bases in several British territories in exchange for fifty old United States destroyers of World War I vintage.[2] The British government found itself in the precarious situation of having to engage in the aforementioned negotiations because it was not fully prepared for the war with which it was confronted. Britain was somewhat handicapped, partly owing to the disarmament policy of the 1920s and 1930s,[3] and with insufficient destroyers and other suitable craft, it was ill equipped for naval warfare against the German fleet. It was noted that during World War I, Britain had over 400 destroyers in service, whereas in September 1939 there were only 153 in operation.[4] One has to acknowledge that the United States' willingness to engage in this agreement spoke to the geopolitical significance of the European colonies, given the then existing global conditions. Of course, in the West Indies several of the colonies possessed primary products such as petroleum and bauxite, products vital to the operationalization of the "new warfare".[5]

THE NEGOTIATIONS

Noteworthy is the fact that negotiations which preceded the agreement were fraught with challenges at the diplomatic level. Conclusively, it can be stated that Britain's prime minister, Winston Churchill, and the president of the United States, Franklin Roosevelt, were principals throughout the negotiating process over the Destroyers for Bases deal.[6] In the United States there were divergent views regarding the domestic and foreign policies of the nation. While Roosevelt was appreciative of the need to provide Britain with the required military assistance, there were politicians in the United States who held a starkly different stance. A staunch opponent of Roosevelt's foreign policy was the Irish-American chair of the Senate Committee on Naval Affairs, Senator David Walsh.[7] Roosevelt attempted to court Walsh, in order to ensure that he did not impede progress of the Destroyers for Bases deal, but Walsh was unrelenting. In order to have the Destroyers for Bases deal materialize, Roosevelt used executive decree as a means of circumventing the determined isolationists.[8] Since the first quarter of the twentieth century, Roosevelt had demonstrated an interest in the West Indies, as evidenced by a presentation he made before the House National Committee in 1916. Roosevelt articulated the position then that in the event of war with Germany, that power would attempt to strike in the Caribbean and western Atlantic.[9] Hence the Destroyers for Bases Agreement was a realization of his vision.

The British too had some degree of reservations about the Destroyers for Bases Agreement. Churchill viewed Roosevelt's demand for bases as crude bargaining and thought it humiliating to Britain and not in the spirit of the Anglo-American relationship.[10] Actually Churchill advanced the position that Britain was willing to continue the lease of facilities in Bermuda, St Lucia and Trinidad under the 1939 agreement and to extend the arrangement to include Jamaica, British Guiana and Newfoundland.[11] He reiterated that this could have been granted without even the concession of the destroyers because he perceived it as being of necessity.[12] However, Roosevelt was adamant that the bases were the "molasses" which would placate his constituency. It was obvious that the leasing of territory for bases within British colonies to the United States was a sensitive matter. Essentially, the Destroyers for Bases Agreement meant the continued growth of US influence in the region, and this was rooted in the principle of Manifest Destiny and the Monroe Doctrine; but it was injurious to British pride and prestige and to some extent was indicative of the declining fortunes of Britain.

In the colony of Trinidad, some concerns were expressed in relation to the negotiations which were centred on the Destroyers for Bases Agreement. Reflecting later on in a 1959 speech, the then premier of Trinidad and Tobago, Eric Williams, stated emphatically that the governor, Sir Hubert Young, was opposed to the agreement.[13] Young endeavoured to have the United States consider alternative sites for its bases in order to mitigate the disruptions which the community would experience.[14] An alternative scheme was championed by Young and Sir Lennox O'Reilly, a prominent member of the Legislative Council, at the negotiations in London. Young stated to the Legislative Council on 16 March 1941: "Rest assured that Sir Lennox O'Reilly and I did our utmost to secure for the people of Trinidad such modifications in the original proposals as were in our opinion desirable."[15] However, the alternative scheme was not accepted by the US government. Young also indicated that his contribution to the Destroyers for Bases Agreement was reflected in the preamble, which provides that "it shall be fulfilled in a spirit of good neighbourliness and the details of its practical application shall be arranged by friendly co-operation".[16] One might deduce that Young was hopeful that the statement would have guaranteed that the Trinidad government retain a voice in developments relating to the US presence and disruptions to the community.

Actually, Williams commented that the governor preferred to have the US military use a specific location instead of accessing several locations. According to Williams, the Trinidad government suggested that the United States reclaim the Caroni Swamp and construct its facilities there.[17] It was also reported by Williams that Young had stated that if the colony "wanted to give up territories for 99 years [it should] . . . make sure that it satisfied the Legislative Council of 1941 and the Legislative Councils to come for 99 years thereafter".[18]

Young purported that

> the British government has just sent out a Royal Commission, it came in 1939, to take positive steps towards removing the social and economic discontent and removing some of the political disabilities which our people face. You cannot say Constitution Reform, with a Commission coming out from Britain, and at the same time say that the Americans are to have what they want, where they want, how they want, when they want, against the wishes of the representatives.[19]

There were other members of the Legislative Council who expressed concerns over the Destroyers for Bases Agreement. One such person was Dr Adam Rankine, the director of medical services, who focused on the point that the facilities of the north-western peninsula were viewed as indispensable to the continued well-being of the colony's inhabitants.[20] Rankine stated that the loss of facilities "would have a most deleterious effect on the health and well-being of a large section of the population".[21] A contribution was also made by Adrian Cola Rienzi, trade unionist and the member of the Legislative Council for Victoria, who saw it necessary to record "that the people were not directly consulted".[22] He further remarked, "I hope, Sir, that the Americans in coming to Trinidad will not bring to this colony some of the objectionable practices in the Southern States of America. I refer to 'Jim Crowism'."[23] Councillor T.M. Kelshall addressed his concerns as well. He presented the view that "there are many people who will feel the taking from them of bays and houses that they have owned for many years".[24] Later he commented, "I hope that they will (I mean particularly the people who will be dispossessed) at no time, Sir, regret this transaction."[25] The several councillors registered their views, which, even though subtle, indicated some degree of scepticism about the Destroyers for Bases Agreement.

There were other issues which were aired. In the *Vanguard*, a weekly newspaper, it was purported that "we should like to make it perfectly clear, that as it is necessary to make this sacrifice, we are not opposed to the granting of portions of our territory to the Government of the United States of America. But what we do object to is the way in which the negotiations have been conducted, resulting in the lease."[26] The article also expressed the opinion that "it would have been a fitting gesture and earnest of the intention of our masters in Downing Street to extend Democracy to the West Indies, if they had consulted us instead of opening the way to the suggestion that the "Democracy" which we are being called upon to make sacrifices to preserve, is one which is only intended for Europe and the Americas.[27]

On 14 February 1941 a meeting, organized by the Public Works and Public Service Workers' Union, was held at the Princes' Building, where it was suggested that the Legislative Council and the dailies were mistaken when they claimed that they expressed the thoughts of the people about the agreement. The union postulated, in fact, that there was an "absence of a coherent mass expression on the grant of sites for bases to the United States until the Princes' Building meeting".[28] Several points which were raised by Adrian Cola Rienzi prior to the signing of the agreement addressed the manner in which the negotiations were conducted. He focused on Churchill's statement that "no action would be taken against the wishes of the Colonies concerned", and he asked for clarification on Churchill's statement in order to ascertain whether he meant that "the Governors in Executive Council in these [colonies] or . . . the people were to be consulted through their elected representatives and public bodies? The latter surely does appear to be the only democratic way of consultation. How else could the wishes of the Colonies be ascertained?"²⁹ Obviously, he articulated the position that the only democratic way would have been identifiable with the latter of the two suggestions. Such were the positions which were being advanced by people who inhabited Trinidad.

LAND AND LEGISLATION

Ultimately, the US authorities required a vast amount of property for the bases and other facilities for the duration of their stay in the colony. Therefore, this translated into both state and private lands being employed for this purpose. The land acquired for the bases and facilities spanned northwestern, eastern, central and south-western Trinidad. It is important to note that two principal sites were selected for the bases: the north-west peninsula was reserved for the naval base and naval airbase while Cumuto in the east was to be the military and military airbase.³⁰ The land which was to be used for naval purposes was approximately twelve square miles, and included areas such as La Retraite and the Point Gourde Peninsula.³¹ Basically, the lands which were desired by the US authorities were located in several wards. They were situated in the wards of Diego Martin and Arima in the county of St George and the wards of Valencia, Tamana and Manzanilla in the county of St Andrew.³² In the ward of Chaguanas, in the county of Caroni, lands were also identified for use by the US authorities.³³ Additionally, the US authorities were leased no less than seventy-four acres in the capital city of Port of Spain, and this included King George V Park, which was situated in the residential area of St Clair, for a period of three years.³⁴ Another site was also identified for the US authorities, but it would require reclamation; interestingly, it was valued at ten thousand pounds but was rented at a dollar per year for the whole period of the agreement.³⁵

Given the nature of the Destroyers for Bases Agreement, which was signed between the governments of the United States and Britain in London on 27 March 1941, not only crown lands were required for the purpose of fulfilling the obligations of His Majesty's government;³⁶ there were some other matters which had to be addressed at the Legislative Council, which met on 17 January 1941 to amend the Land Acquisition Ordinances.³⁷ This amendment was intended to ensure that the acquisition of land for fulfilling the British government's obligations to the United States came under the ambit "for public purposes".[38] The amendment was further aimed at facilitating the acquisition of ancillary areas to the leased areas as well as lands which would have been acquired for subsidiary purposes, possibly as a consequence of the agreement with the US government.[39] It was intended that the Land Acquisition Ordinances provide adequate machinery to meet the aforementioned scenarios. At the sitting of the Legislative Council on 22 April 1941, approval was sought for the governor's decision to acquire all lands, other than Crown lands, in the areas described in an annexed schedule for the purpose of meeting the colony's obligations under the terms of the agreement.[40] In October 1945 a response to questions which arose in the Legislative Council provided a somewhat detailed account of the lands which were acquired in an attempt to fulfil the terms of the agreement between the government of the United States and Britain. It was reported that

1. Of the lands leased to the United States Government for 99 years, approximately 13,000 acres were Crown Lands and approximately 22,000 acres were in private ownership at the time of the Bases Agreement.
2. The U.S. authorities temporarily occupy:
    (a) Crown and Municipal lands in and around Port of Spain at Docksite, Marine Square, St. Clair, Long Circular Road, Mucurapo and also Tobago airport; and
    (b) Private lands from 37 owners at Edinburgh, La Lune, Blanchisseuse, Icacos and Flagstaff Hill (Tobago).
3. All Crown and Municipal lands temporarily occupied by the U.S. authorities are held by them under informal agreements covering the duration of the war and 6 to 12 months thereafter. Private lands so occupied are requisitioned by Government under Defence Regulations.
4. The relinquishment at the earliest possible date of private lands temporarily occupied is being taken up with the United States authorities.[41]

These details allow a more comprehensive insight into the extent of land which was occupied by the US authorities.

The amending of Trinidad's Land Acquisition Ordinances was deemed vital to ensure that they were wide enough to cover the very important purpose of land acquisition for American bases.[42] However, there were those who expressed concerns about the implications of such amendments for the inhabitants of the colony. Lennox O'Reilly figured that the then existing ordinance was sufficient to facilitate the compulsory acquisition of land for the purpose of giving effect to the recent agreement between Britain and the United States in Trinidad. However, O'Reilly expressed the view that it was best to remove beyond the range of possible legal argument that government had the power to authorize the acquisition of land for the purpose of fulfilling its obligations.[43] Thus, Councillor Rienzi aired his concern over the phrase "public purposes". In order to avoid ambiguity regarding the interpretation of the law, Rienzi requested that "public purposes" be defined.[44] Further, he articulated that he was hopeful that the words "public purposes" would not be manipulated for purposes other than those for which they were intended. Importantly, too, Rienzi sought clarification on a constitutional issue which was related to the amendment. He wanted to know whether the piece of legislation could deny the inhabitants of the colony the right to seek redress by the Privy Council, if they were not satisfied with the assessor's valuation of the property. Notably, he further challenged the constitutional right of the Legislative Council to deny inhabitants' access to the Privy Council.[45] Councillor Timothy Roodal registered his disquiet over the legislation by stating that "it will be a dangerous weapon to be placed in the hands of any Governor".[46] Upon hearing the comments of the councillor for Victoria, another councillor, Kelshall, weighed in on the subject and remarked that there was validity in the question which was put forward by the honourable member for Victoria. Kelshall voiced the opinion that "there is some foundation for nervousness on this point".[47] Further issue was taken by Kelshall and Rienzi with other sections of the amendment, articulating the concerns and fears of members of Trinidad's community.

THE QUESTION OF SOVEREIGNTY

Naturally, the question of sovereignty, which surfaced in connection with the Destroyers for Bases Agreement, was of concern to people from various sections of the colony's community. Eric Williams, in his seminal paper "From Slavery to Chaguaramas" in 1959, addressed the issue of Trinidad's sovereignty when he remarked that

> they [Crown lands] were given away free, from all encumbrances, with all other privileges, duty free imports, the exemption from all various charges and taxes, licence fees on cars, radio licence . . . all sorts of privileges, particular privileges

sometimes in respect of jurisdiction over American offenders, particular privileges sometimes in respect to consider Trinidadians working on what we used to consider Trinidad soil, which has now been ceded to the U.S.A.[48]

Williams took issue as well with the view that it was conceived as unthinkable for a non-white policeman to stop a vehicle driven by an American soldier even though there were questionable activities involved such as the smuggling of American products.[49] He was apparently dismayed by the fact that this situation served to undermine a cornerstone of society and challenged the authority of the Trinidad and Tobago government and that of Britain. Indeed, the topic was broached when it was stated in a newspaper article that "it is one thing to say that the existence of U.S.A. naval bases in these islands will not interfere with British sovereignty, but it is another to contemplate the situation realistically".[50]

This viewpoint was advanced in an article in the weekly newspaper, the *People*, and its analysis of the trappings of the agreement was confirmed by the scenario which Williams highlighted. In another instance, it was asserted by sociologist L.E. Braithwaite in an article in *New Dawn*, a newspaper of the National Union of Government and Federated Workers, that "we should not be surprised if under the slogan of defence against totalitarianism these groups should endeavour to gain lasting political control over the British and French West Indies".[51] Here one was confronted with yet another article in 1940 which dealt with the question of sovereignty even before the final signing of the Lend-Lease Act in March of the following year. At the level of the Legislative Council, Rienzi declared, "I hope that our courts here will have jurisdiction over all those who are resident within the leased territories so that no question could ever arise of our courts not having jurisdiction in connection with any matter which happens within the leased territories."[52]

As early as March 1941, reports abounded that many feared that the Americans would demand and obtain extraterritorial rights.[53] This fear was later justified when the United States was actually given jurisdiction over British subjects for military offences on bases.[54] According to a newspaper report at the time, article four of the treaty conferred upon the United States the right of absolute jurisdiction over "United States nationals or non-British subjects charged with committing military offences (such as treason, sabotage, espionage, etc.) either inside or outside the leased areas . . . British subjects charged with committing those offences inside the areas . . . [and] non-British subjects committing any other offence inside the leased areas".[55]

Another article allowed for US counsel to have the right of audience in local courts when a member of the US forces was on trial for specified acts. In *New Dawn*, Braithwaite commented further on the subject of sovereignty when he suggested that it was within the ambit of the United States to claim full political control over the West Indies, based on aspects of the agreement which gave the United States "in case of war or in time of other emergency, power to exercise in the territories and surrounding waters or air spaces all such rights or authority as may be necessary . . . by the United States".[56] Actually, he expounded on possible scenarios, such as war against Germany or of any of the South American republics commencing any activities against the United States (following the example of Rashid Ali al-Gaylani, prime minister of the Kingdom of Iraq[57]), as eventualities which would have allowed for the United States exercising full political control in the West Indies.[58] The issue of Trinidad's jurisdiction as well as that of the other British West Indian colonies was a preoccupation of Braithwaite, who seemed to have contemplated the many implications of the agreement.

Noteworthy too is the fact that the question of sovereignty also featured in the Legislative Council debates in the period after the signing of the agreement. For example Rienzi, the senior member for Victoria, raised the question, "Would Government please state whether it has the legal right to arrest and bring to trial members of the American Forces who commit crimes in the Colony outside of the leased territory?"[59] He also asked, "Would Government please indicate what arrangements, if any, have been made with the Government of the United States of America for the service of legal process and the execution of committal warrants by Marshalls and Bailiffs within the leased Areas?"[60] Rienzi's position, which was representative of many on aspects of the agreements concerning US extraterritorial rights, can be gleaned from the questions which he advanced in the Legislative Council on 28 October 1941. It was observed that the clerk responded at the sitting of the Legislative Council a month later, saying that a reply was not ready to the first of Rienzi's question.[61] No response seemed to have been advanced either in reply to the question or at the meetings of the Legislative Council held in 1942. However, there was a response to the second question, which read: "Pending the enactment of legislation to implement the Bases Agreement, administrative effect is being given to Articles VI and VIII of the Agreement which was published on 13 June 1941, as Council Paper No. 22 of 1941."[62]

At the meeting of the Legislative Council on 28 October 1941, Attorney General L.B. Gibson introduced an ordinance to confer a limited right of audience in the courts of the colony on United States counsel. The bill, which facilitated the implementation of Article VII of the agreement relating to the bases leased to the United States, allowed the US military authorities to appoint US counsel "to act as Counsel and Solicitor in any case in which a member of the United States forces is a party to a civil or criminal proceeding in the Courts of the Colony".[63] Councillor Rienzi proposed that "it seems to me that we ought to have some reciprocal rights from the Government of the United States of America in regard to appearing either in their Civil Courts or before their Courts-Martial in leased areas".[64] Rienzi continued to reaffirm his view by stating:

> I realize that nothing is contained in the lease giving British Counsel a right to appear either before their Courts-Martial or before any of the Courts that the American Government may set up within the leased areas, but I am asking that this Government should use its good offices so as to obtain from the Government of the United States of America reciprocal privileges with a view to enabling the Law Officer or private Counsel to appear if retained by the Crown or if retained by a servant of the Crown.[65]

Councillor Kelshall expressed similar sentiments to Rienzi when he stated, "In regard to the possibility of British subjects being tried by Americans, I[,] like the honourable Senior Member for Victoria, trust that the Government will make some representations to give us the right of audience in American Civil Courts should they ever constitute them."[66]

The positions articulated by the two councillors seem to have been aimed at achieving some degree of parity in the agreement, which when implemented in its original form infringed on the sovereignty of the various arms of the state.

Interestingly, what one might have considered further jurisdictional concession was witnessed in the colony. The US authorities "formed a Civil Police Force for policing the leased areas".[67] However, its powers of arrest were not limited to the leased areas, as it allowed for them to be extended to the portion of the Eastern Main Road running through the leased area at Cumuto and elsewhere in the colony where there was a pursuit from the leased area or from that portion of the Eastern Main Road.[68] This US civil force was granted other powers, such as the ability to execute warrants issued by magistrates in the colony in cases in which local courts had jurisdiction. It appeared as though the US authorities had acquired control of particular spheres; thus some credibility was given to the fears which were put forward by some of the colony's inhabitants.

DISPLACEMENT AND COMPENSATION

Not surprisingly, the Destroyers for Bases Agreement resulted in the dislocation of some of the colony's inhabitants, when compensation was supposed to be forthcoming. Councillor Roodal addressed the subject of compensation for people whose lands were acquired in order to fulfil Her Majesty's obligations to the agreement, and on 1 May 1942 he asked:

> Is the Government aware that there is much anxiety in the minds of land owners who have been dispossessed of their holdings in recent times under the provisions of the Land Acquisition Ordinance as to when final payment, in cases where advances have been made, will be made, and whether appreciable advances will be made against final payment in other cases? In replying will Government state the reasons why there continues to be so much delay in settlement of claims under the said Ordinance, even in cases where titles to the holdings have been approved by the Authorities?[69]

First, the government responded to Councillor Roodal's question by asserting that it was not aware of any such anxiety in the minds of dispossessed landowners as was expressed by the councillor.[70] Second, government declared that it did not accept the position that there was an undue delay in paying compensation. It was estimated that the number of claims related to land acquisitions was 2,371, and as of 31 July 1942, 917 people had received full payment while 247 had received substantial advantages.[71] Those figures for full payment represented only approximately 38.68 per cent of the dispossessed inhabitants. Government endeavoured to clear itself of fault in the matter of settlement of claims by suggesting that some claims were rejected because of their perceived absurdity and by saying that some people did not give the necessary details to facilitate a smooth process for compensation. Councillor

Kelshall contributed to the debate on compensation: "It is almost a scandal the length of time taken to settle claims. We have no right to take people's lands from them and tell them to wait two or three years for payment. . . . Since Mr. Maingot, the Crown Solicitor, has been in charge quite a number of cases have been dealt with . . . but still there are far too many land acquisition claims that are unsettled."[72]

It was observed that Councillor E.V. Wharton shared similar sentiments as Kelshall on the land-settlement issue. Wharton found that land settlements were not processed in a reasonable time. His position can be ascertained from his remarks: "They do not want this matter dragged out . . . what they want to get is their money to apply it for the purpose of producing an income and a livelihood. There are people who were dependent on their properties for their livelihood, and they are now being deprived of the use of their money. . . . What they want is settlement."[73]

The issue of compensation received the attention of several other politicians. Councillor M.A. Maillard emphasized that he was going to make reference mainly to "the Northern Peninsula and of the people living in that area". He said, "I do not think you will find more than five per cent who are satisfied with the amount paid them for their claims."[74] He also declared:

> Many of the land owners are more interested in getting their capital than the interest because they want to do something with their money. Some people believe that proprietors whose lands have been acquired have been generously paid. Some undoubtedly have been: lots of persons who owned properties worth $50 and have been given $200 or $250 did not want the money; they wanted to remain on their lands. Others who owned properties which were invaluable to them for many reasons and with which they would not willingly have parted have been given pre-war price. . . . I do not think it is fair to say that they have been generously treated.[75]

It is important to note that Councillor Maillard, while treating with the issue of compensation, highlighted the fact that there were people who did not have any desire to part with their properties as they were deeply connected to them. Notably, Rienzi did not refrain from expressing his views on the matter. He commenced by stating, "I do not think Government can ever hope to get dissatisfaction eliminated among persons whose lands have been acquired."[76] However, his views at the sitting of the Legislative Council on 13 August 1943 seemed to be a bit more conservative than usual. The conservative nature of Rienzi's comments prompted Councillor G.R. Wight to state that while he witnessed "the Senior Member for Victoria like knight in shining armour drawing the sword to defend Government in this question of land acquisition",[77] it seemed that government had to shoulder responsibility for the unsatisfactory state of the issue revolving around land settlement. Councillor Roodal did not hesitate to echo similar sentiments to Wight's regarding the stance now adopted by Rienzi on this particular subject. Roodal postulated that "since he has been graduated to the Executive Council he has abandoned the interest of those whom he represented in the past and is now championing the cause of government. I am very much surprised, Sir."[78] He articulated further that government,

> realizing that they have to pay such an enormous amount, they are hesitant in paying the compensation which is due . . . I have experience about lands in Cumuto where I know lands were taken nearly two years ago and the claims of the owners have not yet been settled. Representations were made and the people were informed that the claims could not be considered at the moment because they were fictitious. . . . Sir the people of this Colony are highly dissatisfied and I am one of those. . . . I am urging Government to do what is right for the people of this Colony.[79]

Another individual whose views reflected those of Maillard and Roodal was Councillor Fred Grant, who stated that "a great many of these people have been compulsorily dispossessed of their land which provided them a livelihood. Many of these people have no means for the time being of earning money and have to borrow . . . Why should they have to borrow money at high rates and await Government's pleasure to pay them money, to which they are entitled."[80]

While there were several individuals who championed the cause of those dispossessed of their lands, there seemed to be some derision expressed by notable labour leader and Legislative Council member Captain Arthur Andrew Cipriani on the subject of compensation. Interestingly, the person who was once described as the champion of the "barefoot man" adopted a most ardent position on the issue of compensation, which can be inferred from his statement, which read: "The short point is that if the people from whom land was expropriated would take the Government's offer, they would be paid almost on the nail. Our friends at the present moment have got into their minds a fantastic idea of the value of the land today that was worth absolutely nothing yesterday."[81]

Although the issue of compensation was raised at this meeting, it stemmed from the attorney general's desire to make an amendment to the Land Acquisition Ordinance with a view to lowering the rate of interest from 6 per cent. The matter of lowering the interest rate was a keenly contested one, which some viewed as being disadvantageous to the inhabitants of the colony who had suffered the loss of their properties, especially in instances where they did not want to be removed. Such was the nature of some of the technicalities which mushroomed as a result of the Destroyers for Bases Agreement.

TRADE-UNION DEVELOPMENTS

Even though some of the developments and discussions which reverberated in the colony were associated with the agreement between the US and British governments, there were other happenings and parties which served to shape the political landscape at this juncture. A group which featured significantly in the colony during World War II was the trade-union movement, which had emerged particularly after the labour rebellion in June 1937.[82] Its membership comprised, largely, the working class, which meant that it commanded the support of a large cross-section of the society who contributed significantly to the war effort. As early as January 1940, the trade-union movement had denounced vociferously the principles of nazism and Fascism. It purported that "Fascism and Naziism are repugnant to the class conscious workers throughout the world".[83] In his article, Ralph Mentor, journalist and leading trade unionist, stated, "It is confidently expected in the working class circles that no peace will be established unless Hitlerism is completely overthrown. The workers have no particular relish for war. They desire to live in peace and harmony; but they have no alternative but to fight desperately."[84] Unequivocally, Mentor espoused anti-Fascist and anti-Nazi sentiments and endorsed the thinking that the working class should support the Western Allied governments. The aforementioned position was reinforced at a mass demonstration at San Fernando in southern Trinidad in which more than "ten thousand oil, sugar and transport workers as well as shop assistants, clerks, telephone operators, technicians and general workers" participated.[85] At this meeting, several resolutions were adopted by the assembly, and one of them read: "This public meeting of organized workers condemns the philosophy of Hitlerism, Fascism and Imperialism and declares its unshaken faith that the building of a World Socialist Commonwealth is the only guarantee for peace and plenty."[86] Definitely, the trade-union movement displayed a firm commitment against the Fascist and Nazi forces which it conceived as being an immediate threat to the working class. On 2 June 1940 the executive committee of the Trinidad and Tobago Trades Union Council prepared a resolution in which it condemned Hitlerism and Fascism, while expressing its "realisation of the need for mobilizing the moral and material resources of the workers".[87] The Trinidad and Tobago Trades Union Council's resolution read:

> That the Trinidad and Tobago Trades Union Council condemns Hitlerism and Fascism. The Council feels that while the workers in Trinidad do not enjoy the same democratic rights which the workers in Great Britain and other self-governing dominions enjoy, they still enjoy greater rights and privileges than the workers under Nazi Germany or any other Fascist State.
>
> The Council desires to point out that if the rights and privileges thus far won are to be maintained and if the workers are to move forward to the attainment of greater rights, it is essential that Hitlerism and Fascism must be defeated. The Council regards it as a historic mission to mobilize the moral and material resources of the workers for the defeat of Hitlerism and Fascism.[88]

Although the Trinidad and Tobago Trades Union Council displayed solidarity with the Allied governments' war efforts, it did not fail to register that the workers did not enjoy the same democratic rights as those in Great Britain and other self-governing dominions. Even though the Trinidad and Tobago Trades Union Council was pressing the claim for greater democratic rights in a most appropriately couched manner, the attitude of the trade-union movement can be gleaned as well from the governor's comment about the Oilfields Workers' Trade Union. The governor paid tribute to what was perceived as an "unprecedented arrangement recently completed by the Oilfield Employers' Association and the OWTU".[89] Basically, the agreement allowed for an industrial peace in the oil industry of this colony for the duration of the war and six months thereafter.[90] The fact that the OWTU had adopted this position affirmed its commitment to the war effort.

The representatives and organizations of the working class assiduously urged the workers to remain steadfast and committed to the war effort. An example of this commitment was evidenced in the remarks of E.R. Blades, the general secretary of the OWTU, who cautioned workers "that it's no use listening to false propaganda by fifth Columnist in our midst who were out to destroy the morale of the workers by their prediction stating that of ultimate failure of this war. The workers duty is to keep on the alert for these persons."[91] Blades closed by informing the workers that they needed to "be prepared if it comes to the worse to fight to the last man to prevent the spread of Nazism and Fascism which are the enemies of progress".[92] Blades's instruction spoke of a determined resolve to combat Nazism and Fascism, and he expected the workers to take heed and be dedicated to the cause. The stance of Blades and the other unionists was echoed by the *Vanguard*, the organ of the OWTU.[93] It was stated by the *Vanguard* that

> Trinidad workers have been anti-Nazi and anti-Fascist long before the war. Long before Churchill-Eden and Co . . . they advocated stopping the Fascists. . . . In fact they were advocating war on the Fascists since the days of Manchuria, Ethiopia and Austria. . . . Trinidad workers with the class-conscious of other parts of the world were calling attention to the dangers of Fascism. Trinidad workers and this organ make no apology for continuing to advocate total war on Nazism and Fascism . . . the forces of darkness and evil.[94]

Definitely, the *Vanguard* enunciated that the workers and itself were always in the forefront of the fight against Fascism and Nazism, even when the governments of the Western world were pandering to the leaders of Germany and Italy. A comparable viewpoint was conveyed in an article in the 12 April 1941 issue of the *Vanguard*, under the title "The War: An Appeal".

Although the trade-union movement vigorously espoused anti-fascist and anti-Nazi rhetoric, some individuals and bodies in the colony endeavoured to challenge their loyalty to the British Empire and their unswerving dedication to the war effort. Testimony of such a scenario where trade unionism and its adherents were being referred to as disloyal was reported in a May issue of the *Vanguard*. There it was stated that "it is to be expected that the organ of big business will seek every opportunity to create prejudice (if they could) against Trade Unionism and its apostles".[95] The *Vanguard* pronounced on the subject of the disloyalty of trade unionism and its apostles by designating it as "the latest stunt promulgated by the *Trinidad Guardian* . . . to accuse Mr. Roy A. Joseph and the Trade Union Movement with disloyalty because they are advocates of self-government for Trinidad. . . . [With] a war being on they want to pretend they are more loyal to Britain than anybody else."⁹⁶

While the trade-union movement was anti-Fascist and anti-Nazi, it was not prepared to sacrifice the democratic rights of the workers by failing to call for self-government for Trinidad. In order to dispel such propaganda about trade unionism and its apostles, reference was made to the June 1940 resolution of the Trinidad and Tobago Trades Union Council, in which it pledged its loyalty to the war effort in addition to its condemnation of Fascism and Nazism. Certainly, the *Vanguard* was prepared to address and dispel any false accusations which sought to discredit trade unionism and its representatives, since they were merely clamouring for the same democratic principles for which the war was being fought to be extended to the working class. They attempted to dispel the concern that the movement harboured traitors and Fascist sympathizers. The movement was adamant in its propaganda that no such traitor was to be found among members of the working class or among its leadership. The *Vanguard* reaffirmed its position on the war in September 1941 by stating, "We want to make the position superlatively clear – we are supporting local efforts to assist in prosecuting the war . . . everything that can be done, must be done now to defeat the totalitarian dictatorships. We do so, not because we love Crown Colony Government or British Imperialism, but because we hate Fascism and all it represents."⁹⁷ While the advocates of trade unionism supported the war effort wholeheartedly, they grasped at the available opportunity to speak of the need for change in the system of government, as one article said:

> We know now that freedom and liberation, will not come to us as a gift, nor will it be extended to us as a result of the successful conclusion of the war. If we are worthy of freedom, liberty and nationhood, we must achieve them, even as our friends the Americans did, even as the Southern Irish did, may even as the best and noblest in India are at this very moment struggling and fighting to.⁹⁸

Though the trade-union movement was loyal to the war effort, it did not camouflage its demands for self-government. In the midst of war at the May Day celebrations of 1943, Rienzi, president of the Trinidad and Tobago Trades Union Council, bolstered the comments of earlier trade unionists. Rienzi stated that "the trade unions have no desire to take any action, such as calling out workers engaged in essential services, for the purpose of a demonstration, as it would interfere with the war efforts".[99] However, one has to note that Rienzi also voiced his concerns over the political status of the colony's inhabitants. He dealt with the need for the remedying of the political circumstances of the working class of the colony by stating:

> Comrades, today in the midst of World War II, as in World War I, the Fascist Powers pretend that they are fighting for a New Order in Europe and in the world – while the United Nations are proclaiming that they are fighting against subjugation, for the defence of democracy and the democratic way of life. But comrades, it is well to let the United Nations know that the people in Trinidad and the whole Colonial Empire are not at all impressed with the war aims declared by Britain and the rest of the United States. . . . Appeals to sentiment by the use of catch phrases about freedom and democracy are not enough to rally support with which to win the war.[100]

Even though the war effort was being supported by the trade-union movement, there was a denunciation of the Western governments' treatment of the subjugated peoples' calls for more democratic rights. The topic was also delved into by John F. Rojas, vice-president of the OWTU, and he reasoned that

> the British Government is fully aware that it cannot win the war unless it can convince the working people of the Empire that their good is involved in the victory . . .The Government must give expression in constructive action. The democratic ideals and peace of the Empire can be preserved only if the Imperial Parliament set out seriously to solve the problem of economic stability and give full recognition of Labour's aspiration for a full say and share in the governance of our affair.[101]

In an excerpt from a 1944 joint meeting of the executives of the Trinidad and Tobago Trades Union Council and the Socialist Party of Trinidad and Tobago, it was stated that

> the workers of the Colony demand a complete change in the constitution, which will give the people the right to elect on the basis of adult franchise, members to a Legislative Assembly . . . The workers demand the abolition of all property and salary qualifications both for members and voters, and declare that now more than any other time, the British Imperial Government and her Allies should translate their professions of democracy into practical forms by ending

once and for all the most objectionable policy of imposing rulership over other people against their wishes and consent.[102]

As stated earlier, the trade-union movement had a delicate role during World War II regarding the successful prosecution of the war, and even though it did not lose sight of this, it did not camouflage its disdain for imperialism. This contempt and hostility was obvious in its leaders' criticisms of Western governments.

A major issue which was of increasing concern to the trade-union movement and others in the colony was the perceived encroachment on the inhabitants' civil liberties and their freedom of speech. One can deduce that the actions of government during World War II served as a catalyst for expressions of political activism by individuals from a wide cross-section of the society. At the centre of the perceived threat to the inhabitants' civil liberties and freedom of speech were the Emergency Powers (Defence) Act of 1939 and the Colonial Defence Regulations. This perceived challenge to freedom of expression resulted in a heated exchange between a councillor and the mayor of Port of Spain, Captain Cipriani. It was suggested that the mayor was being prejudicial when he denied access to Woodford Square to individuals such as Clement Payne of the Negro Welfare Cultural and Social Association (NWCSA) and Quintin O'Connor of the labour movement, while permission for its use was granted to Algernon Burkett, who used it "to move a resolution of loyalty to His Majesty the King".[103] It was explicitly stated that the war was not a justification for the mayor's actions. In an article, "If They Want Loyalty", the need for preservation of the civil liberties of the working-class movement was similarly echoed.[104]

The discussion which revolved around the subject of civil liberties resulted in the question being asked: "Is Government using the state of war to repress the legitimate expressions of the people of this island? If our normal avenues for expressing our demands and grievances are closed to us, then so much the worse for the much advertised peace of the state in times of national crisis."[105] The tone was a cautionary one, but it aimed at establishing that freedom of speech was an opportunity for release which was therapeutic. Albert Gomes contributed to the discussion, saying, "When the right of public assembly was destroyed in Trinidad, many persons felt that there was hardly need for so drastic a measure . . . since the Secretary of State for the Colonies seems to agree in sentiment that there should be no tightening of the reins during wartime there seems no reason why local governments should act at variance."[106] Gomes expressed his disapproval of the attempt by government to suppress the people's rights to freedom of expression, and he skilfully manipulated the statements of the secretary of state to refute the position adopted by the local government. There was also grave apprehension surrounding the perceived silence of the trade unions in relation to the use of the Defence Regulations to arrest Tubal Uriah "Buzz" Butler, the prominent labour leader blamed for the 1937 labour disturbances,[107] and to curtail the inhabitants' freedom of speech. In an article in the *People* it was stated that "certainly the most serious blunder made by the Trade Union Movement in Trinidad since its inception was that it allowed the arrest of Uriah Butler under the Island's Emergency Powers to pass without protest. . . . Whatever the reasons for such an error, it must be clear by now to all unionists that the factors that operated against Uriah Butler were not for Butler alone."[108] The author's piece also noted that "the industrial movement is inextricably interwoven with the political; and questions affecting the right of assembly, freedom of speech are vital to the political and social advancement of our people".[109] Although the trade-union movement was ardent in championing the cause of the working class in the socioeconomic and political realms, one can ascertain from the article that an attempt was being made to have the trade-union movement address the subject of civil liberties.

There was a sustained effort from some quarters to ensure that the inhabitants' civil liberties were not suppressed through the guise of security during wartime. As a result, questions were posed to the Trade Union Council on the subject of civil liberties because its inaction at this perceived threat was disconcerting. The *People* published the opinion that an experience of the Seamen and Waterfront Workers Trade Union "is more than sufficient proof that the Emergency Powers are operating seriously against the entire trade union movement of the island".[110] It was even suggested that "while we see no other 'Trojan Horse' but that which the businessmen, petty officials and snobs who are out to use the state of war with its excellent opportunities for patriotic overacting in order to break the back of the working class struggle we feel . . . the Trade Union Council should be hammering away at the assaults upon sacred rights and privileges".[111] Most definitely, the author of the piece was issuing a clarion call to the trade-union movement and the working class in order to alert them to the machinations of the business class and politicians. Kelshall, a nominated member of the Legislative Council, "expressed indignation at the extent of censorship activity in Trinidad".[112] Ironically, Cipriani, supposedly pro-labour, was of a different mindset, alleging "that there was not enough real censorship in Trinidad and that the censorship, far from being relaxed, ought to be strengthened".[113] In response to his stance, the question was asked whether "Capt Cipriani is endeavouring to make Government use the state of war against both the critics of the state and the critics of Capt Cipriani himself".[114] Here were two starkly contrasting views, and unfortunately Cipriani's position spoke of a potential betrayal of the interests of the working class.

The subject of civil liberties was also fought in the court, where a judgement proclaimed that the governor had no power to make regulations prohibiting the holding of meetings.[115] This decision meant that Quintin O'Connor, Alexander Duke and Alroy Donawa were successful in their appeal against the decision of the acting chief magistrate, a Mr Boland. Naturally, this could have been conceived as a victory for the cause of the preservation of civil liberties.

Other measures were adopted by the authorities, which were viewed with reservation in some quarters. For example, offices and homes were searched under the Defence Regulations. The office of the *People* was searched on 28 May 1940 by five members of the police force.[116] Also, the homes of Bertie Percival, Jim Barratt, Clement Payne and Councillor Albert Gomes, prominent leaders of the trade-union movement, were searched.[117] It is important to note that all these individuals were associated with the struggles of the working class. There was also the instance where the NWCSA was denied the use of Woodford Square for a public meeting. In a letter to Governor Young, Mrs A. Harrison of the NWCSA reported that the commissioner of police insinuated that the NWCSA "was helping Hitler to win the war and that the said organisation was inciting the public to disaffection".[118] Here was an act which was perceived as seeking to stifle freedom of expression, and it was challenged by the NWCSA, which characterized the official's reasons for banning the group as "untrue and slanderous".[119]

The debate on the question of civil liberties reached its climax at a meeting of the city council. Councillor Gomes dealt extensively with the importance of preserving civil liberties at all times and even raised the motion that "the City Council should pass a vote of censure against Government's actions under the

Defence Regulations on the matter of freedom of assembly".[120] The motion was dismissed by the mayor, and this led to Gomes protesting vehemently. The situation became so inflamed that Councillor Gomes was physically removed from the chamber by several police officers.[121] While being removed from the chamber, Gomes defiantly exclaimed, "All in the cause of democracy." Even the notable Caribbean economist William Arthur Lewis addressed the subject of the Defence Regulations and civil liberties. Lewis identified the Defence Regulations as "the most dangerous threat to the organisation of Colonial Labour".[122] He drew this conclusion based on the fact that governors had taken the power to ban all public meetings. Thus, the question of civil liberty resonated throughout the colony because it was deemed something which needed to be jealously guarded. The preservation of civil liberty was of grave importance to the trade-union movement and the working class, since it ensured that the working class's pursuit of socioeconomic and political advancement remained at the fore. As a result, efforts were taken to protect the working class from the manipulation of the Defence Regulations by the reactionary forces.

CONCLUSION

With the advent of World War II and the Destroyers for Bases Agreement, the lives of British West Indians and their territories were transformed to a significant extent. It was evident that the political landscape of the colonies was affected by the war. Since Trinidad and Tobago was one of the territories selected for the establishment of US bases in the British West Indies, this meant that various constitutional and political accommodations and adjustments had to be made in this territory. These accommodations and adjustments can be viewed within the context of issues such as the question of the British and local governments' sovereignty in relation to US interests, land acquisition, trade unionism, the Defence Regulations and the increasingly agitated working class and their demands for civil liberty. Young's government was opposed to the agreement between the United States and Britain, and his political manoeuvrings reflected this. Furthermore, the question of land acquisition, the accompanying legislation to facilitate it and the intense debate on compensation for those who were dispossessed of their properties were issues that preoccupied legislators, intelligentsia, media and the public. The role of the trade-union movement in the war and the matter of civil liberty also featured in the political landscape of the colony. Hence, World War II had serious implications for the already highly charged political and socioeconomic environment in Trinidad, particularly the engagement of two imperialist powers on such a volatile field.

NOTES

1. The Havana Conference (21 to 30 July 1940) which was called by the United States was attended by the ministers of foreign affairs of the American republics. The conference was primarily geared towards preventing the transfer of colonial possessions in the Western Hemisphere to Germany. At the conference, the Act of Havana was adopted, and it provided for the provisional administration of European colonies and possessions in the New World should a non-American state (Germany) attempt to assert control over them. The conference also adopted a mutual-security resolution which declared that "any outside attack on an American state shall be considered as an act of aggression against all the states which signed this declaration". The declaration was signed by all the American states and it established the foundation for continental solidarity and economic cooperation. "Ministers of Foreign Affairs of the American Republics, Meeting (2nd: 1940; Havana, Cuba). U.S. Delegation (1940–1940)", http://www.research.archives.gov/organization/1170372 (accessed 24 January 2015).
2. Fitzroy Baptiste, *War, Cooperation and Conflict: The European Possessions in the Caribbean, 1939–1945* (New York: Greenwood Press, 1988), 50.
3. Ibid.
4. Ibid.
5. Fitzroy Baptiste, "European Possessions in the Caribbean in World War II: Dimensions of Great Power Co-operation and Conflict" (PhD diss., University of the West Indies, 1981), i.
6. Baptiste, *War, Cooperation and Conflict*, 57
7. Ibid., 53.
8. Ibid., 55.
9. Baptiste, "European Possessions", 3.
10. Baptiste, *War, Cooperation and Conflict*, 58.
11. Ibid.
12. Ibid.

13. Eric Williams, "From Slavery to Chaguaramas" (paper presented at a meeting in Arima by the Premier, Dr Eric Williams, 17 July 1959), 10.
14. Trinidad and Tobago, *Hansard*, 17 January 1941, 2.
15. Trinidad and Tobago, *Hansard*, 16 May 1941, 25. 16. Trinidad and Tobago, *Hansard*, 28 November 1941, 51.
17. Williams, "From Slavery to Chaguaramas", 10.
18. Ibid.
19. Ibid., 10–11.
20. Trinidad and Tobago, *Hansard*, 17 January 1941, 9.
21. Ibid., 9.
22. Ibid., 11.
23. Ibid.
24. Ibid., 10.
25. Ibid.
26. "United States Bases: Message from the Prime Minister to the Governor and the people of Trinidad on signing agreement", *Vanguard*, 29 March 1941, 1.
27. Ibid.
28. "A Socialist Party", *New Dawn*, March 1941, 2–3.
29. Adrian Rienzi, "Government and the American Bases", *New Dawn*, February 1941, 29.
30. Trinidad and Tobago, *Hansard*, 16 May 1941, 25.
31. Trinidad and Tobago, *Hansard*, 22 April 1941, 20.
32. Ibid., 21.
33. Ibid.
34. Trinidad and Tobago, *Hansard*, 28 November 1941, 152.
35. Ibid., 52.
36. Trinidad and Tobago, *Hansard*, 22 April 1941, 20.
37. Trinidad and Tobago, *Hansard*, 17 January 1941, 2.
38. Ibid.
39. Ibid.
40. Trinidad and Tobago, *Hansard*, 22 April 1941, 20.
41. Trinidad and Tobago, *Hansard*, 19 October 1945, 295.
42. Trinidad and Tobago, *Hansard*, 17 January 1941, 2.
43. Ibid., 5.
44. Ibid.
45. Trinidad and Tobago, *Hansard*, 5 September 1941, 116.
46. Ibid.
47. Ibid., 118.
48. Williams, "From Slavery to Chaguaramas", 12.

49. Ibid.
50. "U.S.A. Bases in the Caribbean", *People*, 14 September 1940, 6.
51. L.E. Braithwaite, "America, Over the West Indies", *New Dawn*, 1 November 1940, 11.
52. Trinidad and Tobago, *Hansard*, 17 January 1941, 11.
53. "Startling News of U.S. Powers in Trinidad: Announcement Made in Washington, Mr. Churchill Bans Debate on Leasing of Sites to Americans, Extra Temporary Site for U.S. Naval Camp in Port-of-Spain", *Vanguard*, 1 March 1941, 1.
54. "U.S. Given Jurisdiction Over British Subjects For Military Offences On Bases: Treaty Signed, American Counsel to Have Right of Audience in Local Court Hearings", *Evening News*, 27 March 1941, 1.
55. Ibid., 1.
56. L.E. Braithwaite, "The Yanks Have Come", *New Dawn*, June 1941, 22.
57. Rashid Ali al-Gaylani, Prime Minister of the Kingdom of Iraq and instigator of a coup d'etat in April 1941, attempted to weaken British influence in the territory by forging stronger ties with Nazi and Italian Fascist regimes.
58. Ibid.
59. Trinidad and Tobago, *Hansard*, 28 October 1941, 134.
60. Ibid.
61. Trinidad and Tobago, *Hansard*, 28 November 1941, 169.
62. Ibid.
63. Trinidad and Tobago, *Hansard*, 28 October 1941, 141.
64. Ibid.
65. Ibid., 142.
66. Ibid.
67. Trinidad and Tobago, *Hansard*, 3 May 1942, 66.
68. Ibid.
69. Trinidad and Tobago, *Hansard*, 31 July 1942, 122.
70. Ibid.
71. Ibid.
72. Trinidad and Tobago, *Hansard*, 13 August 1943, 378.
73. Ibid., 379.
74. Ibid., 380.
75. Ibid., 381.
76. Ibid.
77. Ibid., 382.
78. Ibid., 383.
79. Ibid.

80. Ibid., 385.
81. Ibid., 379.
82. O. Nigel Bolland, *The Politics of Labour in the British Caribbean: The Social Origins of Authoritarianism and Democracy in the Labour Movement* (Kingston: Ian Randle, 2001), 281.
83. Ralph Mentor, "Candid Comments", *Vanguard*, 6 January 1940, 11.
84. Ibid.
85. "Mass Demonstration at San Fernando: Over Ten Thousand Workers Take Part", *People*, 3 February 1940, 11.
86. Ibid.
87. Trinidad and Tobago Trades Union Council, Colonial Office despatch, 2 July 1940, no. 222.
88. Ibid.
89. Trinidad and Tobago, *Hansard*, 1 March 1940, 9.
90. Ibid.
91. "The Allies Must Win: Says the General Secretary", *Vanguard*, 1 June 1940, 10.
92. Ibid.
93. "British Communists' Defeatist Policy: Mass Action Necessary, Nazism, Fascism and Imperialism Must Be Fought", *Vanguard*, 12 April 1941, 1.
94. Ibid.
95. "Mischievous Propaganda: Bourgeois Press Launches Indecent Attack", *Vanguard*, 17 May 1941, 1.
96. Ibid.
97. "Where Do We Stand?", *Vanguard*, 13 September 1941, 4.
98. Ibid.
99. "Mr. Rienzi's Stirring Address: Workers Told to Close in Their Ranks", *Vanguard*, 15 May 1943, 1.
100. Ibid., 1–2.
101. John F.F. Rojas, "Socialism the Real Alternative", *Vanguard*, Yuletide Number. 1941, 7–8.
102. "Southern Unions and Socialist Party Taking No Part in Election", *Vanguard*, 25 March 1944, 2.
103. "Woodford Square", *People*, 3 February 1940, 6.
104. Ibid., 7.
105. Albert Gomes, "Let the Speaker Speak", *People*, 13 April 1940, 5.
106. Ibid.
107. Tubal Uriah "Buzz" Butler was a Grenadian who migrated to Trinidad in 1921. In 1929 Butler was involved in an industrial accident which left him unfit for

continued employment in the oil industry. He was a member of the Spiritual Baptist Church, and he later formed the Butlerite Moravian Baptist Church. He was once a member of the Trinidad Labour Party, but his relationship with the organization was severed because of a difference of opinion regarding tactics between Butler and Cipriani. Butler, responsible for organizing workers in the oil industry between 1935 and 1937, emerged as a labour leader after the 1935 Apex Strike. Butler was considered to be the most prominent figure in the labour disturbances of 1937.

108. "Uriah Butler and the Trade Unions", *People*, 16 March 1940, 6.
109. Ibid.
110. "Police Interference", *People*, 11 May 1940, 6.
111. Ibid., 6
112. "Towards a Fascist Trinidad?", *People*, 4 May 1940, 6.
113. Ibid.
114. Ibid.
115. "Governor Has No Power to Ban Meetings: Important Appeal Decision", *People*, 11 May 1940, 11.
116. Ibid.
117. "Office of 'The People' Searched: Other Premises Also Visited", *People*, 1 June 1940, 2.
118. Mrs A. Harrison, "The Right to Hold Meetings in the Square: Association Writes the Governor", *People*, 5 October 1940, 3.
119. Ibid.
120. "Five Policemen Play 'Basket O'Lady' with City Councillor: Climax to Freedom of Assembly Debate", *The People*, 2 November 1940, 2.
121. Ibid.
122. W. Arthur Lewis, "Civil Liberty and Labour in the Colonial Empire", *Vanguard*, 14 June 1941, 3.

8.

WORLD WAR II AND ANTIGUA'S SUGAR INDUSTRY

GELIEN MATTHEWS

For almost three hundred years before the arrival of the United States in Antigua during World War II, the island's economy and, by extension, the working life of locals, were almost completely dominated by sugar. Today, apart from the many mills dotting the island, there is hardly anything to suggest from the largely uncultivated state of agricultural land that Antigua once boasted a history of profitable sugar estates. By the end of the nineteenth century, along with most other West Indian sugar producers, sugar in Antigua had declined to ruinous levels, made worse in the following century by the Great Depression of the 1930s. By 1965, twenty years after the end of World War II, Antigua Sugar Estates (or Antigua Sugar Factory or Gunthorpe's, as it was known to the locals), the central factory of the island, had sunk to its lowest level, and although Antigua's colonial government attempted to rescue the company through a buyout, this failed. Within four years, Antigua Sugar Estates had closed its doors and the movement of sugar from its position of absolute economic centrality to marginality was completed. However, it was in the beginning of this economic slump in the sugar industry that the United States of America during World War II stepped onto the island of Antigua. It is the overarching conclusion of this chapter that the American presence in Antigua during World War II was instrumental in completing the downward slide of the island's sugar industry. The resources that the Americans brought to Antigua and the employment opportunities they created, both in the island and in the United States, finally crippled the island's sugar industry, which was already on its last legs when the war began.

Historians have shaped several popular themes in their interrogation of the history of the United States in the Caribbean during World War II. One such theme is the hegemonic control that the former exerted on the latter during and since this war. In his assessment of the manner in which the United States entered Trinidad, for example, Maurice St Pierre is perturbed that almost no attempt was made to consult the locals, making the Anglo-American Destroyers for Bases Agreement in Trinidad high-handed, unilateral and insensitive to West Indian self-respect and budding aspirations for federation and self-government.[1] In a similar vein, Anthony Maingot pointed out that the agreement confirmed that the United States was the new and "undisputed military power in the whole Caribbean".[2] Another common perspective from which the history of the United States in the Caribbean during the war has been gauged is that locals in the various territories benefited materially from the presence of the American servicemen and civilian contractors. Gail Saunders, for instance, convincingly demonstrates, in both her doctoral dissertation and her *Journal of Caribbean History* article, that at least on a temporary basis the Americans brought relief from poverty, unemployment, underemployment, slum dwellings and even starvation.[3]

With particular reference to the Antigua case, the historiographical analysis of the legacy of the US presence in Antigua since World War II is very slim. The leading scholar in this field is Susan Lowes. Her social analysis focuses extensively, though not exclusively, on the ways in which the arrival of the Americans cheated locals of an entire dwelling space – that is, Winthorpes Village – and brought social disruption to the island largely through a marked increase in prostitution.[4] Despite Lowes's solid academic contribution to this dimension of Antiguan history, several important questions remain unexplored. Central among the overlooked areas in this historiography is the connection between the arrival of the Americans and the island's changed economy and employment situation. However, this chapter does offer an economic analysis of the impact of the Americans on Antigua's sugar industry during World War II.

THE ANGLO-AMERICAN DESTROYERS FOR BASES DEAL AND THE IMPACT ON THE SUGAR INDUSTRY

The presence of the United States in Antigua, the most north-easterly Caribbean island in the chain of the Lesser Antilles, was formalized on 27 March 1941 during World War II. On this date the United Kingdom and the United States of America signed a lease agreement permitting the latter to establish military bases on Antigua for ninety-nine years, while the former received fifty over-aged destroyers to assist in the war effort. The lease was part of a wider pact entered into by the two world powers on 2 September 1940, involving not only Antigua but also Jamaica, St Lucia, Trinidad, the Bahamas, British Guiana, Bermuda and Newfoundland.[5] The two American bases in Antigua were constructed on the eastern and western sides of Parham Harbour. The army airbase on the west of the harbour was named Coolidge Airfield and included a runway that was later used as Antigua's national airport. A naval air station was also built on the east side of the harbour at Crabs (or Crabbs or Crabbes) Peninsula, which was used during the war as a Caribbean communication and tracking centre to monitor German submarine operations in the region. Antigua was one of the smallest of the sites selected for the planned military operation of the United States in the Caribbean, though it is the largest island in the Lesser Antilles chain of the West Indies. For the United States, nevertheless, Antigua's geographical position, climatic conditions and terrain made it of prime strategic importance. In the words of David Rollinson, "Antigua lies in the heart of the Caribbean, almost equidistant from Florida and Venezuela."[6]

On the whole, however, the Anglo-American Destroyers for Bases Agreement involving Antigua and the other base sites of the region was valued for two main reasons. As noted in other chapters of this work, on the one hand, the military resources of the United Kingdom, carrying the brunt of the fighting against Germany, Japan and Italy in World War II before 1942, were in considerable need of reinforcement. Weakened by the war, Britain was unable to effectively defend its Caribbean colonies, and the deal formalized the United States as Britain's war ally. On the other hand, the United States valued the opportunity to establish bases on the aforementioned British Caribbean colonies as crucial to the strategic defence of its east coast. German submarine activity in the Caribbean, especially by 1942, threatened to expose and undermine both British and American shipping routes, particularly in the transportation of such vital war products as bauxite from Jamaica, Suriname and British Guiana and oil from Trinidad, as well as from Aruba, Curaçao and Venezuela, which often passed through the Panama Canal.[7] President Franklin Roosevelt described the agreement as "an epochal and far reaching act of preparation for continental defence in the face of grave danger . . . the most important action in the reinforcement of our national defence that has been taken since the Louisiana Purchase".[8]

As previously indicated, the initial economic impact of the coming of US servicemen and civilians to Antigua during World War II was that it catapulted the island's economy from literal doom and gloom to buoyancy. In his analysis of five of the economies of the Leeward Islands in the immediate post-emancipation era, historian Douglas Hall discusses the adverse effects of free trade and the Sugar Duties Equalisation Act of 1846, competition from Cuba, Brazil, Louisiana and beet sugar in Europe and the Encumbered Estates Act of the 1850s on West Indian sugar producers.[9] The Leeward Islands faced shrinking markets, falling prices and foreclosure of their enterprises. Depression in the sugar industry from the second half of the nineteenth century, aggravated by the Great Depression of the 1930s, left Antigua as well as other British West Indian sugar islands in dire economic straits. Moreover, Antigua, one of the driest islands in the West Indies, suffered the unique disadvantage of drought in the 1930s, which gravely affected its sugar crop in this period. Correspondence lodged at the Colonial Office in London as early as 1916 described Antigua as the "Cinderella of the West Indies",[10] and Antiguan historian Novelle Richards observed that Antigua in the early twentieth century was "a land of misery and depression, an island of slums and hovels, of barefooted, unkempt people".[11] Desmond Nicholson reinforces this assessment when he points out that extreme poverty in Antigua was apparent in the wattle cottages, burlap sacks or crocus- and flour-bag clothing, flambeau lighting and calabash utensils of the ordinary local in the 1930s.[12] In his book *From Columbus to Castro*, Eric Williams notes that in the hundred years since full freedom in 1838 (the end of the apprenticeship system), the daily wages of manual workers in Antigua's sugar industry remained stagnant at twenty-eight cents, while skilled workers seldom received more than thirty-six cents. Williams's statistics demonstrate that Antiguan skilled and unskilled plantation workers received the lowest wages in the region.[13]

There were a few bright spots for the sugar industry during the pre-war era in this overwhelming situation of hopelessness. The Antiguan sugar industry, as was the case in the other British Caribbean colonies, enjoyed modest recovery when, in 1905, Britain, the mother country, allocated sugar quotas,[14] providing a fair measure of security in the export market. Furthermore, Antigua came on stream with other British West Indian producers of sugar when from 1903 to 1905 it embraced the trend of factory centralization. By 1904 the smaller of the two central factories, Bendals, located south of St John's, the capital, had begun its operations. In the following year the larger factory, the privately owned Antigua Sugar Estates, was ready to receive the canes of the many small estates dispersed around the Antiguan landscape since the seventeenth century.[15] Furthermore, Britain offered a grant of fifteen thousand pounds as start-up capital for Antigua Sugar Estates and three thousand pounds for Bendals.[16] Still, as indicated by the statistics Williams provides, whatever fortune sugar produced for Antigua by the turn of the twentieth century, scarcely any went to the workers. The white expatriate planter class exploited the people and appropriated a large portion of sugar profits for themselves and their overseas dependents.

The piecemeal revival of the economy by the turn of the twentieth century was nothing in comparison to the stimulus provided by the $4 million that the Americans intended to invest in the Antiguan bases in the early 1940s.[17] It was the single largest capital injection into the Antiguan economy since recession had hit the sugar industry towards the end of the nineteenth century.

The construction of the American bases at Coolidge and Crabs changed the employment situation in Antigua drastically, though only on a temporary basis. An unmistakable characteristic of this short-lived change was the dislocation of labour from the sugar plantations, similar to what occurred in Trinidad, as Lovell Francis describes in chapter 1. For the first time since the seventeenth century, the stranglehold that sugar planters exerted over the labour market was broken. It must be noted, however, that a few did remain on the sugar estates, and throughout the war years sugar continued to be the main income-provider of the average worker in Antigua. Up to 1945, 90 per cent of the island's exports consisted of sugar.[18] Yet, as Brian Dyde notes, by the end of May 1941 there were not enough workers available to reap the cane harvest. Dyde also mentions that while in previous years workers tolerated the rejection of their requests for increased wages, in 1941, when sugar employers brushed aside the workers' demands, many simply walked off the plantations and found ready employment on the American bases.[19] Hundreds of both unskilled and skilled Antiguans from villages, even those who lived significant distances away from the bases, as well as from neighbouring islands, found work. Some worked at the bases as carpenters, mechanics, maintenance and artisanal crews, clerks, drivers, motor mechanics and operators of heavy equipment such as bulldozers, huge trucks and steam shovels. The locals under American supervision constructed several barracks to accommodate the American servicemen, a pier, a concrete apron and seaplane ramps, as well as the runway at Coolidge. They also dredged channels and blasted reefs for seaplane runways, a turning basin and a shipping channel, and they erected an observation tower at the tip of Crabs Peninsula. There was also room at the bases to absorb hundreds in ancillary occupations such as laundrymen and -women, cooks and those in the field of nursing.[20]

Simultaneous with the significant movement of labour away from the plantations to the bases, the American presence in Antigua contributed significantly to the reduction in the number of functioning estates on the island, reinforcing a trend evident from the mid-nineteenth century. In addition to gobbling up shrubs and mango marshes, the American bases in Antigua were constructed partly on prime canefields. To establish the army airbase and runway at Coolidge, the Americans appropriated the existing 929 acres that constituted Millars' Estate, located in the parish of St George.[21] From 1860 to 1890, Sir Oliver Nugent, family to the long line of Nugents of Antigua, lived on and managed Millars' Estate. It was a thriving estate which as far back as 1836 was credited with producing more sugar than any other on the island, and which had grown from 406 acres in 1829 to 929 acres by 1921. During World War II, the owners at the time, John and May Camacho, leased Millars' to the United States Air Force.[22] The Americans used bulldozers to flatten the old plantation, eradicating in a brief, clean sweep one of the few sugar plantations in operation in the colony by the twentieth century. In the Antiguan historic memory, Millars' Estate was lost to the erection of the US officers' club.[23]

Another economic enterprise swallowed up by the American army airbase in Antigua was High Point Canefield and High Point Canefield Number II owned by Clytie McDonald, which were taken out of sugar cultivation and converted into the main runway of the Coolidge Airfield.[24] Yet another manifestation of the shrinking size of the sugar industry in Antigua which perhaps was not caused by but was certainly simultaneous with the Anglo-America Destroyers for Bases Agreement was the absorption of the second most important estate in Antigua at the time, the Bendals Sugar Factory. In her research on Bendals in the 1920s, Lowes observes that in the view of several officials on the island including the governor, Bendals had grown into a monopoly controlling the price of sugar, labour and Antigua itself.[25] In the Camacho petition to the governor of 3 December 1925, the Camacho brothers, John and Alexander, argued that Bendals should give way to the larger and more efficient Antigua Sugar Estates, established in 1905, since the latter was in a position to absorb more canes to match its grinding capacity of three thousand tonnes while the former was overloaded.[26] The Camacho brothers eventually had their way. Bendals had lapsed into inactivity by 1936 and Antigua Sugar Estates had taken it over by 1944.[27]

Betty's Hope was another sugar estate that folded soon after the arrival of the United States. This was Antigua's pioneer plantation. It had been founded in 1651 by Colonel Chris Keynell, Antigua's governor from 1653 to 1660, and it had changed hands by 1674, following the return of Antigua to the British after a short period of French occupation.[28] The new owner of Betty's Hope was Christopher Codrington, who at the time was settling in Barbados. Under his management, Betty's Hope became Antigua's flagship sugar estate. By 1935 Betty's Hope had in its employ the second highest number of workers on the island of Antigua, but this also all came to an end in 1944, the penultimate year of World War II, when, almost in ruins, the Codringtons sold it to Antigua Sugar Estates.[29] By 1945, the last year of the war, more estates surrendered their independence of operation, and there was further amalgamation. In this year Antigua Distillery Limited took over Montpelier, Lynch's, Colebrook, Brown's, Walrond's, Harman's and Hope's estates, concentrating on the production of molasses for the manufacturing of rum.[30] The United States in Antigua during World War II facilitated and, in part, completed the reduction in the number of small but self-contained sugar estates in operation on the island, promoting amalgamation, centralization, specialization and diversification but in many cases forcing outright closure.

The American bases drove the final nail into the coffin of Antigua's dying sugar industry by trumping the wages of estate employees, which forced many to leave for work on the bases. Susan Lowes records that locals working on the bases exulted in their new "princely pay" and in their newfound ability to participate more extensively in the local market economy.[31] With the sudden increase of money in circulation, the government found it necessary to introduce into the island denomination bills of larger value.[32] Some locals suspected that the Americans were willing to offer even higher wages, but their new employers explained that rates were set in consultation with the British colonial government of the island, in whose interest it was to keep as narrow as possible the gap between wages in the sugar industry and the American bases.[33] Another drawback to the relatively attractive conditions of employment that locals enjoyed on the bases was that the American servicemen insisted that under no circumstances would employees be allowed to operate under the cover of a union.[34] In general, however, higher wages on the American bases made other inconveniences preferable to lower wages and exploitation in the sugar industry. It is ironic that while the Antigua Trades and Labour Union came into existence before the arrival of the Americans, and despite the fact that workers at the bases were prohibited from becoming unionized, the bases were instrumental in invigorating the labour movement of the island, and, of course, this development did not augur well for sugar plantation managers.

The Trade Union Act of 1939 was one of the major outcomes of the labour riots that swept across the British West Indies in the 1930s.[35] With the passage of this act, for the first time Antigua workers had the legal right to unify to demand increased wages, improved work conditions and shorter workdays. Determined to take advantage of these provisions, in 1940 Antiguan labour leaders registered the Antigua Trades and Labour Union, the membership of which was dominated by sugar workers. By 1943 Vere Cornwall Bird, who was to become the first and longest-serving prime minister of the country, emerged as the president of the union.

The construction of the US bases was instrumental in generating further worker discontent within the sugar industry, which led to the multiple strikes from 1939 until the 1960s. The most significant of these strikes occurred in the post-war period and was led by workers of the Antigua Sugar Estates. Bird confronted the manager of the estate, Alexander Moody Stuart, on behalf of the sugar workers with the resolve that "no crop would start until the workers were told their rates of pay". Stuart retaliated by threatening starvation within three weeks and assured police protection for management, who intended to bring in scab workers. Bird and the workers, however, resisted. Beneath an old tamarind tree north-east of Bethesda on what was then the old Betty's Hope Estate, the strikers resolved to maintain their demands and to eat "wilk and cockles" or other shellfish and drink "widdy widdy bush", which was a local plant that grew wild in Antigua, if they had to. The strike lasted just under one year and for their personal sacrifices, the workers enjoyed modest victory. The Antigua Sugar Estates conceded by giving a pay increase of 25 per cent. Though the increase was slight, moving the average daily wage of the manual sugar worker from about twenty-five cents a day to twenty-five cents and sixpence, the moral victory was great.

Moody Stuart had failed to keep the workers in check, and he retreated to England soon after the resolution between management and workers had been reached.[36] Those who had to return to employment on the sugar estates or the central factory in the years after the war, when work on the base had been reduced, welcomed the return to slightly higher wages. However, the war and the presence of the Americans emboldened the resolve of workers to unite for the right to cross the threshold of the relatively higher standard of living that the Americans had introduced as a possibility for locals in Antigua.

COOLIDGE AIRFIELD AND THE CHANGING ECONOMY

The single most significant development emerging out of the presence of the United States in Antigua during World War II that marginalized sugar in the island's economy was the construction of the Coolidge Airfield on the western side of Parham's Harbour. The island benefited from other World War II infrastructure, such as roads and water piers, but these were less influential in undermining the future of sugar than the building of the airfield. The airport was completed in just one year, from May 1941 to May 1942. It was named after American World War I Air Force veteran Hamilton Coolidge, of the 94th Air Squadron, who was killed in action in France in 1918,[37] but was renamed the V.C. Bird International Airport in 1980 after the country's first prime minister. Brian Dyde astutely observes that the building of the airport was the first stage of the revolution of Antigua's economy. After three hundred years of sugar being the main cash crop of the island, agriculture in general became the least important and most rejected, neglected and despised enterprise among locals, with only 5 per cent of the population dependent on this sector from the second half of the twentieth century.³⁸ Dyde goes on to explain that in the short space of twenty-five years after World War II, tourism dominated the economy.³⁹

But, of course, tourism was not uppermost in the minds of the US government when Antigua was included in the Destroyers for Bases deal of World War II. The primary intention of the Americans in constructing a wartime airfield in Antigua was military defence. According to Dyde, "Antigua made the ideal place from which air surveillance of the whole north eastern Caribbean could be mounted."⁴⁰ The island's relatively dry climate and accompanying clear skies, along with a terrain capable of sustaining a long runway, made it crucial to the American strategic priorities in the Caribbean during and after World War II.⁴¹ It was partly from Coolidge Airfield during the war that the American servicemen attempted to keep track of German submarine activity in the region.

Importantly, during the war years it became apparent that simultaneous with serving the hegemonic ambitions of the United States in the Caribbean, the airport could be a most convenient channel through which the island's economy could be diverted from sugar to tourism. The antecedent to the heavy traffic in commercial flights that became a regular feature in Antigua in the post-war period consisted of the thirty military aircraft that the American servicemen landed on the Coolidge Airfield each month during the war. These military aircraft included five medical flights bound for Puerto Rico and twenty-five C-130 and C-141 used to drop paratroopers into the ocean and to keep track of developments down the chain of Atlantic islands.⁴² These military expeditions became the forerunner of the British West Indian Airways Viscount route, launched in 1955 from Antigua to Barbados, Bermuda and New York. As the international airport in Antigua widened its operations, becoming the major port of five entries into the island, it absorbed a greater share of the workforce, which in turn reinforced the failing fortunes of sugar. Today tourism has superseded sugar as the main revenue earner of the island, the foundation for this shift first laid during World War II, when the Coolidge Airfield was constructed.

American-led development of seaports in Antigua during World War II also contributed significantly to steering the island's economy away from sugar and agriculture in general towards tourism. Technical and semi-technical skills which Antiguan locals acquired during the construction of the two bases proved critical to the establishment of the harbours. The use of tractors, bulldozers, cranes and other large vehicles which facilitated dredging and blasting, skills which locals would not have learned during the era when sugar was king, proved crucial to the development of Antigua's seaports. By 1968 the waters which now constitute the St John's Deep Water Harbour had been dredged to a length of six hundred feet, extending to Rat Island, and from 1968 onward it became possible for large cruise ships to drop anchor in Antigua's capital.[43]

Americans contributed significantly to Antigua's transformation into a sand-and-sea destination for international tourists, clearly evidenced in one of the island's first exclusive getaways, Mill Reef Club, which was built just after World War II. American civilians who came to the island alongside the servicemen were fascinated by the island's sandy beaches, turquoise water and steady breeze and began to invest in the colony. Robertson Ward, an American architect, bought Mill Reef from the Sheriff family in 1947 and changed its name to Mill Reef Club. He paid thirty-eight thousand dollars for the property, which consisted of twelve hundred acres with a seafront extending just over five miles. Ward, who intended to develop the spot as a post-war tourist vacation and relaxation resort through a joint capital venture, advertised for prospective investors in the US Northeast and Midwest as well as across the British Commonwealth. Each of the forty-five investors paid seventy-five hundred dollars for a lot on the resort. Ward gave them simple construction guidelines; the homes should contain no more than two bedrooms and should be simply built so as to preserve as much as possible the natural tropical beauty of the reef. By 1949 non-residents were invited to spend their holidays in the newly erected multi-room clubhouse. With more than three hundred beaches, it was not long before resorts, beach hotels, guest houses, commercial villas and apartments competed with sugar mills as characteristic features of the Antiguan landscape.

OVERSEAS OPPORTUNITIES AND EMPLOYMENT

While opportunities created and skills acquired within Antigua during World War II made it possible for locals to turn away from sugar and towards tourism, others resorted to temporary and permanent migration, international military service and agricultural and industrial employment abroad.

Altogether, 16,000 West Indians volunteered to serve alongside the British in World War II, which included over 600 women. The latter served either in the Women's Auxiliary Air Force or the Auxiliary Territorial Service. Of the West Indian veterans of World War II, 6,000 served in the Royal Air Force or the Royal Canadian Air Force as fighter-pilot bomb aimers, air gunners, ground staff or administrative staff, while a much larger number joined the merchant navy, although they were often subjected to racism and limited to menial tasks such as shovelling coal below deck.[44] By April 1944 the Caribbean Regiment had been formed, eventually consisting of 1,226 West Indian volunteers, including a handful of Antiguans.[45] By May of 1944 the First Battalion of the Caribbean Regiment had been transported to the United States and then to Italy for continued training. Despite their enduring six months of overseas drills, their white officers and other superiors held the view that the West Indians were still not ready for active service, and in October of 1944 they were transported to Egypt, where they guarded prisoners of war. In December 1945 the Caribbean Regiment was ultimately disbanded.[46]

One female World War II veteran from Antigua, Leah Bascus Nanton (born 1 June 1925), enlisted in the British Army in 1943 while still living in Grenada. To begin her military training she was deployed to Trinidad and became a member of the all-female branch of the Auxiliary Territorial Service, and on the successful completion of her training, Leah Bascus Nanton was stationed in London, where her substantive position was intelligence officer. On several occasions during her military career, she was posted to various stations in Europe,[47] and following her return to her native Antigua, Nanton became a member of the Antigua and Barbuda Ex-Servicemen and Women's Association. In 2013, in recognition and honour of her service as a World War II veteran, the national government bestowed upon her the Most Illustrious Order of Merit. A year later Nanton died, at age eighty-nine. While for Nanton and her colleagues there was social elevation and prestige to be enjoyed through their new military ranks, as well as opportunities to travel and broaden their understanding of the world, racial prejudice was often a barrier to the realization of their full potential.

Another avenue away from the sugar industry that World War II provided was civilian work in agricultural and industrial sites in the United States. Unemployment in the West Indies on the one hand, especially after the bases were near completion, and the drain on manpower resources that the war exacted in the United States on the other hand, created new employment opportunities for West Indians on the whole. Thousands were needed to cultivate and harvest seasonal crops, especially vegetables.[48] It was ironic that the abandonment of agriculture in Antigua facilitated its sustainability in the United States. Thousands more found ready employment in war-related industries, such as in the production of grey-iron castings for heavy trucks and tanks, ammunition and chemicals, camouflage materials, pulp, lumber, food processing and the manufacture of woollen cloth.[49] The War Food Administration (later renamed the Production and Marketing Administration of the US Department of Agriculture) and the War Manpower Commission of the United States (later renamed the United States Employment Service), as well as the British West Indian governments of the various islands and the British West Indian Central Labour Organization (established 1 November 1944), were responsible for the recruitment, transportation and work contracts, including wages, repatriation and compulsory remittances, of the workers.[50] In 1945 alone the United States recruited as many as forty-six thousand West Indian workers to make up for the local manpower shortfall in agriculture and expansion in industrial production that the war occasioned. Though specific numbers of migrants from Antigua are not available, the reports reveal that locals from the British West Indian islands were employed in thirty-eight out of forty-eight states in two thousand cities, towns and villages.[51] Sugar could hardly compete on the labour market in Antigua with an option that provided not only more attractive wages but also the golden opportunity of migration to the United States on either a temporary or permanent basis.

CONCLUSION

The government of the United States made every effort to contain its operations in Antigua during World War II. No more than 282 American servicemen were deployed to the island, outnumbering only the St Lucia US contingent.[52] Additionally, speed and cost minimization were prioritized in constructing the Coolidge Airfield and the naval air station at Crabs Peninsula. Furthermore, on the eve of the war's end, the whole of the American war project in Antigua was formally reduced to caretaker status.[53] Yet the economic impact of the United States in Antigua during and since World War

II was nothing short of revolutionary. The American presence finalized the collapse of the Antiguan sugar industry, and it provided the critical incentive for and means by which Antiguan labour could finally participate in the exodus from the estates which other ex-enslaved West Indian populations had made about a hundred years before.[54] Most significantly, the United States in Antigua, more than any other single factor, provided a whole new revenue earner for the island, which was tourism.

NOTES

1. Maurice St Pierre, "The Chaguaramas Affair in Trinidad and Tobago: An Intellectual Reassessment", *Journal of Caribbean History* 40, no. 1 (2006): 92–116.
2. Anthony Maingot, *The United States and the Caribbean*, Warwick University Caribbean Studies (London: Macmillan Caribbean, 1994), 52.
3. Gail D. Saunders, "The Social History of the Bahamas, 1890–1953" (PhD diss., University of Waterloo, 1985); Gail Saunders, "The 1942 Riot in Nassau: A Demand for Change?", in *Journal of Caribbean History* 20, no. 2 (1985–86): 117–46.
4. See Susan Lowes, "The U.S. Bases in Antigua and the New Winthorpes Story", http://antiguahistory.net/the-us-bases-in-antigua.html, and "Rum and Coca-Cola: The Arrival of the Americans and the Restructuring of Social Relations in Antigua in the 1940s", http://www.uwichill.edu.bb/bnccde/antigua/conference/papers/lowes.html (accessed 24 January 2015).
5. See "Destroyers for Bases Agreement 2 September, 1940", http://www.history.navy.mil/faqs/faq59-24.htm, for original text of agreement; see M.P.W. Stone, "Defense of the Americas: The US Army Campaigns of World War II", http://www.ibiblio.org/hyperwar/USA/USA-C-Americas/index.html (accessed 17 November 2014).
6. David Rollinson, *Railways of the Caribbean* (London: Macmillan Education, 2001), 79.
7. See "Antigua at War", *Nugents of Antigua*, http://www.nugentsofantigua.net/wordpress/?page_id=421 (accessed 18 November 2014).
8. "Message of President Roosevelt to the Congress, September 3, 1940", *Department of State Bulletin* 3: 201, https://www.ibiblio.org/hyperwar/Dip/PaW/179.html (accessed 1 April 2009).
9. Douglas Hall, *Five of the Leewards 1834–1870: The Major Problems of the*

Post-Emancipation Period in Antigua, Barbados, Montserrat, Nevis and St Kitts (Bridgetown: Caribbean Universities Press, 1971), 125–27.
10. National Archives of the United Kingdom (NAUK): CO 152/153, 3 May 1916.
11. Novell Richards, *The Struggle and the Conquest* (St John's, Antigua: Worker's Voice Printery, 1964), 1.
12. Desmond Nicholson, *Antigua, Barbuda, Redonda: A Historical Sketch* (St John's, Antigua: Museum of Antigua and Barbuda, 2001), 15.
13. Eric Williams, *From Columbus to Castro: The History of the Caribbean 1492–1969* (London: Andre Deutsch, 1970), 44.
14. Rollinson, *Railways of the Caribbean*, 79.
15. Ibid.
16. Desmond Nicholson, *Heritage Landmarks: Antigua and Barbuda* (St John's, Antigua: Museum of Antigua and Barbuda, 2001), 47.
17. *Life Magazine*, 7 April 1941.
18. Brian Dyde, *A History of Antigua: The Unsuspected Isle* (London: Macmillan Education, 2000), 32.
19. Ibid., 232.
20. Lowes, "U.S. Bases in Antigua".
21. Ibid.
22. "Nugent Homes and Estates", *Nugents of Antigua*.
23. "Antigua at War", *Nugents of Antigua*; *Life Magazine*, 7 April 1941.
24. Lowes, "U.S. Bases in Antigua".
25. Susan Lowes, "A Bit of Railroad History", Museum of Antigua and Barbuda, *Historical and Archaeological Society Newsletter*, no. 117 (April–June 2012), 6, http://www.antiguanice.com/v2/documents/HAS%20Newsletter%202012-2.pdf (accessed 19 November 2014).
26. NAUK: CO 152/395, Camacho to Governor, 3 December 1924.
27. See Agnes Meeker, "Sugar Memories", Museum of Antigua and Barbuda, *Historical and Archaeological Society Newsletter*, no. 115 (October–December 2011), 4, http://www.antiguanice.com/v2/documents/HASNewsletter2011-4.pdf (accessed 19 November 2014).
28. Desmond Nicholson, *Antigua and Barbuda: Place Names and Their Stories* (St John's, Antigua: Museum of Antigua and Barbuda, 2002), 6.
29. See "A Chronological History of Betty's Hope with an Index to References", http://antiguahistory.net/Museum/bettyshoperesearch.htm (accessed 19 November 2014).
30. Nicholson, *Heritage Landmarks*, 49.
31. Lowes, "U.S. Bases in Antigua".
32. Ibid.

33. NAUK: FO 371/A3382/20/45, A4526/20/45, "Building the Navy's Bases in World War II History of the Bureau of Yards and Docks and the Civil Engineer Corps 1940–1946", http://www.ibiblio.org/hyperwar/USN/Building_Bases/ (accessed 17 December 2014).
34. Dyde, *History of Antigua*, 232.
35. See Richard Hart, *Labour Rebellions of the 1930s of the British Caribbean* (Kingston: Caribbean Labour Solidarity and Socialist History Society, 2002).
36. Nicholson, *Antigua, Barbuda, Redonda*, 16.
37. Nicholson, *Antigua and Barbuda*, 8–9.
38. Dyde, *History of Antigua*, 32–34.
39. Ibid., 36.
40. Ibid., 32.
41. Robert Coram, *Caribbean Time Bomb: The United States' Complicity in the Corruption of Antigua* (New York: William Morrow, 1993), 128.
42. Ibid., 124.
43. Brian Dyde, *Antigua and Barbuda: Heart of the Caribbean*, 2nd ed. (London: Macmillan, 1993), 67.
44. "Caribbean Participants in World War II", http://www.mgtrust.org/car2.htm (accessed 17 December 2014).
45. Elvey Watson, *The Carib Regiment of World War II* (New York: Vantage Press, 1964), 14–15.
46. Dyde, *History of Antigua*, 233.
47. "Front 5 Nanton Funeral", *Antigua Observer*, http://antiguaobserver.com/world-war-ii-veteran-laid-to-rest/front-5-nanton-funeral (accessed 15 December 2014).
48. Report of the Anglo-American Caribbean Commission to the Governments of the United States of America and Great Britain for the Year 1942–1943 (Washington, DC: Anglo-American Caribbean Commission, 1943).
49. Report of the Anglo-American Caribbean Commission . . . for the Year 1945, 15.
50. Report of the Anglo-American Caribbean Commission . . . for the Year 1944, 29; Report of the Anglo-American Caribbean . . . for the Year 1945, 13.
51. Ibid., 13.
52. Mark Skinner Watson, *Chief of Staff: Prewar Plans and Preparations*, http://www.history.army.mil/html/books/001/1-1/CMH_Pub_1-1.pdf (accessed 14 December 2014).
53. See chapter 18, "Bases in South America and the Caribbean Area, Including Bermuda", *Building the Navy's Bases in World War II: History of the Bureau of Yards and Docks and the Civil Engineering Corps 1940–1946*, vol. 3, pt. 3

(Washington, DC: Government Printing Office), http://www.ibiblio.org/hyperwar/USN/Building_Bases (accessed 18 November 2014).

54. O. Nigel Boland, "Systems of Domination After Slavery: The Control of Land and Labour in the British West Indies After 1838", *Comparative Studies in Society and History* 23, no. 4 (October 1981): 591–619.

9.

BODY POLITICS OF PUERTO RICAN PARTICIPATION IN THE US MILITARY DURING WORLD WAR II

DANNELLE GUTARRA

Una tarde me fui
hacia extraña nación
pues lo quiso el destino
pero mi corazón se quedó frente al mar
en mi Viejo San Juan.
—"En mi Viejo San Juan", Noel Estrada[1]

The song "En mi Viejo San Juan" is one of a few songs that have become anthems of Puerto Rican identity. This song, written by Noel Estrada, a Puerto Rican World War II veteran, encapsulates the perpetual feeling of attachment and longing that is constantly referenced in Puerto Rican culture. Its narrative centres on a Puerto Rican young man who is forced to leave the island because of compulsory recruitment to war. At the beginning of the song, the future soldier sings farewell to his hometown, Old San Juan, promising to return. The ending elucidates that the man was unable ever to go back and that the aged man painfully yearns to return to "where he had left his heart"; he is "drafted" once again, but this time, by death.

Today "En mi Viejo San Juan" is typically sung in harmony during informal gatherings of Puerto Rican acquaintances and families. Whether in the island or in the diaspora, the collective celebration of this song tends to be a cathartic instant of cultural nationalism. If in the diaspora, the group identifies with the chronicle of an excruciating yearning for return. Nevertheless, the reaction tends to be just as or even more emotional when performed on the island; the teary-eyed members of that group either terribly miss a loved one who has left, fear having to depart the island, interpret the song as a consecration of cultural nationalism or, most frequently, are concerned for the future and the quality of life in their beloved Caribbean island. This Puerto Rican anthem about a draft to World War II encompasses the psychological impact of involuntary military service in the United States territory's popular culture. The lyrics seem to hit an emotive spot because they address the reception of the "involuntary" in the history of United States intervention in Puerto Rico.

This chapter intends to capture the reaction of Puerto Rican veterans of the body politics exercised during their participation in the United States military during World War II; that is to say, special attention will be paid to policies concerning the structures of power intended to regulate colonized bodies. This study is largely based on oral-history reports available in the Veterans History Project Archive at the Library of Congress and the VOCES Oral History Project Archive of the University of Texas at Austin, paying close attention to how the participants conceived their role in the war and the idea of national territoriality. This investigation also explores the paradigms of racial segregation and human experimentation in the United States military during World War II, while also deconstructing implemented politics according to race and primary language. This research project aims to identify the discourses of race and colonial subordination that were part of this microcosm in order to contextualize these discursive paradigms with body politics in contemporary Puerto Rico and within the diaspora in the United States.

THE PRELUDE TO THE WAR

In the book *Empire in World History: Power and the Politics of Difference*, Jane Burbank and Frederick Cooper state that the "concept of empire presumes that different peoples within the polity will be governed differently".[2] According to the authors, empires are sustained by the intrinsic element of their "politics of difference"; politics of difference are imposed through a premeditated racialization of colonial hierarchies. Most empires of the nineteenth and twentieth centuries benefited from racialized differences, since they justified their policies in terms of wealth distribution and military recruitment. In this sense, it was of vital importance for imperial powers to promote "loyalty" from colonial subjects, even though this conviction would be representative of metropolitan sovereignty and not of "likeness". Politics of difference were fundamental not only for colonial exploitation but for the international projection of the progression of the empire and its power. The authors point to the United States as a peculiar example of imperialism, since even though its political history was distinguished by a rapid and bellicose acquisition of territories, the nation aimed to avoid the perception of itself as an imperial power with colonies.[3]

Nonetheless, the United States had indeed extended its power overseas at the end of the nineteenth century and intervened in the Caribbean throughout the twentieth century. Before the invasion of Puerto Rico as part of the Spanish-American War in 1898, the United States had already nurtured an economic dependency in the Spanish colony, to the extent that many Puerto Rican colonial subjects, whether in resistance or in subordination, regarded both Spain and the United States as "sources of authority and power".[4] After the 1898 invasion, a short-lived military government was imposed until the 1900 Foraker Act granted a civilian government, with its governor being selected by the president of the United States and initiating a lengthy history of political ambiguity in Puerto Rico as an unincorporated territory. During the early twentieth century, politics of cultural assimilation were enforced by colonial authorities, such as the imposition of English as the language of public education, indoctrination of American heroes and tales and the ban of Puerto Rican nationalist symbols.[5] These experiments failed miserably, as the colonial population persisted at that time in the defence of the Spanish language and Puerto Rican hybrid customs as unalterable components of national identity.

In 1917 the Jones Act was implemented, providing the Puerto Rican population with United States citizenship; the "most palpable significance of their newfound citizenship" would be the immediate eligibility for obligatory military service in World War I.[6] Tens of thousands of Puerto Rican men emerging from impoverished populations fought during World War I, despite the lack of voting representation in the political arena of the United

States. The first four decades of the twentieth century represented a time of economic hardship and hunger in Puerto Rico; the financial limitations imposed by the Foraker Act, the deterioration of the coffee industry, the elevated levels of anaemia and the impact of destructive hurricanes (San Felipe in 1928 and San Ciprián in 1932) aggravated the severe effects of the Great Depression in the island. Nevertheless, during most of the twentieth century the metropolitan and colonial governments would repeatedly concede absolute blame to "overpopulation" in Puerto Rico and deviate attention from the imperialistic intervention of the United States.[7]

The primary sources evaluated in this study evidence the multiplicity of circumstances in the lives of future Puerto Rican veterans of the United States military during the prelude of World War II, whether residing in the island or in the diaspora. Nonetheless, what these oral histories have in common is the profound effect of the historical juncture of the Great Depression in their quality of life. Juan Báez described his youth in Ciales, Puerto Rico, as one marked by extreme poverty; he further said that his family's overwhelming economic situation negatively affected his academic performance in a public high school.[8] Meanwhile, Octavio Negrón spoke about feeling compelled to leave elementary school after the fourth grade to contribute economically to his family as a sugar-cane field worker, labouring from seven in the morning until eight at night. The veteran communicated that his constant concern for survival was only alleviated by Puerto Rican traditional celebrations.[9] Joaquín Santiago's tale is comparable in the manner that he felt forced to leave school after the seventh grade owing to the economic circumstances of his family, but his desolation was lessened by his fond reminiscences of Puerto Rican Catholic culture, the fantasies of the celebrations of Three Kings' Day, and the protection received from his parents during the devastating hurricanes of the historical juncture of the Great Depression.[10] José Blas García also saw Puerto Rican festivities as a symbolic refuge while residing in poor conditions without access to electricity or clean water.[11]

On the other hand, other oral histories of the prelude to World War II would be narratives of mobility and adscription to the emerging Puerto Rican diaspora in the United States. Fernando Pagán explained how, after a childhood handling temporary jobs in order to survive, he relocated to New York City to work as part of the Civilian Conservation Corps, where he recognized only one other Latino with whom he could speak in Spanish.[12] Félix López, another immigrant, described how his family lost their home in the 1928 hurricane, and after their matriarch became ill, moved to Connecticut, where the future soldier would be the only Latino student in his school. Another future Puerto Rican veteran, Luis Ramírez, left Lajas, Puerto Rico, indefinitely when he travelled to New York City in his early thirties to obtain proper health care for malaria.[13]

The grant of United States citizenship in the 1917 Jones Act did not only impose the duty of military draft, but also ignited the peculiar transnational history of Puerto Ricans, since it guaranteed mobility into the United States without the requirement to apply for a visa, generating a "nation of commuters".[14] According to Jorge Duany, Puerto Rican transnational history is distinguished by "circular migration" and "functional bilingualism" in order to maintain communication between Puerto Rican residents and the diaspora.[15] Transnationalism and political ambiguity cultivate the complexity and the multiplicity of symbolic definitions of the "Puerto Rican Nation".[16]

Several of the oral histories of Puerto Rican veterans of World War II highlight the problematic race relations in the diaspora. Raúl Ríos emphasized racial tensions among "minorities" in New York City. "As kids, we'd fight with the blacks, fight with the Italians. Some were friends, but it didn't matter when you go to different areas. It was about territories and cliques."[17] Ríos had relocated with his brothers and sisters to Spanish Harlem at the age of fourteen, only to find a microcosm disturbed by racial rival gang confrontations, one of which left him injured. Meanwhile, Higinio Albelo narrated how he travelled to New York City because he wanted to experience what was outside of the confines of his small farm in Aguadilla, Puerto Rico. "I had an ambition to see the world."[18] What he found was very distant from what he envisioned: a New York City visibly affected by the Great Depression and racial divide. Albelo remembered feeling constrained by his inability to locate a job because of mass unemployment and racial discrimination towards non-white populations. Frank Bonilla, born and raised in East Harlem, identified racism in the New York City instruction system. "We had very good teachers, but they were in many ways racist."[19] Santos Deliz recounted how he and his siblings were sent to an orphanage in Staten Island after their mother's passing; his father, who had earned a law degree from Cornell University, battled in court for their custody for two years. Nevertheless, it would be four years after their mother's death until the family would be reunited, only to be plummeted into the bleak reality of the Great Depression.[20] The reactions of future Puerto Rican soldiers, whether from the island or the diaspora, to instances of racial discrimination in the United States military would inevitably be part of a lengthier narrative of exposure to racism and colonial desolation.

The advent of diasporic communities in the history of the United States had not engendered a correlation between the monetary benefits of their labour and the tolerance towards their cultural singularities.[21] Definitions of race and ethnicity in the United States have been distinguished by a "virtual obsession with hyphenated identity".[22] Hyphenation represents the linguistic concretization of politics of difference, establishing a simplistic hierarchy of Americanness. Interestingly enough, the Puerto Rican diaspora has not been attributed, nor has it claimed, a hyphenated identity. Nonetheless, the colonial politics of difference and their imbrications with the convenient racialization of Puerto Ricans were manifest during the debates that led to the creation of the Jones Act. "Their notions about the 'mongrel' Puerto Rican people, and the presumed incapacity for self-government that resulted from their racial deficits, were repeated ad nauseam throughout debates over Puerto Rico's status in relation to the United States."[23]

In *The Location of Culture*, Homi Bhabha argues that the dynamics of power in colonialism revolve around the concept of mimicry; this mimesis could be described as a premeditated cultural assimilation that simultaneously perpetuates an inescapable difference. In the case of Puerto Ricans, one of the marks of inadequacy would be the signifier of poverty as an emblematic trait, not of colonialism but of cultural inferiority.[24] Furthermore, Puerto Rican residents and members of the diaspora were projected as a "dependent" community, fusing the stigma of poverty with a reputation of "welfare dependency".[25] United States citizenship then became, instead of a birthright, a crucial foundation of the racialization of Puerto Ricans.

Before World War II, Puerto Ricans were seldom depicted in Hollywood films and cultural production, producing generalized ignorance about the idiosyncrasies of the population in the United States territory and the members of a growing diasporic community.[26] Nevertheless, twentieth-century journalism and mass media in the United States subscribed to an aggressive agenda to racialize poverty and its arbitrary signifiers, portraying African Americans, Puerto Ricans and other "minorities" as inclined towards criminal activity, drug addiction, low academic performance and sexual precociousness.²⁷ This racializing enterprise was conflictive with definitions of race in Puerto Rico and the "internal cleavages" of national identity.²⁸ As in other Caribbean regions, and contrary to the "one-drop rule" in the United States, designations of race in Puerto Rico presented a varied gradation of colour, having *trigueño/a* as one of the most-named intermediary degrees between the extremes of the racial spectrum, without diminishing the generalized recognition of an Afro-Caribbean identity.²⁹

The racialization of Puerto Ricans evolved as one in which colour did not occupy a dominant position, since the racial category had to fit the variety of phenotypes of this "mixed community", according to arbitrary eighteenth- and nineteenth-century pseudoscientific theories that generated the modern constructions of race. The diversity of colour did not represent an obstacle to establishing phenotypical traits with which to recognize a distinct racialized "other", particularly the celebration of Puerto Rican culture, the employment of Spanish, the usage of two last names, and, more importantly, the accent that is connoted in the racial slur "spik".³⁰ These attributes were conceived as signifiers of indolence, ignorance and intrinsic violence, making it impossible for the United States consciousness to envisage Puerto Ricans as authentic "American citizens".

The racialist currents of geographical and biological determinism influenced the racialization of Puerto Ricans. Geographical determinism proposes an inexorable connection between climates and "progress", typically depicting human groups from hotter climates as lethargic and, in consequence, retrograde; meanwhile, certain pseudoscientific theories of biological determinism, popularized by Arthur de Gobineau, depict miscegenation as a degenerative phenomenon.³¹ These racialist theories justified colonial subordination of "frozen-in-time" territories, however abstruse the degree of interventionism could be. In accordance with the ambiguity of the political status of the island, the relations between the United States and the racialized colonial subjects were ambiguous in multiple negotiations of power, the best example being in the sphere of military service. "Puerto Ricans have fought and died in all the wars the Americans have fought during this century. When it comes to wars, the United States has been ready to recognize Puerto Ricans as full U.S. citizens and to recruit them for military service."³²

The oral histories of the prelude to World War II are marked by destitution, migration and discrimination. Puerto Rico is portrayed as a space heavily affected by the Great Depression and by two major hurricanes; the testimonies contextualize Puerto Rican traditions as escapism from the constraints of poverty. Nonetheless, the structures of power and racial constructions attributed economic conflicts in the island to overpopulation and "intrinsic flaws" of Puerto Ricans. Simultaneously, the diaspora was met with prejudice and scarce opportunities for economic mobility. The prelude to the war is part of the historical juncture of the imperial history of the United States in which there is intensification in the racialization of Puerto Ricans. The politics of difference constantly fluctuate in diverse contexts, and Puerto Ricans gain some Americanness when their military service is needed. The oral histories of Puerto Rican veterans are replete with the lived experiences of war and how they were distinguished by complex colonial relations.

RECRUITMENT OF PUERTO RICAN BODIES

World War II testimonies of Puerto Rican soldiers are diverse in the representation of violence, trauma, racial relations and military ethic. Of the approximately sixty-five thousand Puerto Ricans who were sent to war, many were forced into military service because of the colonial condition, while others volunteered to be a part of it. Juan Báez willingly enlisted in the army as a way to escape from the economic struggles of the Caribbean island; his parents did not respond well to the news that their eighteen-year-old son was leaving Puerto Rico to go to war. "They didn't like it; they thought they were going to kill me."[33] Meanwhile, Juan Medina-Negrón voluntarily put his college education on hold to support the war cause.[34] On the other hand, Fernando Pagán worked at a restaurant in New York City when he heard the news about Pearl Harbor; one year later, he was drafted. "They sent me a token . . . for the subway."[35] Higinio Albelo had recently found a job at a plant that manufactured warplanes in New York City when he was drafted into the military, just nine months after his first child had been born.[36] Likewise, Luis Ramírez and Santos Deliz were drafted into the military within a year of labouring in factories.[37] Frank Bonilla was forced to delay his plans for an academic career, since he was drafted two weeks after his high-school graduation; nonetheless, he contended in his interview that he believed in the war cause and that it was his obligation to serve.[38]

Several testimonies expose tensions and pressures in the process of voluntary enlistment. Joaquín Santiago was battling economic limitations in Puerto Rico when he volunteered to assist in the war; since he was a minor, his father signed his papers.[39] Octavio Negrón declared he enlisted when he was eighteen years old because of the anxieties of Puerto Rican "machismo"; volunteering meant proving his male pride.[40] Raúl Ríos narrated how, after willingly enlisting in war efforts, he attempted to console some draftees who were acutely terrified, wetting their beds and pretending to be inept in order to avoid the war.[41] Fernando Bernacett was homeless when he was picked up by the police and sent to work for the Civilian Conservation Corps; there he was persuaded by a military representative to enlist voluntarily, soon after turning eighteen.[42] Ramón Viera recalled how he lied about his age when he registered because he was unable to find work as a minor, but the army did not solicit any evidence; he also reminisced about how easy it was to pass his medical examination. "I was called for physical examination, and they took me in. I was only 109 pounds, one pound below the limit, which was 110 pounds. They said: we will not reject you because you are one pound short."[43] Various oral histories portray simple medical examinations and brief training periods after the draft or voluntary enlistment. These narratives provide evidence to support the belief that Puerto Ricans were thought to fit the mould of the "docile body".

Michel Foucault identifies the "docile body" of the soldier as the ideal paradigm of the power relations of modern society, replicating a "military dream".[44] This "docile body" is expected to be both forceful and obedient, providing its energy to the utility of the structures of power, which employ history to justify the conceptualization of power relations according to the idea of war, enabling a discursive war of races.[45] Modernity propels an escalation of racial tensions that climaxes in a philosophy of "counter-history", which distances itself from the conception of the homogeneity of the state, stressing its heterogeneity and the role of authority in perpetuating segregation.[46] According to the philosopher, modern discourses have openly displayed the adaptation of historical narratives into discursive weapons that are favoured in the political sphere. This discursive tactic incites in turn passionate clashes about nationalities, social classes, and races. Foucault ties the issue of race to his description of eighteenth-century biopower[47] and proposes that modernity intensifies the notion of the phenomenon of race as biological dissonance. He concludes that racism justifies the murderous politics of the state.[48]

The oral histories of Puerto Rican veterans give evidence that the colonial subjects were both promptly sent to war and expected to serve diligently. Their military service was a duty linked to the grant of United States citizenship, and their discipline would temporarily transform them into an ideal mimetic Other. Puerto Ricans were either required or incited to put their lives in peril for a military cause of the United States. Even though the term *patria* in Puerto Rican culture is a dense signifier of a declaration of love towards the Caribbean island, there are instances of ambivalent patriotism in some of the testimonies. Carmen Contreras, a former payroll clerk in the War Department in Washington, DC, referred to patriotism as one of the motives to enlist voluntarily in the Women's Army Auxiliary Corps.[49] Similarly, Ismael Nevárez declared, "Everybody has to realize that we live in a country that needs to protect itself, and you should honor your country no matter where you are."[50] Both examples exude patriotic sentiment towards an equivocal definition of "nation". On the other hand, Frank Bonilla, a New York City native, alleged that his participation in the military made him embrace a Puerto Rican identity: "The military experience helped to consolidate my sense of being Puerto Rican and also a sense of wanting to study and be a scholar."[51] Meanwhile, Juan Báez claimed military experiences benefited his sense of self-worth as a Puerto Rican. "We were able to know that we were also soldiers."[52] The testimonies substantiate a convoluted usage of the word "country"; this usage is inexorably tied to the political ambiguity in US interventionism, but it is also due to the cultural obfuscation with representation in Puerto Rican colonial history.

THE LIVED EXPERIENCES OF WAR AND DISCOMFORT

The veterans' narratives of war emphasized accounts of brotherhood and episodes of horror, injustice and discrimination. Justo Pérez had some pleasant memories of folk music and dancing among his fellow soldiers,[53] while Arnold Feliú took many photographs and collected much memorabilia in order to capture his military experiences for his family.[54] Santos Deliz recalled an incident while working as a kitchen hand under the supervision of General George S. Patton in Africa in 1943: "He scolded me because I had rations over the amount I should've had. The rations were food the GIs didn't want, so instead of dumping it, I sometimes gave it to the people who were around there."⁵⁵ José Blas García never forgot how a wounded Puerto Rican pilot struggled in agony to request that a Puerto Rican flag be painted on a future military aircraft.⁵⁶ Ismael Nevárez remembered how he had been training to collect lifeless bodies when news of the detonation of the atomic bombs in Hiroshima and Nagasaki abruptly altered the plans; now, instead of collecting bodies, his troops were expected to accumulate supplies in what was now a barren territory: "Okinawa was all destroyed. Not a single tree was left standing."⁵⁷ Nevárez was shocked by the obliteration he saw when he arrived. "The shores were still smoking."⁵⁸

Some testimonies focused on emotional responses to military experiences. For example, Octavio Negrón was sent with the 65th Infantry to Germany for ten months; in his testimony, the veteran expressed his disillusionment when the few letters he wrote to his family were censored because of institutional fear of release of confidential information. He also opened up about the collective anxieties of his infantry during his stay in Germany, particularly the generalized apprehension of being accidentally assassinated by a fellow soldier; he mentioned losing two war friends this way. Lastly, the former soldier recalled feeling ill throughout his twelve-month stay in France but was told that his condition was due to his emotions. "They told me that I wasn't sick, but scared."⁵⁹ Another member of the 65th Infantry, Juan Báez, also spoke of his emotional reactions to military landscapes. "It was incredible, what I saw. The death . . . those who were killed . . . those who killed."⁶⁰ Báez depicted his military incidents as traumatic: "I don't want to remember."⁶¹ Analogously, Fernando Pagán vividly evoked the compelling images he witnessed when he reached Normandy four days after D-Day. "I saw dead paratroopers dangling from the trees. I saw mutilated corpses. . . . They didn't have time to take them away."⁶² Whether their participation in World War II was voluntary or involuntary, the oral histories of Puerto Rican veterans stress the physical and emotional discomforts of war, portraying their experiences as traumatic and feeling compelled to address whether their colonized bodies were serving their "nation" or not.

Luis Ramírez described how his regiment developed a brotherhood and how their stories and internal jokes helped to alleviate the physical discomforts of war. "Those guys are like my brothers; they worry about me, and I worry about them."⁶³ This brotherhood was fundamental for Ramírez to maintain his composure in the grotesque scenes of D-Day in Normandy and

Figure 9.1. Soldiers of the 65th Infantry after an all-day schedule of manoeuvres at Salinas, Puerto Rico, August 1941. (https://commons.wikimedia.org/wiki/File:Soldiers_of_65th_Infantry_after_an_all_day_schedule_of_maneuvers_at_Salinas,_Puerto_Rico._August_1941.jpg.)

German concentration camps. "We saw people walking like skeletons; it made you sick."[64] Ramírez's testimony provides insight into how he confronted the psychological toll of the imagery of war: "I saw people dead on a beach in Normandy. I couldn't believe it. That affects you a lot, but then you keep going. You forget, and you get used to everything that happens to you in life. Sometimes I remember things so vividly; sometimes I get tears in my eyes. . . . I go easy in life; that is the way I live."[65]

Félix López-Santos also recalled censorship of letters, but he concluded that war happenings were mostly incomprehensible and incommunicable. "People in the United States and here in Puerto Rico don't know what a war is."[66] López-Santos himself had great difficulty in verbalizing sights of the Holocaust. The former soldier noted the "stench of death" that pervaded the European theatres in which he was stationed;⁶⁷ he also underlined the sense of disorientation that permeated his military experiences. "There weren't any newspapers or other media outlets to find about what was happening around us."⁶⁸ The veteran Ramón Viera summarized his reaction to the bloody scenes he witnessed by proclaiming, "I continued living, you know."⁶⁹ The testimonies from Puerto Rican veterans elucidate the substantial toll military experiences in World War II took on the psyche of the young combatants. Many of these witnesses emphasized the Holocaust and D-Day as particularly upsetting events; the oral narratives insinuate trauma with the unintelligibility of military landscapes.

It has been documented that Puerto Rican soldiers were subjected to racial discrimination and human experimentation in the historical context of World War II. During the two world wars, the United States army imposed a "one-drop rule" system of racial segregation.⁷⁰ This system arbitrarily divided Latino soldiers by colour, assigning at times Latinos who identified themselves as Afro-Latin to all-white military units.⁷¹ The 65th Infantry, which served in multiple theatres of World War II (particularly Panama, Casablanca and France), stands out as an all-Hispanic unit amid the complexity of partitions that makes it very challenging to attain proper statistics about Latino participation during the two world wars.⁷² On the other hand, the San José Project (1943–47) on the island of San José in the Panama base was centred on the inadvertent exposure of mostly Puerto Rican soldiers to mustard gas and other toxic substances to determine the efficacy of masks and ointments, while also exploring whether Puerto Ricans, as a "mixed" population, reacted differently to mustard gas.⁷³ San José Island had become, in the words of the *Chemical Warfare Bulletin*, a "test tube island".⁷⁴ This project is part of a disconcerting narrative of human experimentation on Puerto Rican bodies that has included interaction with cancer cells, radiation and hormones.

The oral narratives of Puerto Rican veterans present dissimilar experiences of racial segregation and discrimination in the United States military during World War II. Raúl Ríos witnessed discrimination and harsher treatment, particularly from the drill instructors, towards both Latino and African American soldiers; the former combatant articulated his resentment towards discrimination in the military: "We were all soldiers; we were all risking our lives for the United States. That should have never been done. Never."⁷⁵ Joaquín Santiago, for his part, alleged not having being subjected to any discrimination at all. "We shared in all our missions and diversions like good brothers."[76] Félix López-Santos contended that he witnessed racial discrimination towards African Americans, but not against himself because of his "whiter" skin and blue eyes.[77] Gonzalo Villanueva recollected his military stay in Panama and how there were quarrels and friction between Puerto Rican soldiers and the commanders, which would result in severe punishments for Puerto Rican combatants. "Whoever got in a fight, they would only give them bread and water for some days, until they calmed down."[78] The collection of evaluated primary sources presents the paradigm of instances of either racial discrimination or an apologetic view of racism when compared to other environments at the time.

Higinio Albelo deemed his treatment in the United States military more favourable than the relentless racial discrimination he experienced while trying to gain employment in New York City, but he did mention that he was teased because of his native language. "Everything was fine, only sometimes they would criticize me for my accent."[79] On the contrary, Angel Velázquez remembered how he was bestowed with multiple advantages because of his fluency in English, saying, "The colonel would give me special passes to go to Panama City because I was teaching classes."[80] José Blas García vented the frustration of how, in situations of tension, he had to utilize body language to communicate with his superiors, since he did not speak English and they did not speak Spanish.[81] Comparably, Fernando Bernacett felt alienated because of his status as a Spanish speaker: "I had to take my training by guessing because I didn't speak well enough. I never knew one guy in the Marine Corps who spoke Spanish."[82] The war narratives of these soldiers persistently verify the existence of military hierarchies based on accent or language proficiency.

On the other hand, Frank Bonilla, who was born and raised in the diaspora, felt hostility from his Puerto Rican peers, since he was not deemed a "pure Puerto Rican". "We were American G.I. Joes to them and not Puerto Ricans," he said.[83] This conflict arose from disagreeing visions of nationality. The American construction of nationality or ethnicity emphasizes ancestry, which lays the foundation for the phenomenon of hyphenation in the United States, while the Puerto Rican notion of nationality emphasizes the amount of time of residence in the island and public expressions of culture and patriotic affection. This phenomenon, due mainly to the construction of Puerto Rico as a "cultural nation" in response to the vague political status, is exemplified with expressions by Puerto Rican media of "adoption as Puerto Rican" of artists who immigrated to Puerto Rico during adulthood but dedicated the majority of their lives to producing art in the island and about the island. In his testimony, Bonilla's own interpretation of this is that not only was there a divide between native Puerto Ricans and members of the diaspora but that army efforts were driven by a transnational identity. "The soldiers in the regiment, although proud to be U.S. citizens, felt that they were a Puerto Rican army, not a U.S. army."[84] This statement once more reinforces the conception of military efforts being performed for the "Puerto Rican nation".

The reception of racial discrimination in the United States military was diverse: some recalled and resented instances of discrimination, others denied it, and a few minimized it. Multiple accounts referred to discrimination because of primary language, accepting that being bilingual provided privilege while having an accent or speaking only Spanish generated hostility and alienation. Lastly, some testimonies alluded to antagonism from higher military ranks and disquiets generated by incompatible ideas of Puerto Rican identity between natives and members of the diaspora.

Multiple veterans, including Joaquín Santiago, joyfully evoked the post-war welcome to Puerto Rican soldiers in the island. "We returned to Puerto Rico with a warm welcome from the Puerto Rican government. At that time, we were the heroes of the Infantry," said Santiago.[85] Many soldiers, including both José Blas García and Fernando Pagán, returned to Puerto Rico after the war to find the country dramatically transformed because of the modernization politics of Operation Bootstrap (1948). This enterprise, led by the soon-to-be first governor of Puerto Rico elected by Puerto Ricans, Luis Muñoz Marín, initiated the conversion of Puerto Rico to an industrialized "island of cement" by granting incentives for investments from United States companies.[86] Meanwhile, Ángel Velázquez relocated to Puerto Rico and earned a bachelor's degree from the University of Puerto Rico, after which he worked for the Puerto Rican government for thirty-three years.[87] Frank Bonilla said that his military experiences propelled him to cultivate his prolific academic career at the Massachusetts Institute of Technology and Stanford University.[88] In his turn, Fernando Bernacett went from being a vagabond before World War II to being "thrown into the streets" once again, after the war. "I didn't appreciate being dumped with nothing in San Diego. The least they should have done was give us a few bucks and send us back to where we came from to find a relative or something."[89]

Some Puerto Rican veterans, with no other options, re-enlisted in the military to fight in the Korean War. Ramón Viera argued that he took that difficult decision because of an apparent non-existence of alternatives. "My economic situation was really bad."[90] On the other hand, Luis Ramírez happily continued his military career until he was discharged in 1963; afterwards he always encouraged military enlistment, even unsuccessfully trying to persuade his granddaughter to join.[91] Meanwhile, other veterans vehemently resisted going back to war. In his testimony, Gonzalo Villanueva joked about never leaving Arecibo again until his death and also professed his affection towards his country when he narrated his homecoming. "I remember when I arrived in San Juan. When I put a foot on my land, the first thing I did was to kiss it."[92] Nevertheless, patriotism was not the only motive behind Villanueva's decision; fear played a leading part as well. "Many went again, and many didn't come back."[93]

During the historical juncture of World War II, Puerto Rican popular music encapsulated the complex notions of war and country in the island. The most memorable Puerto Rican song to allude to World War II, besides "En mi Viejo San Juan", has to be "Despedida", written by famed composer Pedro Flores. It was popularized by the impassioned interpretation of World War II draftee and Puerto Rican nationalist Daniel Santos. The song starts by establishing that the male protagonist is departing Puerto Rico to serve in the military.

> Vengo a decirle adiós a los muchachos
> porque pronto me voy para la guerra
> y, aunque vaya a pelear en otras tierras,
> voy a salvar mi derecho, mi patria y mi fe.[94]

The soldier alleges that, even though the war would advance in "other lands", he would be protecting his "country"; just as in testimonies from the veterans, this popular song presents a problematic denotation of the word *patria*. The rest of the song intends to be compelling by elaborating on the soldier's unease on leaving his mother:

Sólo me parte el alma y me condena
Que dejo tan solita a mi mamá,
Mi pobre madrecita que es tan vieja.
¿Quién en mi ausencia la recordará?
¿Quién me le hará un favor si necesita?
¿Quién le hablará de mí si preguntara
Por este hijo que nunca quizás volverá?
¿Quién me le rezará si ella se muere?
¿Quién pondrá una flor en su sepultura?
¿Quién se condolerá de mi amargura
Si yo vuelvo y no encuentro a mi mamá?[95]

Both "En mi Viejo San Juan" and "Despedida" portray leaving Puerto Rico as a highly distressing event; in the case of "Despedida", the potent narrative intertwines patriotic nostalgia with the dread of perpetually losing maternal love.

CONCLUSION

The oral histories of Puerto Rican participation in the US military during World War II present nuances in both reception and storytelling. While some of the testimonies distil military pride, others insist on the psychological impact of war. Nonetheless, some paradigms are identified. For example, the narratives emphasize the matter of privation of options, whether the enlistment was voluntary or not. The Caribbean space is depicted as one marked by extreme poverty and climatological unrest that is tolerated because of idiosyncratic commemorations. Meanwhile, the diasporic reality in the US Northeast is portrayed as detrimental because of discrimination against "people of color". Soldiers who were drafted stressed the involuntary aspect of their enlistment, referring also to the inappropriate timing of the summons, since they had struggled to finally attain a source of income, or they had recently started a family. On the other hand, the majority of the veterans who voluntarily enlisted highlighted the fact that they believed military service was the only alternative. Therefore, most oral histories underlined the "involuntary" elements of Puerto Rican participation in the United States military. Many testimonies also alleged expedited enlistment that defied regulations and improper treatment of diseases and physical discomfort that emerged in the field of war.

The reception of racial discrimination was quite varied. Testimonies elucidated instances of discrimination because of colour and primary language. While some narratives accentuated the resentment towards the injustice of racial discrimination, others either negated it or underestimated it, owing to conformity or in comparison to prejudice within the diaspora of the US Northeast. Several former soldiers articulated a sense of dislocation and peril because of not being able to communicate with the chain of command. While being bilingual was believed to be functional and even amusing, to be solely a Spanish speaker was a sign of disparity and inferiority, reflecting race relations in the twentieth-century United States. Racial tensions in the oral histories of Puerto Rican veterans were not limited to discrimination from the military structure of power but also projected problematic race relations among "minorities" in New York City and dissimilar constructions of identity between Puerto Rican natives and members of the diaspora.

Most testimonies intertwined the historical account with the respective emotional responses to the experiences of war. The oral histories evoked moments of paralysing fear in the storytellers or Puerto Rican peers. The content indicates that multiple war experiences were traumatic, since the veterans did not fully describe what they observed but instead portrayed these happenings as emotional blows with an overwhelming psychological effect. In the context of World War II, the Puerto Rican witnesses distinguished D-Day in Normandy and the Holocaust as unrepeatable and unintelligible historical events. On the other hand, the oral histories of Puerto Ricans also depicted separation from the island and from the opportunity to speak Spanish as cultural anguish; narratives of return migration, or the impossibility of deviating from the diaspora after the war, presented cathartic and emotional imagery in a manner analogous to Puerto Rican popular music of this historical juncture.

The displays of patriotic sentiment in the testimonies alluded to conflicting definitions of nation and frontier. On the one hand, some of the veterans verbalized the longing for Puerto Rico during their service in war. Simultaneously, several former soldiers praised the significance of "fighting for your country", when in reality they were aiding the United States military; this becomes even more problematic when considering that throughout the twentieth century the term *afuera* (outside) became a synonym of the United

States in the Puerto Rican context. This catachresis is evidently tied to the ambiguity in political relations between Puerto Rico and the United States; on the other hand, it discovers new definitions of frontier in the historical juncture of the dawn of Puerto Rican transnational identity. The psychological elements of this trope can be clarified by looking at the impact of the history of lack of political representation of Puerto Rico; some testimonies argued that the military experience offered a sense of self-worth and pride because, in the perspective of the veterans, they were being projected as deserving of the rank of soldier. Just as citizenship became, instead of a right, a burden that hindered Puerto Rican reputation throughout the world, various former soldiers conveniently constructed military service as a privilege instead of a duty, promoting thus their loyalty towards the United States. The testimonies not only cast a light on the reception of military experiences but can also insinuate an exposure to discourses of the structures of power. It could seem that military ethic and an appreciation of belonging to a "Puerto Rican army" could rationalize the narrative of the "involuntary" in order to become "imperial docile bodies", both disciplined and useful.

Resistance to cultural assimilation was conceived as an integral defect of the Puerto Rican population; this cultural specificity made Puerto Ricans unfit to be a colonized mimetic Other. At the same time, the arbitrary quality of Puerto Ricans as a "mixed" population was based on modern racialist theories; by being marked with the stigma of miscegenation, the Puerto Rican population was constructed as a backward and degenerative group. This discourse justified the politics of difference that categorically discarded Puerto Ricans as unquestionably un-American. Nonetheless, the politics of difference oscillated when military service was needed. Puerto Rican participation in the United States military during World War II is part of the historical juncture of the emergence and expansion of its diasporic community in the United States; it is also the era of the escalation of the racialization of Puerto Ricans.

The colonial condition of Puerto Rico and its diaspora was widely portrayed as an incomparable advantage of the colonial population, even being depicted as a "near-celestial privilege" by pan-Africanist historian C.L.R. James.[96] Puerto Rican economic conflicts then seemed to be due to a pathology that inhibited progress on the island and justified United States interventionism. This global representation of Puerto Rican actuality enabled a fluid racialization of the colonized, a racialization that was at the same time fuelled by the historical processes of the prolonged continuation of limitations to the citizenship of "people of colour" after a chaotic emancipation process in the United States. Puerto Ricans were one more population affected by the racialization of poverty in the twentieth century. At the same time, cultural resistance, the Puerto Rican accent and insistent usage of Spanish as primary language were considered confirmations of inadequacy.

The racialized Puerto Rican body was deemed ideal for projects of human experimentation during the twentieth century, since it could deliver data on the "effects of miscegenation". The historical juncture of World War II corroborated the climax of modernity, in which the body of the soldier increasingly structured the archetype model of a society distributed by a racial hierarchy. As such, the body politics of Puerto Rican participation in the United States military during World War II encapsulate the discursive paradigms of body politics of the Puerto Rican colonial actuality and the diaspora in the United States at the time. Imperialistic agency constructed Puerto Ricans as the racialized/colonized who could automatically serve the United States as "docile bodies". Military ethic would then stabilize apparent contradictions of colonial relations. The Puerto Rican body would be expected to direct emotional energy to compliance with the regime of the involuntary. Just as with colonial relations between Puerto Rico and the United States, the failure of colonial subjects to assimilate American culture would serve as sufficient validation to enhance isolation and disoriented subordination. When Puerto Rican bodies failed to fulfil the expectations of military docility and colonial obedience, they would then be disciplined with a regimen of bread and water for a couple of days until it was determined that they had calmed down.

NOTES

1. Gary Morales, "History of Puerto Rican Music", in *Puerto Rico Encyclopedia* (San Juan: Fundación Puertorriqueña de las Humanidades, 2014). "I left one afternoon / to a strange nation / because destiny wanted so / but my heart/ stayed by the sea / in my Old San Juan" (translated by author).
2. Jane Burbank and Frederick Cooper, *Empire in World History: Power and the Politics of Difference* (Princeton, NJ: Princeton University Press, 2010), 8.

3. Ibid., 6.
4. Astrid Cubano-Iguina, "Visions of Empire and Historical Imagination in Puerto Rico under Spanish Rule, 1870–1898", in *Interpreting Spanish Colonialism: Empires, Nations, and Legends*, ed. Christopher Schmidt-Nowara and John M. Nieto-Phillips (Albuquerque: University of New Mexico Press, 2005), 89.
5. Ramón Grosfoguel, Frances Negrón-Muntaner and Chloé S. Georas, "Beyond Nationalist and Colonialist Discourses: The Jaiba Politics of the Puerto Rican Ethno-Nation", in *Puerto Rican Jam: Rethinking Colonialism and Nationalism*, ed. in Ramón Grosfoguel and Frances Negrón-Muntaner (Minneapolis: University of Minnesota Press, 1997), 11.
6. Nicholas de Genova and Ana Y. Ramos-Zayas, *Latino Crossings: Mexicans, Puerto Ricans, and the Politics of Race and Citizenship* (New York: Routledge, 2003), 8.
7. Carmen T. Whalen, "Colonialism, Citizenship, and the Making of the Puerto Rican Diaspora: An Introduction", in *The Puerto Rican Diaspora: Historical Perspectives*, ed. Carmen T. Whalen and Víctor Vázquez-Hernández (Philadelphia: Temple University Press, 2005), 17.
8. VOCES Oral History Project Archive, Benson Latin American Collection, University of Texas at Austin, folder 647 (hereafter VOCES).
9. Ibid., folder 397.
10. Ibid., folder 483.
11. Ibid., folder 256.
12. Ibid., folder 400.
13. Ibid., folder 405.
14. Elizabeth M. Aranda, *Emotional Bridges to Puerto Rico: Migration, Return Migration, and the Struggles of Incorporation* (Lanham: Rowman and Littlefield, 2006), 2.
15. Jorge Duany, *The Puerto Rican Nation on the Move: Identities on the Island and in the United States* (Chapel Hill: University of North Carolina Press, 2002), 213.
16. Grosfoguel, Negrón-Muntaner and Georas, "Beyond Nationalist and Colonialist Discourses", 15.
17. VOCES, folder 290.
18. Ibid., folder 232.
19. Ibid., folder 329.
20. Ibid., folder 26.
21. Leonard Dinnerstein and David M. Reimers, *Ethnic Americans: A History of Immigration* (New York: Columbia University Press, 2009), 2.
22. John D. Garrigus and Christopher Morris, *Assumed Identities: The Meanings of*

Race in the Atlantic World (Arlington: University of Texas at Arlington Press, 2010), 2.
23. Lorrin Thomas, *Puerto Rican Citizen: History and Political Identity in Twentieth-Century New York City* (Chicago: University of Chicago Press, 2010), 5.
24. Laura Briggs, *Reproducing Empire: Race, Sex, Science, and U.S. Imperialism in Puerto Rico* (Berkeley: University of California Press, 2002), 14.
25. Genova and Ramos-Zayas, *Latino Crossings*, 7.
26. José R. Sánchez, *Boricua Power: A Political History of Puerto Ricans in the United States* (New York: New York University Press, 2007), 89.
27. Louis Kushnick and James Jennings, *A New Introduction to Poverty: The Role of Race, Power and Politics* (New York: New York University Press, 1999), 2.
28. Eileen J. Suárez Findlay, *Imposing Decency: The Politics of Sexuality and Race in Puerto Rico, 1870–1920* (Durham: Duke University Press, 2000), 4.
29. Ileana M. Rodríguez-Silva, *Silencing Race: Disentangling Blackness, Colonialism, and National Identities in Puerto Rico* (New York: Palgrave Macmillan, 2012), 5.
30. Grosfoguel, Negrón-Muntaner and Georas, "Beyond Nationalist and Colonialist Discourses", 21.
31. Philip D. Curtin, *The Image of Africa: British Ideas and Action, 1780–1850* (Madison: University of Wisconsin Press, 1964).
32. Grosfoguel, Negrón-Muntaner and Georas, "Beyond Nationalist and Colonialist Discourses", 18.
33. VOCES, folder 647.
34. Ibid., folder 572.
35. Ibid., folder 400.
36. Ibid., folder 232.
37. Ibid., folders 405 and 26.
38. Ibid., folder 329.
39. Ibid., folder 483.
40. Ibid., folder 397.
41. Ibid., folder 290.
42. Ibid., folder 328.
43. Ramón Viera Collection, Veterans History Project (VHS), American Folklife Center, Library of Congress, AFC/2001/001/74655.
44. Michel Foucault, *Vigilar y castigar: Nacimiento de la prisión* (Buenos Aires: Siglo XXI, 1976), 173.
45. Michel Foucault, *Genealogía del racismo: La guerra de las razas al racismo del Estado* (Buenos Aires: Altamira, 1993), 65.
46. Ibid., 54.

47. Michel Foucault, *Historia de la sexualidad I: La voluntad del saber* (Buenos Aires: Siglo XXI, 2002), 168.
48. Foucault, *Genealogía del racismo*, 183.
49. VOCES, folder 237.
50. Ibid., folder 638.
51. Ibid., folder 329.
52. Ibid., folder 647.
53. VHS: Justo L. Pérez Collection, AFC/2001/001/14054.
54. VOCES, folder 622.
55. Ibid., folder 26.
56. Ibid., folder 256.
57. Ibid., folder 638.
58. Ibid.
59. Ibid., folder 397.
60. Ibid., folder 647.
61. Ibid.
62. Ibid., folder 400.
63. Ibid., folder 405.
64. Ibid.
65. Ibid.
66. Ibid., folder 272.
67. Ibid.
68. Ibid.
69. VHS: Ramón Viera Collection, AFC/2001/001/74655.
70. Patrick Manning, *The African Diaspora: A History Through Culture* (New York: Columbia University Press, 2009), 262.
71. Maggie Rivas-Rodríguez and B.V. Olguín, eds., *Latina/os and World War II: Mobility, Agency, and Ideology* (Austin: University of Texas Press, 2014).
72. Gilberto Villahermosa, *Honor and Fidelity: The 65th Infantry in Korea, 1950–1953* (Washington, DC: Center of Military History, 2009), 5.
73. John Lindsay-Poland, "U.S. Military Bases in Latin America and the Caribbean", in *The Bases of Empire: The Global Struggle against U.S. Military Posts*, ed. Catherine Lutz (New York: New York University Press, 2009), 75.
74. John Lindsay-Poland, *Emperors in the Jungle: The Hidden Story of the U.S. in Panama* (Durham: Duke University Press, 2003), 44.
75. VOCES, folder 290.
76. Ibid., folder 483.
77. Ibid., folder 272.
78. Ibid., folder 428.

79. Ibid., folder 232.
80. Ibid., folder 307.
81. Ibid., folder 256.
82. Ibid., folder 328.
83. Ibid., folder 329.
84. Ibid.
85. Ibid., folder 483.
86. Ibid., folders 256 and 400. Fernando Picó, *Historia general de Puerto Rico* (Río Piedras: Editorial Huracán, 2008).
87. VOCES, folder 307.
88. Ibid., folder 329.
89. Ibid., folder 328.
90. VHS: Ramón Viera Collection, AFC/2001/001/74655.
91. VOCES, folder 405.
92. Ibid., folder 428.
93. Ibid.
94. Morales, "History of Puerto Rican Music". "I come to say goodbye to my boys / because soon I leave for war / and, although I will fight in other lands, / I will save my right, my country, and my faith" (translated by author).
95. Ibid. "The only thing that breaks my soul and tortures me / is that I leave my mother so alone, / my poor mother who is so old. / Who will remember her in my absence? / Who will grant her favours if she needs them? / Who will speak of me if she asked / for this son who maybe will never return? / Who will pray for her if she dies? / Who will put a flower in her grave? / Who will condole with my grief / if I return, and I do not find my mother?" (translated by author).
96. C.L.R. James, *The Black Jacobins: Toussaint L'Ouverture and the San Domingo Revolution* (New York: Vintage Books, 1963), 409.

PART

3.

ENGAGEMENT AND DISPLACEMENT

10.

EUROPEAN REFUGEES IN THE WIDER CARIBBEAN IN THE CONTEXT OF WORLD WAR II

CHRISTIAN CWIK AND VERENA MUTH

"It was never migration, it was always flight."
—Adrienne Thomas (1897–1980), German writer[1]

To date, flight from war is one of the most important unsolved social problems of humanity. According to the United Nations high commissioner for refugees in 2015, nearly 51.2 million people are currently refugees around the globe, 16.7 million of them recognized as refugees, according to international law definitions. From the wars in Afghanistan, Syria and Somalia alone, 6 million people escaped to such neighbouring countries as Pakistan, Iran, Lebanon, Jordan and Turkey. Beside these numbers there are about 14 million internally displaced people from only three countries in 2015, Syria, Colombia and Sudan.[2] Those who suffer are primarily civilians – children, adolescents, women and men. Fifty per cent of them are minors.[3] They were robbed of their belongings, uprooted and their livelihoods destroyed. Involuntarily, refugees are thus responsible for the spread of local and regional wars on a global level, as the recent wave of refugees from the Middle East demonstrates. Consequently there are many similarities between the situation in the twenty-first century and World War II.

Estimates of the total number of refugees in the context of World War II range from 30 million[4] up to 50 to 60 million,[5] if one includes the millions of refugees after 1945. The majority of the refugees were victims of the Fascist governments of Germany, Austria, Italy and Spain, and more than a hundred countries all over the world became their places of exile. This makes World War II, hitherto not only the "greatest military conflict"[6] in human history on a global scale with the largest number of victims (estimates of total dead ranging from 50 million to more than 80 million[7] including the 12 to 14 million Holocaust victims[8]) but also a conflict that led to a mass exodus of people, which made the war a global issue on a social level.

If one looks closer at the period of World War II, it becomes clear that the mass exodus of European refugees, accepted as a component of war, started some years earlier than the official beginning of the combat operation on 1 September 1939 (the German occupation of Poland). The war in Spain (1936–39), the Anschluss of Austria as well as the occupation of parts of Czechoslovakia in 1938 and, in general, the early militarization and radicalization of the societies in many European countries provoked the flight of hundreds of thousands of persecuted citizens.[9] However, it is difficult (if not to say impossible) to draw a clear line between flight as an immediate consequence of World War I and flight on the eve of World War II. The situation is comparable to the time after the end of World War II, owing to the differences in the development of European countries and in particular of the Cold War.

This chapter will give an overview of the role of the Caribbean as a place of exile and a space of transit for European refugees fleeing from totalitarianism between 1933 and 1945. It will then examine the social profile and origins of the refugees as well as the manner of their escape from Europe to the Caribbean. It will draw special attention to "German" refugees for two reasons. First, the German Reich was the main motor behind the refugee crisis during World War II,[10] and second, because the "Germans" were one of the largest refugee groups to reach the Caribbean. In order to provide a better understanding of this refugee group, the chapter particularly explores the subgroup of the Austrians, who were (and sometimes still are) perceived and treated by the outside world as "Germans". As such they became subject to further persecution and repression in their Caribbean exile countries, until the governments gradually began to distinguish between the two groups.

THE CARIBBEAN AS A PLACE OF EXILE

The Caribbean served for numerous European refugees as a place of exile. Caribbean countries allowing a noteworthy number of Nazi refugees were Aruba, British Guiana (present-day Guyana), Cuba, Curaçao, the Dominican Republic, French Guiana, Haiti, Jamaica, Martinique, Suriname and Trinidad and Tobago. Other European colonies in the Caribbean such as Barbados, British Honduras (present-day Belize) on the Central American coast, the Bahamas and French Guiana admitted refugees as well, but only in small numbers.[11] With regard to Puerto Rico, the arrival of Jewish Nazi refugees is reported,[12] although neither an estimate of their number exists nor has any study been published that deals with this topic. Of the around five hundred thousand refugees from the Spanish Civil War, a considerable number fled to the Caribbean region, mostly to the Spanish-speaking countries of Mexico, Cuba and the Dominican Republic, but also to Puerto Rico.[13] In addition, many Europeans fled to ports located on the continental shores of the Caribbean Sea and the Gulf of Mexico, such as La Guaira and Puerto Cabello in Venezuela, Cartagena de Indias and Barranquilla in Colombia, Colón in the Panama Canal Zone, Veracruz and Tampico in Mexico as well as Key West and Miami in the United States.

A significant number of European refugees made one or even more stopovers at Caribbean ports on their flight to exile countries in continental South, Central or North America. Among them was the German writer Anna Seghers (1900–83). In 1934 she started her flight from Germany to Zurich and onward to Paris. After the German invasion of France, she had to move on to Marseille in Vichy France in 1940. In 1941 she decided to escape to Mexico via the so-called Martinique route leading from Marseille via Casablanca to Fort-de-France.[14] In Martinique Seghers was detained for four weeks before she sailed on to the Dominican Republic, where she was detained another two weeks. After three months of travel Seghers eventually reached New York.[15] From here she continued her flight to the port of Veracruz, crossing the northern Caribbean Sea once more, and travelled overland to Mexico City.

Among other remote sites in the Americas, Africa, Asia and Australia, places in the Caribbean such as the US Virgin Islands, the Dominican Republic, Jamaica, Haiti and Mexico were even considered for resettlement of Jewish refugees in the 1930s,[16] and as late as April 1943 the participants of the Bermuda Conference took account of British Honduras as an option for refugee settlement.[17] Of uppermost importance, however, were three continental Caribbean colonies located in the most north-eastern part of South America, that is the Guianas. French Guiana had been proposed as early as 1936, followed by British Guiana in 1939 and eventually Dutch Guiana (present-day Suriname) in 1947.[18] The British government planned to divide its colony, British Guiana, into two separate territories, one of which should have served as a Jewish state for the large-scale settlement of about a million refugees from middle European countries,[19] making this the most significant project in the Americas.

During World War II, only three "sovereign" countries existed in the insular Caribbean: Cuba, Haiti and the Dominican Republic. Apart from the Caribbean mainland colonies mentioned above, all other islands were colonies of Great Britain, the Netherlands, France or the United States. Therefore, the question arises as to why the Western governments did not admit more refugees, even though most were highly skilled and although settlers were lacking in most colonies. The example of the steamer *Königstein*, which left Hamburg for Barbados in February 1939, shows that the adult refugees aboard had been physicians, lawyers, peasants, apparel manufacturers, watchmakers, gardeners, hairdressers, domestic workers, cooks and bakers, as well as mechanics.[20]

It seems unlikely that all the governments were only interested in "settlers trained in agriculture or engineering", such as was the case in the Dominican Republic.[21] On the contrary, the demand for skilled workers was high, so it is no surprise that the only refugees France admitted to its colony, French Guiana, were a few engineers and physicians.[22] Also, it is well known that in the nineteenth and early twentieth centuries many Latin American countries and colonial powers in the Caribbean were trying to "import" or attract as many free or bonded labourers from Europe and Asia as possible. It remains all the more mysterious why exactly these states and colonial powers did not admit the masses of Europeans when they reached the Caribbean borders. And finally, one can assume that refugees should have served as "frontier peasants" against the "uncivilized" indigenous and Maroon population such as had occurred in British and Dutch Guiana with the establishment of Jewish homelands. British Guiana was planned as a settlement of refugees in the Rupununi Savannah, a region between the Caroni and the Essequibo

Rivers that is inhabited primarily by Makushi (a Carib tribe), and the latter in the territory of the Saramacca, one of the six Maroon people in this region. Some historians have argued that the British refugee policy was "designed to keep out large numbers of European Jews – perhaps ten times as many as it let in"[23] and thus may have been of an anti-Semitic and an anti-Communist nature.

The Caribbean in particular, as well as the Western Hemisphere in general, was in most cases not the first choice for the millions of European refugees. Of the 120,000 categorized as Jews who left Nazi Germany between 1933 and 1937, approximately 40,000 fled to other European countries, a further 40,000 to Palestine (despite horrible newspaper reports on the bloody conflict between Arabs and Jews) and only the remaining third to other continents.[24] Numerous people tried to reach neighbouring countries, especially Great Britain, France, the Netherlands, Switzerland and Belgium in order to wait there until the situation had eased (see table 10.1). Some even fled to Fascist Austria, where the Nazi Party was forbidden until 1938, but with the Anschluss in March 1938, this proved to be an unfortunate decision. Likewise, the situation in Europe never eased – on the contrary, it got worse each day and Fascism as well as anti-Semitism was prevalent virtually everywhere.

For the refugees, the Americas became more important beginning in 1938, with the United States being the main target. South and Central America and the Caribbean were, in their imaginations, simply too "exotic". Therefore, except for Palestine, the United States took (in absolute terms) more refugees than any other country in the non-European world. It was followed by Latin

Table 10.1. Main European Exile Countries of Nazi Refugees

Country	Estimated Number of Refugees (rounded)
Great Britain	42,000
France	30,000
Netherlands	27,000
Switzerland	25,000
Belgium	15,000

Source: Based on Gleizer, Unwelcome Exiles, 19–20.

Table 10.2. Main Extra-European Exile Countries of Nazi Refugees

Country	Estimated Number of Refugees (rounded)
United States	140,000
Latin America	112,000–135,000
Palestine	66,500
Shanghai	16,300

Source: Based on Gleizer, *Unwelcome Exiles*, 20; Haim Avni, "Los países de América Latina y el Holocausto", in *Shoá – Enciclopedia del Holocausto*, ed. Efaim Zadoff (Jerusalem: Yad Vashem and E.D.Z. Nativ Ediciones); Marion A. Kaplan, *Zuflucht in der Karibik: Die jüdische Flüchtlingssiedlung in der Dominikanischen Republik 1940–1945*, Hamburger Beiträge zur Geschichte der deutschen Juden 36 (Göttingen: Wallstein, 2010), 3; Robert M. Levine, *Tropical Diaspora: The Jewish Experience in Cuba* (Princeton, NJ: Markus Wiener, 2010), 132; Patrik von zur Mühlen, "Deutsches Exil in Lateinamerika: Kulturelle und politische Aktivitäten nach der Flucht", *Lateinamerika-Nachrichten* 251 (1995); American Jewish Joint Distribution Committee (2010).

America (especially Argentina and Brazil) and Japanese-controlled Shanghai, which admitted refugees without any visa regulation (see table 10.2).

The non-Spanish-speaking Caribbean played an important yet little studied role as places of exile, before, during and after World War II, though there is no general agreement about the number of European refugees they absorbed. However, there are more statistics pertinent to the Spanish-speaking Caribbean as part of Latin America. According to Robert M. Levine, Cuba alone received about 8,000 Holocaust refugees from Europe between 1933 and 1942,[25] whereas the American Jewish Joint Contribution Committee claims to have aided "most of the 12,000 refugees who arrived in Cuba from 1938 [to] 1944".[26] It is important to note that one of the largest of all Caribbean territories, the Dominican Republic, granted proportionally more Jews asylum than any other state in the Western Hemisphere.[27] During the Evian Conference in July 1938, only the Dominican Republic was willing to admit 100,000 refugees, while representatives of other states declared a refugee limit far below that number (for example the United States, South Africa and Australia) or allowed the arrival of refugees only for transit purposes or even entirely refused them. But the number of people fleeing to the Dominican Republic was far from reaching 100,000. According to the estimates of Marion A. Kaplan, just about 3,000 Jews,[28] and a further 3,000 refugees from the Spanish Civil War,[29] actually managed to reach the Dominican Republic and relocated in the eastern part of the island of Hispaniola. With regard to Haiti, the western part of Hispaniola, the records of the American Jewish Joint Distribution Committee are the only reliable source to date. They determine that approximately 150 Jewish refugees entered during World War II.

Bernard Wasserstein quoted the official estimate of people who fled to the British colonial empire between 1933 and 1939 as "in the neighbourhood of 3,000".[30] Apparently this estimate increased dramatically during the following years. Claus and Katja Füllberg-Stolberg, for example, numbered the refugees in the three different sections of the internment camp of Gibraltar in Jamaica at 4,800, as Suzanne Francis-Brown also establishes in chapter 11 in this volume.[31] Simone Gigliotti mentions an additional "1,131 prisoners of war and enemy aliens ... interned in the Up Park military camp in Kingston" by January 1944.[32] According to Tony Martin, 585 refugees had entered the British colony of Trinidad and Tobago in February 1940[33] and 130 entered British Guiana as late as 1942.[34] And these examples refer only to three colonies in the British Caribbean.

As for the French colony of Martinique, Eric Jennings stresses that it is almost impossible to reconstruct reliable numbers. From his detailed explanation, however, it can be assumed that approximately 3,000 refugees (Jewish and others) arrived between 1938 and 1942.[35] Although French Guiana had been proposed as the place for Jewish settlement in 1936, a surprisingly small number of 30 refugees (mostly Austrians) were accommodated in this extreme part of South America between February and April 1939.[36]

According to Liesbeth van der Horst, the Dutch Caribbean colonies granted asylum to 1,200 to 1,400 refugees.[37] But there is debate over the numbers that enter the Dutch colonies of Aruba, Bonaire and Curaçao. Gigliotti (referring to Oscar E. Lansen) states some 422 enemy aliens were interned on the island of Curaçao in 1940, with 77 German and Austrian Jews among them.[38] Junnes E. Sint Jago, by contrast, specifies all 422 as Germans and Austrians and explains that they had been arrested on Curaçao and Aruba and were transferred to the internment camp on the island of Bonaire.[39] Lansen himself reported that the 422 people arrested (202 of whom he declared

Germans), in addition to another 17 German and Austrian Jewish refugees, were transported from Panama to Curaçao in 1940 after they had been refused refuge there. The number of incarcerated also included 30 "Jewish West Indian residents of German, Austrian, Polish, and Romanian origin" who had been living in the Caribbean for an unknown period.[40] Lansen, in his abstract, actually mentions that 77 of the 422 internees were Jewish, but this was never further explained nor referenced. As there is no exact number of refugees per Dutch colony, it must be assumed that the remaining 700 to 900 refugees entered Suriname. What is known for sure is that the governor of Suriname counted 138 Germans in Surinamese internment camps in 1945.[41]

As for the continental Caribbean ports in North, Central and South America, it is equally difficult to tell how many refugees remained in these ports and how many migrated onward, especially to the capitals or other important cities such as Caracas, Bogotá, Panama City, Mexico City or New York, nor is there an estimate of how many refugees actually reached these ports. Before 1942 all refugees to Venezuela and most refugees to Colombia, Panama and Mexico had to enter via the Caribbean ports unless they were coming from a third-party country in the Americas to which they had initially fled. Veracruz became an important Mexican port of entry, in particular for about 6,000 refugees of the Spanish Civil War in the year 1939.[42] Mexico accommodated approximately 20,000 refugees from the Spanish Civil War,[43] but in contrast only some 1,500 to 1,850 Holocaust refugees.[44] Some of the refugees labelled as Spanish Civil War refugees may also have been Holocaust refugees, explaining the disparity in the figures. In fact, many escaped first from Spain to France but were persecuted there by Hitler after the successful German occupation of France in 1940. On the other hand, it has to be borne in mind that some refugees entered Mexico as tourists in order to avoid the status of refugee. For Colombia, Puerto Colombia (Barranquilla's Caribbean seaport) played an almost exclusive role as a port of entry until 1943, when it was shut down by the Colombian government. Colombia is supposed to have admitted 9,502 refugees, of whom 7,878 were Germans,[45] 526 Austrians and 1,098 from other Eastern European countries such as "Poland, Romania, Bessarabia, Czechoslovakia and Hungary".[46] Apart from these exceptions, there is no further accurate data, only general estimates (see table 10.3).

Table 10.3. Main Caribbean Exile Countries for European Refugees

Country	Estimated Number of Nazi Refugees (rounded)	Estimated Number of Refugees from the Spanish Civil War (rounded)
British Guiana	130	unknown
Colombia*	9,500	†
Costa Rica*	300	unknown
Cuba	8,000–12,000	†
Curaçao, Aruba, Bonaire	500	unknown
Dominican Republic	3,000	3,000
Jamaica	4,800–6,000	unknown
Martinique	3,000	unknown
Mexico*	1,850	20,000
Panama*	600	unknown
Trinidad and Tobago	600	unknown
Suriname	700–900	unknown
Venezuela*	600	†

*The number refers to the entire country, not specifically to their Caribbean regions.
†For Colombia, Cuba and Venezuela together, 2,000 refugees are specified.

Source: Siglinde Bolbecher, "Österreichische Emigration in Kolumbien" (Salzburg: Universität Salzburg, 2002), 4, http://www.literaturepochen.at/exil/l5040.pdf (accessed 29 March 2015); Geneviève Dreyfus-Armand, *L'exil des républicains espagnols en France: De la Guerre civile à la mort de Franco* (Paris: Albin Michel, 1999), 80.

To sum up, estimates of the number of refugees only to the insular Caribbean in the context of World War II range from at least 24,000 up to 28,000. One of the main problems is that statistics include primarily Jewish refugees, and in this context it remains unclear whether these numbers also include their non-Jewish family members. Only few statistics consider other refugee groups, such as escapees of the Spanish Civil War. Besides, the numbers of the arrested occupants of the internment camps usually also include deported prisoners of war and other groups such as labourers or residents, who did not necessarily have to be refugees.

An additional difficulty arises in reconstructing the post-war migration in particular,[47] but also the migration from 1933 to 1937. Regarding German-speaking Jews especially, Patrik von zur Mühlen assumes that as many as 7,500 went to Cuba and the Dominican Republic between 1933 and 1945.[48] In the context of interned Germans and Austrians on the islands of Aruba, Bonaire and Curaçao, Sint Jago talks of about 404 peeople, Lansen of about only 77, as already mentioned above. As Austrians are both "absorbed" within the group of Germans, or generally subsumed as "German-speaking", and estimates on other Caribbean islands are missing, a reliable estimate on the migration of Austrians to the Caribbean has not been provided to date.

As mentioned, the Caribbean was not the first place of exile for a significant number of European refugees, as many had initially fled to other (primarily European) countries. Likewise, the Caribbean was not the last place of exile, as it remained for a significant part of the refugees only a temporary stopover on the way to such actual target countries as the United States, Canada, Mexico or Venezuela.[49] In many cases, the location of the Caribbean encouraged refugees to make use of these islands as stepping-stones to North America and South America. But facts indicate that the onward migration depended on the lack of women (gender imbalance), internationality, educational opportunities for children, urbanity and other prospects, and conflicts among the refugee groups and additional limitations altogether became quite frustrating.[50] Moreover, other factors that explain why the refugees did not remain in the Caribbean have to be taken into consideration. In some cases they did not leave voluntarily but were deported.[51] It is well known that numerous people fled from dictatorship, persecution and repression of the "fascist terrorism"[52] in Europe with the hope of finding a safe haven in the Caribbean, so it is unfortunate that they were again confronted with persecution and repression. As in Europe, Fascist regimes had taken power in many Latin American (inclusive of Caribbean) countries, as a consequence of the Fascist German and Italian policy. Thus, dictatorships existed in the Dominican Republic and Haiti, rudimentarily also in Cuba and Venezuela. Similarly, multiple armed conflicts in the Caribbean host countries (for example the anti-Trujillo invasion in the Dominican Republic in 1948) persuaded many refugees to migrate onward or to migrate back to their home country.

Uncertainty arose in the Dutch and French colonies after the German occupation of the Netherlands and France in 1940, since Nazi takeover of the colonies was feared and deportation to European concentration camps seemed imminent. Similarly, the serious fear of a Nazi invasion in the Caribbean was growing after the German navy (mostly submarines) had entered the Caribbean Sea and attacked enemy ships. An additional uncertainty accrued from the hesitation of many Caribbean and Latin American countries, as well as the United States, to declare war on Germany.

Furthermore, German-speaking migrants were registered as "enemy aliens" in the British, Dutch, French and US-American colonies and territories. Shortly after the beginning of the occupation of Poland by Nazi Germany on 1 September 1939, Jewish refugees were deemed to be enemy aliens. In Trinidad and Tobago, for instance, the colonial government decided to detain all Germans, Austrians and Italians in 1940, as has been confirmed by various refugee accounts. As Hans Stecher, an Austrian of Romanian origin who had fled to Trinidad in 1938, remembers, "It was on my birthday the 16 June 1940 when the police knocked on our door and proclaimed the order of the acting Governor George F. Huggins: 'you are going to be interned at the governors pleasure'."[53] Shockingly, the refugees were held in the internee camps together with German merchant seamen, U-boat crews and some actual Nazi spies, even after the end of World War II. Internment camps existed in Bonaire, Cuba, Curaçao, Jamaica, Martinique, Trinidad and Suriname. It is no surprise that anti-Semitism was omnipresent in the camps. Gerhard Frey, a former internee at Camp Copieweg, Suriname, related that "wer sehr gelitten hat im Camp war Bruder Ehrhardt. Viele Lagerinsassen haben damit gedroht nicht in die Kirche zu gehen, wenn dieser 'Halbjude'predigt [The one who really suffered in the camp was father Ehrhardt. Many internees threatened not to go to church when this 'half-Jew' was preaching]."[54]

Anti-Semitism was not only prevalent in internment camps among Germans and Austrians but also in Caribbean societies, where policies against Jews can be traced to the Spanish inquisition in the Caribbean since 1492. Likewise, Nazi parties and sympathizers existed in the Caribbean exile countries. In right-wing-government countries such as Cuba, a clearly anti-communist tendency was visible, and anti-communism was often synonymous with anti-Semitism. The Cuban journalist José Ignacio Rivero, for example, commented on Jewish refugees, "Not that every Jew is a communist nor every communist is a Jew, but . . . every Jew is a potential communist."[55]

EUROPEAN REFUGEES AND THEIR ORIGIN

Numerous European refugees came as families to the Caribbean. A considerable number were children, inclusive of unborn children. The few existing photographs that have been taken aboard ships before, during and after the crossing of the Atlantic document the faces of many children, especially toddlers. They suggest that families with toddlers formed a substantial part of the refugees who escaped to the Americas, but in some cases the families got separated during their flight to the Caribbean. The Viennese family Mechner, of Romanian origin, provide such a case. In 1938 the family managed to obtain visas for and tickets to Cuba. While the physician Adolph Mechner and his wife left for Havana, their seven-year old son Franzi remained with Adolph's sister in Paris. After the invasion of France in 1940, the child and his aunt had to flee to Vichy France, where they left for Cuba in October 1941 aboard one of the last ships able to leave Europe for the Western Hemisphere; they were eventually reunited with the rest of the family.[56]

The majority of the refugees were Jewish or people deemed to be "Jewish", according to the Nuremberg Laws (14 November 1935). They were often accompanied by their non-Jewish family members. In addition, other victims of persecution, such as socialists, communists, social democrats, anarchists, dissidents, Roma, Sinti, homosexuals, conscientious objectors, and economic refugees, were seeking a safe haven in the Caribbean. It is important to stress the strong heterogeneity among European refugees. Further, it is necessary to emphasize the intersections between the different refugee categories so that an exact distinction is neither possible nor desirable. A considerable number of refugees were thus exposed to multiple types of discrimination, for example, female Jewish communists. They shared, however, collective experiences and thus a common history.

World War II (including its pre-war conflicts) as well as the phenomenon of Fascism (as one of its major causes) generated millions of refugees. Many of them were Europeans, but millions of refugees were to be found on other continents as well. For instance, between only 1937 and 1939 around 30 million Chinese refugees (mostly internally displaced people) were the result of the Second Sino-Japanese War.[57] While the Spanish Civil War (1936–39) caused about 500,000 refugees, the same number of people fled from Germany, plus another 150,000 from (former) Austria, between 1933 and 1939.[58]

During World War II, approximately 10 million people were displaced to *Arbeitslager* (labour camps), 2.5 million to *SS-lager* (SS camps) and 1.5 million "Jews" to extermination camps.[59] In Poland, the country with the largest Jewish population in 1939 (more than 3 million), almost 350,000 people fled from the German-occupied parts during the war.[60] Even after World War II, an estimated 25 million people were still affected by flight and displacement,[61] among them around 14 million German *Heimatvertriebene* (expellees).[62]

Although people fled from almost every European country, a total estimate is lacking. In Caribbean countries, refugees of most European nationalities were to be found during and immediately after World War II. Some groups were, however, bigger than others. The major refugee groups in Mexico, for instance, were Spanish, German, Austrian, Dutch, French, Belgian, Polish, Czech and Hungarian.[63] In Martinique, "Germans, Austrians, Czechs, Spaniards" outnumbered surprisingly "only a few French people".[64] The West Indian Census 1946 lists the following European nationalities of the "foreign-born population" in the British colony of Trinidad and Tobago: Belgium, Czechoslovakia, Denmark, France, "Germany and Austria", Greece, "Holland" (Netherlands), Italy, Poland, Portugal, Spain and Soviet Union, with Germans and Austrians being the biggest group (120), followed by the French (115), Poles (92) and Russians (72).[65]

The flow of European refugees which also affected the Caribbean can be divided into three waves. The first wave of flight began in 1933, immediately after Hitler took power in Germany. As many as 51,000 to 53,000 Jews and 9,000 to 10,000 non-Jews fled Nazi Germany and until the end of 1937 were followed by a further 95,000 people.[66] During the same period, approximately 200,000 people also fled from the Fascist countries Italy, Austria and Spain. The actual refugee crisis started, however, in 1938. It was provoked by the Anschluss of Austria to the German Reich on 12 March 1938, followed by public humiliations of Jews such as the cleaning of sidewalks and mass deportations to concentration camps and which culminated in Kristallnacht on 9–10 November 1938, with its violent programmes against Jewish civilians as well as the demolition of Jewish synagogues, cemeteries, homes, stores, hospitals and schools across the German Reich (inclusive of Austria). The aryanization of flats, businesses and motorized vehicles, as well as dismissals and the prohibition of any further employment, deprived Jews of their livelihood.

By December 1938 about 400,000 non-Jewish people in Germany and former Austria were arrested in concentration camps for political reasons.[67] This development caused the flight of over 63,000 people in 1938 and another 54,500 in 1939 from Austria alone.[68] It can be traced back to the fact that the occurrences in Vienna, the former capital of Austria, in 1938 were described by eyewitnesses as much more radical and violent than in Berlin. Hitler's invasion of Poland, Denmark, Norway, Belgium, the Netherlands, Luxembourg and France between September 1939 and June 1940 caused the third big wave of refugees. Many people from Germany, Austria and Poland had found refuge there but had to then flee again. A considerable number decided to seek refuge further afield and took one of the last opportunities to get on board a steamer to be taken as far away as possible from Europe. In October 1941 any further emigration from Nazi-occupied territories was forbidden by law; the number of refugees emigrating between 1939 and October 1941 comprised an estimated 71,000 persons.[69]

FLIGHT TO THE CARIBBEAN

There were a number of reasons for the flight of European refugees to the Caribbean. Very often personal relations were the catalysts for choosing the country of emigration. These could be friendship with Caribbean diplomats, consuls working in Europe or family members who had already emigrated to the Caribbean. Emmy Rosenbaum, for example, noted in her diary[70] that the consul of the Dominican Republic in Austria was a business friend of her husband's. With his help, the couple, because of pending expropriation and deportation, escaped in 1938 from Gmünd (a small border town in the province of Lower Austria with 5,727 residents in 1939[71]) via Vienna, Switzerland and France to the Dominican Republic, where they settled and began a new life in 1939.

The Viennese Zeisel family decided to flee to the Colombian port city of Cartagena de Indias in 1939 because their son Heinrich, after pending deportation to a concentration camp, had already been there since 1938. His early flight, his already-acquired knowledge of the country and its people and his established business contacts helped his later-arriving family members to integrate more easily both culturally and economically into the Caribbean exile.[72] Similarly, the father of Heinz Schwarz had fled from Vienna to Trinidad and Tobago in December 1938 after his dismissal, arrest, harassment and pending deportation to a concentration camp. Heinz and his mother Hermine followed via the Netherlands in July 1939, which was even more problematic, since by that time the Netherlands did not permit transit to German Jews any more. Fortunately, they had no "J" stamped in their passports, which was the official identification for "Jewish".[73] Since Heinz was coming from a non-religious household but his father was of Jewish descent, he was deemed to be a *mischling* (mixed breed).

The family of Hans Stecher was informed about the uncomplicated immigration process to Trinidad and Tobago in 1938 by an uncle who was living in the Caribbean port city of Maracaibo, Venezuela. The original plan was to flee from Vienna via Amsterdam to Port of Spain by the end of 1938 and continue from there to Maracaibo, which route seemed to be easy. It was, however, not so easy. In Trinidad, to earn money the Stechers had to open a small watch shop, which could not simply be abandoned. Even after their internment between 1940 and 1943, first on Nelson and Caledonia islands, and later in the St James Barracks, the family decided to stay in Trinidad.[74]

In many cases, flight to the Caribbean was dependent on the receipt of a visa. In Austria, for instance, a visa for Colombia could be received quite easily after presenting the required papers (generally a valid passport, medical certificate, character reference, vaccination certificate, proof of citizenship and proof of profession, as well as proof of liquidity).[75] After the Anschluss the situation changed, as Vienna was no longer the capital; the different consulates closed down, and usually the next consulate was in Hamburg, Berlin or Milan. Receiving a visa in Nazi Germany became additionally complicated after September 1939, since the war cut most diplomatic relations. Nevertheless, some refugees, such as Erwin Sensel from the Austrian province of Styria, who left Hamburg for Barbados in 1939, related how the Jewish aid organizations and passenger lines organized visas directly at the ports of embarkation as well.[76]

Quite often, however, visas were disavowed, sometimes during the passage, in other cases upon arrival. The most famous example is the passenger liner the SS *St Louis*. The steamship carried over nine hundred passengers from Hamburg to Havana, mostly those categorized as Jews. While the ship was crossing the Atlantic, Cuba changed its immigration laws, the visas of the passengers became void and the refugees were denied entry. The captain and the crew then tried to call at the United States and Canada, but most of the refugees were, dramatically, sent back to Europe, where many were killed by the Nazis.[77]

Norbert Adler, a German Jew who fled from Berlin to Cuba in July 1938, explains another strategy to apply for a visa:

> I heard about the possibility of immigrating to the United States via Cuba, by first securing a tourist visa at the American Consulate. It was possible to buy a "vacation" round trip from Europe to New York, plus an additional "cruise" from New York to Havana, and pay for all this in German marks. The plan would be to get a visitor's visa from the U.S. Consulate in Berlin, find an American in New York to sign an affidavit to guarantee I would not become a public burden, take these papers to Cuba, and magically get my immigration visa.[78]

Many refugees booked a cruise ship with a stopover in New York, where they tried to receive an invitation letter or a labour contract from a US enterprise. With this document in hand, they would apply at the next US consulate in the Caribbean for a US visa and then wait there until their quota number came up. Cuba became the most important country for accessing these visas, though many refugees never received their visas and remained in Cuba.

For a period of time, some Caribbean countries, for instance Trinidad and Tobago, did not require a visa at all. The already mentioned Austrian Heinz Schwarz related that his father escaped to Trinidad in December 1938 after "posting the equivalent of a $250.00 deposit required for immigration".[79] Equally, Hans Stecher confirmed this regulation and narrowed down the period from September to December 1938.[80]

Generally, however, it proved to be much more difficult to get a travel permit in Nazi Germany than a visa. The refugees were redirected frequently to different public authorities and banks and had to pay a great deal of money. As all the public authorities were located in bigger cities, people had to travel from the countryside, often for an entire day, to get to them. In the end, if they were successful, refugees were not allowed to travel with any of their personal assets.

The majority of refugees to the Caribbean left Europe via German ports such as Hamburg and Bremen. Others fled from Amsterdam or Le Havre. Refugees who were already in France, in particular those who were interned in camps in southern France, left via Marseille. Passenger-ship lines serving the Caribbean included the Dutch Koninklijke Nederlandsche Stoomboot-Maatschappij, the British Royal Mail Steam Packet Company and the German Hamburg-Amerikanische Packetfahrt-Actien-Gesellschaft (also known as Hamburg America Line), as well as the French Compagnie Générale Transatlantique and Compagnie Française de Navigation à Vapeur Cyprien Fabre & Compagnie (also known as Fabre Line). However, from September 1939, passenger liners from these companies gradually stopped their service.

As the former Austria lacked access to the sea, which it had since 1918, the flight from there proved to be much more complicated, and it generally involved crossing several countries to reach the final port of embarkation to the Caribbean. Thirty-five-year-old Viennese Alfred Steckerl, for instance, fled together with his brother Rudolf and his brother-in-law Emil in June 1938 by train to Switzerland and onward to Paris. There he reunited with his thirty-three-year-old wife Rosa, who had fled together with their eight-year-old daughter, Gisl, and their three-year-old daughter, Susie, as well as her sister-in-law Ottilie and her two little daughters, Renate and Franziska, by train via Strasbourg. In Paris, they bought tickets to Colombia for the steamer *Cuba* which left Le Havre on 25 June 1938.[81] The island of Cuba was reached by Edith Osinsky, née Fink, from Vienna via Milan and Paris and by Ralph Peter Gray, who was born Otto Felix Goldstein, from Vienna via London.[82] But flight routes to the Caribbean did not only involve stopovers in one or more European countries but also within the Caribbean. When the Viennese Zeisel family, for instance, fled in May 1939 from the German Reich, they did so via Barbados and Venezuela to Colombia.[83] The author Egon Eis fled from Vienna to Czechoslovakia in 1938, then to France, to Morocco in 1940, to Cuba in 1941 and finally to Mexico in 1942.

From 1940, it became increasingly difficult to find ships to cross the Northern Atlantic because of the maritime battles, and most connections were only possible from ports located in the South of France, Spain and Portugal – besides Marseille, from Barcelona, Vigo, Bilbao and Lisbon. After their deportation from the German city of Worms to the French internment camp of Gurs in 1940, Miriam Gerber, née Mirjam Sondheimer, and her family managed to flee via Marseille and Lisbon to the Dominican Republic in May 1941.[84] Similarly, Leonhard Spatz, who had left Vienna for Switzerland in 1938 and fled onward to Paris in 1940, was able to escape from a French camp to Marseille, from where he travelled with his parents by train via Spain to

Portugal and by ship to Cuba. He eventually reached Havana in March 1941, when he was eighteen years old.[85] Alfred Unger, an Austrian of Polish origin, was twenty years old when he ended his flight to the Dominican Republic via France, Spain, Portugal and the United States by the end of 1940. Together with his cousin Karl Pick, Alfred had left Vienna in July 1938 for Switzerland, and while they ended up in a work camp, although with minimal wage, his parents were killed in the Holocaust.[86]

A random sample in the *German Biographical Lexicon* demonstrates that famous personalities often belonged to the group of refugees which fled Europe very late. In almost all cases France served as a hub for them on their way to the Caribbean, and most did not stay permanently in their Caribbean exile but either migrated onward to the United States or returned to their home country after 1945. Many of them were members of the anti-Fascist opposition, as well as Jews, such as the social-democratic journalist Robert Breuer, alias Lucian Friedlaender, who fled in 1940 to Martinique and died of starvation under the difficult conditions in the Antillean Vichy colony. Another example shows the fate of the Austrian resistance fighter Lisa Fittko, who fled from Berlin to Zurich, Amsterdam, Paris, Marseille and later to the Pyrenees, where she escorted refugees into Spain between 1940 and 1941. In 1941 she escaped with her German husband, Hans, a communist resistance fighter, to Cuba. Likewise, Otto Eis, a screenwriter, fled via France, Spain and Portugal to Cuba in 1941, and the German art historian Curt Glaser escaped to southern France and Portugal in 1940 before he eventually reached Cuba.

Flight became additionally complicated by the prohibition of emigration from the German Reich in October 1941. Simultaneous to this, several countries of the Americas banned immigration of refugees from Axis countries – for example, Cuba in April 1942[87] – and by the middle of 1942 Atlantic connections came to a standstill. Further flight to the Americas was possible almost exclusively via the Asia-Pacific route. The 1900-born Jewish woman Sidonie Csillag from Vienna – the famous lesbian patient of Sigmund Freud – received a visa for Cuba as well as a ship ticket to leave Germany via Hamburg in early 1940. Her younger brothers, Ernst and Robert, had already escaped to Cuba and were waiting there. However, Sidonie's plan failed at the last moment and she had to return to Vienna in April. Later in August she travelled via Berlin and Königsberg to Moscow, where she took the Trans-Siberian Railway and reached the shores of the Pacific at Harbin (Manchuria) nine days after her departure from the Soviet capital. She embarked to Japan, and after two months of waiting she was able to get aboard a ship, crossed the Pacific to Hawaii and later to San Francisco. In California Sidonie boarded again and travelled onward to Balboa, Panama. After crossing the isthmus, she reached Havana in December 1940.[88]

Lilly Gottlieb was one of the last refugees who managed to get to the Caribbean via the Atlantic in 1942. Her adventurous route took her from Vienna to Antwerp in Belgium and from there on to Paris and Nice. She left France, together with her parents, on 9 January 1942 for Casablanca. In Morocco the refugees were held in a "beach resort" until, on 26 January 1942, they were able to board the SS *Serpa Pinto*, which took the refugees to Cuba via Jamaica, and on 14 February 1942 they reached Havana harbour. The conditions aboard must have been terrible, since the ship was constructed to hold approximately 350 passengers, but there were about 800 refugees, mostly Jewish, aboard. Needless to say there was overcrowding, with 25 people sharing a cabin; also, men and women were separated from each other, and suspicions prevailed. According to Lilly Gottlieb, the stopover in Kingston on 13 February 1942 was made simply to remove a German man suspected of being a spy.[89]

When European refugees managed to reach their Caribbean destinations, it was not uncommon for ships carrying them to be denied entry. A famous case is the SS *Caribia*. Scheduled for Trinidad, the ship left Hamburg in January 1939 with about 450 refugees on board, but in February 1939 the ship was refused permission to land in Port of Spain. An attempt to call at the nearby Venezuelan port of La Guaira was also unsuccessful. While already on the way to Panama, and after numerous interventions by the Jewish community of Valencia, the refugees were finally permitted to land at the Venezuelan port of Puerto Cabello.

A similar fate was suffered by the 165 Jewish passengers of the SS *Königstein*. Coming from Hamburg in February 1939, the ship was scheduled to land in Barbados; however, the officials there as well as in British Guiana and French Guiana did not allow the refugees to enter the countries. Once again it was Venezuela which granted the refugees asylum, in March 1939.

But some refugees who tried to flee to South America finally ended up on Caribbean islands. The Austrian "Jewish" passengers of the SS *Ulysses* were left stranded in the Panama Canal Zone after Chilean immigration authorities refused to admit them. Other Austrian and German passengers from other ships followed. Those with money were able to buy visas for Bolivia and Ecuador, but the rest were shipped to Willemstad, Curaçao, eventually being interned in Bonaire together with other Austrians, Germans, Poles and Romanians.[90] Likewise, Lilly Schock, née Lebenhardt, and her husband, Ernst, tried to flee from Vienna to Mexico in 1938 but were not permitted to land. They had to travel to Cuba, where they spent two years in Havana before they received an affidavit for the United States in 1940.[91]

An incredible odyssey was the fate of some dozens of Nazi refugees. They left Marseille aboard the SS *Alsina* in January 1941 for Brazil, but were detained for more than four months in Dakar and were sent to a detention camp in Casablanca. In October 1941, they finally managed to sail to Brazil aboard the SS *Cabo de Buena Esperanza*. In Rio de Janeiro, however, their visas were declared invalid, and the ship was sent to Buenos Aires, from where the refugees, after a brief stop and the refusal of their request to land in Trinidad and Tobago, were sent back to Europe. They eventually tried again to reach Buenos Aires and were finally admitted to Curaçao, in November 1941.[92]

CONCLUSION

This chapter presented an overview of the role of the Caribbean as a place of exile for thousands of Europeans, especially for Austrian and German refugees, in the context of World War II. Refugee waves reached the Caribbean from at least 1933 and continued for several years after 1945. A high percentage of the refugees were families, pregnant women and children, and many were Jewish or political refugees from the different Fascist regimes. The flight from Europe across the Atlantic (and also the Pacific) lasted weeks, occasionally months or even years. There existed real flight routes from Europe to the Caribbean, such as the "Martinique route", leading from Marseille via Casablanca to Fort-de-France. Furthermore, this chapter also deconstructed romanticized images of the Caribbean as a "tropical paradise" where the refugees found a safe haven. Instead, they were often confronted with similar problems to those in their home countries, such as anti-Semitism, anti-communism, repression and persecution. Sometimes even the attempt to find refuge in the Caribbean ended unsuccessfully, with only some refugees admitted while others were sent back to Europe, where many of them became victims and were often murdered by the Nazi regime. In contrast, Europeans who were trying to flee to South or Central America in some cases ended up in the Caribbean. The uncertainty of acceptance in the Caribbean exile countries was a constant problem, the difficult and sometimes arbitrary legal situation producing fear and misery.

Nevertheless, while many European refugees did find a new home in the Caribbean the flight from Europe was the privilege of the lucky few: for various reasons the majority of the Nazi victims did not manage to flee, either to the Caribbean or elsewhere, and almost all became part of the estimated 12 to 14 million killed by the Nazi regime between 1933 and 1945.

NOTES

1. Cited after Roland Paul, "'Es war nie Auswanderung, immer nur Flucht': Zur Emigration der Juden aus der Pfalz im Dritten Reich", in Alfred Hans Kuby, *Juden in der Provinz – Beiträge zur Geschichte der Juden in der Pfalz zwischen Emanzipation und Vernichtung* (Neustadt an der Weinstraße: Pfälz, Post, 1988), 157.
2. "World Refugee Day: Global Forced Displacement Tops 50 Million for First Time in Post–World War II Era", UNHCR – UN Refugee Agency, http://www.unhcr.org/53a155bc6.html (accessed 19 March 2015).
3. "Kinder auf der Flucht–Flüchtlingskinder", http://www.uno-fluechtlingshilfe.de/fluechtlinge/themen/fluechtlingskinder.html (accessed 19 March 2015).
4. Tony Kushner and Katharine Knox, *Refugees in an Age of Genocide: Global, National and Local Perspectives during the Twentieth Century* (London: Frank Cass, 1999), 172.
5. Klaus J. Bade and Jochen Oltmer, *Normalfall Migration: Texte zur Einwanderer Bevölkerung und neue Zuwanderung im vereinigten Deutschland seit 1990* (Bonn: Bundeszentrale für Politische Bildung, 2004), http://www.gla.ac.uk/rg/dmigrgra.htm (accessed 19 March 2015).
6. Jörg Echternkamp, *Die 101 wichtigsten Fragen – Der Zweite Weltkrieg* (München: C. H. Beck, 2010), 11.
7. "Source List and Detailed Death Tolls for the Primary Megadeaths of the Twentieth Century", http://necrometrics.com/20c5m.htm#Second (accessed 19 March 2015).
8. Dieter Pohl, *Verfolgung und Massenmord in der NS-Zeit 1933–1945* (Darmstadt: Wissenschaftliche Buchgesellschaft, 2003), 153.

9. See also the Japanese invasion of Manchuria in 1931, the Second Italo-Ethiopian War from 1935 to 1936 and the remilitarization of the Rhineland in 1936.
10. Daniela Gleizer, *Unwelcome Exiles: Mexico and the Jewish Refugees from Nazism, 1933–1945* (Leiden: Brill, 2014), 3.
11. Tony Martin, *Caribbean History: From Pre-colonial Origins to the Present* (Boston: Pearson, 2012), 243. Michael R. Marrus, ed., *The Nazi Holocaust, Part 8: Bystanders to the Holocaust*, vol. 1 (Westport: Meckler, 1989), 391.
12. Eli Ross, "Puerto Rico", *American Jewish Year Book* (1970): 365–68, http://www.ajcarchives.org/ajc_data/files/1970_8_latamerica.pdf (accessed 25 March 2015).
13. Arnau Gonzàlez i Vilalta, *Cataluña bajo vigilancia: El consulado italiano y el fascio de Barcelona (1930–1943)* (Valencia: Publicacions de la Universitat de València, 2009), 215.
14. Eric Jennings, "Last Exit from Vichy France: The Martinique Escape Route and the Ambiguities of Emigration", *Journal of Modern History* 74, no. 2 (2002): 300.
15. Ruth Schwertfeger, "Simultaneity of Past and Present in Mexico", in *The Jewish Diaspora in Latin America and the Caribbean*, ed. Kristin Ruggiero (Eastbourne: Sussex Academic Press, 2010), 9–10.
16. William R. Perl, "The Holocaust and the Lost Caribbean Paradise", 1 January 1992, https://fee.org/articles/the-holocaust-and-the-lost-caribbean-paradise/ (accessed 30 January 2015); Simone Gigliotti, "'Acapulco in the Atlantic': Revisiting Sosúa, a Jewish Refugee Colony in the Caribbean", *Immigrants and Minorities* 24, no. 1 (2006): 26; Henry L. Feingold, *The Politics of Rescue: The Roosevelt Administration and the Holocaust, 1938–1945* (New Brunswick, NJ: Rutgers University Press, 1970), passim; Peter Hoffmann, *Carl Goerdeler and the Jewish Question, 1933–1942* (New York: Cambridge University Press, 2011), 171; Vicki Caron, *Uneasy Asylum: France and the Jewish Refugee Crisis, 1933–1942* (Stanford: Stanford University Press, 1999), 222–23. Jennings, "Last Exit", 295; Adam L. Rovner, *In the Shadow of Zion: Promised Lands before Israel* (New York: New York University Press, 2014), 183–84, 188; Dirk Hoerder, *Cultures in Contact: World Migrations in the Second Millennium* (Durham: Duke University Press, 2002), 459.
17. William R. Perl, *The Holocaust Conspiracy: An International Conspiracy of Genocide* (New York: Shapolsky, 1989), 77. The question of British Honduras as settlement for Jewish refugees was in fact discussed as early as 1938. National Archives of the United Kingdom (NAUK): CO 123/370/2.
18. Rovner, *Shadow of Zion*, Chapter 6, provides the most comprehensive account on this topic. See also Alexander Heldring, *Het Saramacca project: Een plan van*

Joodse kolonisatie in Suriname, 1946–1956 (PhD diss., University of Groningen, 2010; Hilversum, Netherlands: Verloren, 2011); Martin, *Caribbean History*, 244; and David Popper, "A Homeland for Refugees", *Annals of the American Academy of Political and Social Science* 203 (1939): 175. According to Popper, a League of Nation's mission canvassed British Guiana as a site for Christian Assyrian refugees from Iraq as early as 1935.

19. NAUK: CO 111/765/1.
20. Jacqueline Goldberg, *Tierra de gracia, tierra prometida* (2000), http://www.analitica.com/bitblioteca/jgoldberg/tierra_de_gracia.asp (accessed 17 November 2012).
21. Robert M. Levine, *Tropical Diaspora: The Jewish experience in Cuba* (Princeton, NJ: Markus Wiener, 2010), 135.
22. Caron, *Uneasy Asylum*, 222.
23. Louise London, *Whitehall and the Jews 1933–1948: British Immigration Policy and the Holocaust* (Cambridge: Cambridge University Press, 2003), 12.
24. Gleizer, *Unwelcome Exiles*, 16.
25. Levine, *Tropical Diaspora*, 132.
26. American Jewish Joint Distribution Committee, 2010.
27. Anthony P. Maingot, foreword to Levine, *Tropical Diaspora*.
28. Marion A. Kaplan, *Zuflucht in der Karibik: Die jüdische Flüchtlingssiedlung in der Dominikanischen Republik 1940–1945* (Göttingen: Wallstein, 2010), 3.
29. Kaplan, *Zuflucht*, 141.
30. Bernard Wasserstein, *Britain and the Jews of Europe, 1939–1945* (Oxford: Oxford University Press for the Institute of Jewish Affairs, 1979), 28.
31. Claus Füllberg-Stolberg and Katja Füllberg-Stolberg, "Jüdisches Exil im Britischen Kolonialreich – Gibraltar Camp Jamaica 1942–1947", in Marlies Buchholz, Claus Füllberg-Stolberg, Hans-Dieter Schmid, eds., *Nationalsozialismus und Region: Festschrift für Herbert Obenaus zum 65. Geburtstag* (Bielefeld: Verlag für Regionalgeschichte, 1997), 100.
32. Gigliotti, "Acapulco in the Atlantic", 25.
33. Martin, "Jews to Trinidad", *Journal of Caribbean History* 28, no. 2 (1994): 253.
34. Martin, *Caribbean History*, 243.
35. Jennings, "Last Exit", cf. Gigliotti, "Acapulco in the Atlantic", 25.
36. Caron, *Uneasy Asylum*, 222–23, 311.
37. Liesbeth van der Horst, *Wereldoorlog in de West: Suriname, de Nederlandse Antillen en Aruba 1940–1945* (Hilversum, Netherlands: Verloren, 2004), 116.
38. Gigliotti, "Acapulco in the Atlantic", 25.
39. Junnes E. Sint Jago, *Wuiven vanaf de Waranda: De interneringskampen op Bonaire en Curaçao tijdens WO II* (Amsterdam: Gopher, 2007).

40. Oscar E. Lansen, "Victims of Circumstance: Jewish Enemy Nationals in the Dutch West Indies 1938–1947", *Holocaust and Genocide Studies* 13, no. 3 (1999): 441–42.
41. C. Lamur and H.E. Lamur, *Duitse zendelingen in interneringskamp Copieweg, Suriname 1940–1947: Vrijlating en uitwijzing* (Paramaribo: Herrnhutter Archieven Suriname, 2008), 78.
42. Bernardo García Díaz, *Puerto de Veracruz* (Xalapa, MX: Gobierno del Estado de Veracruz, 1992), 102.
43. Gleizer, *Unwelcome Exile*, xiii. In addition, see José Antonio Matesanz, *Las raíces del exilio: México ante la guerra civil española, 1936–1939* (Mexico City: El Colegio de México and Universidad Nacional Autónoma de México, 1999).
44. Gleizer, *Unwelcome Exiles*, 23.
45. Gerhardt Neumann, "German Jews in Colombia: A Study in Immigrant Adjustment", *Jewish Social Studies* 3, no. 4 (1941): 387n2.
46. Siglinde Bolbecher, "Österreichische Emigration in Kolumbien" (Salzburg: Universität Salzburg, 2002), 4, http://www.literaturepochen.at/exil/l5040.pdf (accessed 29 March 2015).
47. As Gigliotti, "Acapulco in the Atlantic", 42 shows, the flight of Europeans was not over after 1945. She mentions the arrival of a group of ninety refugees in the Dominican Republic, coming from their first exile in Shanghai.
48. Patrik von zur Mühlen, "Deutsches Exil in Lateinamerika: Kulturelle und politische Aktivitäten nach der Flucht", *Lateinamerika-Nachrichten* 251 (1995), http://lateinamerika-nachrichten.de/?aaartikel=deutsches-exil-in-lateinamerika (accessed 29 March 2015).
49. Martin, "Jews to Trinidad", 253. Levine, *Tropical Diaspora*, 85.
50. Gigliotti, "Acapulco in the Atlantic", 39–42.
51. Kaplan, *Zuflucht*, 89.
52. Hoerder, *Cultures in Contact*, 456.
53. Hans Stecher, interviewed by authors, Carenage, Trinidad and Tobago, 21 October 2013.
54. Lamur and Lamur, *Duitse zendelingen*, 46 (translated by author).
55. Cited after Levine, *Tropical Diaspora*, 113–14.
56. Levine, *Tropical Diaspora*, 84–85 (Levine misspelled the family's name). Leo Baeck Institute, Austrian Heritage Collection, AHC 3663, Francis Mechner, interview, New York, 2008.
57. Howard Adelman and Elazar Barkan, *No Return, No Refuge: Rites and Rights in Minority Repatriation* (New York: Columbia University Press, 2011), 30.
58. Dirk Hoerder, *Geschichte der deutschen Migration: Vom Mittelalter bis heute*, Beck'sche Reihe 2494 (Munich: C.H. Beck, 2010), 97.

59. Ibid., 99.
60. Elżbieta Trela-Mazur, Włodzimierz Bonusiak, Stanisław Jan Ciesielski, Zygmunt Mańkowski, Mikołaj Iwanow, eds., *Sowietyzacja oświaty w Małopolsce Wschodniej pod radziecką okupacją 1939–1941* (Kielce, Poland: Wyższa Szkoła Pedagogiczna im. Jana Kochanowskiego, 1998), 43, 79.
61. Mathias Beer, *Flucht und Vertreibung der Deutschen. Voraussetzungen, Verlauf, Folgen* (Munich: C.H. Beck, 2011), 9.
62. Hoerder, *Geschichte der deutschen Migration*, 102.
63. Gleizer, *Unwelcome Exiles*, 1.
64. Jennings, "Last Exit", 309.
65. "Table 43 – Foreign-Born Population of Each County or Other Major Divisions, by Age and by Country of Birth", in Central Bureau of Statistics, "Barbados, British Guiana, British Honduras, Leeward Islands, Trinidad & Tobago, Windward Islands", *West Indian Census 1946*, vol. 2, pts C–H (Kingston: Government Printer, 1948–1850), 49–50.
66. For the lower estimates, see Yvonne Kapp and Margaret Mynatt, *British Policy and the Refugees 1933–1941* (Abingdon, UK: Routledge, 2013), 34 (note 10); for the higher estimates see Gleizer, *Unwelcome Exiles*, 14.
67. Kapp and Mynatt, *British Policy*, 34 (note 9).
68. Gleizer, *Unwelcome Exiles*, 17.
69. Ibid., 19.
70. Leo Baeck Institute LBI Archives: ME 1440, MM III 16, diary by Emmy Rosenbaum, Ciudad Trujillo, 1939.
71. "Statistik Austria, 31.10.2011", http://www.statistik.at/blickgem/rg3/g30908.pdf (accessed 27 March 2015).
72. Cwik and Muth, *Von Wien nach Barranquilla*, 168.
73. Heinz Schwarz, interviewed by Hans R. Weinmann (Farmington Hill, MI: Holocaust Memorial Center, Zekelman Family Campus, 18 February 2009).
74. Stecher interview, 21 October 2013.
75. Cwik and Muth, *Von Wien nach Barranquilla*, 79.
76. Ibid., 96. Sensel was one of the passengers aboard the SS *Caribia* and eventually landed in Venezuela instead of Barbados.
77. See, e.g., Scott Miller and Sarah A. Ogilvie, *Refuge Denied: The St. Louis Passengers and the Holocaust* (Madison: University of Wisconsin Press, 2006).
78. Levine, *Tropical Diaspora*, 99–100.
79. Heinz Schwarz, interviewed by Hans R. Weinmann, Holocaust Memorial Center, Zekelman Family Campus, 18 February 2009.
80. Stecher interview, 21 October 2013.
81. Cwik and Muth, *Von Wien nach Barranquilla*, 114.

82. Leo Baeck Institute, Austrian Heritage Collection: AHC 3344, Edith Osinsky, interview, Paramus, NJ, 2013; Leo Baeck Institute, Austrian Heritage Collection: AHC 3171, Ralph Gray, interview, New York, 2006.
83. Cwik and Muth, *Von Wien nach Barranquilla*, 119.
84. Leo Baeck Institute, LBI Archives: AR 25503, MF 1428, reels 1–2, Jack and Miriam Gerber Family Collection 1801–2002.
85. Levine, *Tropical Diaspora*, 151.
86. Leo Baeck Institute, LBI Archives: ME 1301, MM III 6, memoirs of Alfred Unger.
87. Levine, *Tropical Dispora*, 152.
88. Ines Rieder and Diana Voigt, *Sidonie Csillag: la "joven homosexual" de Freud* (Buenos Aires: El Cuenca de plata, 2004).
89. United States Holocaust Memorial Museum, Lilly Gottlieb, interview with Bernard Weinstein, 7 February, 1989, http://collections.ushmm.org/search/catalog/irn504782 (accessed 28 March 2015).
90. Lansen, *Victims of Circumstance*, 441–42.
91. Leo Baeck Institute, LBI Archives: AR 11174, questionnaire filled out by Lilly Schock, 2000.
92. Perl, *Holocaust Conspiracy*, 78.

11.

JAMAICA
Fixed-Term Haven and Holding Tank during World War II

SUZANNE FRANCIS-BROWN

During World War II, Jamaica became a temporary haven, or holding tank, for a variety of displaced people on both sides of the conflict, including evacuees from the western Mediterranean, refugees from across Europe, German and Italian civilians interned in British West African colonies and mainly German merchant seamen captured in or near Caribbean waters. While the colonial government in Kingston invited or otherwise agreed to these groups, it never intended even the fellow British colonials to mingle with the local population, and it certainly had no intention of supporting settlement. The offers were made to support the imperial cause, with some local economic spillover by way of construction and other jobs and payments for the care of camp residents; and they were generally without reference to the increasingly feisty local population.

The limited local recollection or memorialization of the thousands of white foreign incomers may reflect the success of government policies to limit interaction or even interface.[1] Nonetheless, oral-history interviews, in addition to media reports and secondary and primary sources, still enable one to conjure not only the camps and their residents but also some of the local context within which the camps were created and existed over several years. The result is a grainy image of specially created spaces within a colonial landscape in a time of distanced war, tinted with paternalistic and authoritarian governance amid more generalized racial, gender and class notes.

These considerations are most clearly visible with respect to Gibraltar Camp, which was a civilian-run camp initially conceived for evacuees from the British Mediterranean fortresses of Gibraltar and Malta but whose eventual spare capacity attracted refugees from wartime Europe, especially Jewish refugees – or those who were deemed Jewish as discussed by Cwik and Muth in chapter 10. Government efforts to buffer the camp and its residents from the local environment led to its being described on occasion as a semi-internment camp. Whereas Gibraltar Camp was a temporary home for free Europeans, the other camps were military-run internment camps for enemy civilians, and one also a camp for POWs but never fully identified as such. In these camps, security considerations understandably affected any contact with the local population. Under military control were the main internment camp at Up Park, adjacent to the military headquarters, whose population included POWs; a small women's internment camp in downtown Kingston which became a subject of tension between Britain and Germany; and by way of eventual replacement mid-war, a third, low-security family internment camp on the Gibraltar Camp compound.

Even given the clear security considerations which affected the operation of these military camps, the level and type of control exercised by the colonial

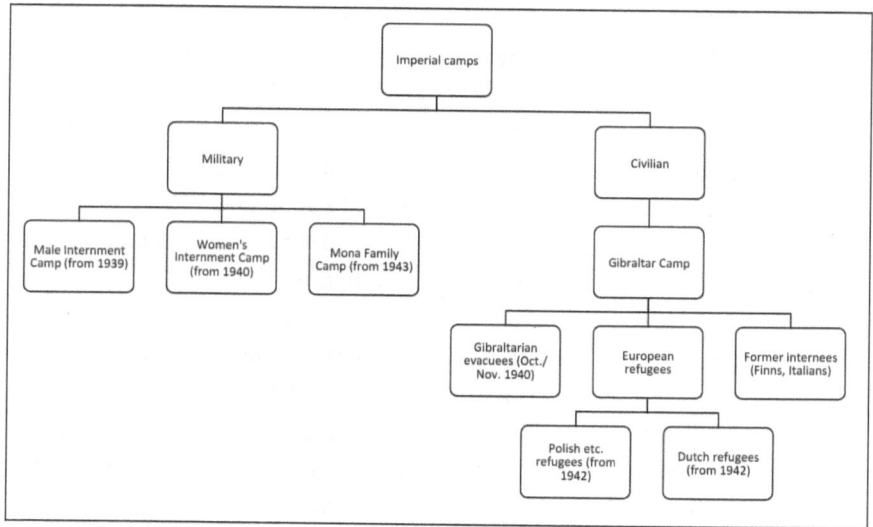

Figure 11.1. Imperial camps in Jamaica during World War II

government, during the early wartime governorship of Sir Arthur Richards, raised comments in the United Kingdom and elsewhere. Questions were raised particularly in regard to German Jews, some of whom were naturalized in the pre-war period as British citizens, after fleeing rising Nazism, but who ended up in the same camp with Nazi merchant mariners. Questions were also raised about German women and children separated from their husbands and fathers and kept in close quarters in downtown Kingston.

THE JAMAICAN CONTEXT

The camps were created by fiat; wartime facilities offered in support of the imperial government by the new governor, Sir Arthur Richards, who had replaced a careworn Sir Edward Denham when he died in office.[2] Richards came to Jamaica determined to deal with labour issues and nascent political activism. A hands-on governor with a somewhat combative style – frequently on show through the media – he rejected any criticisms of the colonial government, the constitution and demands for greater self-government, and he detained several critics, including members of the People's National Party, the leader of the union movement and journalists and commentators.[3] He argued that it was not the people in general who wanted change but just a small group desiring power. He also accused Jamaicans, both specific opponents and the general population, of disloyalty. The People's National Party, founded in 1938, which agreed in 1939 to put aside its political agenda during wartime, was by the end of 1940 at loggerheads with the governor.

Even before the war was declared, Governor Richards had asked for emergency powers, and these were granted on 25 August through the Westminster Parliament's Emergency Powers (Defence) Act, which was applied to the colonies through an Order in Council and became the basis of the Jamaica Defence Regulations. However, his widespread use of these powers caused reverberations which reached London. A February 1941 conference on civil liberties in the colonial empire heard a resolution which called attention to the shortcomings of law, justice and administration in the colonies. Director of the newspaper the *Gleaner* and wealthy local solicitor Leslie Ashenheim, responding to the detention of *Gleaner* columnist G. St C. Scotter, contended that safeguards contained in equivalent British legislation were missing from the local defence regulations.[4] At the third annual conference of the People's

National Party in August 1941, the party argued that "the use of the regulations to create a special body of law to deal with the ordinary peacetime incidents which are unaffected by any war risk, however remote, goes beyond the intention and scope of the Legislative sanction from which the above regulations derive force".[5]

Challenged in 1941 regarding the Jamaica Defence Regulations, Colonial Office under-secretary George Hall denied any suggestion of injustice, but noted that some of the provisions had been amended to better conform to provisions in the United Kingdom.[6] The Colonial Office would also pressure Richards in 1942 with respect to the use of the regulations for activities that they feared might be construed as anti-union.[7]

"Govanah", one of several wartime poems written by Jamaican poet Louise Bennett-Coverley, included the lines "as a po' man meck mistake . . . him gawn a jail" and "Me did bex wid him bout dat fe true / for talking not noh crime".[8] Gordon Lewis noted that "the colonial power . . . in the shape of Sir Arthur Richards' administration, became more authoritarian than ever under the pressures of the war after 1940, characterized by wholesale internment . . . repressive censorship legislation and the use of the law of seditious libel to silence outspoken critics".[9]

A thorny issue raised throughout the period was race discrimination, a complex matter threaded with socioeconomic elements and one that made the governor uncomfortable. Debates within the Legislative Council about possible race-related restrictions on the use of local forces to guard the camps and staff the women's camp were reported in the media. Also reported were the discussions of apparent British unwillingness to recruit non-white forces. There were also blatant racist incidents reported during early 1942, notably clashes involving white US soldiers based in south-central Jamaica.[10]

The long delay in sanctioning the enlistment of black Jamaican soldiers was a particularly sore point, which frequently made the local news in 1940 and 1941. In 1939 the governor had acknowledged a wave of loyalty expressed in Jamaica and willingness to set aside domestic differences to face the war united, and he had advised those trying to enlist to be patient. However, as months passed and patience ran out, the political activism, particularly in support of constitutional change and economic advancement, was the issue used to accuse Jamaicans of disloyalty and of being too concerned with internal affairs during a time when Britain was at war. However, columnist

Morris Cargill was among those who put his pen into the fray in defence of Jamaicans. "Jamaicans on the whole are tremendously patriotic", he argued, but they had been told "often and clearly" that the country's help was not required.[11]

Many Jamaicans interviewed in later years reported that they felt distant from the war, seeing little connection beyond inconveniences such as shortages, which led to food and petroleum rationing and lessened economic opportunity.[12] Apart from those who went to Canada to volunteer for the Royal Air Force, the main direct involvement would come through the Caribbean Regiment, as noted here by Matthews in chapter 8, which was only formed in 1944 but saw no fighting, while RAF ground crews were also recruited in 1944.

Interaction with refugees could have been an opportunity for the local population to get first-hand details about the war; however, the camps, with their populations of people who had been actively involved in or were connected to the war theatres, were buffered from the local population. Even those evacuees and refugees who did not constitute a security risk were held in camps run by Colonial Office functionaries. Issues of paternalism, race and class influenced decisions to limit interface and interaction especially for the Gibraltarians, who were mainly white Catholic females. With respect to the other camps as well, the presence of a large population of whites in subordinate positions – as prisoners and internees – would surely have seemed to potentially undermine the colony's tradition of white control. Similarly, the possibility of a white working class mingling with a local population threatened the notion of white superiority. Certainly there would have been concern over Italian construction workers from West Africa who were interned in Kingston until the 1943 Armistice and who took up jobs normally done by black and non-white Jamaicans.

Many of Governor Richards's concerns about the situation in Jamaica climaxed in mid-1942, when he sent the Colonial Office a long typewritten letter, followed by a handwritten letter, in which he railed against the opposition and political and union activity. He furthermore complained about rising race consciousness and the "skein of racial hatred . . . skilfully woven into the pattern of the incompetent Englishmen in selfish and autocratic control for his own good and the people's detriment".[13]

The Colonial Office, which had dealt previously with complaints from, as well as about, the governor, was alarmed. File notes responding to his first letter expressed concern that there was "a good deal more than mere blind discontent going on in Jamaica", as well as the danger of "serious trouble", and noted that Governor Richards had "got into the position of being supported by no active and vocal section of the population . . . hardly a situation which we should like to see continue indefinitely".[14] There was also a comment that "considerable responsibility rests with the local Government for having failed to emphasize sufficiently the potential dangers of the situation, thereby failing to get an active popular interest in the remedial measures which are possible and at the same time giving an opportunity to the opponents of the Government to make profitable capital out of the situation".[15]

With a raging war going on, in January 1943 Governor Richards was summoned to London for talks and subsequently reassigned to Nigeria. By July, Jamaica had a new governor, in the more diplomatic person of Sir John Huggins, who served for the rest of the war. With the change in governors, a major decision was made with respect to the camps: the long-sidelined notion of a family camp, to reunite civilian internees separated since 1940, was brought to the forefront, and subsequently the Mona Family Camp was established at the northern extremity of Gibraltar Camp. Work to ameliorate the conditions of enemy aliens who were Jewish, or otherwise patently anti-Nazi, continued, while some locally based people were gradually allowed to return home.

When the Armistice was declared in September 1943, the Italian civilian internees moved from the male internment camp into a sort of semi-internment facility, initially located at the military hill station of Newcastle and later as a section of Gibraltar Camp.[16] Many of the Italians did work, particularly in making concrete and clay products. However, the government maintained the position that they would not be allowed to stay.

INTERNMENT CAMPS

The need for an internment camp was considered beginning in July 1939, and plans commenced for a camp that would hold 96 men, with room for doubling. By September the first group of foreign-born internees was already housed, detained under the island's Emergency Defence Regulations. They were initially Germans already living in Jamaica, some of them Jews.[17] A September 1939 newspaper story titled "All Is Well with Interned Germans" assured the sympathetic public that all was indeed well with this group. Later a few Italians also joined the detainees. This local civilian group, however, was soon outnumbered by foreigners loosely described as POWs. In March 1940 a newspaper story informed readers that "Enemy Aliens at Camp Number Close on 140",[18] and by July 220 German merchant seamen had been brought north for detention from Curaçao, where the British and French had occupied Dutch Antillean territories with Free Dutch involvement. Other groups of mainly German merchant seamen were brought in to Kingston by the British navy throughout the first half of the war, including two groups of 48 and 43 respectively on 8 and 13 December 1940, and a group of 84 was transferred from Bermuda in the third quarter of 1941.

The largest single group detained at the male internment camp comprised 447 men from a group of 564 German and Italian civilians interned in West Africa and shipped to Jamaica in December 1940. These were men who, often with their families, had been living and working on plantations and engineering projects or as missionaries in Nigeria, Sierra Leone, British Cameroon and the Gold Coast. They were rounded up within those particular colonies and sent to Nigeria, from where they were dispatched to Jamaica.[19]

With the southern African colonies already overpopulated with internees from East Africa, the War Office had appealed for a colonial location that could accommodate these internees from West Africa, and Sir Arthur Richards, the governor of Jamaica, agreed to accept them as an imperial liability;[20] upgrading and expanding the military internment camp to accommodate the men and creating a facility for the women and children.[21] Later a Colonial Office document explained that the transfer was "to help Sierra Leone, Nigeria and Gold Coast to get rid of some of their more dangerous internees" by moving them further away from the fighting. There was particular concern with respect to such countries/territories as British Cameroon, which had former German allegiances. Other concerns in Nigeria included the potential effects of the climate and the guards available to oversee these white internees.[22]

By the end of 1941 there were more than a thousand mainly German internees in the camp, and the numbers were still around twelve hundred in 1943.[23] The largest non-German group comprised 224 Italians, most of them with experience in construction-related fields. A detailed list of the occupations of some half of the Italians, prepared in 1944, indicated that there were miners, some with experience in road and concreting, carpenters, merchant seamen, mechanics, builders, contractors and masons.[24] The thousand-plus men at the Male Internment Camp were a mixed bunch (as discussed by Cwik and Muth in chapter 10), and the decision to hold them all together, Jew and Nazi, Germans and allies or former allies, Nazi and non-Nazi supporters, raised issues beyond Jamaica.

In February 1941 a parliamentary question was broached in London by member of Parliament Philip Noel-Baker with respect to the Jamaican internment camps for Germans and Italians. The MP asked the undersecretary of state for the colonies, George Hall, to urge on the governor of Jamaica "the very grave injustice of interning Nazis and anti-Nazis together" and encouraging, at the least, "effective separation" if the anti-Nazis must be interned. Hall, however, supporting the governor, argued that one could not discriminate among enemy seamen and others without some corroboration with regard to their political views.[25] A month later, there would be similar complaints with regard to the women's camp.[26]

This insensitivity towards European differences which was rooted in political and military views and ethnic ignorance was reflected in different sources. One exploration of the men's camp, through philately, showed that few of the Africa-born Germans, traders and planters, were ardent Nazi Party members, "unlike some of the Prisoner-of-War captives, most of whom were from the Mother country". However, Hall also quoted a former camp official who thought that some of these internees "might have been Nazi agents sent to West Africa in preparation for the outbreak of war".[27]

There was ongoing public discussion, in Jamaica and the United Kingdom, on the co-internment of people of severely opposite views, and critics urged the review of cases where anti-Nazi or anti-Fascist sympathies were not seriously in doubt. One example was the case of Jewish doctor Rudolph Aub, who had been interned in West Africa, where he had fled to escape Nazi persecution in Germany. Nonetheless, the governor was adamant that all such people transferred to Jamaica from West Africa would remain in internment while in Jamaica, and he telegraphed the secretary of state for the colonies that adequate arrangements to supervise released internees were not possible, especially since there was danger of their being pressured through relatives still in enemy territory. He reiterated that he could not consent to release them.[28] The secretary of state for the colonies did not agree that these were sufficient reasons for keeping interned people who did not qualify as being of enemy status, and he requested an early review and report.[29] Eventually, the governor relented somewhat. With respect to internees who had been locally resident before the war, a local advisory committee established by the governor reviewed and made determinations with respect to twenty-seven internees, as Governor Richards reported to the secretary of state for the colonies in September 1942.[30] However, regarding the civilians who had been interned in West Africa, the committee was "unable to make any recommendation or otherwise as to the desirability or otherwise of their release from internment", given that relevant documents had apparently been lost at sea. Nonetheless, by September 1942 it did recommend that a few interned men, including Dr Aub, be allowed to enlist in the Auxiliary Military Pioneer Corps, which ameliorated their living and working conditions.[31]

While they remained in the male internment camp, German Jews were eventually allowed to share a compound with the Jamaican political detainees. Interviewee Richard Hart, one of the Jamaican detainees, recalled that he and his countrymen shared one of several huts in a compound which also housed the German Jews, some other non-military Germans and a group of Norwegians.[32] A July 1942 Red Cross report stated that the camp, the site of which is now Jamaica's National Stadium complex, had the following sections: two sections for Germans, one for Italians, one for Jews and one for British subjects, along with a hospital, administration area and sections for provisions, canteen and workshops.[33] Besides incidents of physical confrontation, some Germans refused to attend movies at the camp if Jews were also invited, and others even refused the offer of a radio receiver to listen to any news because they could not listen to German transmissions.[34] By mid-war the more violent Nazis among the German internees were segregated, as a result of which, according to a 1943 report, there was "a marked improvement in the discipline of the Camp. Intimidation and physical violence against non-Nazi German internees has practically ceased".[35]

Another issue in the running of the male camp revolved around its status, that is, whether it was a designated internment or prisoner-of-war camp. A Jamaican Legislative Council minute of March 1940 referred to sixty-five prisoners of war, sixteen locally interned civilian enemy aliens, one enemy alien who had been interned in British Honduras, one internee being held in the mental hospital and one female internee held at the YWCA in

Kingston.[36] Just five months later a telegram from the officer commanding troops, Jamaica, noted that there were 429 detainees, including forty-five enemy aliens and 384 merchant seamen, of whom three were claiming POW status.[37] By December 1940 the War Office was requesting that the term POW not be applied to enemy merchant seamen or civilian internees at the male camp. The correspondence noted that the director of prisoners of war was responsible for POWs as defined under articles 1 and 81 of the relevant convention, and for enemy merchant seamen captured on the high seas, but not for civilian internees.[38] One part of the confusion lay in the differential understanding of the term "merchant mariner" for the British and the Germans, one considering them as civilians and the other as military.[39] However, there are other references to the male camp as a prisoner of war camp. A.P.D. Sutcliffe, in his *Military Mail in Jamaica*, referred to stamps marked "Internment & P. of W. Camp, Jamaica" as late as 22 November 1944.[40]

Later on, a 1945 War Office document clarified that German merchant seamen landing in Jamaica had originally been told that they were prisoners of war but that they had subsequently been installed in the male internment camp with civilian internees and treated as such. When the question of their status was raised in 1944, "it was considered that after nearly four years it was not possible to set up a separate Camp for them, or advisable to treat them other than as internees".[41]

Racial issues arose with respect to internees, both in official correspondence and in the local media. Early complaints about the guarding of white, especially German, civilian internees by non-white troops were discussed in the context of POW conditions. Articles 9 and 10 of the 1929 Geneva Convention had proposed the separation of different races and nationalities to the fullest extent. However, the Colonial Office pointed out that relevant POW provisions did not apply to guards and that the internees were not designated prisoners of war but rather enemy aliens.[42] Another minuted note underscored the political implications of its becoming locally known that there were objections to "native troops" being guards for internees, and discussions were held on the difficulty of guaranteeing that European troops based in Jamaica would always be available for this duty. British officials were receptive to this private correspondence with local officials and advised that it was undesirable to use black guards.[43] The urgency of the situation was heightened as it was known that there were merchant seamen in the camp who resented

Jamaican guards.⁴⁴ The discrimination against local forces was discussed among Jamaican members of the Legislative Council when the matter of the internment camp arose, as reported in the local newspapers.⁴⁵

THE WOMEN'S CAMP

The internment camp for female enemy aliens, which also held their children, was located on Hanover Street in downtown Kingston and was a reconditioned and enlarged compound that had housed an Anglican deaconess house and chapel. A YWCA report described the compound, centred on the church building, which had been repurposed as a dining room, as having "several separate buildings, each with several rooms but none of them very big; an open space . . . the usual outhouses etc. . . . There are guards at the gate and high fences with barbed wire around the property."⁴⁶

Police cars escorted the first residents, in January 1940. These were the wives and families of "13 prominent local Germans".⁴⁷ They had previously been allowed to remain at home, under restricted conditions, when their husbands were interned after war was declared. By year end the Hanover Street camp's population had been swollen by the addition of seventy-eight German and Italian women and their thirty-nine children, transferred from West Africa, which brought the total to eighty-nine women and forty-three children. Another six babies would also be born in the camp later on.

As with the male camp, 1941 saw the start of expressions of concern over relations between camp residents, and discussions were held over issues of ethnic discrimination. British member of Parliament Eleanor Rathbone, a member of the Parliamentary Committee on Refugees, wrote to the governor of Jamaica regarding complaints by a Jewish resident, who lamented that most of the women were Nazis, making life particularly difficult for Jewish internees.⁴⁸ The 1941 YWCA report confirmed that the small Italian group was most contented, but that there did appear to be conflict between them and German residents, despite efforts by the matron to divide them in the most helpful way. However, the YWCA report added that the main irritants were limited space, heat and frustration over lost possessions.⁴⁹

There were limited efforts to ameliorate conditions for these internees. Taking them on outings and blocking an adjacent street to expand available space were considered, but the authorities appeared to have been concerned about possible complications, particularly the negative local comments and media coverage.[50] Indeed in 1941–42, the two local newspapers, the *Gleaner* and *Public Opinion,* carried adverse stories on proposed and actual privileges allowed German internees. The *Gleaner* also covered debates among members of the Legislative Council on possible racial overtones in decision-making for the camps, in particular a decision to replace a non-white Jamaican matron with a white English one, ahead of the arrival of a group of internees from West Africa. As one member argued, "If they were going to say that a German alien was too good to be taken care of by a Jamaican, a loyal Britisher, because of colour, then the time had come when they must call a halt."[51]

Meanwhile, internee complaints about conditions continued. In June 1943 twenty-three women signed a letter requesting speedy repatriation, complaining that some of the children were permanently ailing and that after three years "in thickly crowded internment camps in a tropical climate, we were all subjected to great psychical stress; some of us had a nervous breakdown".[52]

THE MONA FAMILY CAMP

Such complaints regarding conditions at the women's camp, and related German reprisals, were factors influencing the decision to establish the Mona Family Camp at the north-eastern end of the Gibraltar Camp in August 1943. The camp reunited sixty-seven interned and divided families who had been transferred to Jamaica from West Africa in December 1942 and then separated into the existing gender-specific camps at Up Park and Hanover Street.

The idea of establishing a family camp or compound for married internees had arisen as early as March 1941 but was not pursued owing to the opposition of both the governor and the officer commanding troops. They did not favour creating a separate camp, nor did they agree with the Home Office practice of segregating a small area of the main camp. They therefore put in place a practice of allowing the men to visit at "reasonable intervals", intervals which were, among other things, affected by gasoline rationing, as a 1942 Red Cross report noted. The report also observed that permission to send packages between the camps was halted owing to security concerns.[53]

Additionally, the Colonial Office noted that correspondence sent to Jamaica in 1942 seeking to create a uniform imperial approach to internees, based on the practice in Britain, where the Home Office had primary responsibility, garnered little response. Instead, pressure from the International Red Cross, in favour of family camps, influenced the attitude in Jamaica:

> There is little doubt that the handing over of male civilian internees to the military and the segregation of the sexes in separate camps had proved a cheaper and more labour-saving system than the establishment of a family camp, or of family quarters within a larger camp. But it does not follow the policy adopted by this country, by most other colonies and partially even by Germany herself. It also entails the danger of anomalies which may give a handle for complaint and reprisal.[54]

This fear of reprisal by Germany was, unfortunately, realized. Conditions at the Liebenau camp for British women and children, in Germany, were allowed to deteriorate "on the pretext that the contrast between Liebenau and Vittel on the one hand, and the Female Internment Camp, Hanover Street, Kingston on the other, was too marked to be any longer tolerated by Germany".[55]

This occurred around the time when Governor Sir Arthur Richards was called to London for talks on the situation in Jamaica. Since he was subsequently sent to Nigeria, the new governor, Sir John Huggins, was put in charge when the new camp opened. Though under military control for security reasons, the camp had a far more relaxed environment. After extensive correspondence, it was agreed that internal staff would be European civilians and external guard duties would be carried out by local forces,[56] a compromise aimed at toeing the line of international conventions while appeasing the Germans as well as considering possible local sensibilities.

By September 1943 a YMCA report noted great excitement among the affected male and female internees over the prospect of a family camp, and the men moved into the compound first to ready things for the women and children. The report added, "About 160 men, women and children will be affected. Families separated some three years and more are to be reunited."[57]

A further report in 1945 stated that the camp's 186 internees included 56 men, the balance being women and children, including some single women and a doctor. There was also one stewardess in the category Merchant Seamen (P/W). It noted that the "married families give no trouble at all. The men have excellent allotments in full production."[58] The internees lived in wooden barrack-style buildings, built as part of Gibraltar Camp. However, they were buffered from the rest of the camp by fencing and an empty area of land.

GIBRALTAR CAMP

Gibraltar Camp differed markedly from the internment camps in that it was designed and run for civilian evacuees. Originally scaled to accommodate thousands of civilians from the Mediterranean fortress colonies of Gibraltar and Malta, its initial population was affected by the Maltese refusal to leave home and the fact that large numbers of the planned Gibraltarian occupants, routed via England, remained there in the face of escalating transatlantic threats posed by German U-boats. Two shiploads, sailing straight to Jamaica from Gibraltar, arrived in October/November 1940 (1,093 on the SS *Neuralia*; 393 on the SS *Thysville*), while a few others trickled in thereafter. The estimate of fifteen hundred to sixteen hundred is supported by a typewritten report at the Catholic Chancery in Kingston, which stated, "About 1,500 evacuees, practically all Spanish speaking, have taken refuge in the Island Mission of Jamaica. They constitute one of the largest cities of Jamaica and certainly the largest exclusive Catholic Settlement of the island."[59]

The Catholic church was asked to be involved with the day-to-day operation of Gibraltar Camp even before it was built, given the strong religious roots of the Gibraltar people, and perhaps also owing to the fact that the majority of these evacuees were women and children. However, the Gibraltar Camp did not remain exclusively Catholic, as even at the start there were a few Jewish evacuees among the Gibraltarians. Additionally, there were dozens of Spanish refugees from General Franco's Spain, a fact that the British were not too anxious to advertise, given the delicate balance of British-Spanish relations relating to the actual Gibraltar, the strategically located British fortress at the southern tip of Spain.

The semantic distinction between evacuees, who were sent away from home for their safety by their government, and refugees never really permeated Jamaican society, though the evacuees tried to make it clear in their limited interactions with the public. An article in *Catholic Opinion* of December 1940 recalled that Gibraltarian women shopping at Issa's store in downtown Kingston had been called "Spanish refugees" by Jamaicans in the store: "Ofelia and Euralia turned around, and Ofelia said 'First of all, we are not Spanish, we are British. And secondly, we are not refugees, we are evacuees'."[60] Nonetheless, they continued to be thought of as refugees, and sixty years later most Jamaicans interviewed remember the entire camp population as refugees.[61]

But hundreds of refugees from Nazi-occupied areas of Europe were about to arrive (as discussed by Cwik and Muth in chapter 10). The existence of significant spare capacity at Gibraltar Camp drew the attention of British and other officials and of refugee groups seeking sanctuary away from the diminishing areas of Europe remaining free from Nazi or Fascist influences.[62] The first successful refugee group consisted of mainly Polish Jews who had reached Lisbon and run out of overland escape options. They appealed to Winston Churchill, who agreed to allow them sanctuary at Gibraltar Camp, but his agreement was rooted in more layered correspondence that involved the Polish Embassy in London, the British Foreign Office and also the Colonial Office. In an effort to make way for Portuguese acceptance of other Poles and Czechs clinging to the remains of unoccupied France, the British government asked whether Jamaica "could accommodate them temporarily either in an existing camp or by building additional huts".[63]

The Colonial Office agreed to forward the request on the basis of a guarantee of the refugees' removal after the war as well as an assurance that expenses would be covered by the British government. They added that refugees would probably be accommodated in "semi-internment conditions", which would entail confinement to camp at night and prohibitions on working or establishing businesses without the permission of the colonial government. They also wanted to reserve the right to fully intern any refugees the colonial government deemed fit.

Under these conditions, the details of which had not been conveyed up front to the refugees, the first group of 153 arrived in Kingston aboard the SS *Serpa Pinto* on 7 February 1942. There were 147 Polish men, women and children; 3 Dutch and one each Belgian and German. An American, Bertrand Jacobson, representing the American Jewish Joint Distribution Committee, which had agreed to underwrite the group's expenses, accompanied them. A second group, in March, included 14 Poles, 9 Czechs, 4 Dutch, 7 Luxemburgers and a single Austrian. The German from the first group was eventually sent to the male internment camp, and the others were placed at Gibraltar Camp, initially in quarantine, as there was a case of typhus aboard the *Serpa Pinto*, and then because a camp resident contracted dengue fever.

Camp life proved frustrating for most of the Poles, whose distress was made worse by the lack of Polish government (in exile) representation in Jamaica and the consequent difficulty of gaining visas to permanent destinations. The Poles were vociferous in their complaints about Gibraltar Camp, which did not endear them to the governor. For instance, file notes at the Jewish Joint Distribution Committee revealed that while the British authorities "stressed that the refugees were treated as guests of a friendly power . . . the Polish refugees were disposed to compare camp conditions with those of a concentration camp".[64] In correspondence with the secretary of state for the colonies during 1942–43, the governor indicated his refusal to loosen the restrictions on their conditions of stay.

The Dutch refugees, most of whom arrived in late 1942 and early 1943, were a completely different story. First of all, they were for the most part better off, and they were from the start designated as transients, en route to one of the Dutch Caribbean territories or elsewhere. Importantly, they also had Dutch representation, and this would have influenced their treatment. Several of them, who were then youngsters in the camp, have positive memories of attending local schools, of outings and of enjoyable times living in the camp, such as using a pulley to hang a big bunch of ripe bananas from the roof of the verandah that ran outside their rooms.[65]

The British Foreign Office had asked the Colonial Office to find temporary accommodation for Dutch refugees en route to Suriname, suggesting Trinidad. They wanted to oblige the Dutch government, which had helped the British with refugees who had overstayed their time in Curaçao the previous year. As the Foreign Office pointed out in correspondence, "Unless we can help them over their party of Jews for Surinam [sic], they will certainly be averse to turning a favourable ear to any appeals we may make to them in the future."[66] However, the Colonial Office responded by saying that having succoured more than fifteen hundred seamen rescued from ships sunk in Caribbean waters, plus hosting British and American service personnel, Trinidad was overcrowded. They suggested Jamaica or British Guiana as alternatives.[67]

The first Dutch group referenced was some 150 to 200 Dutch subjects travelling from Spain on the *Transatlantica*. The details surrounding this group are sketchy, however. What is sure is that a group of around 225 travelling on the *Marques de Comillas* from Vigo, Spain, arrived in Kingston in November 1942, and correspondence suggests that a second group followed on its heels.[68] A Dutch Jewish camp resident, who was then a young girl and who has further researched the experience and maintained communication with other residents, quotes an older refugee: "Our convoy of 172 people left

Vigo 16 November and arrived in Kingston on December 4, 1942. The second convoy consisted of 110 people."[69]

The difference in approach to these Dutch refugees is made plain in a telegram to the governor of Jamaica advising that while currency limitations would be applied to this group, they were "not (repeat not) to be searched for other unauthorised valuables".[70] There was subsequent reference to at least one Dutch refugee's proposal to establish a diamond-cutting enterprise in Jamaica, which was refused by the governor.[71] At least one other Dutch group, of around 70 persons, arrived in March 1943; and there was correspondence in August relating to another party of 50 or 60 Dutch refugees. A camp resident recalled that there was one group of mainly young gentile men, en route to join the fighting forces.

The exact numbers of Dutch refugees is therefore still questionable. Statements from the Dutch consul, who left Jamaica in November 1943, confirmed a group of 173 sent to Kingston in December 1942 and another 79 sent temporarily in March 1943. He claimed that 154 of the refugees had already moved on or identified jobs they would fill; 81 would go to Curaçao, and some young men had gone to join the armed forces.[72] Figures prepared by the Gibraltar Camp officials to gain reimbursement for refugee residents during the 1942–43 financial year appear to confirm the consul's figures. However, further statements were also submitted for December 1943, after the consul's departure from Jamaica, so the numbers may have been more.[73]

Father William Feeney, the resident chaplain who wrote an article on the camp in 1989, estimated that as many as 2,000 Jewish refugees were accommodated at Gibraltar Camp.[74] Claus Füllberg-Stolberg estimated up to 4,800 refugees of various nationalities, arguing that the documents at hand are incomplete. He relied more on the recollections of eyewitnesses from the period.[75] Joanna Newman, using figures from the Jewish Joint Distribution Committee, referred to five groups of Dutch refugees at Gibraltar Camp: two, of 250 and 175 people respectively in December 1942; one in April 1943 of 305 people; one in October 1943 of 60 people and one in December 1943 of 300 refugees.[76]

For certain, at least some hundreds of Dutch refugees at a time lived at Gibraltar Camp, in relatively unruffled transience that lasted a year in some cases, between the years 1942 and 1944. What seems equally certain is that the Jewish refugee group may at times have been just as large as the

Gibraltarian one at Gibraltar Camp. It must be noted that some geographical separation was maintained between the first comers and those who followed. Camp 1, where the Gibraltarians had been settled when they arrived in 1940, was on a higher elevation than Camp 2, which had been unoccupied and where the refugees and other small groups were later accommodated. However, access was through the same gate and all official facilities like the commissary and recreation spaces were common. One of those other small groups sharing the camp for a time was a group of Finnish sailors, interned at the male internment camp while war raged between Finland and Britain's ally, the Soviet Union. A policy change, however, in 1942 led to their transfer to Gibraltar Camp.[77] The wife of the commissary officer at Gibraltar Camp remembered blond men scything grass at Mona, an indelible picture, she said.[78]

GIBRALTAR CAMP LAYOUT AND LIVING CONDITIONS

Gibraltar Camp was set on some two hundred acres of relatively flat land that was surrounded by hills, around seven miles from downtown Kingston, between two semi-rural outposts, Papine and August Town. The land was part of the Mona property, an old sugar estate subsequently acquired by the National Water Commission, which made the land available to the Colonial Office for the setting up of the camp. The market community of Papine, which lay about a mile north of the camp, was the terminus for public transport into the city – first the tram and then, from 1944, the bus. Papine was a well-known location – important for travel from the surrounding hills but also a popular drinking place on weekends, when it also attracted market traffic. In addition, it was near to the popular Hope Botanical Gardens.

The camp layout and construction were simple. Given a tight time frame and limited resources, the Public Works Department designed barrack structures, each 150 feet long and 25 feet wide, which could be subdivided as necessary. Each pair of barrack buildings was linked by covered walkways to a shared sanitation block, and walkways linked the rows of housing units to kitchen/dining halls and other facilities.

Within the housing units, an internal passageway provided access to fourteen rooms on each side, with adjacent rooms allocated to families and linked as necessary to create self-contained flatlets. There was also an effort to allocate the barrack rooms strategically, so where possible single people, for instance, might be in different buildings from families and the Gibraltarian Jews could be housed together. Internal walls stopped short of the roof, for ventilation, but also limited privacy. Verandahs on the long sides of the buildings meant that all rooms had some external as well as internal space.

The camp was built to be self-contained; it had a shop where residents could purchase common necessities, including fabric and thread as well as snacks and toiletries. A 1941 report referenced a dry-goods canteen and a grocery canteen, including a "much patronised" bar, which served beer but not stronger spirits. There was a Catholic church, a recreation hall, a school for the young children, a hospital, a dispensary and dental office, a police station with cells, workshops for sewing and other activities and its own water tank, fed from the nearby Hope River. When necessary, empty buildings were allocated as worship spaces for Jewish and Anglican residents. Since meals were provided in dining halls, each with a modern kitchen, personal cooking was unnecessary, though those with the taste and the means could, and did in fact, add to the fare provided. The camp also included a barber shop, a shoemaker's shop, a beauty parlour and a dry cleaner, which generally provided an employment opportunity for residents, as they were not allowed to work outside. Miriam Stanton, a young woman among the Polish refugees who subsequently wrote a book on her war experiences, described Gibraltar Camp as a lively and self-sufficient little town. "There was always something happening, concerts, weddings, fights, scandals and unfortunately, funerals as well. We had beautiful gardens; everybody tended his own little patch."[79]

Gibraltar Camp was well provisioned and advertisements throughout the war testify to the ongoing importance of ensuring that supplies for the camp were available. Allan and Daphne Rae, whose father, Ernest, was camp commandant for some time, and Priscilla Harris, whose husband was commissary officer, recalled that whatever the shortages outside the camp, the residents were well provisioned even if the quality might have diminished somewhat for some items such as when, at a point during the war, fresh eggs were replaced with powdered egg.[80]

Although Gibraltar was a civilian camp run through the Colonial Office, it is noteworthy that the camp officials included a commandant and deputy commandant and a commissary officer. The senior staff was all resident, as was a Catholic establishment which included a priest and a corps of eight nuns, two each from the Franciscan, Sisters of Mercy, Dominican and Native

Sisters communities. The nunnery was the only two-storey building in the camp. Apart from the rows of barrack buildings, there were bungalows for the staff and a set of small cottages which had been built for families but were eventually used otherwise, to avoid jealousies over who got what type of housing.

The camp was fenced and guarded, and though it was officially a civilian camp, it was governed within the context of the Defence Regulations then in force. Signboards warned that trespassers would be prosecuted, but the restrictions of the camp were most clearly set out in a warning notice that ran several times in the *Gleaner*, drawing attention to Evacuees (Defence) Regulations made on 18 October 1940. The main points reiterated were that members of the public entering the camp without a valid pass signed by the commandant would be prosecuted and fined up to twenty-five pounds or imprisoned for up to three months, and it was stressed that passes would not normally be granted to members of the public. A *Gleaner* story set out other regulations pertinent to residents, who were prohibited from any work and who could be fined up to five pounds, imprisoned in the lockup for up to a week and have their freedoms and diet rights restricted. They could also be arrested and handed over to the police. The public was, therefore, made aware of the status of the residents within the camp.

The initial intention was to keep the residents in and the Jamaicans out, other than the few employed in the kitchens and other facilities and those working in the offices, who were expected to be prompt in their arrival and departure times. Evacuees, however, complained at the restrictions, which the Camp Committee chairman subsequently described as "prudent reluctance on the part of the administration to allow the evacuees to leave the camp at will".[81]

Eventually a pass system was put in place, and residents could sign out using a registration number but were required to return by 5:00 p.m. unless they had previously secured special permission. By the end of January 1941 they were shown more leniency and could leave camp from 8:00 a.m. and remain out until 10:00 p.m., or even longer with special permission.

Prosecutions did occur, however. Vendors seeking to make contact with potential customers and camp employees remaining at the camp after hours were among those prosecuted under the regulations, especially during the first few months of the camp opening. Several interviewees, including some who attended local high schools with the evacuee and refugee teenagers, understood that Jamaicans were not welcome in the camp. There was intense scrutiny of those entering the camp, and locals competing with camp teams, entertainers and other invitees had to be escorted, observed and returned to the gate.

A young evacuee who finished school while in the camp and who was given special permission to intern at the local public works department commented in an interview that "Camp Commandant Ernest Rae (and) . . . the religious group – Jesuits from Boston; they ruled very nicely". He said that most of the Gibraltarian residents had husbands and families back home and explained the "great stress put on keeping us apart" from the Jamaicans.[82] Jamaicans had packed the sidewalks to cheer on the Gibraltarians when they arrived, and some young men were attracted to the "very nice girls indeed", as evacuee Frank Tucker described some of his camp mates. However, the governor stood firmly against contact between these women and local men.

Asked in 1942 to respond to a complaint that residents in Gibraltar Camp had "no right to entertain anybody" in what was supposed to be their home, the governor told the secretary of state for the colonies, "It is not possible to allow evacuees to have their friends to their own huts in the Camp, as the Administration would obviously lose all control of Camp discipline and order if this were allowed, other than in very special cases."[83] Indeed, in 1941 a Colonial Office minuted comment had described the camp as having "semi-internment conditions", including confinement at night, lack of facility for visitors and the banning of internees from engaging in any business without special permission.[84]

Local response to the camp varied, but in general there was interest in these "exotic" visitors. There was always great eagerness to engage with them in sporting and other activities, as well as the usual efforts to sell them goods and services. Interaction occurred on the roads, in the markets and the shops of Papine, at nearby Hope Gardens and elsewhere. There was, however, significant respect for the regulations, especially in the context of the authoritarian governor. With regard to the interaction which did occur, social class and religion were also factors. The majority of Gibraltarians were Catholic, many spoke Spanish among themselves and many, if not most, were working class. Based on several interviews, it appears that middle- and upper-class Jamaicans were more interested in the better-off among the refugees, some

Table 11.1.

Name	Location	Residents	Oversight	Date Opened	Closure
Gibraltar Camp	Mona, outskirts of Kingston Jamaica	– Gibraltarian Evacuees (arrived October/November 1940) – Jewish Refugees (arrived 1942–43)	Civilian – Colonial Office commandant and establishment/Catholic establishment	1940	Taken over by military after main Gibraltarian group left in October 1944. Still termed Gibraltar Camp until 1947
Mona Family Camp	Mona, outskirts of Kingston, Jamaica. Physically, part of Gibraltar Camp	Civilian internees (mainly German) comprising families and single women transferred from main male and female internment camps.	Military	1943	Camp remained in hands of military post-war; remaining internees gradually found new homes and left Jamaica
Male Internment Camp	Up Park Camp, Kingston, Jamaica	– Local German and Italian internees (1939–) – Civilian internees transferred from West Africa (December 1940) – Merchant seamen and other wartime prisoners (1940–41) – Jamaican civil internees	Military	1939	Married civilians (German and Italian internees) transferred to Mona Family Camp in 1943. Last major overseas group shipped out 1946
Female Internment Camp	Hanover Street, Kingston, Jamaica	– Local German and Italian women and children (1940 – German and Italian women and children interned in West Africa (Dec 1940)	Military oversight	1940	1943, when population transferred to Mona Family Camp

of whom were reportedly entertained in private homes and many of whom also reported outings to Kingston's nicer facilities, such as the Myrtle Bank Hotel in downtown Kingston.[85]

CONCLUSION

The decision of Governor Sir Arthur Richards to offer to host the Gibraltarians was a fixed-term response to an imperial concern. They could come for the duration of the war, they would be cared for and returned to their families. The considerations were economic, logistical and imperial; the approach paternalistic and authoritarian. The building of the camp would provide some jobs, albeit for the short term. Similar considerations were taken into account for the refugees, who were offered what were effectively semi-internment conditions.

Governor Richards offered to accept at least one other large group, Italian prisoners of war whom the War Office was seeking to move from locations in North Africa. In an April 1941 missive, Governor Richards advised that he could accept four thousand Italian POWs the following month and another six thousand three and a half months after that.[86] It was argued that the use of non-white guards would not be an issue, as the prisoners were then being supervised by Indian guards. The logistics were discussed, including the building of a new camp for the Gibraltarians and using Gibraltar Camp for the POWs. But the British government proved unwilling to find funds for a new camp, though it was inclined to keep open the possibility of moving further Gibraltarian evacuees, then in London, on to Jamaica.

In no case did the governor recommend that the people for whom camps were proposed or actuated should stay in Jamaica beyond the end of the war; hence there was no thought to their interface with, and even possible incorporation into, the society. Therefore, even those who offered skills or business opportunities were discouraged. The refugees stayed for varied times, depending on their individual networks and the possibility of getting jobs and visas elsewhere – and also depending on the involvement of their governments. Some stayed for weeks, others for months or years. A small group was still there more than a year after the war ended.

Most of the evacuees were sent home to Gibraltar in October 1944. A few young men who had joined the Pioneer Corps remained to complete their duties, and a few returned to Gibraltar later with Jamaican wives. Like the refugees, some of the German and Italian civilians were able to get visas and jobs that took them elsewhere, some to Cuba, Latin America or the United States, and others returned to Africa or Europe. A large group of mainly German internees and people who might have been named POWs, mostly with military connections, were finally shipped home in November 1946. They had remained incarcerated beyond the end of the war because the Jamaican security authorities refused the responsibility of supervising them once released. A few of the residents of the various camps did, however, manage to stay in Jamaica, often by marrying Jamaican women.

The distinction between haven for displaced friends or allies and holding tank for enemy aliens, whether civilian or state agent, was rooted in the camp conditions. The strict conditions imposed at civilian-controlled Gibraltar Camp, in the interest of order and a paternalistic control, blurred that distinction. The regulatory context, even for this population of fellow colonials and, later, refugees was the governor's emergency regulations, though the local context also suggests race and class considerations. With added requirements forbidding business or work and mandating nightly presence, the description of conditions as generally semi-internment was apt. The Gibraltar Camp experience is relevant to a period that has been underexplored in twentieth-century Jamaican historiography and significant to the role that Jamaica and the Caribbean played in the crisis.

ACKNOWLEDGEMENTS

This chapter draws on the author's PhD thesis from the University of the West Indies in 2008: "Gibraltar Camp, 1940–1947: Isolation and Interaction in Colonial Jamaica".

NOTES

1. PhD research on Gibraltar Camp, Mona, Jamaica, revealed limited local recollection, in terms of consistent quality of information during interviews conducted as well as references located in local cultural material such as books, songs, heritage performances, etc. Such texts as exist include references in three wartime poems by Jamaican Louise Bennett-Coverley ("Jamaica Patois", "Po Mufeena" and "Govanah") and a poem by Nobel laureate Derek Walcott,

who was an undergraduate at the University College of the West Indies at Mona when the Gibraltar Camp barracks were still in use, in the late 1940s and early 1950s. Many Jamaicans in the World War II age group had a general recollection of refugees and prisoners of war, often conflating their separate camps into one.

2. Denham died in office, and his colonial secretary, C.C. Wollery, filled in until Richards's arrival.
3. Jamaicans detained at the male internment camp were Alexander Bustamante, leading trade unionist from 1940 to 1942; journalist G. St C Scotter from 1941; and, in 1942, People's National Party propaganda secretary Samuel Marquis, trade unionist Arthur Williams, New York–based Jamaican political activist W.A. Domingo and People's National Party radicals Ken and Frank Hill, as well as Arthur Henry and Richard Hart.
4. Leslie Ashenheim's "The Pathway to Detention", originally published in the *Gleaner*, 27 May 1941, was discussed in "Detention", *Public Opinion*, 31 May 1941, 3.
5. People's National Party, Annual Report, 1941, quoted in Richard Hart, *Towards Decolonisation* (Kingston: Canoe Press, 1999), 125. Hart, an avowed communist and then a member of the People's National Party, was himself detained and was one of four subsequently booted from the party.
6. *The West India Committee Circular*, 13 November 1941, 274.
7. Hart, *Towards Decolonisation*, 194–208.
8. Louise Bennett, "Govanah", *Jamaica Labrish* (Kingston: Sangsters Book Stores, 1972), 124. Bennett's other wartime poems included at least one that mentioned the Spanish-speaking residents at Gibraltar Camp.
9. Gordon Lewis, *The Growth of the Modern West Indies* (New York: Modern Reader Paperbacks, 1968), 182.
10. Relevant files include National Archives of the United Kingdom (NAUK): CO875/13/16 PR, Jamaica 1942, telegram from Governor of Jamaica to Secretary of State for the Colonies, 30 May 1942 re the clash between police and American soldiers in the town of May Pen.
11. "Through the Looking Glass", *Public Opinion*, 26 April 1941, 12.
12. Interviews conducted between 2001 and 2007 towards a thesis on Gibraltar Camp.
13. NAUK: CO 137/854/14, Situation in Jamaica, Richards, letter to CO, 1 June 1942, handwritten letter of 7 July 1942.
14. NAUK: CO 137/854/14, Situation in Jamaica 1942 and 1943, minuted notes dated 26 June and 2 July 1942.

15. NAUK: CO 137/854/14, Situation in Jamaica 1942 and 1943, minute re Sir Arthur Richards's letters.
16. While several interviewees confirm that the Italians lived and even started a business making and selling clay and cement garden and other fixtures, the exact location in the camp, the timeframe and conditions of their presence remain unclear.
17. The distinction of foreign-born is made because there were several high-profile Jamaican internees detained between 1940 and 1942, for activities considered inimical to the war effort, the best known being trade unionist and subsequent prime minister Sir Alexander Bustamante.
18. "All Is Well with Interned Germans", *Gleaner*, 14 September 1939; "Enemy Aliens at Camp Number Close on 140", *Gleaner*, 5 March 1940.
19. "More Enemy Aliens Arrive", *Gleaner*, 5 December 1940.
20. Jamaica National Archives: WO 216/149, Jamaica General: letter from Officer Commanding Troops Jamaica to War Office, 14 August 1940.
21. NAUK: WO 216/149, Jamaica General: report by secretary, Local Defence Committee, on events from 1 October to 31 December 1940, noted completion of a sixth extension to the male internment camp at an estimated cost of £14,500.
22. NAUK: CO 323/1798/1, Internment of Enemy Aliens Jamaica, individual cases: minuted note #29, August 1940; CO 968/45/3 WO to CO, 23 May 1941.
23. *Report of YMCA War Prisoners Aid Office* (Kingston: YWCA, 1943).
24. NAUK: HO 213/183, Italian Internees: telegram from Governor of Jamaica (Sir John Huggins) to Secretary of State for the Colonies, 6 October 1944.
25. NAUK: FO 916/71, Internment Camps for Germans and Italians in Jamaica 1941 (pt. 2 of file): Parliamentary Question: Jamaica (Refugees), 6 February 1941.
26. NAUK: CO 968/35/13, Treatment of Enemy Aliens, Jamaica 1941: letter from MP Eleanor Rathbone, Parliamentary Committee on Refugees, to the CO, 8 August 1941.
27. A.P.D. Sutcliffe, *Jamaica: A Philatelic Handbook*, Roses Caribbean Handbook no. 5 (United Kingdom: Roses Caribbean Philatelic Society, 1982), 66.
28. NAUK: CO 968/64/11, Internment of Enemy Aliens (policy): telegram from Governor of Jamaica to Secretary of State for the Colonies, 8 April 1942.
29. NAUK: CO 968/68/11, Internment of Enemy Aliens (policy): telegram to Governor of Jamaica from Secretary of State for the Colonies, 13 June 1942.
30. NAUK: CO 968/68/11, Jamaica Detainees: telegram from Governor to Secretary of State for the Colonies, 21 September 1942 re internees; NAUK: CO 968/68/13,

Jewish Internees: telegram from Governor of Jamaica to Secretary of State for the Colonies, 21 September 1942.
31. The Pioneer Corps, which also included mainly young men from among the evacuees at Gibraltar Camp, did guard duties in non-sensitive areas in Jamaica.
32. Richard Hart, e-mail correspondence with author, 2005.
33. Red Cross Archive, M. Roth, Red Cross Report on the Male Internment Camp, 8 July 1942, 1.
34. Ibid., 7.
35. NAUK: CO 980/35, Civilian Internees in Jamaica 1943–1944: extract from Jamaica Security Report, 31 May 1943.
36. Jamaica: Legislative Council Minutes, 5 March 1940, 79.
37. NAUK: WO 216/149, Jamaica General: officer commanding troops Jamaica to WO, 26 August 1940.
38. NAUK: WO 216/149, Jamaica General: WO to officer commanding troops Jamaica, 21 December 1940.
39. Bob Moore and Kent Fedorowich, *The British Empire and its Italian Prisoners of War, 1940–1947* (Basingstoke: Palgrave, 2002), 18.
40. Sutcliffe, *Military Mail in Jamaica*, 75, fig. 112.
41. NAUK: WO 106/5124A, Report on Visits by Lt Col N.J. Darling to Trinidad, Jamaica and Bermuda, March–May 1945, 10.
42. NAUK: CO 323/1800/4, Removal of Internees from West Africa to Jamaica 1940–1941: minuted note, November 1940.
43. NAUK: CO 323/1800/4, Removal of Internees from West Africa to Jamaica 1940–1941: minuted note K.E. Robinson, 31 October 1940.
44. NAUK: WO 106/5124A, Report on Visits by Lt Col N.J. Darling to Trinidad, Jamaica and Bermuda, 10.
45. "Estimates of Government Departments", sections subheaded "Internment Camp" and "The Local Forces", *Gleaner*, 15 March 1941, 10.
46. NAUK: CO 968/35/13, Treatment of Enemy Aliens Jamaica 1941: extract from YWCA report on the camp by M.M. Mills of the YWCA, who visited Jamaica 3–26 February 1941.
47. *Jamaica Times*, 15 June 1940, 1.
48. NAUK: CO 968/35/13, Treatment of Enemy Aliens, Jamaica 1941: letter from MP Eleanor Rathbone, Parliamentary Committee on Refugees, to the CO, 8 August 1941.
49. NAUK: CO 968/35/13 Jamaica: YWCA Report, 1941.
50. "Can This Be True? Reported Move to Reserve Rockfort Mineral Bath for Exclusive Use of German Internees", *Gleaner*, 30 May 1941; "German Women Internees to Use Bath at Rockfort", *Gleaner*, 3 June 1941; "Current Items",

Gleaner, 19 July 1941; "Enemy Internees", *Public Opinion*, 31 January 1942; "Enemy Internees"; "Amends and Protest", *Public Opinion*, 7 February 1942.

51. "Estimates of Government Departments", subhead "Internment Camp", *Gleaner*, 15 March 1941, 10.
52. Jamaica Archives and Record Centre: CSO 1B/5/77/217, Enemy Aliens (Females), Complaints From: letter to the Colonial Secretary from the Women's Internment Camp, 22 June 1943.
53. Red Cross Archive: Roth Report, 6.
54. NAUK: CO 980/35, Civil Internees: note on civilian internment in Jamaica, undated document.
55. NAUK: CO 980/35, Civil Internees in British Territories, Jamaica – Family Camp: correspondence re German Camp conditions, including note on civilian internment in Jamaica, undated document; and telegram from Berne to Foreign Office, 20 February 1943.
56. NAUK: CO 980/35, Civil Internees: telegram from Commander, North Caribbean Area, to War Office, 6 May 1943.
57. NAUK: FO 916/202, Jamaica, 5–16 September 1943: KW4/4. Report on Visit to Jamaica by Conrad Hoffman Jr. of the YMCA War Prisoners Aid fund.
58. NAUK: WO 106/5124A, Report on Visits by Lt Col N.J. Darling to Trinidad, Jamaica and Bermuda, 10. These observations were corroborated in reports from the Swiss Consul in Jamaica, 1943, held in the Swiss Federal Archive.
59. Catholic Chancery: Gibraltar Camp 1940–1945: typewritten report, n.d., 3.
60. "From Gibraltar Rock to Gibraltar Camp", *Catholic Opinion*, December 1940, 25. Evacuees were groups of people who left their home countries in response to external threat, in this case at the insistence of their government, which arranged for them to be accommodated elsewhere; while refugees escaped religious or political persecution by gaining permission to stay in another country. The internees were detained, usually under police or military powers, in response to a state perception that they might pose a security threat.
61. With respect to other camp populations of the time, many local interviewees also made no distinction between civilian internees and prisoners of war.
62. The camp was originally designed to hold four thousand evacuees, a number subsequently increased and then reversed when war conditions made transport difficult and the Maltese, for whom space had been planned, refused to travel to Jamaica.
63. NAUK: CO 137/854/7, Refugees 1941: 8 November 1941, Rogers, CO, to Randall, FO.
64. American Jewish Joint Distribution Committee: file notes 884–885 Jamaica, 1941–1944.

65. Bananas, by then an important export, were a casualty of diminished transport for non-essentials in wartime, and hence extremely cheap, yet still a delicacy for foreigners living in the island.
66. NAUK: FO 371/32677, Refugees 1942: letter from FO to P. Rogers, CO, 6 August 1942.
67. NAUK: FO 371/32677: Refugees 1942: letter from CO to Randall, FO, 7 August 1942.
68. NAUK: FO 371/32677, Refugees 1942.
69. Correspondence with Inez Baker, 2004.
70. NAUK: FO 371/32677, Refugees 1942. telegram to Governor of Jamaica from Secretary of State for the Colonies, 5 November 1942. Valuables including diamonds were often sewn into hems by wealthy Dutch refugees.
71. Tomasz Potworowski, "The Evacuation of Jewish Polish Citizens from Portugal to Jamaica 1941–1943", *Polin* 19 (2007): 155–82, 171.
72. "Dutch Consul Leaving Island Deals with Refugee Problem", *Gleaner*, 30 November 1943, 6.
73. NAUK: FO 371/42826, Political General, Refugees (WR): telegram 362 of 20 November 1943, apportionment of expenditure from 5 December 1942 to 31 March 1943 for Dutch Refugees ex SS *Marques de Comillas*.
74. Catholic Chancery, Gibraltar Camp, typescript of article for *Gleaner* newspaper, 1989.
75. Claus Stolberg and Katja Füllberg-Stolberg, "Jewish Exile in the British Colonial Empire – Gibraltar Camp, Jamaica, 1942–1947" (translation by Alfred Gutmann), *Hannoversche Schriften* 11 (1996): 85–102.
76. Joanna Newman, "Nearly the New World: Refugees and the British West Indies, 1933–1945" (PhD diss., University of Southampton, 1998), 265.
77. Suzanne Francis-Brown, "Finnish Sailors among World War II Internees", *Jamaica Journal* 29, no. 3 (2006): 60–62.
78. Priscilla Harris, interviewed by author, 2004.
79. Miriam Stanton, *Escape from the Inferno of Europe* (London: M. Stanton, 1996), 217. In the camp, Stanton was still known as Myriam Sandzer.
80. Allan Rae, interviewed by author, 2001 and 2002; Daphne Rae, interviewed by author, 2006; Priscilla Harris, interviewed by author, 2004.
81. Catholic Chancery: Gibraltar Camp file, untitled typewritten document describing the camp.
82. Frank Tucker, interviewed by author, London, 2007.
83. Jamaica Archives and Record Centre: CSO 1B/5/77/264, Camp for Imperial Government at Mona: miscellaneous (personal), 14 July 1942, Secretary of State for the Colonies Lord Cranborne to Governor of Jamaica Arthur Richards,

enclosing 19 May 1942 letter to British Ministry of Health from Gibraltarian evacucee to London Joseph Sanchez.
84. NAUK: CO 137/854/7, Refugees 1941: P. Rogers, CO, to Randall, FO, 8 November 1941.
85. Daphne Rae Morrison, interviewed by author, 2006.
86. NAUK: WO 216/150, Jamaica General Administration 1940–1942: Jamaica Command Intelligence, 1 April–30 June 1941.

12.

BODIES IN CONFLICT
Policing Sexual Liaisons in Jamaica during World War II

DALEA BEAN

While Jamaica was not involved directly as a belligerent nation in World War I (1914–18) and World War II (1939–45), various aspects of the society were affected by these near-global conflicts. The tendency has been to study the effects of these wars on the country's economy and its place in the shifting geopolitical landscape, which (particularly in World War II) saw the United States expanding its sphere of influence into the Caribbean. Where individuals have been examined, the inclination is a focus on the thousands of Jamaican men who participated at various levels in battles on the side of the Allied powers. However, there is an often overlooked dimension to World War II, that is, the impact of public wartime ideology on the private sexual activity of local women and soldiers in transit.

Historically, the excitement of war as well as the realization that both military and civilian life could be cut tragically short tended to erode inhibitions. However, evidence from Jamaica during World War II indicates that women's bodies were *punished* for engaging in prostitution while men's bodies were *protected* via various means. In this way, soldiers and local women's bodies were not only involved in activities of pleasure but were in ideological conflict with each other. This chapter will examine this dialectical approach to men's and women's bodies in Jamaica during World War II and illustrate the extent to which the private became the source of very public discourse.

COLONIZATION AND SEXPLOITATION

Historically, discourse on sex in the Caribbean context has been intertwined with control of one race/people by another. The power that European colonizers exerted over colonized peoples was not only for financial aggrandizement but also included rights to sexual access to those considered to be subordinate. As Verene Shepherd indicates, male plantation proprietors such as Thomas Thistlewood used their position as owners or managers of the subaltern to render colonized women sex objects over whom they could exercise power.[1] "Sexploitation" of indigenous, African enslaved and Indian indentured women was critical to the project of colonization. As Hilary Beckles convincingly argues, "This meant . . . the slave-owners' right to extract a wide range of non-pecuniary socio-sexual benefits from slaves as a legitimate stream of returns on capital, and an important part of the meaning of colonial mastery."[2] Such was the experience of the enslaved woman in the colonized Caribbean, and this legacy of the perceived right that the white male had to the body of the black woman was evident in twentieth-century Jamaica.

The exploitation of indigenous, enslaved and later indentured women by European men emerged from a concept of "exoticization" of the cultural Other. Kamala Kempadoo contends that this "exoticization" continued to dictate sexual relations in the Caribbean after slavery.[3] This exotic label given to the women of colonized peoples was an attempt on the part of colonizers to understand what was considered strange, exert power over their bodies, legitimize them as sexual fantasies and undermine the masculinity of their partners.[4] Indeed, prostitution in the Caribbean has been grounded in racialized interactions predicated on the Caribbean woman as raunchy and sexually enticing. Black and brown women were viewed by soldiers in transit as alluring representations of uninhibited sensuality. During World War II, Jamaica was a hotbed for sexual liaisons between soldiers and local women of an ephemeral nature. Though prostitution of this nature was illegal in Jamaica, Beckles suggests that there was no vehement enforcement of the laws even during the period of enslavement.[5] Establishments such as lodging houses that catered to visitors, which were primarily owned by women in twentieth-century Jamaica and were located close to areas frequented by military men, are widely assumed to have doubled as inconspicuous brothels. Indeed, if Paulette Kerr's analysis is correct, though brothels were never overt operations, it is likely that prostitution was a feature of the lives of these hospitality establishments. As Kerr opines, "There is little concrete evidence to suggest that prostitution was institutionalised in lodging houses in Jamaica. But it is true that many lodging housekeepers were . . . maintained by the support of white men who also formed the bulk of their clientele and for whom they provided sexual favours among their services."[6]

While predicated on centuries of racism and sexism and unequal power relations, the interaction between these black and white bodies, when left to their own devices, was seemingly harmonious. Some liaisons proved to be a mutually advantageous arrangement for women as well as their travelling patrons. Usually motivated by economic considerations, the women accrued monetary benefits and some even amassed wealth, while the men involved gained short-term companionship and an outlet for sexual fantasies. But these private relations were often a source of great public concern. For legislators and self-proclaimed upholders of moral codes, they were simply inimical to public order and were intimately associated with drunkenness and indecency. However, black and white bodies were not held equally culpable for depravity. Not surprisingly, social evils that resulted from prostitution, were pegged on "fallen" black womanhood.

Definitions of prostitution signify how closely related it was to femininity and not to masculinity. As Joanna Phoenix suggests, typical definitions explained the phenomenon as a woman offering her body commonly for lewdness for payment in return.[7] Particularly when white foreigners were involved, local black and brown female bodies bore the brunt of the blame for prostitution's decadence. This was exacerbated by the presence of military men, whose bodies were conceptualized as fundamental to successful war campaigns and which had to remain paragons of strength and prowess. While it was accepted that military personnel should have regular sexual outlets (of a heterosexual nature), the women who provided these services were condemned as treacherous.

THE WAR APHRODISIAC

There is a strong connection between war and sexual behaviour as far as the military complex is concerned, and it has been believed that military personnel should have access to sex as frequently as possible. Sigmund Freud argued that the connection between acts of violence and eroticism was evident in the tendency of war-torn societies to discard the repressions which civilization has imposed on the human sex drive.[8] While a society at war might not totally abandon its moral codes that control sexuality in the Freudian sense, the methods of sexual repression are often diluted. This "war aphrodisiac"[9] as John Costello terms it, is usually associated with army life. Costello explains that the urgency and thrill of war, as well as the realization that both military and civilian life can be cut tragically short, erode moral restraints. Other writers such as George Hicks indicate that the military community of men is often obsessed with sex, particularly when they are confined to a regimented situation and deprived of normal emotional outlets.[10] Ronald Hyam, writing about the connections between the British Empire and sexuality, draws a similar conclusion, though more coloured by an intrinsic objectification of women. He notes: "War always tends to increase sexual activity because of the general heightening of nervous tensions and because the beauties of the fleshpots made a wonderful contrast to the horrors and absurdities of war."[11]

While Caribbean bases were not usually the scenes of open warfare, this mentality ostensibly accompanied military personnel stationed in the region. What Jamaica lacked in the urgency of battle, it made up with its so-called exotic women, tropical climate and a cultural and physical distance from the homes of troops. Indeed as Harry Benjamin and R.E.L. Masters argue, military camps, bases and ports were prime targets of brothels, taverns and prostitutes the world over. They said:

> The men stationed there are frequently . . . off from their normal sources of sex gratification: wives and girlfriends. Moreover, there are likely to be many young males, away from home for the first time, the incidence of whose sex contacts rises sharply in the sudden absence of parental supervision. Particularly in wartime, men live "as if there is no tomorrow" and squander their money as they never would do at home.[12]

The soldier was expected to assert his masculinity and virility as an extension of his wartime duties. It was also understood that some leisure time was given to him as a reward for the intense discipline, hard work, exposure to danger and self-sacrifice associated with his service to the army and to encourage his spirits in the midst of death and destruction. The ideology was explained by a US Infantry journal published during World War II in this way: "The army does not officially condone profanity; unofficially, it knows it can do little to stop it. The society of soldiers is not polite. It is a society of men, frequently unwashed, who have been dedicated to the rugged task of killing other men, and whose training has emphasized that a certain reversion to the primitive is not undesirable."[13]

Associated with the penchant of armies to encourage sexual licence among its men was the incongruous policing of the women who provided the services. At best, men were encouraged to use prophylactics and cautioned against visiting areas of cities that were deemed as harbouring particularly large numbers of infected women. However, laws such as the Defence of the Realm Act and the Contagious Disease Acts in Britain – the latter having been instituted in Jamaica in 1864, 1866 and 1869 – were introduced to control the bodies of women thought to be propagators of harm to otherwise healthy men.[14] Cantonment acts permitted colonial police to conduct compulsory genital examinations on women around bases to allow British soldiers to have sexual relations with local women without fear of contracting venereal diseases.[15] Interestingly, these female-gender-specific penal codes made no mention of detaining or testing men's bodies.

The Contagious Disease Acts and Defence of the Realm Act (Regulation 40D)[16] were eventually repealed. Feminist groups convincingly argued that women were attacked to protect men from infections, while they were not protected from the infections from men. The Contagious Disease Acts in particular came under scathing attack from the Social Purity organization in England headed by Josephine Butler. She and others were deeply troubled by the double standards to which men and women were held, which made "a large section of female society . . . minister to the irregularities of the excusable man".[17] The aim of these feminists was not only to remove the scourge of blame from womanhood but also to get men to engage in more responsible behaviour and self-control.

Therefore, the tendency to regulate prostitution and particularly the women involved in the transaction was not endemic to Jamaica or to the war years. Indeed, a study of the history of the oldest profession alludes to numerous strategies to control, punish and protect various bodies involved. What made the need to police these liaisons even more pertinent during wartime, however, was the great significance placed on the young, healthy male body through which wars were lost and won. Any threat to the physical capabilities of masculine fighting power was construed as directly inimical to a nation's ability to be successful in battle. Male bodies were tropes for victory and national pride, while female bodies became representative of destruction of not only the empire's war effort but also the colony's fight against indecency and moral decay. These bodies involved in physical acts were at the same time ideologically in conflict and faced vastly different consequences for their actions.

POLICING PROSTITUTION DURING WORLD WAR II

In Jamaica during the war, the amateur prostitute was far more prevalent than any militarily established brothel. This amateur prostitute was defined as a "woman who is prepared for reward to engage in acts of lewdness with all and sundry or with anyone who may hire her for that purpose".[18] She was perceived by local and international policymakers as the greatest threat to decency, public order and the health of the military for two main reasons. First, professional prostitutes were thought to be the primary vectors of venereal diseases, such as gonorrhoea and syphilis, as discussed by McCollin in chapter 13, but amateurs suggested a freedom from disease because their sex work was sporadic.[19] This afforded soldiers a false sense of security in interacting with them. Second, while brothels and professional prostitutes were in theory easier to control and regulate, the young woman who occasionally roamed the streets looking for a "good time" for a minimal fee was elusive. Theodore Rosenthal and Julius Vandow, researchers into prostitution and venereal diseases during and after World War II, indicated that from their findings, "the prostitute is no longer the major vector of venereal disease. Her place has been taken by the promiscuous amateur, usually referred to as a 'pick-up' or a 'friend'."[20]

Sailors seemed particularly fond of these women, who were often servant girls, market women and banana carriers at docks. This fondness was not overlooked by lodging-house proprietors, who set up establishments to cater to the growing need presented by travelling sailors. As a representative from the Jamaica Constabulary Force indicated, "many of the so called-Brothels and Lodging Houses are used for the purpose of prostitution and the latter is rampant on the Water front, especially when Naval Vessels are in port".[21] These alleged brothels were safe havens for "wayward" women, who were perceived as walking the streets looking for clients like "professional prostitutes" but were harder to identify. As the director of medical services put it: "VD in Kingston is not so much a question of the professional prostitute (housed or street walker) as of the amateur or semi-professional. VD appears to me to be spread primarily by the domestic servants, half starved dressmakers and under paid clerks."[22]

Shortly before the outbreak of World War II, the Moyne Commission[23] also gave credence to this idea by arguing that women who acted as prostitutes were not professionals but mainly did so to supplement their daily wages. The report explained that prostitution is "usually for economic reasons and because the wages earned by the woman in her other occupation are often too low to obtain the necessities of life for her. She is therefore found at night at the docks when ships put in, while carrying on her own work as well in the daytime."[24]

As a result of these perceptions, during World War II not all women were targeted for repressive regulation and intense scrutiny but, more specifically, women of the working class and those of African descent. As Kempadoo informs us, Europeans placed social emphasis on the "inherent" promiscuous, immoral and unclean character of working-class women and non-white peoples who did not, or refused to, adhere to European bourgeois family norms.[25] These constructions of African-descended women as being of a different stock from her pure European counterpart were present from the days of colonization and slavery and altered little in the twentieth century. Historians have now attributed this thinking to a need to justify white masculine promiscuity by a fabricated inherent immorality of the black female,[26] but in the midst of World War II white male technocrats, such as the medical officer in the country, were content with believing that working-class women of African descent were the prime sources of VD and therefore should be targeted by the law. In his mind, the small number of decent (insert "European-descended" here) female companions in Jamaica and the ever-decreasing moral code of the "female descendant of the slave days" made Jamaica a haven for VDs.[27]

Prevailing European stereotypes of the "proper" manifestations of sexual behaviour in men and women influenced the policing of female bodies. These stereotypes accepted that men were lecherous. As Joan French and Honor Ford-Smith argue, "Women were the repositories of chasteness, virtue and purity and a superior civilizing force, while men were creatures of unlimited sexual appetite and the source of vice which had to be controlled."[28] The burden was placed on women to keep this sexual unrest in males at bay. Overt female sexuality was considered a corruption and the female body, often the source of male lust and admiration, was condemned as the source of downfall of the superior and highly esteemed male form.

The conceptualization of the venerated male body was even more essential to maintain when these bodies were expected to be at their healthiest in order to secure victory in battle. Cartesian ideas about the weakness of the corporeal (closer to femininity) and the strength of the mind (closer to masculinity)[29] were buttressed in the early twentieth century by medical practitioners who argued that women could carry syphilis and gonorrhoea with no symptoms of their infection. This led to the myth that all women potentially carried the disease inherently without being infected from an external source. As Brandt explains, "The asymptomatic nature of the disease in women even led to the idea that virtually all women carried gonorrhoea without damage and could transmit to their partners... she was contagious without having been contagioned [sic]. The woman was considered dangerous ipso facto."[30]

Controlling women's sexual outlets was therefore seen as the most effective way to curb the spread of diseases, as they were labelled as inherent disease carriers and disseminators. In a world where the dominant rhetoric held that morally questionable women were inherently diseased, both amateur and professional prostitutes were branded as "dangerous". They threatened the vitality of the male physique, endangered the collective worth of the country's female virtue and situated the country's reputation on a perilous cliff. As if this was not enough, the various vices that accompanied the commercial sexual transactions meant that soldiers in Jamaica were also vulnerable to criminal activities. Prostitution was frequently linked with such other illegal acts as petty theft and other forms of harassment, all of which were inimical to the comfortable shore-leave of sailors. As the *Gleaner* lamented:

> From Orange Street to the western end of the Harbour and Port Royal Streets members of the criminal and prostitute elements of the Kingston's population

are to be found night and day. . . . Some of these prey upon sailors who have shore-leave; when they can do so with a fair hope of success they rob these sailors, and we have even heard of one or two cases of beatings-up. Clearly the situation calls for more police activity than we have had.[31]

Ostensibly, sexual relations were not the only activities that needed policing during World War II, but there was a distinct effort to protect the military from diseased bodies and other corrupting influences. Apart from independent streetwalkers, sexual relations between women and military personnel in Jamaica also occurred in establishments that doubled as unofficial brothels as well as legitimate licensed hotels, taverns and inns. As E.A. Glen Campbell informed Governor Edward Denham, "The half has not yet been told of these places, some under the guise of Hotels, Board and Lodgings and others with no sign at all, only a collector at the gate who receives the fares and delivers the keys."[32] It was theorized that two major types of brothels existed: tenement yards, with girls of all ages who freely engaged in prostitution, and houses run by older women (following in the tradition of nineteenth-century lodging houses), who employed young girls from twelve to sixteen as prostitutes.

However, of equal importance to legislators were the temperance bars that were prevalent in towns in Jamaica. These bars were not allowed to sell spirits but sold beer and other liquors. This enabled them to have trade licences, which did not allow police entry, rather than spirit licences, which made provision for police entry at their discretion. Under section 56 of the spirit licence, people were not allowed to make taverns, inns or hotels the habitual resort of reputed prostitutes. However, the law did not prevent the owner from allowing such people to visit the establishments to purchase food and drink.[33] As a result, officials complained that the women in question would still frequent the establishments and wreak havoc on "unsuspecting" troops. These bars and restaurants were seen as breeding grounds for illicit behaviour because they served alcohol and could remain open all night. It was therefore suggested by various committees that temperance bars be forced to take out spirit licences and fall under the purview of police patrol.[34]

From as early as 1915, authorities were able to identify fifty-three common houses where alleged "loose" women lived and entertained sailors in Kingston. These establishments were also cause for concern during World War II and were frequently policed to stem the rising tide of "amoral" women. These were mainly on Luke Lane, Matthew's Lane, Water Lane, Princess

Street, Orange Street and West Street, among others.[35] United States Marines and British soldiers were also spotted at the Kit Cat bar, Double B bar and Queensbury, which were allegedly run by prostitutes who catered specifically to soldiers and sailors.[36] Closer to the outbreak of World War II, it was even alleged by the inspector general that one particular woman was the source of all the cases of infection on the HMS *Dragon* in 1934. In response to this, the ship's authorities put the Breezy Cottage, where she worked, out of bounds to their men.[37] This official ban continued during World War II but there is little evidence to suggest that sailors did indeed obey the prohibition. Regardless of whether the decree was obeyed, however, the critical point is that both Jamaican and non-Jamaican officials engaged in various acts of policing local women's bodies and that this can be compared to the rhetoric of protection of men's bodies and welfare.

The rhetoric in dealing with military personnel was one of protection rather than policing, as a result of the ideology that men were merely following "the very necessary call of nature".[38] As Glenford Howe explains, "sailors, volunteers and members of the military forces being male, were not held responsible for their actions. It was as if they had a right to engage in prostitution without risk."[39] To reduce this risk, however, officials such as Lieutenant Colonel Anderson of the Jamaican Command advocated the provision of condoms to military personnel, and this suggestion influenced the policy of protection of soldiers who visited Jamaica during World War II.[40] Legislators did their part by lobbying for tighter restrictions on women considered to be dangerous. Indeed, protecting the troops from diseased women preoccupied military and political authorities for much of the 1930s and 1940s. For instance, officials suggested that a system of compulsory examination of women should be instituted to rid the island of the women "rotten with disease and capable of infecting every male [they] may meet".[41] It was also suggested that fines for soliciting should be raised from forty shillings because women could easily afford this paltry sum and then resume their activities on the same day as their arrest.

Women were unequally burdened with causing the spread of VDs; however, it is undeniable that unprotected sexual liaisons were prevalent between military men and civilian women globally. Indeed, Jamaica was not the only site of conflicting representations of the bodies during World War II. Perhaps in an attempt to shift focus from Jamaica's growing embarrassment over the local rates of the spread of VD, leading newspapers regularly published evidence of rising rates of the disease worldwide. In December 1942 the *Gleaner* reported that the spread of VDs in Britain had increased 70 per cent since the beginning of the war. Close to the war's close in 1945, the newspaper reported that the VD rate among US Army ground forces in the European theatre increased more than 300 per cent between April and May.[42] There is, therefore, evidence to support the "war aphrodisiac" theory during World War II.

In the case of Jamaica, it should not be assumed that the documented infections originated with Jamaican women, but the level of VD transmission in the country was admittedly disturbing, as tables 12.1 and 12.2 indicate. The prevalence of the spread of diseases gave Jamaica the reputation for being a hotspot with regard to infection rates. The *Gleaner* in particular was distressed to report that many ships refused to call in at Jamaica owing to the rate of VDs contracted by previous vessels. As an editorial noted:

> It seems clear that only two or three of the smaller units of the British fleet visiting the West Indian waters will be permitted to call in Jamaica. . . .The larger ships will go elsewhere . . . the Admiral (Plunkett-Ernle-Erle-Drax) frankly, does not consider it safe for his men to be given shore leave in Kingston because of the prevalence of VD in the brothels of the town: on previous occasions too many sailors contracted . . . "unmentionable complaints" in Kingston.[43]

Women's bodies were, therefore, construed as not only dangerous to male bodies, which needed to remain at the peak of physical health, but were blamed for making Kingston a port of ill repute at a time when officials were keen on portraying Jamaica as critical to the Allied war effort. Protecting both the reputation of Jamaica and the bodies of those men of use to the king and empire from being irreversibly damaged by an army of "loose diseased women" was a priority.

Those charged with safeguarding the health of transient populations during the war also had every right to be concerned about VDs in general. The immediate and long-term effects of VDs were debilitating and affected the health of men, women and even unborn babies, who could be infected by their mother. Men and women who carried the diseases were equally susceptible to sores, rashes and hair loss. The long-term effects of VDs if untreated were critical. Syphilis could develop into a cardiovascular problem and result in loss of muscular coordination, partial paralysis, insanity and failed organs.

Gonorrhoea, which was initially seen as a trivial disease, joined syphilis as a most serious malady. It could result in arthritis, meningitis and inflammation of the tissue around the heart.[44]

In addition to the physical effects of the diseases, the methods of proper treatment also posed a problem for military officials.[45] As Howe informs us, the close quarters in which soldiers lived necessitated the segregation of those infected, to guard against cross-infection. However, the army was against long-term hospitalization of troops, since this would apparently give rise to "enforced idleness and the wastage of much needed manpower".[46] Inevitably, these patients had to be quarantined and would be removed from front-line duty. It was these effects of the diseases on soldiers and sailors that spurred officials to brand some women as dangerous and having enormous powers to cripple military efficacy and ruin the colony's reputation. The issue was further compounded by the military's concern about the effect of these diseases on the population back home. Men in the early stages of the diseases could unwittingly transmit them to wives and girlfriends, and, worse yet, to their unborn children, who could die from the infection. Those children who survived the contagion at birth faced lives of suffering from congenital syphilis in the form of severe mental retardation, meningitis and, most commonly, blindness.[47] It was therefore deemed necessary to control those women who represented a source of pollution for civilians in the soldiers' homes. As Howe explains, "The army felt it had a moral and patriotic responsibility to protect the soldiers so that they could return home healthy, and reduce the risk of their families and communities being 'innocently' infected."[48]

As concerned as military officials and legislative arbitrators were about the matter, the public was equally, if not more, vociferous about the spread of VDs by "dangerous" women in the country. Demands ranged from a fairly reasonable suggestion of mobile VD clinics to bizarre ideas of flogging the women in public. A contributor to the *Gleaner*, James Herbert, suggested, "Flog the girls caught with tamarind rods in public. This might sound drastic but an evil of this sort which is spreading like measles and is undoubtedly playing havoc with thousands of men deserves a drastic remedy . . . after two or three of these public birchings you wouldn't get many of these Scarlet girls willing to risk the indignity."[49]

Suggestions of this nature signalled the very real conceptualization of women as vectors who indiscriminately damaged wholesome, innocent men who visited the island. While these suggestions were never given much credence, they nonetheless underscored the high value that was placed on the men's bodies compared to the disdain with which women were treated, both of whom were involved in the same activity.

As the war progressed, the Port Welfare Committee was formed to secure the health of seafarers in connection with the Brussels agreement. The Brussels agreement of 1924, according to Johannes Huisman, allowed for the "treatment of venereal diseases, free of charge and open to all merchant seamen regardless of nationality", in the ports of the supporting countries.[50] It was felt that regulatory campaigns against women and VDs should also be considered a wartime measure to safeguard the efficiency of the military. The committee was of the opinion that several laws required strengthening to deal with VDs, prostitution and the sale of alcohol, as it was felt that much of the disease contracted after 1939 was as a result of the men becoming intoxicated. As a naval commander argued, "There is always the difficulty that a naval rating, after partaking of cheap liquor, is not in complete possession of his senses and falls as easy victim to the allurements of a woman."[51]

When surveying the archival documents of the period, one is hard pressed to find evidence of any view or legal framework, which signalled that both military personnel and female prostitutes were part and parcel of a potentially dangerous activity in which they were both culpable. The Port Welfare Committee sang the same tune as others before it. The suggestion was that any woman seen soliciting or loitering with the intent of soliciting in any public place should be arrested without a warrant. The committee also felt that VDs should be made legally notifiable diseases, so that those who deliberately concealed the infection could be penalized. It was also suggested by the Port Authority that stipendiary magistrates should try cases, as according to the research conducted by the authority, other magistrates tended to be lenient towards the women.[52]

Along with the sanctioning of women, a few other suggestions surfaced, including making recreational spots available for troops as alternatives to bars. Entertainment centres, including the Silver Slipper Plaza in Cross Roads as a dance hall and the YMCA and playing fields, were provided. In addition, the Victoria League agreed to entertain the naval ratings with trips and other expeditions at the expense of the league. A canteen committee was also organized to cater to North American sailors' recreational needs. This was headed by Mrs Hugh Watson, wife of the US consul general in Jamaica, and other wives of military personnel.[53] These social groups comprised women from the United States and Canada who organized clubs, including the United Service Organization and the Maple Leaf Club, to entertain men from their countries stationed in Jamaica.[54] The groups intended to give the military the feeling of being at home away from home and certainly attempted to provide what was considered to be more wholesome entertainment for the men by women of their own race and nationality, similar to the activities in Trinidad, as discussed in chapter 14.

It was clear, however, that the schemes were not very successful, as troops continued to frequent brothels and temperance bars. What the committees neglected to consider was that troops hardly engaged in sex for lack of anything better to do. Fraternizing with women in a sexual manner was deemed necessary, regardless of the presence of other opportunities for entertainment. Indeed, it is also not far-fetched to assume that soldiers may even have viewed contracting VDs as a positive (even if uncomfortable) marker of their frequent sexual activity, virility and prowess. As the acting VD officer, Dr Wedderburn, explained in an extensive piece in the *Gleaner* in 1945, "There is a prevailing belief among the male members of a certain section of the community that the contraction of a venereal disease is inevitable and the earlier acquired the better. Indeed some relate with pride their numerous previous infections as evidence of virility."[55] Rather than shame and concern, a typical response was to view VDs as tools for bragging rights. Dr Wedderburn was referring to the general civilian population, but the soldiers' eager disposition, and even desperation, to bed as many local women as possible, indicates that similar thoughts may have entered their minds.

The importance of the company of women to the army is very well illustrated in the novel *Small Island*, where the character Gilbert Joseph (a Jamaican RAF member stationed briefly in a military camp in Virginia, United States) explains how disgruntled men in the army became when they were barred by the authorities from socializing with American women. He said:

> With our stomachs full, our thoughts had all returned to women. Although I did not want to be turned round having come so far, this war business was getting me down. No one knew how long we would be immured on this camp without seeing a curvaceous bosom, a rounded hip, a shapely leg. How long

without female company? A week, a month? No American girl was to see me in uniform – oh boy this was serious.[56]

Though fictional, this illustrates a very real sentiment among military personnel. Rooted in what Kempadoo calls the masculinist definition of the issue (that non-marital sexual relations corrupted womanhood but were necessary for the healthy development of manhood),[57] the army was concerned about recreation that involved the company of women, who were concomitantly condemned for participating. This trend undoubtedly resulted in high rates of infection. While it is difficult to obtain rates of infection of women, details on the infection of the military are accessible and were often used as a blight on Jamaica's reputation, even though it could not be proven that the diseases were contracted in the colony. Reports were that men from HMS *Orion*, *Ajax* and *York* contracted diseases quite rapidly in Jamaica, as table 12.1 illustrates. Without a doubt, the contraction rate on the HMS *Orion* was the most alarming, with a reported fifteen cases during a two-day visit.[58]

Table 12.1. Total Cases of Venereal Diseases on Three Ships, 1939

Ship	Syphilis First Record	Syphilis Later Record	Acute Gonorrhoea	Gonorrhoea
Orion	4	1	70	21
Ajax	3	138	3	3
York	3	0	15	6

Source: Compiled from CSO: 1B/5/77/1937 #2, Venereal Disease in Jamaica Representations of the Port Welfare Committee, 1937–1941.

Table 12.2 also confirms that up to 1942, troops were still being admitted for VDs.

Even with evidence of the high rates of infection, signalling that men were not refraining from random sexual liaisons, authorities refused to sanction the naval ratings, seeing indulgence in alcohol and women as a natural part of their military lives. The commander-in-chief noted, "Kingston may have to be used as a base in wartime. The psychological state of the liberty men, after many days at sea in war routine is likely to result in indulgence with wine and women."[59] Also, reports from individual members of the Port Welfare Com-

Table 12.2. The Medical History of Troops

Period Ending (date)	Number of Admissions	Admissions for Venereal Diseases	Local Forces (general illness)	Other forces admitted (general illness)				
				British	Dom	RN	RAF	ATS
30 June 1943	296	59	42	45	152	25	–	–
30 September 1943	330	82	126	62	81	35	–	–
31 December 1943	382	80	134	76	97	36	–	4
31 March 1944	393	107	184	62	66	34	13	3
10 June 1944	498	134	183	88	81	51	57	11

Source: Compiled from NAUK: WO 222 905: Medical Quarterly: Jamaica Military Hospital October 1941–September 1944.

mittee continued to propagate the double standard between the behaviour of men and women in the island. As one member, Dr Ferreira, explained,

> The control of the prostitute is best enforced by legal enactments, and efficient police action. The control of the sailor, including his prophylaxis is a matter for the navy. It is up to the navy to regulate shore-leave and enforce prophylaxis . . . . May I urge that more effective legal power be provided to deal with the whole question of VD . . . until much wider legal powers be provided to deal with this problem, progress will continue to be lamentably slow.[60]

Naturally, these legal enactments were to be geared towards women, rather than to the men who willingly participated in the act of prostitution. Ten women from various bars were listed as possible carriers of diseases in 1940 by C.T. Hyatt, surgeon commander of a British ship. The majority of these women were Afro-Jamaican women.[61] Again, these women were stigmatized as "possible" carriers of disease. There was very little evidence presented relating to specific women who could then be treated for diseases. The tendency was to characterize all women in a particular locale and occupation as disease carriers and enact legislation in an attempt to restrict the spread of infection, and many ships refused to call at Jamaica for fear that their men would contract VDs. An admiral in the British fleet labelled Kingston as worse than Port Said in Egypt and stated plainly he would not permit the fleet to enter.[62] This compounded the already existing levels of embarrassment Jamaicans felt at their "fallen" women during World War II.

During the war, many secret meetings were held with leading figures in the Canadian, Jamaican, English and American armies regarding the health of the military. In these gatherings, the danger of women was usually the focal point. Inspectors Drake and O'Connor from the Jamaica Constabulary, for instance, gave the assurance that the police would arrest women when the act of solicitation for the purpose of prostitution could be established.[63] To this end, Law 51 of 1941, to amend the Offences against the Person Act, was passed to give the police greater powers in dealing with brothel proprietors and patrons. Particularly under Sergeant Major T.M. Cole, the police waged a campaign against brothel owners in 1942. Ione Biggs and Joycelin Johnson were two female owners who were accosted in this move. The women were ordered to pay fines totalling seventy pounds for managing a brothel, Hotel Bims, on John's Lane. Their case was seen as a landmark one, as it was the first to be taken to court in a decade.⁶⁴ This gave reformers hope that some end could be put to the scourge of brothels in the city and, in turn, the termination of the centres of VD infection.

Moreover, the military was sure that brothels, disguised as lodging houses and hotels, were still established on the waterfront to accommodate naval vessels, a practice rampant in World War II. It was also noted by the All Jamaica Youth Movement and the Bustamante Industrial Trade Union that establishments such as these which doubled as brothels were steadily growing in the corporate area. Over sixty-two were estimated to operate, under the guise of hotels and boarding houses, close to churches and elementary schools.⁶⁵

CONCLUSION

Between 1938 and 1945 there was no obvious legislation or discourse related to the sanctioning of military personnel who engaged in ephemeral sexual relationships in the country. Policing and punishment were reserved for women suspected of luring sailors to their beds. It is undeniable that some women in Jamaica capitalized on the willingness of some military personnel to spend money for sexual favours. There is no doubt that businesses thrived off the sale of sex and liquor when military personnel disembarked in Jamaica. It was also inevitable that any act of sexual intercourse without the use of prophylactics would be a likely source of VDs and other infections. This would prove to have deleterious effects on the health and efficiency of these men and women. However, the fact that prostitution and VDs were seen as synonymous with women of compromised moral fibre was the major hindrance to a successful campaign against the spread of infection. The focus of legislators and military authorities was on policing women, lessening temptations, protecting soldiers from themselves and blaming alcohol and natural urges for the spread of VDs. Most of the attention was diverted away from the problems involved in the sexual relations on the part of both sexes to figuring out how to rid the streets of dangerous women. For the most part these recommendations were not overwhelmingly successful in their aims. Even when women were sanctioned, fined, controlled and examined, troops always found a way to satisfy their sexual appetite. These men viewed access to alcohol and heterosexual activities as a part of their military lives, and they were subtly encouraged, by the army, to enjoy these recreational activities.

The paucity of sources that would allow the voices of these women to be heard does not permit a full assessment of the impact of the legislative response on their lives. What is clear, however, is that the conceptualization of poor, mainly black women in the urban centres who worked in inns, taverns and bars, as conduits of diseases was rampant during World War II. Their bodies were targeted with misguided, oppressive legislation that served to perpetuate the myth of their inherent diseased status but did nothing to curb the spread of diseases in the country and little to assist the women, who may have actually been suffering from VDs and who may have indeed been infected by their military partners.

Despite the fact that the control of prostitution in its entirety could have curbed the spread of diseases, the error of administrators was to ignore men as part and parcel of the sexually motivated transaction. The twin obstacles of hypocrisy and false modesty that hampered the campaign prevented real progress from being made.[66] Local regulations did nothing to protect the parties involved, not because prostitutes were allowed to practise their trade but largely because even when these women were sanctioned, troops were not deterred from seeking regular sexual outlets. During World War II, military men's bodies were positioned as being in conflict with women's, rather than their being situated as two halves of one activity. Policies that focused less on blame and more on multifaceted constructive measures might have borne more fruit in curbing the social ills associated with the act of prostitution, especially if they mandated the troops to take some responsibility for their own actions.

NOTES

1. Thomas Thistlewood was a manager and enslaver who lived in Jamaica from 1750 to 1786. Brief extracts of his journals have been published by Douglas Hall in the book *In Miserable Slavery: Thomas Thistlewood in Jamaica, 1750–86* (London: Macmillan, 1989). Verene Shepherd, "'Sex in the Tropics': Women, Gender and Sexuality in the Discourses of Asian Labour Migration to the British Caribbean", in Verene Shepherd, *I Want to Disturb My Neighbour: Lectures On Slavery, Emancipation and Post-Colonial Jamaica* (Kingston: Ian Randle, 2007), 31–32.
2. Hilary Beckles, "Property Rights in Pleasure: The Marketing of Enslaved

Women's Sexuality", in *Caribbean Slavery in the Atlantic World: A Student Reader*, ed. Verene Shepherd and Hilary Beckles (Kingston: Ian Randle, 2000), 692. In other works Beckles, Kempadoo, Bush and others have also argued that though prostitution was a basis for domination over women during slavery, it was also manipulated by the women (particularly mulattoes) who sometimes made strategic use of their "exoticized" status to further their status and that of their children. See Hilary Beckles, *Natural Rebels: A Social History of Enslaved Black Women in Barbados* (New Brunswick, NJ: Rutgers University Press, 1989); Kamala Kempadoo, "Continuities and Change: Five Centuries of Prostitution in the Caribbean", in *Sun, Sex and Gold: Tourism and Sex Work in the Caribbean*, ed. Kamala Kempadoo (Lanham: Rowman and Littlefield, 1999) 3–36; and Barbara Bush, *Slave Women in Caribbean Society, 1650–1838* (Kingston: Heinemann Caribbean, 1990).

3. Kamala Kempadoo, "Theorizing Sexual Relations in the Caribbean: Prostitution and the Problem of the 'Exotic'", in *Confronting Power, Theorizing Gender: Interdisciplinary Perspectives in the Caribbean*, ed. Eudine Barriteau (Jamaica: University of the West Indies Press, 2003), 160.

4. See, for example, Fernando Henriques, *Prostitution and Society: Europe and the New World*, vol. 2 (London: MacGibbon and Kee, 1963); Bush, *Slave Women in Caribbean* Society; Shepherd, "Sex in the Tropics"; Beckles, "Property Rights in Pleasure"; and Kempadoo, "Theorizing Sexual Relations", 159–85.

5. Beckles, "Property Rights in Pleasure", 694.

6. Paulette Kerr, "Victims or Strategists? Female Lodging-house Keepers in Jamaica", in *Engendering Caribbean History: Cross-Cultural Perspectives*, ed. Verene Shepherd (Kingston: Ian Randle, 2011), 467. Similar analysis has also been done by Marietta Morrissey, who concludes that, in the nineteenth century, domestics in the British Caribbean tended to double as prostitutes sporadically. See Marietta Morrissey, *Slave Women in the New World: Gender Stratification in the Caribbean* (Lawrence: University Press of Kansas, 1989).

7. Joanna Phoenix, *Making Sense of Prostitution* (New York: Palgrave Macmillan, 1999), 24.

8. Sigmund Freud, *Reflections on War and Death* (1918), quoted in John Costello, *Love, Sex, and War: Changing Values, 1939–45* (London: Collins, 1985), 10.

9. Costello, *Love, Sex, and War*, 17.

10. George Hicks, *The Comfort Women: Sex Slaves of the Japanese Imperial Forces* (St Leonards, Australia: Allen and Unwin, 1995), 3.

11. Ronald Hyam, *Empire and Sexuality: The British Experience* (Manchester: Manchester University Press, 1992), 151.

12. Harry Benjamin and R.E.L. Masters, *Prostitution and Morality: A Definitive*

Report on the Prostitute in Contemporary Society and an Analysis of the Cases and Effects of the Suppression of Prostitution (New York: Julian Press, 1964), 132.

13. Quoted in Costello, *Love, Sex, and War*, 115. So concerned were armies with the sexual satisfaction of their soldiers that many made provisions for official military brothels. The French, for instance, experimented with *maisons tolérées* or military brothels in World War I. However, the Japanese were probably the most notorious in this regard, with a system of providing "comfort women" for their troops; a system that was far from comforting for the enslaved women. It is estimated that some 140,000 comfort women serviced up to thirty men a day after being abducted and sold into a lifetime of sexual slavery. See Hicks, *Comfort Women*.

14. Under the Contagious Diseases Acts women had to endure mandatory medical inspection, and if found to be infected with a disease, they could be detained for up to three months. The Contagious Diseases Acts were repealed in 1886, but they resurfaced in World War I in the form of Defence of the Realm Act. Clause 40d of the act, for example, mandated the incarceration of women for medical examination. See Sheila Jeffreys, "Women and Sexuality", in June Purvis, *Women's History: Britain 1850–1945* (New York: St Martin's Press, 1995).

15. Cynthia Enloe, *Bananas, Beaches, Bases: Making Feminist Sense of International Politics* (London: Pandora, 1989), 82.

16. Regulation 40D of the Defence of the Realm Act stated that any woman who solicited, spoke to or had sexual intercourse with a soldier or a sailor could be arrested. See Jeffreys "Women and Sexuality".

17. Jeffreys, "Women and Sexuality", 195. Also see Judith Walkowitz, *Prostitution and Victorian Society: Women, Class, and the State* (Cambridge: Cambridge University Press, 1980).

18. Phoenix, *Making Sense of Prostitution*, 24.

19. *Gleaner*, 30 July 1917, 11.

20. T. Rosenthal and J. Vandow, "Prevalence of Venereal Disease in Prostitutes", *British Journal of Venereal Diseases* (1958): 94.

21. Colonial Secretary's Office Correspondence (CSO): 1B/5/77 #95 1936, Brothels Control Of (Regarding Law 51 of 1941): letter from Commissioner of Police to Private Secretary, 30 November 1939.

22. CSO: 1B/5/77 #2 1937, Venereal Disease in Jamaica, Representations of the Port Welfare Committee, 1937–1941, Director of Medical Services report, 9 February 1938.

23. In the aftermath of the widespread protest movements in the British West

Indies between 1937 and 1938, the British government set up a royal commission, led by Lord Moyne as chair, to investigate social and economic conditions in the colonies and make recommendations to improve the socioeconomic conditions in the islands.

24. *West India Royal Commission 1938–1939 Report and Recommendations* (London: His Majesty's Stationery Office, 1940), 239.
25. Kamala Kempadoo, "Continuities and Change", 10.
26. See Henriques, "Prostitution and Society".
27. CSO: 1B/5/79 #258 1934, Venereal Disease in Jamaica: letter from the superintendent Medical Officer to the Colonial Secretary, 27 March 1936. This tendency to link sexual reputations to race was also prevalent in the regulatory campaigns of Puerto Rico and has been well explored by Eileen J Suárez Findlay in *Imposing Decency: The Politics of Sexuality and Race in Puerto Rico 1870–1920* (Durham: Duke University Press, 1999).
28. Joan French and Honor Ford-Smith, *Women and Organization in Jamaica 1900–1949* (The Hague: Institute of Social Studies, 1985), 169.
29. René Descartes (1596–1650), dubbed the father of modern philosophy, was a French philosopher. His thesis was that mind and body are really distinct – a thesis now called "mind-body dualism." René Descartes, *The Philosophical Writings of Descartes*, 3 vols., trans. John Cottingham, Robert Stoothoff, Dugald Murdoch and Anthony Kenny (Cambridge: Cambridge University Press, 1984–1991).
30. Allan Brant, *No Magic Bullet: A Social History of Venereal Disease in the US since 1880* (New York: Oxford University Press: 1985), 10. Brant highlighted the views of a French physician in this passage. However, this myth may have been predominant because the female reproductive system, being largely concealed, may not have been as obviously diseased as the male. In men, early symptoms of syphilis and gonorrhoea become visible and uncomfortable soon after infection.
31. *Gleaner*, 8 April 1940, 10.
32. Letter from E.A. Glen Campbell, Office of the Chief Sanitary Officer, to Edward Denham, 1 January 1938, CSO 1B/5/77 #2 1937: Venereal Disease in Jamaica Representations of the Port Welfare Committee, 1937–1941.
33. Laws of Jamaica: Spirit Licence Act, 1 February 1928.
34. See, for example, CSO: 1B/5/77 #2, 1937, Venereal Disease in Jamaica: Port Welfare Committee memorandum, Representations of the Port Welfare Committee, 1937–1941.
35. CSO: 1B/5/76/ 3 #219, Venereal Disease: list from the Detective Office, Kingston, 20 March 1915.

36. CSO: File 1B/5/77 #95.
37. CSO: 1B/5/79 1934 #258, Venereal Disease in Jamaica: letter from Inspector General to the Colonial Secretary, 14 March 1934.
38. CSO: 1B/5/76/ 3 #219, Venereal Disease.
39. Glenford Howe, *Race, War and Nationalism: A Social History of West Indians in the First World War* (Kingston: Ian Randle, 2002), 145.
40. CSO: 1B/5/79 #258, 1934, Venereal Disease in Jamaica.
41. CSO: 1B/5/76/ 3 #219, Venereal Disease.
42. *Gleaner*, 22 December 1942, 6; 26 June 1945, 4.
43. *Gleaner*, 17 January 1941, 12.
44. See Brant, *No Magic Bullet*, particularly 10–15, for the effects of these diseases on the human body.
45. In Jamaica, syphilis was treated over long periods with irrigation and regular doses of Salvarsan, mercury, Sulfarsenol, Amarsan or mapharsen. Antigonorrohoeal medications included: Proseptasine, Uliron and urinary antiseptics, and albucid and later penicillin. The minimum time a syphilitic should receive treatment is two years, during which time he should have received no fewer than 50 injections. See CSO: 1B/5/77 1937 #209, Venereal Disease Clinic report on results of treatment 1937–1939, and the *Gleaner*, 4 August 1942, 10.
46. Howe, *Race, War and Nationalism*, 146.
47. Brant, *No Magic Bullet*, 14.
48. Howe, *Race, War and Nationalism*, 145. Congenital syphilis was also a cause for concern in Jamaica. A large number of cases of syphilis between 1907 and 1914 were inherited. While there were 49 cases of primary syphilis, 43 cases of secondary infection, there were 58 reported cases of inherited syphilis, which led to 29 deaths. See CSO: 1B/5/76/ 3 #219, Venereal Disease and Social Hygiene Report on Jamaica.
49. James Herbert, "Do You Agree with This?", *Gleaner*, 12 February 1938, 25.
50. J. Huisman, "Venereal Diseases ('Sexually Transmitted Diseases': STD)", in W.H.G. Goethe, E.N. Watson, D.T. Jones, eds., *The Handbook of Nautical Medicine* (Berlin: Springer-Verlag, 1984), 207.
51. CSO: 1B/5/77 #2, Venereal Disease in Jamaica: Representations of the Port Welfare Committee, 1937–1941, memorandum from Inspector W.A. Orret, 1937.
52. CSO: 1B/5/77 #2, Venereal Disease in Jamaica: Representations of the Port Welfare Committee, 1937–1941, Port Welfare Committee memorandum, 1937.
53. See *Gleaner*, 20 April 1940, 10 and 27 September 1941, 12, for information on the activities of the Victoria League in this regard.

54. See Mrs Robert Watts, ed., *The Victory Book: A Patriotic Publication* (Kingston: Gleaner, 1941 and 1945).
55. *Gleaner*, 24 September 1945, 7.
56. Andrea Levy, *Small Island* (London: Headline, 2004), 107.
57. Kempadoo, *Sun, Sex and Gold*, 10.
58. CSO: 1B/5/77/1937 #2, Venereal Disease in Jamaica: Representations of the Port Welfare Committee, 1937–1941, dispatch from the Commander in Chief, America and West Indies Station, to the Secretary to the Admiralty, 3 January 1939.
59. CSO: 1B/5/77 #2 1937, Venereal Disease in Jamaica: Representations of the Port Welfare Committee, 1937–1941, dispatch from the Commander in Chief, America and West Indies Station, to the Secretary to the Admiralty, 3 January 1939.
60. CSO: 1B/5/77 #2 1937, Venereal Disease in Jamaica: Representations of the Port Welfare Committee, 1937–1941; ibid., letter from Dr Ferreira, medical officer in charge of VD Clinics, to Director of Medical Services.
61. CSO: 1B/5/77 #2 1937, Venereal Disease in Jamaica: Representations of the Port Welfare Committee, 1937–1941; ibid., letter from C. T. Hyatt to the Medical Officer of Health, Jamaica, 10 April 1940.
62. *Gleaner*, 4 August 1942, 10. Port Said in Egypt is geographically isolated, situated on low, sandy ground west of the Suez Canal and east of Lake Manzila, which was notorious for high infection rates of VD.
63. CSO: 1B/5/77 #95 1936, Brothels Control Of (Regarding Law 51 of 1941): minutes of a conference on measures to combat VD among troops, 8 December 1941.
64. *Gleaner*, 22 January 1942, 5.
65. CSO: 1B/5/77 #95 1936, Brothels Control Of (Regarding Law 51 of 1941): letter from the All Jamaica Youth Movement Institution to the Colonial Secretary, 6 September 1941 and letter from the Bustamante Industrial Trade Union, 26 March 1947.
66. *Gleaner*, 20 January 1938.

13.

RAVAGES AND REJUVENATION
World War II and Public Health in the British Caribbean

DEBBIE McCOLLIN

The atmosphere created by conflict has always been one where public health and medicine both floundered and flourished, where the ravages of war on communities were countered by innovation, volunteerism and cooperation that advanced public health systems and territories. Steve Gower asserts that "the major wars of the last 100 years have driven advances in treatment . . . and . . . preventative measures against disease and infection [but] nonetheless, continue to inflict their toll of carnage and human misery on not just combatants but also civilians".[1] World War II is considered one of the most dramatic of such examples. Even as military forces and civilian populations around the world between 1939 and 1945 were physically enfeebled by attacks, malnutrition, disease and emotional distress, they rallied because of the home front and war efforts of public health professionals and volunteers.

In the British West Indies this dichotomy was keenly experienced. Though it was only a peripheral theatre of war, the desperation created by rationing, sanitation problems and the disruptive movements of refugees and foreign militaries all generated periods of crisis. Reaction to these crises ensured a rejuvenation of interest in enhancing public health systems, as British and American efforts created opportunities for information gathering, training, infrastructural development and the establishment of sanitation and disease campaigns that would continue to buttress the public health systems of these territories after the war. In this period, as Berridge et al. explain, public health transitioned from the responsibility of the local community to the duty of large government and international groups, clearly evidenced in the Caribbean.[2]

Considering its obvious impact, the stark rarity of studies on World War II and public health in the Caribbean is stunning. Other than this author's work on venereal diseases and the American presence in Trinidad and Tobago and *World War II to Independence: Health Services and Women in Trinidad and Tobago 1939–1962*, Harvey Neptune's "Love American Style" in his 2007 *Caliban and the Yankees* and David Clyde's occasional insertions in his 1985 work *Health in Grenada*,[3] this aspect of the war has been largely unexplored. In an abbreviated yet herculean effort to fill this vacuum, this chapter will attempt to draw the reader's attention to the most significant consequences of the war on British Caribbean public health infrastructure and its people and the reactionary contribution of foreign entities to the preservation and propulsion of public health in the region. The chapter also explores the ultimate consequences of such involvement on local autonomy, the strength of the local practitioner and the health services, and it further posits that engagement over public health helped to cement World War II alliances and, as a result, opened the door to neo-imperialism in the region.

The limitations of such an attempt, however, must be acknowledged. It is impossible to comprehensively, and thus accurately, assess the collective consequences in these territories. A single chapter is certainly insufficient to analyse societies that vary markedly in their history, culture, geography, resources (and thus their wealth) and specifically their experience during the war. Nonetheless, the current work, *World War II and the Caribbean*, an innovation in the historiographic trend itself, demands a chapter that reveals the depths of the impact on public health within the British Caribbean[4] of this most significant conflict.

PUBLIC HEALTH PRIOR TO WORLD WAR II

The war, as well as creating its own public health problems, also exacerbated those already in existence. By 1939 the British Caribbean sadly represented the crises of the colonial empire – largely impoverished, debilitated by the pre-war depression and in the midst of political and social readjustment and agitation for reform, as reflected by waves of unrest during the late 1930s. In particular, health conditions, though differing greatly from territory to territory, fell short of the ideal. All territories by the 1930s possessed centralized institutions in urban centres and district services that serviced rural communities, but these were, routinely, insufficiently supplied with medical personnel, overwhelmed with patients and generally dilapidated.

Compounding these problems was the fact that the disease profile of British Caribbean territories was distinctly varied, with ailments reflecting a myriad of sanitation problems. Infectious diseases and diseases caused by contamination of water, food and the environment were the chief causes of morbidity and mortality in the Caribbean. Tuberculosis and malaria typically vied for the position of principal cause of death in these territories, with ailments such as dysentery, typhoid fever and enteritis also featuring prominently on the cause of mortality lists. The 1938–39 Moyne Commission,[5] examining the reasons for this trend, was scathing in its assessment that the "housing accommodation for the poorer people in the West Indies is generally deplorable, general sanitation is often primitive in the extreme and the diet of the poorer people is often insufficient and usually ill-balanced".[6] Additionally, degenerative diseases were also on the rise – with heart and malignant ailments quite prevalent in various territories. Systems put in place failed to effectively stem the tide of disease, focused as they were on curative rather than preventive solutions.[7] Despite general declines in the mortality rates in the early twentieth century, death and infant-mortality rates in British Caribbean territories remained high (in some territories more than others[8]), reflecting the poor socioeconomic conditions as well as cracks in the public health framework of these colonies. The death rate in St Kitts, for instance, did not indicate a pronounced decline during the 1930s, as by 1937 it remained relatively high at 36.5, as compared to 39.8 in 1928. Infant mortality was also a disturbing 209 per 1,000 live births.[9] Thus, the potential for deterioration once the Caribbean was thrown into crisis was considerable, and the public health conditions within the British Caribbean, already precarious, certainly crumbled further in the disorder of World War II. The renewed interest and involvement of imperialist nations within these vulnerable yet crucial territories also contributed to the decline of public health within the region during the war.

THE BRITISH CARIBBEAN IN WORLD WAR II

It must be noted that the attention focused on this region by these powerful nations was indeed merited, as the British Caribbean played a considerable role in World War II. These territories were instrumental in securing the sea route to critical theatres of the war. They were launch pads for the protection of the Atlantic, as well as the first line of defence in an eastern attack on the crucial Panama Canal, the opening to the Pacific. The southern coast of the United States and the northern coast of South America were also made vulnerable by instability in the British Caribbean. As a supplier of food, oil (via Aruba and Trinidad) and bauxite from Jamaica, they represented an essential supply base for the British. Thus, ensuring the stability of the British Caribbean, by shoring up security, systems and services, was vital to winning the war. Public health was a significant aspect of this matrix of stability and, as such, was an emphasis of the war effort.

Additionally, as the ferocity of attacks against the British heightened after the fall of France in June 1940 and negotiations to secure the acquisition of fifty destroyers from the United States, which had been ongoing from May 1940, threatened to stall, the British successfully offered the use of bases in their colonies of Newfoundland and the Caribbean in exchange for the destroyers.[10] It is through this agreement that the protection, and therefore the control, of the British Caribbean were largely relinquished to the United States beginning in 1941. Though restrictions were placed on their leases and projects that would encroach on the public, the establishment of American bases in the British Caribbean allowed the Americans considerable access to their weakest systems, of which healthcare was a prominent example. Nonetheless, it would first be the collapse of systems that highlighted critical weaknesses and ensured the deterioration of public health within the region.

THE RAVAGES

The war's effect on public health in the British Caribbean resulted first in serious disruptions within systems and services intrinsic to the maintenance of public health (nutrition, water and medical supplies and sanitation). Additionally, the tightening of the German hold in the Atlantic and Caribbean and the political restructuring and decisions made to secure the area, both

Anglo-American and French, generated demographic crises (due to inter- and intra-island migration) and actual casualties of war. Lastly, the disruption of systems and populations led to a rise in social diseases, outbreaks of infectious diseases and as will be seen an upsurge in mortality.

Disruption of Essential Systems

Food Shortage and the Cry for an Agricultural Revolution

At the onset of the war, government officials were quick to reassure the West Indian public that food supplies would not be severely affected by the war. This was necessary, as all were aware that the dominant weakness of the region was its dependence on the importation of food. As a result, a desperate discourse began in British parliamentary circles and colonial governments about increasing domestic production to support the war effort and supply local communities. Almost immediately agrarian reforms and schemes were endorsed, efforts were made to convert arable and crown land and food comptrollers were appointed throughout the region. Warren Alleyne describes the strict measures taken in Barbados, one of the most vulnerable colonies:

> The Vegetable Production (Defence) Control Order of 5th September [1939] required all planters to submit a monthly report of all acreages planted with vegetables and where appropriate, the acreage planted with each kind of vegetable, stating the date or dates of planting. Planters were also required to furnish details of any arable land lying uncultivated. All plantations were made subject to inspection, and Inspectors were empowered to enter on any plantation at any time between six o'clock in the morning and six o'clock in the evening to ensure that the Order was being complied with.[11]

Between 1939 and 1945, arable land under food cultivation in this territory was increased from 5 to 35 per cent.[12] In 1943 in St Kitts the government established a pig and dairy farm, Bayford Dairy, in an attempt to alleviate the shortage of meat and dairy products.[13] There were also attempts in the colonies to fix the prices of wholesale food items, and Grow Your Own Food campaigns began almost immediately as well. In Trinidad and Tobago, for instance, the public was encouraged through newspaper advertisements to design and create home gardens.[14]

It was clear, however, by 1942 that the West Indies' food supply was at risk and that food prices were skyrocketing, as Rita Pemberton notes in chapter 4. The presence of German U-boats, a direct attempt to disrupt the supply routes, particularly after the American entrance into the war, began to escalate. It became increasingly difficult to acquire rice and other staples or vegetables. Arthur Creech Jones, the member for Shipley, explained the gravity of the situation in a House of Commons debate:

> There are shipping difficulties. We have not mobilised the production of food to anything like a sufficient degree to meet the needs of this population of nearly 3,000,000, and so far as rice is concerned, although the Under-Secretary said that certain things had been done, I doubt if they are adequate to feed the populations of our own territories. I put it that we are face to face with a very grave situation which calls for the gravest attention from the Government at the present moment.[15]

At the local level, residents of the colonies were forced to find innovative means of surviving the war food shortages. As one rural Trinidadian resident recalls:

> Life became a lil tough, before that we had cows and a garden but during the war years we had to have more than one garden; we had four or five gardens because we used to plant ground provisions, plant all kinds of things in order to survive because things were hard to get. . . . I had to go and hunt as a young boy at night in the week; sometimes I would go twice a week to hunt manicou in the night to provide meat; on Saturday I would go to fish in the swamp, Nariva swamp . . . our staple diet consisted of corn and cassava . . . you couldn't get rice so we had to plant rice . . . for instance you couldn't get oil; you had to use coconut.[16]

The fact that the first few years of the war recorded extremely low rainfall also affected agricultural production and food supplies. Rice production in British Guiana, for instance, was reduced in 1941 to nine thousand tons owing to drought. With the demand for rice in the West Indies at forty thousand, it was obvious that the major supplier could not fulfil the demand.[17] As a result, black markets in food supplies emerged, and rationing was implemented in all British Caribbean territories.

Complicating the situation was the unrest within the agricultural sector due to low wages, poor working conditions and lack of unionization, complaints effectively continuing from the 1930s. The need for stability within this sector was critical to protect and continue to ensure consistent food production in the West Indies, which would support the British war effort. Additionally, though by June 1942 a convoy system (John Whitney Hall argues, belatedly[18]) was established to protect merchant vessels moving into and through the region, there were accusations that the focus, because the United States had been instrumental in organizing the convoy system, was to supply largely those territories which harboured American bases. Alleyne notes in *Barbados at War* that, at first, the convoy system "did not provide service to the islands in the eastern region and thus the areas of critical scarcity experienced little relief initially".[19] However, Claus Füllberg-Stolberg explains that by October 1942 efforts had been made to reinvigorate the importation of food into territories of the West Indies, with the support of the convoy system. The West Indian Schooner Pool, he notes, organized by "the governments of Cuba, Haiti and the Dominican Republic, with the support of several American institutions . . . acted speedily to construct road and rail networks for efficient overland transport, and to set up stockpiles at strategic points".[20] The governments of the smaller islands were also heavily involved, as goods moved not only from Puerto Rico in the north but also from Barbados and Trinidad in the south to the rest of the Leeward and Windward islands.[21] It was this pool, largely facilitated by local efforts, that helped to alleviate food shortages in the British Caribbean during the war. Nonetheless, many colonies, particularly at the height of the U-boat war in 1942, struggled to provide a consistent and diverse supply of food for their people. These import challenges, as well as the aforementioned unrest within the agricultural sector, presented difficulties in reducing the soaring food prices and the ailments caused by malnourishment or undernourishment.

Medical Shortages

The difficulty in acquiring goods and materials did not simply affect food but also the procurement of pharmaceuticals, medical supplies, instruments and equipment. With the hindrance of British and South American supply routes, the West Indies depended for pharmaceuticals increasingly on the United States, a country which would establish itself as the primary supplier during and beyond the war. Specifically, the drugs and equipment used in American-controlled programmes, whether military or philanthropic, were acquired solely through the United States. The Caribbean Medical Centre located in Trinidad, for example, an institution developed to combat the rise of venereal diseases in the territory, was supplied with stores, worth sixty thousand dollars, purchased by the colonial government from the US Army, as "such supplies, of course, in the quantities needed, were unobtainable at this time from any other source".[22]

Drugs, particularly those of paramount importance in the West Indies, such as quinine used to combat endemic malaria, were rationed to ensure some level of availability in the region. The control of drugs was the designated responsibility of the officer in charge of bulk purchasing in the various territories. In Trinidad fifteen distributors (thirteen drug firms and two opticians) were designated under the Control of Medical Supplies Regulation, instituted on 7 September 1942, to supply businesses recognized by the Control Board: "Owners of drugs stores and other medical supply businesses registered with the Control Board and sent in applications with the names and quantity of drugs required and the name of the chosen distributor. Prices were fixed by the Board to prevent exploitation by distributing firms during this period of shortage."[23]

It was, therefore, obvious that the procurement and availability of drugs and medical supplies was of paramount concern to British and local authorities during the war, attested to by the attention given to organizing and controlling their distribution.

Water Supplies

Climatic conditions also effectively added to the public health woes of West Indians during the war. The first two years of the war experienced abnormally low rainfall, and by early January 1941 it had become clear that water supplies were adversely affected, and efforts were being made to prevent wastage. In Barbados a public appeal was made in mid-January, and repeated at the end of February, to conserve water. By September the situation had become so dire that the government voted £31,000 to build a second reservoir at Castle Grant, St Joseph.[24] In Antigua the Annual Medical Report for 1944 noted that "many villagers were obliged to resort to drinking water from untreated sources".[25] Similar problems were experienced in Trinidad, where by 1 January 1942 a committee, the Special Water Advisory Committee, had been established and water schedules were put in operation, with water being generally shut off daily from 2:00 p.m. to 5:00 p.m.[26]

The shortage of water did not only affect consumption supplies but also compromised agricultural production, an essential focus of the war effort. Thus, with such a crisis, Britain, through a revised colonial-welfare policy, was tapped by many territories to assist with water problems. In 1942, at the height of the water shortage, a loan of £382,000, initially free of interest, was approved for the construction of a reservoir at Mona, Jamaica, to augment the Kingston supply and assist with irrigation. Furthermore, the year afterward a grant of £60,000 was issued to improve country water supplies by constructing "tanks for the catchment and storage of rain water".[27] Nonetheless, the construction of most of these reservoirs and the development of water schemes were regularly obstructed by difficulties of importing materials and equipment.

Housing, Living Conditions and Sanitation

The impact of the deteriorating housing and living conditions during the war was particularly evident in St Kitts, one of the Leeward territories. A housing survey conducted in 1943 to determine the impact of the war shortages on the local population revealed that the quality of housing in rural St Kitts was poor and even more so in the capital, Basseterre.[28] It reported that there was a large number of "beggars" in Basseterre, and pervasive poverty was evident in both Basseterre and the countryside.[29] Though not originally spawned by the war (labour issues and cries for increased wages had been ongoing since the 1930s), living conditions and the cost of living were certainly exacerbated by the shortages generated by the war. The fact that St Kitts was one of the wealthiest of the Leeward Islands gives some indication of the severe impact of the war on Leeward territories in the West Indies. The escalation of all forms of migration, urbanization and overcrowding throughout the region further assisted in the deterioration of housing and sanitation conditions within the British Caribbean.

Population Disruptions

The movement of people throughout the region due to the disruption of the war severely affected health conditions, increasing the demographic burdens of some societies and reducing the working and breeding population of others. The attraction of the growing oil industry in Aruba, Curaçao and Trinidad, and the American bases in the last, encouraged significant emigration into these territories. For Trinidad, this had particular implications for overcrowding, sanitation and disease control within Port of Spain. Dr Santon Gilmour, for instance, who conducted a survey of tuberculosis in the territory in 1943, noted that "a large number of workers migrated into the colony from other islands and within the colony itself there has been considerable migration of the more susceptible people from rural areas into the towns where provision of additional accommodation could not keep pace with the increase in population".[30]

For the Leeward and most of the Windward territories this emigration brought severe complications. The natural population increase of most of these colonies was stunted as a result of the out-migration to base territories. Through these demographic movements, the natural increase of the Windward Islands was reduced by approximately 48 per cent. Unfortunately, the worst estimates were in Grenada, which suffered an 80 per cent reduction. St Vincent faced a 40 per cent decline, Dominica 35 per cent and St Lucia 25 per cent. Even Barbados saw a decrease of 7 per cent.[31]

One Windward colony without an American base that had a similar demographic pattern to base colonies was Dominica. Situated between two French territories, which from the fall of France in 1940 were under the pro-Nazi Vichy government (as Eric Jennings details in chapter 5), Dominica became the unwilling host of thousands of French refugees. Lennox Honychurch explains that "the trickle became a flood and before the end of 1942 the number of refugees became unmanageable".[32] Local law enforcement had to be buttressed by a detachment of the South Caribbean Forces, and eventually commanders of the Free French army were deployed to supervise the refugees. Nonetheless, this incredible influx of refugees led to severe overcrowding of the capital, Roseau, in which it was estimated there were over five thousand refugees at the peak of the movement. French refugees received free food and lodging and one dollar a week, ultimately paid by the Free French government,[33] but nonetheless the escalation of population put pressure on housing and limited food supplies. Honychurch gives insight into the severity of the housing situation: "Houses, small shops and offices had been lined with bunks to provide sleeping space, anyone who could rent space for a bed made room. For a time the government was fearful of disease and epidemics."[34] Prices also skyrocketed, despite price-control measures, as the French pockets remained full and merchants and vendors sold vegetables at exorbitant prices, effectively compromising the nutrition of the inhabitants.[35]

Temporary migration to the United States also caused significant issues with public health in such colonies as Jamaica and Barbados. War industry programmes organized by the United States War Food Administration and the War Manpower Commission led to, for instance, thirty-six hundred Barbadian labourers[36] and approximately sixty-four thousand Jamaicans[37] (who made up the majority of the migrants) migrating to work temporarily in the United States beginning in 1942. The vulnerability created in the public health service by these schemes is evident in the case of Barbados. Already-overstretched local medical practitioners were required to examine these men before assignment,[38] which unfortunately exacerbated the inadequacy of service provision to the local community.

Furthermore, in Barbados the consequences were even direr, with temporary migrant workers responsible for transferring viruses from the American mainland to Barbados upon their return. On 17 December 1944, 1,507 labourers returned to the colony and by 22 December the first cases of an outbreak of cerebrospinal meningitis had been reported. No notification had been given by American authorities and this, coupled with the sizeable number of returning labourers, ensured that by March 1945 there were 119 cases and 19 fatalities within the colony.[39] Assistance from the United States and British army stationed in Trinidad was received, but as the Annual Report of the Colony recognized, the credit for eventually controlling the outbreak had to be given to the "Parochial Medical Officers, private practitioners, bacteriologists, nurses and sanitary inspectors",[40] the true heroes of the day.

The Battle of the Caribbean, Dealing with Casualties of War

Though there was no fighting on the shores of the British West Indies, local governments had to be ready to deal with the consequences of battles in one of the most significant maritime theatres, the Caribbean Sea. With a third of all fuel used by the British in the World War coming from Trinidad, Venezuela and Aruba, the West Indies was a major shipping lane for vital resources. Moreover, with nonstop movements of military and cargoes of food, equipment and supplies, the Caribbean became a major target for a German U-boat incursion, code named Neuland, in 1942. Another offensive also occurred in July 1943. Gaylord Kelshall reports that by the end of 1942 "thirty-six percent of all world-wide merchant shipping losses had occurred in the Caribbean theatre".[41]

As ships were torpedoed and sunk in the seas and harbours surrounding West Indian territories (such as in Castries, St Lucia, in March 1942) and bodies floated to shore days after these attacks, or were brought in by rescue operations, local systems were burdened with the care and treatment of the wounded. In 1942 in Barbados, approximately 203 survivors within a seven-day period, 5–12 May, washed up along the coast, "with 86 on 21st May alone".[42] The St John's Ambulance Association, doctors, nurses and law enforcement were all part of the critical structures that ensured the care of the wounded. Significantly, however, in this area the women's involvement in the war effort was very evident. Women's volunteer organizations and government nursing personnel were frequently tasked with assisting in the care of the wounded from shore to hospital. The Red Cross Women's Brigade, which was established in many territories at the onset of the war under the auspices of the British Red Cross, was often charged with the erection of casualty clearing stations and first-aid posts, which helped to treat the washed-up wounded.[43] Youth organizations also worked to alleviate suffering; the Girl Guides in Barbados, for instance, created an emergency unit which ran a canteen service for survivors, as Karen Eccles also details in chapter 14.[44]

Disease Escalation

War Aphrodisia and the Upsurge of Venereal Diseases

From the beginning of the war British and foreign troops flooded the British Caribbean. The United States in particular opened bases in St Lucia, Trinidad, Jamaica, Antigua, the Bahamas and British Guiana, leading to troops stationed regularly throughout the West Indies. The rapidity with which the influx of foreign military occurred only encouraged what can be referred to as "war aphrodisia", a relaxing of sexual behaviour and restraints during wartime, very common in territories with a strong presence of foreign forces, as Dalea Bean explains in chapter 12.[45] Patterns of sexual behaviour morphed and increased with the expansion of the military, placing significant pressure on the existing medical service. Though VDs, particularly syphilis and gonorrhoea, were by no means new to the British West Indies, such a relaxing of sexual attitudes encouraged their escalation. The movement of troops into the region and the intensification of visits of naval vessels to the shores of these colonies from 1937 complicated and escalated the spread. In Jamaica, for instance, a report by the commander-in-chief of American and West Indian stations revealed that contact with the territory generated significant cases on the vessels:

> During 1938, the visits of HM Ships ORION, AJAX and YORK to Kingston, Jamaica, were all followed by a large number of cases of venereal diseases. ORION reported 27 cases during a 12 day visit. During the crisis in September, ORION visited Kingston for 2 days and 15 cases were contracted in the short stay. AJAX contracted 18 cases during a stay of 4 weeks. YORK contracted 5 cases during a 7 day visit out of 14 cases for the whole quarter.[46]

Nonetheless, the problem of VDs was exacerbated by the stationing of British, Canadian and particularly American soldiers and sailors on colony bases. Young and old West Indian women were attracted to the men in uniform, who seemed different from the typical local males, and the men were lured by the seeming "exoticness" and availability of local West Indian women (neither of which was a new phenomenon). Many West Indian women became the temporary wives and girlfriends of these men and many also engaged in sexual exchanges for money or security. This atmosphere certainly led to a rise in violence (sexual and otherwise) against local women, as well as the constant communication and reinfection of sexually transmitted diseases throughout the ranks of foreign soldiers and the local communities.

Compounding the problem was the fact that the British government could not afford to stretch its resources to treat VDs in its colonies. Medical personnel and supplies were "required not only by the British military services but on the bombed-out home front",[47] leaving local communities wanting. Thus, these diseases continued to escalate, reaching tens of thousands within territories such as Trinidad where American bases were established. By 1942, for instance, in Trinidad it was clear that VDs were "the major cause of sickness and disability among both [American] troops and construction workers" on the bases.[48]

Outbreaks of Infectious Diseases and Mortality

With compromised public health infrastructure and water and food supplies, unfortunately coupled with irregular ingress patterns in many colonies, it was inevitable that there would be outbreaks and epidemics in the British West Indies during the war. Typhoid, a bacterial infection caused by ingestion of faeces-contaminated water, was typically present in most territories but rose to epidemic proportions in many areas during the war, since as water supplies and sanitary conditions declined, West Indians were forced to find innovative means of sourcing water and available water sources became overused. Typically, many across the West Indies used water sources – wells, rivers, ponds – that were easily contaminated and in the midst of war not effectively regulated. Women, men and children, many of whom were already affected by typhoid, used these sources for their daily ablutions alongside washerwomen and laundresses who engaged in washing contaminated clothing at times. In 1940, Grenada reported a typhoid outbreak of 54 cases and 6 deaths, a jump from 25 cases and 6 deaths the previous year.[49] Carriacou, an island off the coast of Grenada, provided 50 per cent of the notifications of typhoid cases for the entire colony in that year. Clyde describes the behaviour of the first victim in one village, La Resource in Carriacou: "Ill for three weeks before the district medical officer was approached, the initial victim (one of the two who died) continued to wash herself and her clothes alongside the upper well and, together with others, frequently stood in the well itself to draw water. The bucket in which she washed her clothes was also used to carry drinking water."[50]

Subsequent to the initial outbreak, the local medical officer ordered the cleaning of the well and environs and established treatment structures and routines within the local community to curtail the spread. Of the contacts of the typhoid cases, 250 were identified and inoculated and warned to boil water.[51] In 1942 a tuberculosis hospital at Cherry Hill had to be converted to a typhoid centre to deal with the escalation. Despite these measures, by 1945 typhoid peaked in the colony at 158 cases and 21 deaths.[52] Panicked authorities finally traced this latter outbreak to returning labourers from Trinidad. It was only with the advent of antibiotics in the years succeeding the war that numbers dramatically declined. It should be noted that many British Caribbean colonies, such as St Vincent and St Lucia, suffered severe typhoid epidemics as well during the war, with St Vincent, in fact, leading in typhoid mortality in the West Indies.

At the peak of the war, another severe disease outbreak occurred in Trinidad. Poliomyelitis had been consistently present in relatively low numbers in the decades prior to the war, with an average of 3 cases per year except in periods of outbreak. The third and fourth years of the war saw one of the worst outbreaks of poliomyelitis that had ever been recorded in the twentieth century in the colony. Beginning in October 1941, the number of cases increased to 135 by the end of 1942, occurring throughout Trinidad and even in Tobago.[53] With no known effective means of controlling polio and inconclusive evidence as to the vector of the disease, preventive control took the form of isolation of cases and sanitary measures. Before the war was over another outbreak occurred, in 1945, resulting in 99 cases.[54] The fact that this would be the last major polio outbreak for the next ten years emphasizes the extent of the deterioration of social conditions during World War II.

Outbreaks of other communicable diseases continued unabated between 1940 and 1945. Dysentery, primarily, presented a challenge to many communities, with Barbados being one of the most affected: from 1940 to 1941 cases more than doubled, moving from 35 to 92.[55] In Antigua an influenza outbreak ravaged communities in 1944, with "the number of deaths from influenza . . . higher than in any of the previous 17 years or more".[56] The shortage of doctors, a pervasive problem, also exacerbated the incidence of disease, as seen in the case of yaws in Grenada.[57]

Mortality rates as well reflected the dilemma faced by Caribbean societies during the war. The most vulnerable groups, the elderly and the very young, were most affected. As figure 13.1 shows, infant mortality rates, typically an apt indicator of home and community health,[58] spiked in various territories between 1941 and 1942, and in the case of British Guiana, 1943. The Grenadian Medical Report in 1942 explained that "the deterioration in the state of public health can be correlated with a higher death rate at the extremes of life and it is obvious that these classes of the community are most hard hit by the economic adversities inseparable from war conditions particularly in the way of nutrition".[59]

The war thus became the bane of public health authorities, ravaging these societies already in social and economic crises. Food, water and medical-supply shortages coupled with the disrupted migratory patterns provoked

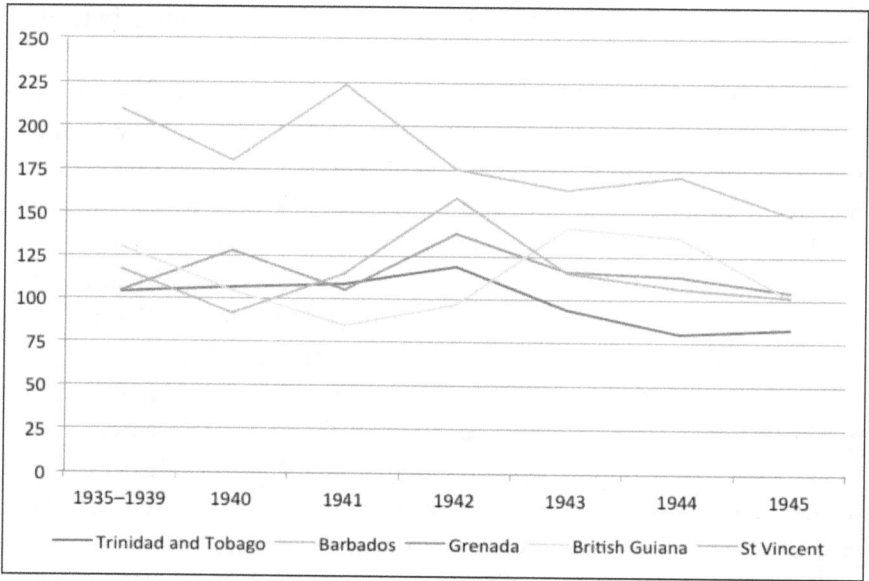

Figure 13.1. Infant mortality rates for select British Caribbean colonies during World War II. (Statistical Unit, Research Branch, Central Secretariat, Caribbean Commission, *Caribbean Statistical Digest: Demography and Finance*, issue 1, vol. 2 [February 1952]

disease escalations and ensured substandard delivery of services and lack of implementation of critical public health initiatives.

REJUVENATION

Despite the aforementioned ravages, the dichotomy in the effect of the war on public health was also clearly evident. World War II, though devastating to the British Caribbean, also laid the foundation for unprecedented progress in public health in the post-war era and cemented the involvement of United States personnel, arguably the foremost experts in this field, in health in the Caribbean. The implications of this involvement, however, must never be underestimated, as the era also re-established the superiority of the foreign worker in healthcare in the precursor period to decolonization within the region. Nevertheless, it was the imperial government that in part created the financial basis for this progress.

The Colonial Development and Welfare Fund

The British government, catalysed by the 1937 unrest in the West Indies and recommendations made in subsequent investigative commissions such as the Moyne Commission of 1938–39, engaged a funding tool to assist in the development of the region, especially as its "merits as compared with those of Germany in colonial administration [would] soon be under the public eye".[60] Through the Colonial Development and Welfare Fund the government worked to buttress the region's social services by inviting governments to apply for financial assistance for specific developmental projects. This fund, though limited, established a fiscal basis for some advancement in public health in the region during the years of the war. The first Colonial Development and Welfare Act in 1940 provided funds for British Caribbean territories for a five-year period, and this was followed in 1945 with a second act of ten years' duration. Sir Rupert Briercliffe, former director of the Nigerian Medical Service, was appointed medical adviser to the comptroller of the fund. This fund pledged millions for use by British Caribbean governments for approved programmes and research and many of them took advantage of the opportunity. For instance, it was noted that by March 1942 the Colonial Development and Welfare Fund had reported that British Guiana had applied for twenty-two grants, the vast majority for public health development, as revealed in the *Hansard* record below:

> Appointment of a malariologist, extension of campaign against yellow fever mosquito, medical service for the aboriginal Indian population, material for health education instruction, equipment for a venereal diseases clinic, apparatus for the diagnosis of tuberculosis, broadcasting, lady health officer, training for sanitary inspectors, school medical officer, improvements in irrigation in West Demerara, model houses for health centre staff at Anna Regina, animal husbandry, livestock officer, marketing officer, sister tutor, survey, improvement of river communications, experimental community centre, principal and instructor at Kingston trading centre, stock farming, buildings and equipment for Georgetown and Kitty boys' clubs, boys' work secretary, hospital secretary.[61]

By 30 June 1942 it was clear that British Guiana was not the only territory in such a situation; the majority of applications concerned public health, indicative of the fact that the greatest need was in this sphere. Twenty-six applications out of eighty-three were approved for "Medicine, Public Health and Sanitary" schemes (exclusive of the six water-improvement schemes) and were in various degrees of implementation in the entire British Caribbean by this date.[62]

The fund was also used to develop the human resources at all levels. The education of subordinate medical personnel was certainly a priority, however. For instance, a grant of £15,000 for a large permanent training school for health personnel in Jamaica, including courses in public health nursing, laboratory techniques and the duties of sanitary inspectors, was approved in 1943. Similarly, a grant of £1,290 was provided for training courses in British Guiana for sanitary inspectors and health visitors from the Leeward Islands.[63] The products of these training schemes supported malaria campaigns across the region in the latter years of the war. Additionally, the fund provided for the education of doctors, supporting promising West Indian students in medical schools in Britain, including female candidates. One such prominent example was Grenadian Hilda Gibbs, later Hilda Bynoe, who received her award in 1944 and went on to study at the London University Royal Free Hospital. After completing another degree at the London School of Medicine in 1951, she returned in 1953 to the region, where she became a renowned general practitioner and eventually the governor of Grenada, Carriacou and Petite Martinique.[64]

The war, however, presented obstacles to the implementation of many of the programmes approved by the Colonial Development and Welfare Fund authorities. In Grenada, for instance, projects were sanctioned in four categories: anti-malaria work at the cost of £10,000, a mobile anti-yaws unit, the development of a maternal- and child-welfare education and demonstration health centre and the reconstruction of the Sanitary Department.[65] The escalation of the war brought almost all of these projects to a standstill, and as with many other territories, Grenadian authorities were only able to commence with anti-malaria work and the training of personnel for other approved projects. Nonetheless, this fund would be credited with providing the foundation for development within the region during and in the aftermath of World War II, extracting to a measured extent many British West Indian territories from the abyss of poor sanitation and health infrastructure at all levels.

Reconnaissance and Planning

Reconnaissance during World War II was not confined to information on human forces but also on enemy pathogens. Diseases were enemy agents which had to be studied before they could be engaged or opposed. Consequently, a vast number of surveys were conducted throughout the war in an attempt to create a knowledge base from which to launch disease and general public health programmes. It can also be argued that in the midst of the stagnation generated by the war due to lack of supplies and experts, governments could only resort to gathering information and planning for post-war execution. Additionally, the Caribbean, as a peripheral theatre of conflict, presented a fairly stable environment in these crucial years to study "tropical diseases".

Whatever the catalyst, World War II was arguably, in the case of healthcare, the most concentrated and diverse period of information gathering in the West Indies in the twentieth century. Surveys were conducted before troops were deployed into the region to discover the extent of the malaria threat or after deployment to determine the prevalence of VD infections. Experts were funded by governments, the Colonial Development and Welfare Fund or philanthropic organizations commissioned by governments or the military. They surveyed the territories, assessed and made recommendations to control endemic diseases such as leprosy and tuberculosis and, as mentioned, malaria and VDs. Dr Lawrence J. Charles of Dominica, malariologist with the Colonial Development and Welfare Association, conducted a survey of malaria in Grenada in 1945 confirming conclusively *Anopheles aquasalis* as the main vector of the disease.[66] Another, Dr E. Muir, studied leprosy extensively in British Guiana, Jamaica, Barbados, Antigua, St Kitts, Nevis, St Lucia and Trinidad, beginning in the second year of the war. In addition, the Council of the National Association for the Prevention of Tuberculosis in Great Britain, after being approached by local governments and guaranteed funding by Colonial Development and Welfare, agreed to send tuberculosis expert Dr Santon Gilmour to the region in 1943 to conduct tuberculosis surveys and produce the most comprehensive report on this ailment in the region at that time. Surveys for infrastructural development also took place during the period. Financed by a Colonial Development and Welfare Fund grant, hospital architects William Watkins and Stuart Gray (of Watkins Gray) entered the West Indies in 1940 and conducted surveys of hospital buildings in the eastern Caribbean colonies and British Guiana, producing plans for the building and renovation of facilities such as Antigua's Holberton Hospital and the San Fernando Hospital in southern Trinidad. Thus, it is obvious that though the war stymied action in public health, it also, as a result (since little else could be accomplished), laid the foundation for major developments in the aftermath of the war.

Foreign Intervention and Disease Campaigns

Military and Philanthropic Organizations

The presence not only of foreign troops but of United States medical professionals of all levels had a profound impact on the development of public health in the region. The first wave could be attributed to the United States Army. For the first two years of the war, before the United States officially declared war on Axis forces, the Caribbean was second only to the Pacific in terms of deployment of US medical personnel overseas. By the war's peak in 1943, there were 6,063 members of the US Army Medical Department (which included doctors, nurses, laboratory technicians and other medical personnel) employed within the Caribbean region.[67] Their engagement within the colonies ensured that local medical professionals were exposed to training opportunities through the Medical Department. The Americans, by necessity, generally established a policy of using local labour when appropriate "to prevent diminution of the efficiency of their troops" or to appease local governments who were somewhat apprehensive about their presence. It was obvious that this use was predicated on the factors that existed within the region that encouraged the use of civilians within the US Army Medical Service. *The History of the US Medical Department* explains, for instance, that "by virtue of their location, relative stability, and type of function, installations in the communications zone or base sections were able to utilize such personnel on a greater scale than those troops in combat areas".[68]

The involvement of such army personnel in wider public health initiatives in these colonies was largely focused on the protection of the forces stationed within the region and the surrounding communities. The British, other than the Colonial Development and Welfare Fund, in many cases abdicated their responsibility to the United States military and their associates. As noted, these foreign authorities were primarily concerned with the safety of their men and hence concentrated on diseases that affected them the most, specifically malaria and VDs.

Army personnel, however, were not the only foreigners involved in healthcare in the British Caribbean during World War II. The war opened opportunities for the large-scale return of the Rockefeller Foundation, an international philanthropic organization, to public health work in the Caribbean. The Rockefeller Foundation had first appeared in the region in 1913, establishing through its International Health Division a comprehensive hookworm campaign throughout the British West Indies. Other vertical campaigns dealing with malaria would follow. But since the 1920s the foundation's involvement had waned considerably in the Caribbean. World War II, however, provided opportunities through invitations by the United States military and collaborations with the British under the Colonial Development and Welfare Act. This group effectively assisted in transforming the public health infrastructure of the territories but was also implicated in abetting the thrusts of neo-imperialists.

Anti-Malaria Offensive

The first major collaboration of governments, US military and the Rockefeller Foundation was aimed at combating the malaria threat. After being approached by US military personnel, the director of medical services in Trinidad and Tobago, Dr Adam Rankine, on 2 May 1941 approved a one-year malaria survey that would initiate malaria control in the colony.[69] This scheme was conducted by members of the Rockefeller's International Health Division – Wilbur G. Downs and Mark Boyd – and H.S. Gillette of the Health Department of Trinidad and Tobago (future head of the Malaria Division).[70] A similar anti-malaria programme, supported by a grant from the Colonial Development and Welfare Fund grant, began in Grenada in 1942 on the "thickly populated west coast from St George's to Sauteurs where vectors bred in stagnant or slow moving water at the mouths of rivers held up by sand bars from flowing into the sea".[71]

Furthermore, a collaborative effort of the Jamaican government, the Colonial Development and Welfare Association and the Rockefeller Foundation led to the establishment in 1943 of training programmes for sanitary inspectors and nurses from various Leeward and Windward territories in Jamaica.

The mobile Windward and Leeward Islands Malaria Control Unit resulted from this initiative and inspired vertical campaigns during the war in these areas. In 1944 the Grenadian malaria unit was merged with a newly formed Windward and Leeward Islands Public Health Engineering Unit, headquartered in Grenada with branches in St Vincent, St Lucia, Antigua and St Kitts, funded by Colonial Development and Welfare and directed by a sanitary engineer, Brian R. Dyer, from the Rockefeller Foundation.[72] By February 1944, funds totalling £72,635 had been allocated for anti-malaria control measures by the Colonial Development and Welfare Act for the West Indies.[73] The history of malaria control in the West Indies during the war, therefore, is clearly a story dominated by Colonial Development and Welfare and the Rockefeller interests in the region.

VD Control and the Caribbean Medical Centre

By 1942 VD units or initiatives had been established in most territories, but it was clear that sexually transmitted diseases were not in decline. This exacerbated the discontent among local practitioners, who felt excluded from these disease-control schemes. The editor of the *Caribbean Medical Journal* complained that the existing provisions for the treatment of VDs by 1942 in most of the British West Indian colonies had "proved a failure in spite of the heavy financial expenditure". He pointed out that in Trinidad only 20 per cent of the patients attending the VD clinics received the full course of treatment and suggested that had local practitioners been involved, this number would have been reduced. He recommended that the cooperation of the medical practitioners be sought in distributing drugs and identifying cases.[74] This lack of utilization of the local medical practitioner in the systems established during the war by British and American authorities would continue to be a problem beyond the war years.

Despite such complaints, the responsibility for effecting change within this sphere was given to the Americans, who, with the approval of the British, were in charge of developing VD treatment across the British Caribbean. This work was conducted principally through a centre for research, treatment and training, the Caribbean Medical Centre. This centre, established in 1944 at 103 Ariapita Avenue on the western outskirts of Port of Spain, Trinidad, was run by Colonel O.C. Wenger of the United States and a twenty-one-strong US medical team that had been imported into the colony.[75] One hundred tons of medical and hospital equipment and material[76] were transported to Trinidad from the United States for the anti-VD campaign in the West Indies and after its first year of existence, the Caribbean Medical Centre was attending to three-quarters of all new cases of VDs in the colony.

Its most successful endeavours, however, were with the military bodies. The centre ran an intensive educational prophylactic programme among the US and British military stationed in the Caribbean, which saw within six months "the contingent with one of the highest rates dropped to one of the lowest rates", according to US officials.[77] By the end of the war the incidence of VDs among the US troops stationed in the British Caribbean was even lower than among forces stationed in the United States. Among British troops there was a similar reduction, from 239 per 1,000 per annum in January 1944 to 71 by January 1945.[78]

The Caribbean Medical Centre also functioned as a training centre for local and regional personnel. By March 1945 the United States military and medical personnel had trained fifty-six Trinidadians as technicians, nurses and clerical workers to take over many of the centre's operations,[79] and in November 1944 a conference was organized to plan for the expansion of the centre's operations and VD programmes to other British West Indian colonies. It was decided that though "the extreme shortage of personnel in all British colonies will handicap the training program for the time being", physicians, nurses, laboratory technicians and others would spend three months to a year, depending on the position, in training at the centre.[80] These men and women would be funded by Colonial Development and Welfare where possible. Colonel Wenger reported that by 1 March 1945 "12 trainees have arrived at the Caribbean Medical Center, . . . two nurses from Dominica; one nurse from British Guiana; 2 student nurses from St. Lucia; 1 laboratory technician each from British Guiana, British Honduras, Dominica, Grenada, and St. Lucia. In addition, a dispenser (pharmacist) and a sanitary inspector from Dominica are undergoing special training."[81] The work of the Caribbean Medical Centre and the US-run VD campaign of 1941–45 made a marked impact on VD treatment and prevention in the region and laid the foundation for the development of effective VD divisions within the health service of the colonies.

The positive contributions made by the Colonial Development and Welfare

Fund and the Rockefeller Foundation during the war cannot be denied. The work of the foundation's Health Division was commended in a 1943 statement in the British House of Commons: "That matter-of-fact, business-like body is always to be found about whenever a real job of work is to be done in research, in promoting public health or in international co-operation; it is the delight and admiration of its friends, I might almost say the envy.... There is no better example in the world of practical co-operation and good will."[82]

However, there was a distinct and growing distrust of the consequences of the work of these groups within the region. In 1947, according to David Clyde, Dr Leonard Commissiong, former director of medical services of Grenada, pleaded in his poem entitled "Whither Grenada":

> Oh my people! Oh my people!
> We are slipping down the hill;
> Waiting for C.D. and W.,
> All they've promised to fulfil...
> Have you never heard the saying God helps those who help themselves?[83]

These groups and initiatives, despite their relative achievements, perpetuated the dependence on foreigners and heightened imperialist notions, entrenching the idea of British and US superiority in the decolonization era.

CONCLUSION

It becomes quite obvious that it was not only the home fronts and public health systems of the European theatres that were compromised by World War II but also the peripheral theatres, the colonial societies that entered the war alongside Britain. The troubles of the first three decades of the twentieth century in the British Caribbean created a foundation for the collapse of essential systems once the pressure of war began to be experienced. The successful German Caribbean offensive which crippled supply lines, coupled with the historic weaknesses of the region, led to shortages of food, water and medical supplies, severely handicapping public health in the Caribbean. Rapid and stunning alterations in demographic patterns as a result of labour opportunities, political upheavals and official displacement also encouraged outbreaks of major contamination and communicable diseases such as typhoid, poliomyelitis and dysentery.

But the inevitable paradox of war pervaded the health sector of the British West Indies. Though not altruistic in their motives, the Allies clearly "allied" to support the colonial home front when distinct challenges arose, especially after the official entrance of the United States into the region in 1941. The Anglo-American Caribbean Commission, a collaboration of the British and American governments, the British Colonial Development and Welfare Act, the US military and the Rockefeller Foundation all ensured that certain initiatives, those most important to securing the war effort, of course, were sustained financially and otherwise. Their support generated a broad base of knowledge, due to numerous surveys and expert reports, which laid the foundation for post-war progress. World War II cemented the involvement of American personnel in public health and redirected the focus of the British on development in the Caribbean.

The initiative of the colonies themselves, despite handicaps, should not be undervalued, as citizens, local governments, indigenous organizations and medical professionals of all levels worked to maintain the health of their populations under the direst circumstances. However, an examination of public health during World War II reveals the deep-rooted problems of the region, which were exacerbated by the conflict and led to an increasing dependence on the support of outsiders. The region's progress in public health was tied intrinsically to this involvement, a problematic development on the eve of post-war decolonization.

NOTES

1. Steve Gower, preface, in *War Wounds: Medicine and the Trauma of Conflict*, ed. Elizabeth Stewart (Wollombi, Australia: Exisle, 2011), 7.
2. V. Berridge et al., *Public Health in History* (Berkshire, NY: Open University Press, 2011), 168–69.
3. Debbie McCollin, "Friend or Foe: Venereal Diseases and The American Presence in Trinidad and Tobago during World War II", *History in Action* 1, no. 1 (2010): 1–12; Debbie McCollin, "World War II to Independence: Health, Services and Women in Trinidad and Tobago 1939–1962", in Juanita de Barros, Steven Palmer and David Wright, eds., *Health and Medicine in the Circum-Caribbean 1800–1968* (New York: Routledge, 2009); Harvey R. Neptune, *Caliban and the Yankees: Trinidad and the United States Occupation* (Chapel Hill: University

of North Carolina Press, 2007); David Clyde, *Health in Grenada: A Social and Historical Account* (London: Vade-Mecum Press, 1985).

4. The British West Indies included the Windward Islands (Grenada, St Lucia, St Vincent, the Grenadines and Dominica [from 1940]), the Leeward Islands (Antigua, Barbuda, British Virgin Islands, Montserrat, St Kitts, Nevis, Anguilla), Barbados, the Bahamas, British Guiana, British Honduras, Jamaica (including its dependencies, the Turks and Caicos Islands and the Cayman Islands) and Trinidad and Tobago.

5. The Moyne Commission, also known as the West India Royal Commission, was sent to the region in 1938 and 1939 to assess the social and economic conditions of the British West Indies.

6. Great Britain, *Report of the West India Royal Commission (1938–1939)* (London: His Majesty's Stationery Office, 1945), 154.

7. Ibid.

8. Ibid., 137, 138. The death rate for Barbados in 1937, e.g., was 18.5 as compared to 30.1 in 1928, while Grenada's death rate declined only from 16.5 to 14.3 and Trinidad and Tobago's from 19.9 to 17.4 in the same years. Detailed rates for all British Caribbean territories can be found on the indicated pages of the Royal Commission's report. It must be noted that the high numbers in the later years may be a result of improved statistical reporting.

9. Ibid., 137.

10. Martin Gilbert and Simon Vance, *Churchill and America* (New York: Simon and Schuster, 2005), 202.

11. Warren Alleyne, *Barbados at War 1939–1945: A Historical Account by Warren Alleyne* (Barbados: Published by author, 1999), 4.

12. Ibid.

13. *Agriculture in St. Kitts Nevis 1991–1995 and Beyond: Working Document #9 of 13* (Port of Spain: Inter-American Institute for Cooperation on Agriculture, 1997), 12.

14. Debbie McCollin, "The History of Health and Healthcare in Trinidad and Tobago 1938–1962" (PhD diss., University of the West Indies, 2010), 105–6.

15. United Kingdom, "Colonial Affairs", *Hansard Parliamentary Debates*, vol. 382 (4 August 1942), 932.

16. John Bramble, interviewed by Lovell Francis, *Project Voices from the Past* (Department of History, University of the West Indies, St. Augustine, 14 July 2008).

17. United Kingdom, "Rice Production", *Hansard Parliamentary Debates*, vol. 380 (24 June 1942), 1959–1960.

18. Hall points out that "the United States was slow to adopt the convoy system and

the U-Boats had a field day against unprotected shipping". John Whitney Hall, general ed., *History of The World: Earliest Times to the Present Day* (Bridgewater, MA: World Publications Group), 725.
19. Alleyne, *Barbados at War 1939–1945*, 14.
20. Claus Füllberg-Stolberg, "The Caribbean in the Second World War", in *UNESCO General History of the Caribbean*, vol. 5: *The Caribbean in the Twentieth Century*, ed. Bridget Brereton (Paris: UNESCO, 2004), 111.
21. Ibid., 14.
22. O.C. Wenger, *Caribbean Medical Center: The Organisation, Development and Activities of the Caribbean Medical Centre at Port of Spain, Trinidad, B.W.I. From 9 February 1943 to 1 March 1945* (Washington, DC: Caribbean Commission, 1946), 8–9.
23. McCollin, "History of Health and Healthcare", 98.
24. Alleyne, *Barbados at War 1939–1945*, 10.
25. *Antigua Annual Medical and Sanitary Report for the Year 1944* (St John's, Antigua: Government Printing Office, 1945), 1.
26. "Special Committee to Probe Water Shortage", *Trinidad Guardian*, 1 January 1942, 2.
27. United Kingdom, "Jamaica Water Supplies", *Hansard Parliamentary Debates*, vol. 401 (12 July 1944), 1728.
28. Vincent Hubbard, *A History of St Kitts: The Sweet Trade* (London: Macmillan, 2002), 126.
29. Ibid., 136, 140.
30. Medical Officer of Health for Port of Spain, Trinidad and Tobago, *Administrative Report of the Public Health Department: Urban Sanitary District of the City of Port Of Spain 1942 and 1943* (Port of Spain: Government Printing Office, 1944), 5.
31. Joycelin Massiah, "Reflection on the Current Demographic Position of Small States in the Caribbean" (paper submitted to the Conference on the Independence of Very Small States with Special Reference to the Caribbean, University of the West Indies, Cave Hill, 25–28 March 1974).
32. Lennox Honychurch, *The Dominica Story: A History of the Island* (Roseau: Dominica Institute, Roseau Division, 1975, 1984), 135.
33. Ibid., 136. French refugees' food and lodging and financial allowance was paid by the Dominican government, which was repaid by the British government once the allowance had been refunded by the Free French government.
34. Ibid., 135.
35. Ibid.
36. *Barbados Annual Report of the Chief Medical Officer for the Year 1944–45* (Bridgetown: Government Printing Office, 1946), 5.

37. Fitzroy Baptiste, "Jamaicans in the United States' Emergency Farm and War Industries Programme, 1942 to 1947" (paper presented at the 39th Annual Conference of the Association of Caribbean Historians, Kingston, Jamaica, 6–10 May 2007), 1.
38. *Barbados Annual Report of the Chief Medical Officer for the Year 1944–45*, 5.
39. Ibid., 9.
40. Ibid.
41. Gaylord T.M. Kelshall, *The U-Boat War in the Caribbean* (Port of Spain: Paria, 1988; repr. Annapolis: Naval Institute Press, 1994), xiv.
42. Alleyne, *Barbados at War*, 14.
43. McCollin, *World War II to Independence*, 82.
44. Alleyne, *Barbados at War*, 14.
45. Joshua S. Goldstein, *War and Gender: How Gender Shapes the War System and Vice Versa* (Cambridge: Cambridge University Press, 2001), 338.
46. National Archives of the United Kingdom (NAUK): CO318/436/18, H.W. Young, *Report to MP Malcolm MacDonald*, 13 August 1939.
47. Wenger, *Caribbean Medical Centre*, 4.
48. Colonel John Lada, ed., *Civil Affairs/Military Government Public Health Activities Preventive Medicine in World War II*, vol. 8 (Washington, D.C.: Office of the Surgeon General, Department of the Army, 1976), 128. See Major Gen Morrison C. Stayer, MC, USA (Ret), "U.S. Possessions and Bases in the Caribbean Area", ibid.
49. *Grenada Annual Medical and Sanitary Report for the Year 1940* (Georgetown: Government Printing Office, 1941), 2.
50. Clyde, *Health in Grenada*, 330.
51. *Grenada Annual Medical and Sanitary Report for the Year 1940*, 3.
52. Clyde, *Health in Grenada*, 331.
53. *Port of Spain Population and Vital Statistics Report 1958* (Port of Spain: Government Printing Office, 1959).
54. Ibid.
55. *Barbados Annual Report of the Chief Medical Officer for the Year 1941–42* (Bridgetown: Government Printing Office, 1943), 5.
56. *Antigua Annual Medical and Sanitary Report for the Year 1944* (St John's, Antigua: Government Printing Office, 1945), 2.
57. Clyde, *Health in Grenada*, 303.
58. Infant mortality is an apt indicator of general health because it gives insight into care in the home, post-partum care of child and mother, conditions of the surrounding environment and general and specific nutrition of the family.
59. *Grenada Annual Report of Medical Services for the Year 1942*, 1–2.

60. Stephen Constantine, *The Making of British Colonial Policy 1914–1940* (London: Routledge, 2005), 221.
61. United Kingdom, "British Guiana, British Honduras", *Hansard Parliamentary Debates*, vol. 378 (19 March 1942), 1680.
62. United Kingdom, "Welfare Schemes", *Hansard Parliamentary Debates*, vol. 382 (29 July 1942), 498.
63. L.P. Mair, *Welfare in the British Colonies* (New York: Oxford University Press, 1944), 78.
64. National Institute of Higher Education, Research, Science and Technology, "Hilda Bynoe, General Practitioner, Lady Health Officer", http://www.niherst.gov.tt/icons/women-in-science/hilda-bynoe.html (accessed 14 December 2014); Suzanne Lopez and Rhona Baptiste, *The 90 Most Prominent Women in Trinidad and Tobago* (Port of Spain: Trinidad Express Newspapers, 1991), 75.
65. Clyde, *Health in Grenada*, 315.
66. Ibid., 320.
67. US Army Medical Department, Office of Medical History, "Strength and Distribution of Military Personnel", pt. 1, chap. 11, in *Medical Department, United States Army Personnel in World War II*, http://history.amedd.army.mil/booksdocs/wwii/personnel/default.htm (last modified 18 June 2009; accessed 24 September 2014).
68. "Procurement of Civilian Personnel", pt. 1, chap. 8, in ibid., 266.
69. Arden Du Bois, *Letter to Dr. Sawyer*, 10 May 1941. Rockefeller Collection: Record Group 1.1, Series 451, box 1 folder 20, Rockefeller Archive Center, Sleepy Hollow, New York.
70. Darwin H. Stapleton, "The Rockefeller Foundation's Experimental Strategies for Using DDT to Control Malaria in the Caribbean Region 1943–1951: The Case of Trinidad and Tobago" (paper presented at the Social History of Medicine and Public Health Policy in the Caribbean Conference, University of the West Indies, Cave Hill Campus, Barbados, 23–26 May 2001), 8. Anopheles mosquitoes had been discovered in 1880 to cause malaria.
71. Clyde, *Health in Grenada*, 320. Work was conducted under the direction of Trinidad Government Engineer C.E. Newbold, at Tempé, at Fontenoy and at Grand Mal.
72. Ibid.
73. Mair, *Welfare in the British Colonies*, 83.
74. Editorial, "Venereal Diseases", *Caribbean Medical Journal* 4, no. 3 (1942): 80.
75. Wenger, *Caribbean Medical Center*. This included a laboratory director, clinicians, dentists, nurses, X-ray and laboratory technicians, a dietician, an educational director, a counsellor and administrative personnel.

76. Peter McKnight, "1,440,000 VD Equipment Coming Here", *Trinidad Guardian*, 24 March 1944, 11.
77. Wenger, *Caribbean Medical Center*, 4. Actually numbers relating to United States forces would be difficult to obtain because during the World War II conflict information relating to this was strictly top secret to be kept from enemy intelligence.
78. Wenger, *Caribbean Medical Center*, 4–5.
79. Ibid., 11–12.
80. Ibid., 13.
81. Ibid., 14. Colonel O.C. Wenger was the Senior Surgeon, United States Public Health Service and United States Venereal Disease Control, Anglo-American Caribbean Commission.
82. United Kingdom, "Colonial Administration (West Indies)", *Hansard Parliamentary Debates*, vol. 387 (16 March 1943), 1108.
83. Clyde, *Health in Grenada*, 321. In L.M. Commissiong, *Whither Grenada* (London: L.M. Commissiong, 1947).

14.

VOLUNTEERISM DURING WORLD WAR II
Trinidadian Women Mobilize in Time of War

KAREN E. ECCLES

The activities of Trinidadian women, the organizations they were engaged in, the totality of their experiences and their overall contributions to World War II are largely still unknown in the historiography of twentieth-century Caribbean history. What prevails, however, about these women is the perception of the "Jean and Dinah" women caught in a euphoria of "rum and Coca-Cola",[1] the derogatory reputation which follows them to this day. Indeed, some lower- and middle-class women engaged in sexual services for military men, as happened globally where servicemen were stationed, but other middle- and upper-class women at the time received glowing praise and attention thanks to the war-related activities in which they were engaged. The number of organizations and the names of the many women who volunteered are too numerous to detail in this chapter, but indeed it was said that there "were over 40 organisations manned by women which supplied vital items to those in war".[2] It would be remiss, however, to discuss voluntary work, which connotes work without pay, without mentioning the paid war work of nurses, women in the postal services and the women who were recruited into the British army under the Auxiliary Territorial Service (ATS). These three salaried services all required uniforms, as well as the even lesser-known unpaid volunteers in the Women's Emergency Corps, the Women's Voluntary Service

(WVS), the Girl Guides and the local branch of the British Red Cross Society. These and other volunteer organizations, such as the Ladies Shirt Guild and the United Service Knitting Association, are the subject of this chapter.

Of course this flood of voluntary endeavours emerged with the wave of volunteerism and mobilization which took place globally, and in its participation Trinidad was no exception. Trinidadians mobilized into action even before Britain's official entry into the war on 3 September 1939, and the following year, in June 1940, the Win the War Association, the umbrella under which many of the colony's fundraising drives operated, was formally inaugurated. Branches of this association mushroomed in all corners of the island, and dozens of voluntary funds were established: to name a few, there were the Fighter Fund, the Spitfire Fund, the Seamen's Fund, the Navy Fund and the Tobacco Fund – there was even a Grapefruit Fund.

Beginning in April 1939, a call was made through the *Trinidad Guardian* for the public to enlist in the new men's voluntary units being established.[3] These units were initially supposed to be purely for Trinidad defence and not for overseas service; however, in September 1939 Trinidad seamen volunteered to serve on British merchant ships when regular crews of foreign nationality declined to continue voyages within the war zone.[4] This hazardous sacrifice did allow many lower-class men to travel abroad, but other options were available, as recruits were needed for the Trinidad Royal Naval Volunteer Reserves, the Trinidad Light Horse Volunteers, the Trinidad Light Infantry Volunteers and for anti-aircraft batteries or coastal batteries. For some there was a local air-training scheme, and many who trained here succeeded in joining the Royal Air Force in England. The Home Guard, similar to a unit in Britain, was brought into existence in 1942, but it was mostly the preserve of upper-class white men, and its secret mandate was really to quell any labour disturbance in the vital oilfields.

Women followed suit. They enlisted in the uniformed services which expanded or emerged calling for service to the war. Women in the existing nursing and postal services received a great deal of attention, as their functions, particularly those of the nurses, were seen as vital. There was even a film, *Vigil in the Night*, which glorified their work,[5] and a publication, *Win Magazine*, played up the role of local nurses.[6] Of course, in Trinidad very few girls of the upper or even middle class would consider nursing, unless it was for the highest ranks, since it involved direct physical contact with the non-white lower class. Therefore, it continued to be a profession which attracted mainly those of the lower socioeconomic class, mostly African women. However, as positive changes did take place in the service, by the end of the war quite a number of middle-class women had entered it.

Dorris Khan, a middle-class Indian girl who signed up for nursing in 1943, explained that the war opened all types of opportunities for women in the hospital service. Nurses were needed for the internment camps set up for enemy aliens, internees, evacuees and shipwreck survivors. Nurses were also recruited for the special camps set up for survivors of ships attacked by submarines in Trinidadian waters; it was estimated that the Germans had sunk over 250. Gaylord Kelshall recalled the experience of his aunt, nurse Edith Dyer, who had witnessed the horrific attack on the ship *Kioto* and seen the burning men, and said she lived with the gruesome memories until the day she died.[7] Nurses also contributed to the various funds in aid of the war effort. In March 1942 a concert in aid of the merchant navy fund was given by the senior nurses of the Colonial Hospital and members of the Nurses Association,[8] and in 1943 another concert was arranged by the Nurses and Midwives Association under the patronage of Lady Alice Devin Clifford, the governor's wife. For the duration of the war it continued to be a profession which garnered debate and sometimes criticism, but it no doubt was recognized to be a crucial service in time of conflict.

Middle-class women were recruited into the postal service to carry out various censorship proclamations during the war. Under the Colonial Defence Regulations of 1939, enacted by the governor under authority of the Emergency Powers (Colonial) Defence Order in Council 1939, the Censorship Office was given the power to impose censorship on all postal matter, telegrams, documents, pictorial representations or photographs, or other articles leaving the colony, and to search anyone leaving the colony for any of these articles.[9] "Censors possessed the power to stop, delay or delete communications."[10] New post offices opened up throughout the island, and major offices now needed special examiners and sorters, as well as staff, for traveller censorship[11] and for the transit room, for sorting, scrutiny, serial numbering, dispatch, checking, indexing, filing and searching.[12] There was also a need for table sorters, and this created an opportunity for young secondary-school girls, who were recruited specifically for this task.[13] To deal with the bulk of mail, the censorship staff also performed night duties on a shift basis and worked on Sundays. However, even in 1944 complaints continued about the need for more staff, as Trinidad had become one of the most important transit stations in the Western Hemisphere. Other opportunities for women emerged, however.

There were new paid services which created unique opportunities for women, and one was entry into the ATS. The formation and inclusion of British West Indian women into the local branch of the ATS South Caribbean Area can be considered a landmark occurrence, not only for Trinidadians but for Caribbean women generally during World War II. Of all the women's services, it was the only one which eventually embarked upon a programme of recruitment within the Caribbean.[14] The local branches of the ATS were designed in the Caribbean to augment the female branch of the British army,[15] and two headquarters were set up, one in Trinidad at the St James Barracks and the other at Up Park Camp in Jamaica. However, owing to private debates between the Colonial and War Offices about the racial composition of the women who should be recruited, recruitment of Caribbean women only started in 1943. The final decision was that lighter-skinned Trinidadian and other Caribbean women would be sent to Washington, while black women would go to London or would serve locally or regionally.

The batches of ATS women sent to Washington from Trinidad also included recruits from the other Caribbean islands within the South Caribbean Area. By August 1943 the third group of women, mostly stenographers, arrived from Barbados to be sent along with other, white women to Kitchener, Ontario, for training under the Canadian Women's Army Corps.[16] Although it is mentioned that six hundred women from Trinidad alone were recruited for the ATS,[17] other accounts suggest that that figure was the total for the entire British West Indies, and of these about one hundred served in Britain.[18] It is more likely that the latter account is more accurate. Some who were included in the early batches from Trinidad for London were Doreen Marcano of San Fernando, the daughter of Captain G.R. Marcano, the city health official; Georgy Masson, the daughter of A.H.L Masson, magistrate of St George West, whose wife was active in the war campaign and is mentioned subsequently; Marjorie Smith of Alexandra Street, who worked as a cipher clerk at the Imperial Censorship Department before joining the ATS; and Vivien Hochoy, Chinese-Trinidadian stenographer from Port of Spain, who worked as a secretary at the US army hospital at Docksite as well as a cipher clerk at the Royal Naval

Station. Others included Sybil Robinson, who was attached to the clerical staff of the Royal Engineers Stores and had been secretary to the commanding officer of the South Caribbean Area, and Leonine Joseph, who was a teacher at St Theresa's Intermediate School in Woodbrook prior to enlisting.[19] These women were included in the first batch of thirty who joined the ATS in London and were featured in a magazine called *Picture Post*. Senior Commander Doreen Venn said that her misgivings about the women waned as soon as they arrived and she saw their "enthusiasm and sound common sense. . . . They are all ambitious to make a career of the ATS and their months training indicates there is every reason why they should succeed. Their officers give them high marks for character, intelligence and educational standard and when they go to a new camp all of them intend to take advantage of the extra educational facilities that will be available."[20] After camp training they were destined for work as stenographers, typists, storekeepers, transport drivers, draughtsmen and other war-related work needed in Britain.

Trinidad was the training ground for women in the South Caribbean Area, but Trinidadians who had reached certain ranks went to islands within the area to assist in the training of the women's battalions which were being formed there.[21] However, there was a wide range of jobs to which ATS women were assigned in Trinidad, such as drivers, messengers in the transport division, stenographers, typists, filing officers, clerks in "stores", canteen workers to run the canteens, "ciphers" in a highly secretive division, switchboard operators, payroll officers in Command Pay, and nurses and clerical staff in the army section of the Port of Spain General Hospital. There were also accounts of these women driving motorcycles. Some worked at St James Barracks or at St George's Camp, which was located at the back of the barracks, and others were sent to the Port of Spain hospital, where there was an area set up only for the military. There were also military camps at Point Fortin and Pointe-à-Pierre, which also had female recruits. According to the ex-ATS women interviewed, however, the south region comprised women recruited from southern Trinidad, but all recruitment took place at the St James Barracks, which operated like the headquarters for the British military in Trinidad.

VOLUNTEERISM

The Women Emergency Corps

Women who worked in the ATS as well as the postal and nursing services were paid workers during the war, but the majority of Trinidadian women occupied themselves in unpaid volunteer work specifically to contribute to the war effort, as women globally were doing. In May 1939 the Women's Emergency Corps (WEC) was formed led by Mrs G.H. Masson, a white Trinidadian and wife of the magistrate of St George West. Lady Margaret Rose Mary Young, wife of the governor at the time, who was very active in voluntary work, later on took up the role of president and was instrumental in the expansion of the corps, and shortly after a branch called the South Women's Auxiliary Corps was formed. Generally this organization was dominated by upper-class white women who received training in driving all types of vehicles, including trams, buses, and ambulances, in running canteens, in first aid and nursing, in ambulance work and in domestic science. The WEC was most active in canteen work, under the training and supervision of Mrs H.B. Lake. In November 1939, on opening a new canteen for foreign troops at the expanded harbour front in Port of Spain, Governor Young paid tribute to the corps and its collaboration with the twenty-one-year old Soldiers and Sailors Club.[22] In a ceremony which included many leading political and military men, the governor lauded the WEC: "The canteen has . . . so far been run by the Women's Emergency Corps and we are all immensely grateful to them for everything they have done. [It] is a group of ladies who banded themselves together before the war – they knew there was going to be a war although we didn't and they turned out to do their bit as soon as the war started."[23]

The WEC got involved in all the other fundraising activities of the Win the War Association. They held a tea party to raise funds for the King George's Fund for Sailors at the home on Sweet Briar Road of Mrs Masson, who, as the chairman of the WEC, undertook to make all the toys for a toy stall at a fundraiser for the Fighter Fund at the country club.[24] Later it was reported by the *Hummingbird*, "when I called on Mrs. Masson . . . I ran into a hive of industry. About 20 or more of the members of the WEC were busy sorting and cutting the materials that have been sent in to make dolls for the toy stall."[25]

The WEC also became heavily involved in training in first aid and home nursing. At the first class, one of Port of Spain's female doctors lectured and two sisters from the medical staff of the Colonial Hospital attended to give practical instruction. Only the members who were enrolled for ambulance training or first aid were eligible to attend the home-nursing class.[26] Training in these areas served well for those who wished to join the Red Cross Society later on, as it was announced that all those members of the corps who took first-aid and home-nursing courses could automatically become members of the Red Cross. It was thought an excellent idea for the two organizations to unite, and the first batches of Red Cross workers were funnelled from the corps.

The British Red Cross Society

This local branch of the British Red Cross Society (BRCS), which was revitalized with the outbreak of war, was another body to receive international attention, particularly since the governors' wives, Lady Young and Lady Clifford respectively, served as presidents. Hence it included many women in the upper echelons but also many non-white middle-class women. In fact, Governor Young wrote at one time that one prominent lady had regarded the Red Cross as "undesirably mixed".[27] However, despite the comments, branches of the Red Cross mushroomed all over the island, as did Voluntary Aid Detachments, which consisted of qualified personnel who could render supplementary aid under the name and banner of the Red Cross. Thousands joined.

Volunteers were a regular sight, giving assistance and training, marching, assisting during blackouts and establishing first-aid posts at public functions. An important milestone was the approval of the local BRCS as an authorized agency for the transmission of postal messages to friends and relatives in enemy-occupied territories.[28] Red Cross training was added to the curriculum of some girls' schools, and for others there were about 215 classes for courses in first aid, home nursing and infant welfare, with about 2,962 women registered.[29] A station was also set up daily at the Piarco Aerodrome while candidates received instruction under the Air Training Scheme, which was said to be a comforting assurance to trainees.

The Red Cross also worked with Air Raid Precautions (ARP), an organization under the Civil Defence Department, in preparation for rendering first aid and dispatching patients to aid posts, what were called "casualty clearing stations" or hospitals, as the case might be. Plans were made for more seriously injured patients to be sent first to casualty clearing stations, from which they would be cleared after treatment and then sent to the hospitals. The Red Cross undertook to conduct the clearing stations on behalf of the Health Department. Fourteen casualty clearing stations were planned, and by 1943 eleven already existed, three of which were in Port of Spain. These stations were equipped with all the necessities for nursing and feeding patients by the Health Department but were operated by the Red Cross personnel. In San Fernando there were five ARP posts from which five first-aid parties worked. Red Cross personnel also volunteered for the private first-aid, ARP posts and casualty clearing stations, which also existed in the oilfields and on estates.

The Red Cross was involved in a number of services for troops and war victims abroad. Shipments of comforts and hospital supplies, such as knitted garments, pillows, bandages, pyjamas, surgical dressings and other articles, "expertly made to specification by the colony's needlewomen", were dispatched to England by the Red Cross supply-packing committee.[30] There was also a branch of the Red Cross called the Trinidad Junior War Workers, which probably comprised teenage girls, who did knitting and helped organize functions for the Red Cross.[31] It seems a blood-transfusion service was also operated in Trinidad by Red Cross nurses, and in 1942 it was reported that the activities of the local Red Cross in enrolling blood donors for transfusion purposes were widely extended through the issue of a circular to members to volunteer for "this important duty".[32]

The Red Cross was instrumental in assisting in the medical services in Trinidad. Many Red Cross members had gladly accepted an invitation from government medical authorities to render auxiliary nursing assistance at the Colonial Hospital in Port of Spain, "where they had been regular in attendance and had done good service".[33] Importantly, Colonel A.R. Robertson of the British army hospital indicated that the facilities of a hospital on the north-eastern side of the city's Colonial Hospital were given to them by the local branch of the Red Cross, who continued to contribute towards its maintenance and supplies of surgical gowns, pyjamas, bandages and dressings.[34]

Women of the Red Cross were active in many other spheres. Aid was given to the Child Welfare League, to the survivors of the *Simon Bolivar* disaster, to sufferers from a fire in Maracaibo and to the local branch of the St John's Ambulance Association. As it was said in a newspaper magazine, "The branch also rendered service by supplying information in response to enquiries received through headquarters regarding aliens resident in this colony and . . . also forwarded . . . enquiries on behalf of local residents in respect of relations and friends in enemy occupied territory."[35] From August 1942 the headquarters in Port of Spain were very diligent in distributing the monthly publication the *Prisoners of War*, the official journal of the prisoners-of-war department of the Red Cross and St John's War Organization of London.[36]

Red Cross nurses were integral to the assistance rendered to many survivors of ships torpedoed around Trinidad. Misses Rice, Norman, and Melville paid daily visits and distributed comforts to merchant seamen in the Colonial Hospital.[37] The publicity officer of the Trinidad branch of the British Red Cross released details in February 1942 of the Red Cross nurses assisting sixty-seven survivors of a torpedoed British warship which had landed in Trinidad from a rescue ship.[38] The report stated that their ship went down in seventeen minutes and how these men, who lost everything, took to sea on rafts. For three days, the report went on, these men, who suffered from wounds, exposure and lack of food and water, drifted about until they were rescued by a passing ship and brought to Trinidad. Immediately after the survivors were brought ashore, relays of Red Cross nurses rushed to render aid and remained on duty for months working on shifts to aid the men. When news of their arrival reached Lady Young, she immediately appealed for fresh fruit, vegetables, cigarettes, pyjamas, towels, magazines and newspapers, as well as for clothing when a few months later twenty-five of the men were ready to leave. The Trinidad Red Cross branch also received thank-you letters from Martinique for the individual parcels they sent for survivors who landed there.[39]

The executive committee of the Red Cross also opened Hillcote, a convalescent home for servicemen at St Augustine.[40] This home was formerly the private residence of D. Hope Ross and was lent to the Red Cross for the duration of the war and a period of six months thereafter. Ross converted the garage into an annex and provided all the necessary furniture. Hillcote stood on three acres and provided a perfect home for about thirty convalescents at a time. In collaboration with the WVS, another volunteer women's group, the Red Cross also handled the medical side of another convalescent home, at St Ann's, called Daljarrock.[41]

The very noticeable volunteer work of first-aid workers stimulated the generosity of the Trinidad population. Edwin Lee Lum, chairman of the Chinese Patriotic Relief Fund Committee and president of the Chinese Association of Trinidad, wrote to Lady Young for permission to organize a Chinese committee to raise a Red Cross fund among the Chinese community in Trinidad.[42] Subsequently, the Chinese Ladies Committee of the British Red Cross Ambulance Fund was formed.[43] By early 1940 it had raised funds for two Red Cross ambulances, one to send to France and the other for use by the local volunteers.[44] The Indian community as well, it was reported, was "responding splendidly to appeals to aid the British Red Cross Society", and Mrs H.C. Mahabir, the daughter of politician Timothy Roodal, was the authorized collector of funds.[45] The French community organized a Flag Day, the proceeds of which were handed over to the Red Cross.[46] Lady Young was presented with numerous cheques from the Portuguese Association.[47] Many other private individuals, organizations and consulates gave generously to the Red Cross.

Praise and letters of appreciation poured in. The secretary of state for the colonies sent a letter of thanks to the people of Trinidad and Tobago on behalf of the Red Cross and the St John's War Fund.[48] George Hall, parliamentary under-secretary of state for the colonies, paid a visit to the ladies at work at the Red Cross hospital supply depot at Government House and commented, "Lady Young, ladies – I have just dropped in to see you working (not that ladies don't usually work, they are always working as a matter of fact. I don't know what we would do without you) but this morning I dropped in to see you doing a special bit of work, and a work for which I have been asked . . . to express . . . our grateful thanks."[49] The Red Cross was recognized by local military authorities as the authoritative organization to render auxiliary medical aid in time of war.[50] The Trinidad branch was also instrumental in stimulating Red Cross work in other islands. When Lady Young met Mrs J.D. Harford, the wife of the acting governor of Antigua, a request was made for the full particulars of Red Cross work in Trinidad in order for work to be organized in Antigua along similar lines.[51] The Red Cross was highly regarded and received a great deal of publicity throughout the war.

The Women's Voluntary Service

A major organization formed in May 1942 by Mrs Joan Huggins, the wife of the colonial secretary, "in an effort to mobilize all the women power of

Trinidad" was the WVS.⁵² This was similar to the organization of the same name which was formed in England in 1938, when the dowager Marchioness of Reading was asked to organize the women of Great Britain for air-raid precaution work.⁵³ In Trinidad an appeal was made to women of every class and creed to volunteer either on a part-time or full-time basis in any of the many spheres for civil defence. Despite this appeal, the higher executive positions were reserved for white women, a few of whom were British; however, the majority of the WVS's ordinary membership seemed to have been middle-class non-white women. Despite the early advisory that it was a volunteer organization and women had to pay for their own uniforms, by late 1942 there were already three thousand members. Women who worked in offices, schools or shops and could only give a couple hours a week of their time were also encouraged to apply, as were those who were able to serve on a full-time basis. The liaison officer at the Colonial Office, Lady Southorn, reported in 1943 that "there are women of every community, class and creed working in the WVS, associating amicably together and giving their time and energy for the common welfare and safety of Trinidad".⁵⁴

The women of the WVS worked with such other groups as the Red Cross and the nurses, they worked with the Commissioner of Civil Defence as well as the Agriculture Department and they rushed to the aid of the military men who docked at the harbour; there was even a telephone-operator service of the WVS, which operated in the Civil Defence Office and the control room.⁵⁵ Actual evacuation camps were set up, as were fully equipped air-raid shelters. The WVS ran the Services Lending Library, with a number of book and magazine depots to supply literature to all the military forces, which passed through Trinidad. During the government's rationing scheme, the WVS was able to staff ten centres and supply about 140 personnel, who distributed over 21,800 ration cards. The WVS made financial donations to the Red Cross and between July and December 1942 dispatched about 647 parcels to members of the forces in England.⁵⁶ By October 1944 this figure had climbed to 5,000 parcels of local sugar, sweets, chocolate and marmalade sent to fighting men overseas by what had became known as the Parcels Section of the WVS.⁵⁷

There were also two mobile canteens operated by WVS members in Port of Spain and San Fernando, with women drivers. On one occasion, as food and drinks were taken out by WVS members in their green and maroon uniforms, one survivor who landed in San Fernando remarked, "Why, this is just like England."⁵⁸ Canteen work eventually recruited about six hundred helpers, and it was reported that

> this is a work which goes on all the time and a great deal has already been done, and is being done, for the many survivors who reach the shores of Trinidad. The WVS members are workers in all the various canteens; i.e. the wharf canteen, and the Royal Naval club which are open to merchant seamen and navy men, and the merchant navy club and part of the internment camp, both used for survivors.⁵⁹

Housewives were asked to enrol in the Home Workers Service of the WVS to perform work such as sewing and mending clothes.⁶⁰ The service did all the mending for the Royal Naval Club and even replenished its linen and chair covers.⁶¹ The members made urgent appeals for used clothing to distribute as well as to keep as a reserve supply,⁶² and they were prepared to make all the darning and mending repairs for clothes which were donated. A receiving depot for clothes was generously established at the Electricity Board Office.⁶³ Food-production efforts received new impetus from the WVS Home Workers Service, as they worked with the food controller in aid of the Grow More Food Campaign. They encouraged garden clubs, they worked with the Horticultural Society and eventually members of the WVS went house to house in various districts advising on the need for provision gardens and for keeping animals for food.⁶⁴

In support of the WVS thrust towards the Grow More Food Campaign, the Jewish Ladies Association organized a new branch of the WVS known as the Housewives Supply, which began the sale of homemade jams, jellies, preserves and sweets on Saturdays.⁶⁵ The Jewish Ladies Association eventually established a central kitchen at a centre on Tragarete Road in Port of Spain called the Suzy Q War Cookery Centre, which had been opened by the WVS around 1943 and enabled them not only to increase their supplies of jams and preserves but also gave them a central location for preparing their supplies.⁶⁶ The centre was financed by the government and fully supported by the food controller and the Department of Agriculture. A number of courses, for a small fee, were offered which taught the use of local produce and cooking for the sick. Some courses and demonstrations, however, were given free of charge to the public.

Similar to the convalescent home established by the Red Cross, the Emergency Care Organization of the WVS was instrumental in opening Daljarrock, a convalescent home at St Ann's for seamen forced to be or stranded in Trinidad. Opened in September 1942, Daljarrock, a two-storey building directly opposite Coblentz House (a local residence well noted for its grandeur, history and famous owners over the decades) and close to the merchant navy club, was open to men of the forces "regardless of colour or creed".[67] It was run by a band of volunteers, with the Red Cross handling the medical side. The WVS was responsible for all the housekeeping, which was under the supervision of Mrs Richard Bradley and Miss Les Chaloupe, while Mrs Errol dos Santos volunteered her services as a qualified dietician, and a Miss O'Reilley, those of a masseuse. In October 1942 Mrs Joan Huggins, who was acknowledged as the founder of the WVS in Trinidad, said that hundreds of survivors had already been helped.[68]

Another important service by the WVS was the establishment of the Citizens Advice Bureau to provide information on civil defence to the public. Everyone who needed information on civil defence or ways they could serve was able to visit the bureau. The Citizens Advice Bureau pressed the Silence for Safety Campaign, while the artist group of the WVS was responsible for nearly all the "Don't Talk" posters.[69] The portrayal of images of women being hanged because they talked too much was a regular feature of this branch of the WVS,[70] as in wartime there was constant fear of spies, traitors and information being leaked to the enemy. In August 1942 there was a "Silence for Safety" rhyming competition organized by the WVS in collaboration with another campaign, called the Anti-Chatter Campaign.

The WVS also formed the Mutual Aid Good Neighbours Association (MAGNA), inaugurated in October 1942 in an effort to encourage neighbours to help each other during and after a raid.[71] In a plea to join MAGNA Mrs Joan Huggins said:

> Every woman rich and poor should take part. . . . If a certain number of women in each street and district in Trinidad prepare a corner in their home . . . they can give shelter to a neighbour who lost everything. Members of Magna must also be ready to give their ARP warden any help which he may require . . . it gives an opportunity to the women of Trinidad in their own homes to offer active help to the Civil Defence during an actual emergency.[72]

The association was encouraging all women to band together to help each other.

Other women in the WVS were entrusted with responsibilities such as censorship for the mail service. As Gaylord Kelshall, former officer in the Coast Guard and pilot, as well as founder and curator of the Chaguaramas Military History and Aviation Museum, said, "Every letter written had to be read before posting, so no secrets could be revealed. It was highly secret work, under military control, and they [the women] worked all hours of day and night."[73] Florrie Kelshall, Thora Dumbell and Jessie Brash were a few of the women who served in the WVS to do censorship duties; Florrie Kelshall recalls the rigours of her duties: "We had to know the names of all the individuals and firms that were black-listed. These were placed in a special box and sifted through carefully for any undercurrents. And if we missed one, God help us, for they were re-checked. . . . Once I got called out 11 p.m. when a plane brought mail, and had to go through all the letters. You had to be prepared at any time."[74]

It is estimated that the WVS trained over five thousand uniformed local women by the end of the war. In fact, by 1943 the women had divided themselves into eighteen sections, including a first-aid section, which established rest centres at various locations all over the island and was ready at a "minutes' notice" to shelter people, as well as a home sewing group responsible for making bandages and other hospital supplies for shipment overseas.[75] The clerical section was actively involved in work for the civil defence service as well as other wartime work.

By the organization's second anniversary the Trinidad WVS was receiving high commendation internationally. Lady Reading, the chair of the Women's Voluntary Services for Civil Defence in England, sent a letter of high praise to the WVS women in Trinidad. "They worked in the Harbour Canteens, R.N. Club, Merchant Navy Clubs and the Rest Camp in St James, and in various places in the South, assisting generally in the comfort and entertainment of the men."[76] These women of the WVS seem to have dominated the war effort in Trinidad; they made a colossal effort, branching out to all spheres, volunteering their time for no monetary gain, raising funds in creative ways and trying to mobilize women into action. However, there were other organizations as well which tried to do the same.

The Girl Guides

The Girl Guides was another of the existing uniformed services which expanded and set up numerous work parties for the duration of the war. One of the Girl Guides' first contributions was a campaign to give half a day's work to the empire or half a day's pay to contribute to the purchase of two air ambulances and a motorized lifeboat for the Royal Air Force Medical Services.[77] They held a children's party in aid of the Fighter Fund; sewed for the Red Cross; started a tinfoil-collection campaign, the proceeds from which they sent abroad to the Lord Mayor's Fund, and by the end of their first year of service to the war, the Girl Guides had made their thousandth pillow.[78] About seventy Guides also staffed one of the Air Raid Relief Centres which had been established by the WVS, and regular visits were made to the soldiers and sailors in hospitals.

Guiding was a very prominent international affair during the war, and the work of Guides was highly recognized. A Guides conference was held in Jamaica in 1940, and a delegate from Trinidad attended the meeting of the Western Hemisphere Advisory Committee of the World Association of Girl Guides and Girl Scouts held in Toronto, Canada, in September 1943.[79] The local island commissioner also received an invitation from the Girl Scouts of America, and two local delegates were sent to an encampment held in the United States. The Trinidad Guides were also visited by the director of international guiding, Mrs Arethusa Leigh-White, whose visit was made into a "grand affair".[80] The Trinidad Guides received global recognition and praise during the war. The lord mayor of London sent a letter to Mrs Maria O. Forbes, the island commissioner, thanking her for all the gifts received, and in the Girl Guides' international publication, the *Guider*, pictures of Trinidad Guides were portrayed. This brought letters from the secretary of the Girl Guides in London, requesting local guides to write to English Guides about guiding in Trinidad.

Private Fundraising

There were other women who made individual, small-group and organizational-type contributions to volunteer work without a trademark uniform, such as those mentioned thus far. One such was the effort made by a particular woman who called herself "Madamme Cooze" and who raised funds for the Fighter Fund through her "Bomber Hut", which she set up at Woodford Square in Port of Spain. Apparently this lady received gifts of "all sorts, handmade needlework, knick knacks, and other articles" which she sold daily, the proceeds from which she donated to the Fighter Fund.[81] Perhaps she was affiliated with the group of city women who had formed themselves into the Trinidad's Women's Effort, which was started by Mrs J. Stanhope Lovell to raise funds specifically for the Fighter Fund, around the same time that the "Bomber Hut" emerged. Whatever her motivation, the volunteer drive and the effort she made is particularly noteworthy, but it is unfortunate that the woman's real name and her identity are still not known.

Three other ladies of the Archibald Institute,[82] which opened in 1931 in St Augustine to train older girls in home economics and to instil the ideals of Christian homemaking, got together to give free demonstrations at the Government Training College on the conservation of locally grown foodstuffs.[83] A cookery book, *The Trinidad Win the War Cookery Book*, was even published in November 1940. This book was compiled by Allison Lavington, the wife of Commander H.V. Lavington, with "tested recipes" of Trinidad's dishes and sweetmeats sent in as a contribution by Trinidadian housewives.[84] This book was publicized as an inexpensive Christmas present and sold at one dollar per copy, the proceeds of which were sent to the King George's Fund for Sailors through the Win the War Association.[85] Every housewife in Trinidad, it was said, should have a copy of the book, which was on sale at the headquarters of the Win the War Association.

The Ladies Shirt Guild

Five prominent white ladies led by Martha Simpson, wife of the chairman of the Committee of Supply and member of the Colonial Board, decided to get together and form an official organization to make garments as a contribution to the war effort.[86] As a result the Ladies Shirt Guild emerged, on 4 September 1939. In less than two months, and despite the membership fees, there were three hundred members, and shortly afterward the organization had grown to include six centres. The objective of the guild was, primarily, to work for hospitals and relief committees in England and to allow women the opportunity to engage in war work in their own homes. A large contingent of supplies were sent by the guild to England, for which a letter of appreciation which Mrs Simpson received from the queen was published in the local newspaper. However, the guild was short-lived, as friction eventually arose between Mrs Simpson and Lady Young, the wife of the governor and president of the British Red Cross Society. Mrs Simpson continued to work with many other funds and activities for the war effort, more so when the new governor, Sir Bede Clifford, and his wife, Lady Clifford, arrived.

The Wives of the Officers of the Second Battalion of Trinidad Volunteers

In the meantime, though, other ventures were a resounding success. The upper-class white wives of the officers of the Second Battalion of Trinidad Volunteers, or the WOFFS, showed a great deal of camaraderie and garnered a great deal of publicity for the numerous fundraising and other war-related activities in which they were engaged. They raised funds particularly for the BRCS, the Fighter Fund and the Bomber Fund, but interestingly they were one of the very few war associations founded by women of the upper class which raised funds for local troops. In March 1943 they held a grand fete at the St James Barracks, one of the major military barracks in Trinidad, under the patronage of Governor and Lady Clifford in aid of the Comfort Fund for local troops in the South Caribbean Area. They received very generous contributions for their raffles and sales from the business class, including – at one time – three motor cars and a yacht. It is indeed difficult to imagine these women on a house-to-house campaign, but this was another of their ventures in an effort to sell tokens for a raffle, ultimately selling over five thousand.[87] The great deal of publicity these women received was due not only to their class position but to the fact that their ventures were undeniably a monetary success, as publicly recognized at the time.

United Services Knitting Association

Lady Young in April 1941 formed a completely female branch of the Win the War Association. Initially this branch included a small committee of about fourteen ladies, but it eventually expanded into the United Services Knitting Association, as the feeling was that "the necessity for this separate organization to make the much needed comforts for those in the services who are sick or wounded has become imperative".[88] Its formation received the full endorsement of the BRCS and positive feedback from an editorial in the *Trinidad Guardian*. Lady Young, being the governor's wife as well as the founder and chairman of the association, was able to secure payment for all supplies of wool from the Central Fund of the Win the War Association. The hundreds of women who knitted for this association included some middle-class non-white women.

Coterie of Social Workers

But it was the middle-class Coterie of Social Workers, led by founder Audrey Jeffers, that attracted the majority of middle-class black women. The Coterie's focus, as it was before the war, was on breakfast sheds, the feeding of poor children, parcels to the poor, day nurseries and assistance to young working-class mothers; however, harsh economic conditions during the war and the redirection of funds which were usually given by the director of education to assist the Coterie put a great deal of strain on the Coterie's work. Nevertheless, with support from people such as labour leader Arthur Cipriani and the mayor of Port of Spain in 1942, there was a small increase in the monetary grant given, while the San Fernando Borough Council allowed the use of Skinner Park for fundraisers. Despite the hardships, the Coterie persevered and was the only women's group in Trinidad to offer assistance to the black American troops stationed there at the time, putting one of their breakfast sheds at the troops' disposal and organizing entertainment for them.[89] The Coterie comprised mostly black middle-class women, and as Jeffers was a Garveyite, it is not surprising that she reached out to the black American troops stationed in Trinidad.[90]

The Home Hospitality Programme

However, the majority of resources, time and effort went into the provision of services for the white foreign military through an organized programme called the Home Hospitality Programme, the successor of the Trinidad Corps of Cadettes,[91] which had been touted as an "opportunity for girls . . . to find entertainment, make new friends and do their share in maintaining the high morale of the armed forces".[92] In 1943, with collaboration between the Huggins family, Mrs L. Fahey and US officials,[93] the Home Hospitality Programme, a volunteer organization of white upper-class women, emerged along the same lines. There were many parties, picnics, cruises, and though the bases were closed to the public, white upper-class women in Trinidad were regular visitors to them as well as to the island's military bases at Chacachacare, Monos, and Patos Islands. Harvey Neptune asserts that this programme was one in which elite white women sought to establish socially and racially acceptable spheres in which white American men could meet young white Trinidadian women.[94] Whatever the reasons, it was recognized as one in which a great deal of volunteer time, effort and resources were given by many women quite willingly.

The Girls Talent Club and the Duration Club

Upper-class women were engaged in other spheres of volunteer work. The Girls Talent Club organized entertainment with the aim of raising funds for the Fighter Fund, the Navy League and Children's War Charities. The Duration Club was formed in October 1940 specifically to utilize the fondness and flair there was for acting and drama to support the war effort. The main objective of this dramatic society was both to produce plays in aid of the war and local charities and also to offer free entertainment to the forces. There were about thirty founding members, and the management committee included the wife of Flight Lieutenant John Carroll. There were quite a number of prominent women who volunteered.

From the Duration Club emerged a branch of the club, the Co-pessimists, organized by Mrs G.R. Longdale "entirely for the benefit of members of the services".[95] Though the membership clearly comprised those of the upper class, an invitation went out to the general public to join either of the clubs in either "active" or "non-active" membership. Active members were those who were willing to take part either on or off stage, while non-active members were those who were willing to support the club by attending the public performances and offering financial aid. The entrance fee for all shows and for all members was one dollar, while non-active members were required to pay an additional annual subscription of two dollars and forty cents. Though the Co-pessimists charged no entrance fee for men of the services, a hat was usually passed around for one of the various funds.[96] As the many military men stationed here were constantly on the lookout for entertainment, these shows put on by Trinidadian women were a popular pastime.

CONCLUSION

Despite all of this, little has been written about the ways in which Trinidadian upper and middle-class women mobilized, and their intense preoccupation with contributions towards the war. However, extensive research has revealed the number of associations, the vibrant activism and the colossal effort Trinidadian women made. In occupations such as the postal and nursing services, women eagerly assumed new roles and responsibilities, working on weekends and at nights. The Girl Guides and the Red Cross manipulated their work to serve the war effort, and the women similarly performed in such new services as the WEC, WVS and ATS. They all generously served the foreign soldiers who came to Trinidad and commanded not only their respect but the respect of the local male forces and indeed the government authorities who acceded to their needs. They rallied and agitated, using their time, resources and homes to make foreign military men feel at home. The number of socials and fundraisers thrown during the war is astounding, and the number of war funds the women contributed to, equally so. Their activities received a great deal of attention in the newspapers. At the end of the war it was said of local women, "Their courage and fortitude [were] a bright chapter in the history of Trinidad that will be read and read again."[97] Unfortunately, the effort of many of these women during the war has not been documented or remembered, and their names are all but forgotten. Slowly, however, Trinidadian and indeed Caribbean women's historiography is being unearthed, and the efforts of Trinidad's women are being posited into the contribution made towards those of the Allies in World War II, just as women's endeavours globally are being recognized.

NOTES

1. Slinger Francisco (The Mighty Sparrow) sang the 1956 calypso "Jean and Dinah", derogatorily describing the wartime prostitute; Rupert W. Grant (Lord Invader) sang the famous 1943 "Rum and Coca-Cola", which was plagiarized by Morey Amsterdam and became a hit for the American Andrews Sisters

in 1945, and which describes a euphoric state of women with American men about.
2. Deborah Samuel, "Honouring Women Who Serve", *Trinidad Guardian*, 28 April 1996.
3. "Voluntary Recruiting in Trinidad", *Trinidad Guardian*, 26 April 1939.
4. "Local Seamen Volunteer for Service", *Trinidad Guardian*, 21 September 1939.
5. "Nurses Glorified In Vigil in the Night", *Trinidad Guardian*, 14 September 1940.
6. "Win Plays Up Local Nurses", *Trinidad Guardian*, 6 March 1941.
7. Samuel, "Honouring Women Who Serve".
8. "Nurses Concert to Aid Seamen", *Sunday Guardian*, 29 March 1942.
9. "Regulations for Defence of the Colony Issued: Censorship Powers Vested in Governor", *Trinidad Guardian*, 5 September 1939.
10. R.G. Wike, *British Empire Civil Censorship Devices, World War II: Trinidad and Tobago* (Perth: Chavril Press, 1993), 6.
11. National Archives of the United Kingdom (hereafter NAUK): W. Watling, Report No. 4, Trinidad Imperial Censorship, Office Accommodation, 27 October 1941, Reports from the Assistant Controller, Trinidad, 1941–1942, United Kingdom, Department of Defence 1/148.
12. Ibid.
13. NAUK: Report No. 5, Trinidad Imperial Censorship, Staffing, 30 October 1941, Reports from the Assistant Controller, Trinidad, United Kingdom, Department of Defence 1/148,.
14. Ben Bousquet and Colin Douglas, *West Indian Women at War: British Racism in World War II* (London: Lawrence and Wishart, 1991), 2.
15. Samuel, "Honouring Women Who Serve".
16. "Caribbean ATS Recruits Arrive", *Trinidad Guardian*, 13 August 1943.
17. Samuel, "Honouring Women Who Serve".
18. Bousquet and Douglas, *West Indian Women at War*, 2.
19. "Trinidad ATS Girls Get London Welcome: Six in West Indies Batch of 30 Settling Down to Camp Course", *Sunday Guardian*, 23 January 1944.
20. Senior Commander Doreen Venn, "West Indian ATS Show Britain They Can Take It", *Trinidad Guardian*, 30 January 1944.
21. "More ATS Get Chance to Go Abroad", *Trinidad Guardian*, 3 September 1944.
22. "Governor Opens New Canteen for Local Troops", *Trinidad Guardian*, 21 November 1939.
23. Ibid.
24. Hummingbird, "Talk of Trinidad", *Trinidad Guardian*, 29 September 1940.
25. Ibid., 12 October 1940.

26. "Nursing Classes for WEC", *Trinidad Guardian*, 7 June 1939.
27. Letter from H. Young to Lloyd of Dolobran, 1940, Correspondence and Papers Concerning a Petition from Major and Mrs Simpson, Colonial Office 295/621/1.
28. Colony Director, "The Work of the Red Cross in Trinidad", *Trinidad Guardian Christmas Magazine*, 8 December 1940.
29. Women's Activities in the West Indies, 1 April 1943, Colonial Office 875/16/12.
30. "Red Cross Notes: More Comforts Shipped to England", *Trinidad Guardian*, 20 October 1940.
31. "WVS Official Reviews Work on Second Anniversary", *Trinidad Guardian*, 12 May 1944.
32. "Local Red Cross Makes an Appeal for Blood Donors", *Sunday Guardian*, 25 January 1942.
33. A. Emlyn, "Letter to the Editor", *Trinidad Guardian*, 25 January 1944.
34. "Army Hospital Treats 1,200 in First Year", *Sunday Guardian*, 4 June 1944.
35. Colony Director, "The Work of the Red Cross in Trinidad", *Trinidad Guardian Christmas Magazine*, 8 December 1940.
36. "Red Cross Circulates First Issue of Prisoners of War", *Sunday Guardian*, 9 August 1942.
37. "Red Cross Pay Daily Visits to Seamen in Hospital", *Sunday Guardian*, 1 March 1942.
38. "Local Red Cross Helps Survivors", *Trinidad Guardian*, 6 February 1942.
39. "Red Cross Help Survivors landed in Martinique", *Sunday Guardian*, 6 September 1942.
40. "Red Cross Xmas Cards on Sale", *Sunday Guardian*, 8 November 1940.
41. "Service Men Convalesce at Daljarrock", *Sunday Guardian*, 28 February 1943.
42. "Chinese to Raise Red Cross Fund", *Trinidad Guardian*, 19 September 1939.
43. "Red Cross Meet Tonight", *Trinidad Guardian*, 3 November 1939.
44. "Local Ambulance for France", *Sunday Guardian*, 21 April 1940.
45. "Indians Help Red Cross", *Sunday Guardian*, 8 October 1939.
46. Colony Director, "The Work of the Red Cross in Trinidad", *Trinidad Guardian Christmas Magazine*, 8 December 1940.
47. "Portuguese Gift to the Red Cross", *Trinidad Guardian*, 29 March 1940.
48. "Red Cross Thanked", *Trinidad Guardian*, 21 November 1940.
49. "Mr. G. Hall Thanks Red Cross Workers for Women and Children of Britain", *Trinidad Guardian*, 7 September 1941.
50. Colony Director, "The Work of the Red Cross in Trinidad", *Trinidad Guardian Christmas Magazine*, 8 December 1940.
51. "Another £2,000 to be Sent to London by Red Cross", *Sunday Guardian*, 5 October 1941.

52. "Women Asked to Enlist in Local WVS", *Trinidad Guardian*, 3 May 1942.
53. "WVS Great Organisation Known All Over The World", *Trinidad Guardian*, 31 January 1943.
54. NAUK: Colonial Office 875/16/12, Women's Activities in the West Indies, 1 April 1943.
55. "WVS Trains Telephone Operators", *Trinidad Guardian*, 23 May 1942.
56. "Lady Young Sends New Year Greetings", *Trinidad Guardian*, 17 January 1943.
57. "WVS Sends 5,000 Parcels", *Sunday Guardian*, 15 October 1944.
58. "Farewell Talk on WVS Work", *Trinidad Guardian*, 7 October 1942.
59. Women's Activities in the West Indies, 1 April 1943, Colonial Office 875/16/12.
60. Ibid.
61. "WVS Official Reviews Work on Second Anniversary".
62. "Appeal for Old Clothes", *Trinidad Guardian*, 12 June 1942.
63. "WVS Well Organised", *Trinidad Guardian*, 4 July 1942.
64. "WVS Can Help Trinidad's Plant or Die Campaign", *Trinidad Guardian*, 28 June 1942.
65. "WVS Plans Sale of Jams", *Trinidad Guardian*, 12 August 1942.
66. "Central Kitchen for Housewives Supply", *Sunday Guardian*, 1 November 1942.
67. "Service Men Convalesce at Daljarrock".
68. "Farewell Talk on WVS Work", *Trinidad Guardian*, 7 October 1942.
69. "Activities of the WVS Are Many and Widely Varied: Eighteen Sections Including Cooking, Sewing, First Aid and Clerical Work", *Trinidad Guardian*, 16 May 1943.
70. "WVS Silence for Safety", *Sunday Guardian*, 2 August 1942.
71. "New Developments in WVS Work", *Trinidad Guardian*, 4 October 1942.
72. "Farewell Talk on WVS Work".
73. Samuel, "Honouring Women Who Serve".
74. Ibid.
75. "Activities of the WVS Are Many and Widely Varied".
76. "WVS Official Reviews Work on Second Anniversary".
77. Hummingbird, "Talk of Trinidad", *Trinidad Guardian*, 30 May 1940.
78. "Lady Young Praises Guides for Wonderful War Work: Spirit of Self-Sacrifice Stressed at Meeting", *Trinidad Guardian*, 14 November 1940.
79. "Guides part in post-war world stressed at Hemisphere parley", *Trinidad Guardian*, 13 November 1943.
80. "South Girl Guides rally", *Trinidad Guardian*, 22 March 1941.
81. "Fighter Fund", *Trinidad Guardian*, 10 September 1940.

82. See Mabel Brandow, *The History of Our Church Women of Trinidad 1868–1983* (Manitoba: Printed by Friesen Printers, 1983), 1.
83. "Canning Show Tomorrow", *Trinidad Guardian*, 7 November 1940.
84. "Win the War Cookery Book", *Trinidad Guardian*, 13 November 1940.
85. "Win the War Cookery Books", *Trinidad Guardian*, 8 January 1941.
86. These ladies' first names are not mentioned in the sources or in correspondence about them, except Martha Simpson, whose name is known as she herself had written a letter to Lady Young. The references to them are only by their husbands' names, indicative of the status of women then, even in the upper class. They were referred to as Mrs Gilchrist, wife of the acting chief justice; Mrs Skinner, wife of the assistant treasurer; Mrs Macgillivray, wife of the director of lands and surveys; and Mrs Gordon, wife of W.B. Gordon of Gordon Grant and Company.
87. Hummingbird, "Talk of Trinidad", *Trinidad Guardian*, 25 January 1941.
88. "United Services Knitting Group for Trinidad", *Sunday Guardian*, 11 May 1941.
89. "Recreation for Volunteers Advocated", *Trinidad Guardian*, 20 June 1942.
90. See Reddock, *Women, Labour and Politics in Trinidad and Tobago* (Kingston: Ian Randle, 1994); Olga Comma-Maynard, *The Briarend Pattern: The Story of Audrey Jeffers O.B.E. and the Coterie of Social Workers* (Port of Spain: Busbie Printerie, 1971).
91. "Girls Auxiliary to Be Formed in Trinidad", *Trinidad Guardian*, 24 February 1942.
92. "News From U.S. Bases", *Trinidad Guardian*, 24 February 1942.
93. Harvey R. Neptune, *Caliban and the Yankees: Trinidad and the United States Occupation* (Chapel Hill: University of North Carolina Press, 2007), 169.
94. Ibid.
95. "New Dramatic Society to Aid War Charities", *Trinidad Guardian*, 20 October 1940.
96. "At the Sailors and Soldiers Club Tonight", *Trinidad Guardian*, 28 September 1940.
97. "Young People of Trinidad Are a Credit to the Forces", *Trinidad Guardian*, 3 January 1945.

SELECTED BIBLIOGRAPHY

ARCHIVES

Archives of the de Gaulle Foundation (FCDG)
French Colonial Archives, Aix-en-Provence (ANOM)
French Gendarmerie Archives, Vincennes (SHDG)
French Naval Archives, Toulon (SHDMT)
French Naval Archives, Vincennes (SHDMV)
Archives départementales de la Guadeloupe (ADG)
Jamaica Archives and Record Centre
Archives de la Martinique (ADM)
National Archives and Records Administration – Northeast Division (New York City) (NARA-NYC)
National Archives of Trinidad and Tobago (NATT)
National Archives of the United Kingdom, Kew (NAUK)
Red Cross Archives

BOOKS

Abenon, Lucien, and Henry Joseph. *Les Dissidents des Antilles dans les Forces françaises libres combattantes, 1940–1945*. Fort-de-France: Désormeaux, 1999.

Ad van den Oord, Jules Rijssen and Ted Schouten. *Een gemeenschappelijke strijd: Tiburg, Suriname, Aruba en de Antillen in de Tweede Wereldoorlog*. Tilburg: Commissie Wereldoorlog II in de West te Tilburg, 2007.

Alleyne, Warren. *Barbados at War 1939–1945: A Historical Account by Warren Alleyne*. Barbados: Warren Alleyne, 1999.

Anthony, Michael. *The Making of Port-of-Spain*. Vol. 2: *Port-of-Spain in a World at War 1939–1945*. Port of Spain: Ministry of Sport, Culture and Youth Affairs, 1983.

Ayala, César J. and José L. Bolívar. *Battleship Vieques: Puerto Rico from World War II to the Korean War*. Princeton, NJ: Markus Weiner, 2011.

Baptiste, Fitzroy. *War, Cooperation and Conflict: The European Possessions in the Caribbean, 1939–1945*. Westport, CT: Greenwood Press, 1988.

Beruff, Jorge Rodríguez. *Strategy as Politics: Puerto Rico on the Eve of the Second World War*. San Juan: La Editorial Universidad de Puerto Rico, 2007.

Beruff, Jorge Rodriguez, and José L. Bolívar Fresneda, eds. *Puerto Rico en la Segunda Guerra Mundial: Baluarte del Caribe*. San Juan: Ediciones Callejón, 2012.

Bolívar, José L. *Guerra (banca) y desarrollo: El Banco de Fomento y la industrialización de Puerto Rico*. San Juan: Fundación Luis Muñoz Marín/Instituto de Cultura Puertorriqueña, 2011.

Bolland, Nigel O. *The Politics of Labour in the British Caribbean: The Social Origins of Authoritarianism and Democracy in the Labour Movement*. Kingston: Ian Randle, 2001.

———. *On the March: Labour Rebellions in the British Caribbean, 1934–1939*. Kingston: Ian Randle, 1995.

Bosque Pérez, Ramón, and José Javier Colón Morera. *Puerto Rico under Colonial Rule: Political Persecution and the Quest for Human Rights*. Albany, NY: SUNY Press, 2006.

Bousquet, Ben, and Colin Douglas. *West Indian Women at War: British Racism in World War II*. London: Lawrence and Wishart, 1991.

Brand, Twan van den. *De strafkolonie: Een Nederlands concentratiekamp in Suriname 1942–1946*. Amsterdam: Balans, 2006.

Breeveld, Hans. *Baas in eigen huis: Wim Bos Verschuur, heraut van Surinames onafhankelijkheid 1904–1985*. Paramaribo: Uitgeverij Djinipi, 2004.

Brereton, Bridget. *A History of Modern Trinidad, 1783–1962*. Oxford: Heinemann, 1981.

Captain, Esther. *Achter het kawat was Nederland: Indische oorlogservaringen en-herinneringen 1942–1995*. Kampen, Netherlands: Kok, 2002.

Captain, Esther, and Guno Jones. *Oorlogserfgoed overzee: De erfenis van de Tweede Wereldoorlog in Aruba, Curaçao, Indonesië en Suriname*. Amsterdam: Bert Bakker, 2010.

Captain, Esther, Marieke Hellevoort and Marian ven der Klein, eds. *Vertrouwd en vreemd: ontmoetingen tussen Nederland, Indië en Indonesië*. Hilversum, Netherlands: Verloren, 2000.

Caron, Vicki. *Uneasy Asylum: France and the Jewish Refugee Crisis, 1933–1942*. Stanford: Stanford University Press, 1999.

Clyde, David. *Health in Grenada: A Social and Historical Account*. London: Vade-Mecum Press, 1985.

Cohen, Lizbeth. *Making a New Deal: Industrial Workers in Chicago*. Cambridge: Cambridge University Press, 1995.

Comma-Maynard, Olga. *My Yesterdays*. Port of Spain: Granderson Brothers, 1992.

Conn, Stetson, Rose C. Engelman and Byron Fairchild. *Guarding the United States and Its Outposts*. Washington, DC: Center for Military History/US Army, 1964.

Constantine, Stephen. *The Making of British Colonial Policy 1914–1940*. London: Routledge, 2005.

Cwik, Christian, and Verena Muth. *Von Wien nach Barranquilla: Flucht ins karibische Exil, 1938/39. De Viena a Barranquilla: Huida al exilio caribeño, 1938/39*. Vienna: Forschungs- und Kulturverein für Kontinentalamerika und die Karibik, 2012.

de Barros, Juanita, Steven Palmer and David Wright, eds. *Health and Medicine in the Circum-Caribbean 1800–1968*. New York: Routledge, 2009.

de Bossière, Ralph. *Rum and Coca-Cola*. London: Alison and Busby, 1984.

Divine, Robert A. *Roosevelt and World War II*. Baltimore: Johns Hopkins University Press, 1969. Reprint, New York: Penguin, 1977.

Dumont, Jacques. *L'amère patrie: Histoire des Antilles françaises au xxème siècle*. Paris: Fayard, 2010.

Fairbank, Miles H. *The Chardón Plan and the Puerto Rico Reconstruction Administration, 1934–1954*. San Juan: Fairbank Corporation, 1978.

Feingold, Henry L. *The Politics of Rescue: The Roosevelt Administration and the Holocaust, 1938–1945*. New Brunswick, NJ: Rutgers University Press, 1970.

Gleizer, Daniela. *Unwelcome Exiles: Mexico and the Jewish Refugees from Nazism, 1933–1945*. Leiden: Brill, 2014.

Goldstein, Joshua S. *War and Gender: How Gender Shapes the War System and Vice Versa*. Cambridge: Cambridge University Press, 2001.

Hagelberg, G.B. *The Caribbean Sugar Industries: Constraints and Opportunities*. New Haven, CT: Yale University Antilles Research Program, 1974.

Hall, Douglas. *Five of the Leewards 1834–1870: The Major Problems of the Post-Emancipation Period in Antigua, Barbados, Montserrat, Nevis and St Kitts*. Bridgetown: Caribbean Universities Press, 1971.

Harmsen, Jolien, Guy Ellis and Robert Devaux. *A History of St Lucia*. Vieux Fort, St Lucia: Lighthouse Road Publications, 2012.

Hart, Richard. *Towards Decolonisation: Political, Labour and Economic Development in Jamaica 1938–1945*. Kingston: Canoe Press, 1999.

Hemingway, Hilary, and Carlene Brennen, eds. *Hemingway in Cuba*. New York: Rugged Land, 2003.

Hoefte, Rosemarijn, and Peter Meel, eds. *Twentieth-Century Suriname: Continuities and Discontinuities in a New World Society*. Leiden: KITLV Press, 2001.

Honychurch, Lennox. *The Dominica Story: A History of the Island*. Roseau: Dominica Institute, Roseau Division, 1975, 1984.

Howe, Glenford. *Race, War and Nationalism: A Social History of West Indians in the First World War*. Kingston: Ian Randle, 2002.

Hubbard, Vincent. *A History of St Kitts: The Sweet Trade*. London: Macmillan, 2002.

Jennings, Eric. *Vichy in the Tropics*. Stanford: Stanford University Press, 2001.

Jones, Guno. *Tussen onderdanen, rijksgenoten en Nederlanders. Nederlandse politici over burgers uit Oost & West en Nederland 1945–2005*. Amsterdam: Rozenberg, 2007.

Kaplan, Marion A. *Dominican Haven: The Jewish Refugee Settlement in Sosúa 1940–1945*. New York: Museum of Jewish Heritage, 2008.
Kapp, Yvonne, and Margaret Mynatt. *British Policy and the Refugees 1933–1941*. Abingdon, UK: Routledge, 2013.
Katznelson, Ira. *When Affirmative Action Was White: An Untold History of Racial Inequality in Twentieth-Century America*. New York: Norton, 2005.
Kelshall, Gaylord T.M. *The U-Boat War in the Caribbean*. Port of Spain: Paria, 1988. Reprint, Annapolis: Naval Institute Press, 1994.
Kushner, Tony, and Katharine Knox. *Refugees in an Age of Genocide: Global, National and Local Perspectives during the Twentieth Century*. London: Frank Cass, 1999.
Lamur, C., and H.E. Lamur. *Duitse zendelingen in interneringskamp Copieweg 1940–1947: Vrijlating en uitwijzing*. Paramaribo: Herrnhutter Archieven Suriname, 2008.
Leighninger, Robert. *Long-Range Public Investment: The Forgotten Legacy of the New Deal*. Charleston: University of South Carolina Press, 2007.
Leonard, Thomas M., and John F. Bratzel, eds. *Latin America during World War II*. Lanham, MD: Rowman and Littlefield, 2007.
Levine, Robert M. *Tropical Diaspora: The Jewish Experience in Cuba*. Princeton, NJ: Markus Wiener, 2010.
Lewis, Gordon K. *The Growth of the Modern West Indies*. New York: Modern Reader Paperbacks, 1968.
London, Louise. *Whitehall and the Jews 1933–1948: British Immigration Policy and the Holocaust*. Cambridge: Cambridge University Press, 2003.
Macey, David. *Frantz Fanon*. New York: Picador, 2000.
Maingot, Anthony. *The United States and the Caribbean*. Warwick University Caribbean Studies. London: Macmillan Caribbean, 1994.
Mair, L.P. *Welfare in the British Colonies, Royal Institute of International Affairs*. New York: Oxford University Press, 1944.
Maldonado, A.W. *Teodoro Moscoso and Puerto Rico's Operation Bootstrap*. Gainesville: University Press of Florida, 1997.
Martin, Tony. *Caribbean History: From Pre-colonial Origins to the Present*. Boston: Pearson, 2012.
Matos-Rodríguez, Félix V., and Pedro Juan Hernandez. *Pioneros: Puerto Ricans in New York City: 1896–1948*. Charleston: Arcadia, 2001.
Meijer, Hans. *In Indie geworteld. De twintigste eeuw*. Amsterdam: Bert Bakker, 2004.
Miller, Scott, and Sarah A. Ogilvie. *Refuge Denied: The St. Louis Passengers and the Holocaust*. Madison: University of Wisconsin Press, 2006.
Morison, Samuel. *The Two-Ocean War: A Short History of the United States Navy in the Second World War*. Boston: Little, Brown, 1963.

Murray, Robert N., and Patrick L. Hylton. *Lest We Forget: The Experiences of World War II West Indian Ex-Service Personnel*. Nottingham: West Indian Combined Ex-Services Association, 1996.

Neptune, Harvey R. *Caliban and the Yankees: Trinidad and the United States Occupation*. Chapel Hill: University of North Carolina Press, 2007.

Oostindie, Gert, and Inge Klinkers. *Het Koninkrijk in de Caraïben. Een korte geschiedenis van het Nederlandse dekolonisatiebeleid, 1940–2000*. Amsterdam: Amsterdam University Press, 2001.

Pohl, Dieter. *Verfolgung und Massenmord in der NS-Zeit 1939–1945*. Darmstadt: Wissenschaftliche Buchgesellschaft, 2003.

Radford, Gail. *The Rise of the Public Authority: Statebuilding and Economic Development in Twentieth-Century America*. Chicago: University of Chicago Press, 2013.

Rijssen, Jules. *Teken en zie de Wereld, oorlogsveteranen van Suriname*. Amsterdam: KIT, 2012.

Rivas-Rodríguez, Maggie, and B.V. Olguín, eds. *Latina/os and World War II: Mobility, Agency, and Ideology*. Austin: University of Texas Press, 2014.

Rivas-Rodríguez, Maggie, and Emilio Zamora, eds. *Beyond the Latino World War II Hero: The Social and Political Legacy of a Generation*. Austin: University of Texas Press, 2009.

Rodríguez-Silva, Ileana M. *Silencing Race: Disentangling Blackness, Colonialism and National Identities in Puerto Rico*. New York: Palgrave Macmillan, 2012.

Roman, Héctor Marín. *Llego la Gringada! El Contexto Social-Militar Estadounidense en Puerto Rico y otros lugares del Caribe hasta 1919*. San Juan: Academia Puertorriqueña de la Lengua Española, 2009.

Ruggiero, Kristin, ed. *The Jewish Diaspora in Latin America and the Caribbean*. Eastbourne: Sussex Academic Press, 2010.

Scholtens, Ben. *Suriname tijdens de Tweede Wereldoorlog*. Paramaribo: Anton de Kom Universiteit van Suriname, 1985.

Scott, James. *Weapons of the Weak: Everyday Forms of Peasant Resistance*. New Haven, CT: Yale University Press, 1985.

Sempaire, Eliane. *La Guadeloupe an tan Sorin*. Matoury: Ibis rouge, 2004.

Shephard, C.Y. *The Sugar Industry of the British West Indies and British Guiana with Special Reference to Trinidad*. Imperial College of Tropical Agriculture Trinidad Economic Series. St Augustine, Trinidad: Imperial College of Tropical Agriculture, 1929.

Sherwood, Marika. *Many Struggles: West Indian Workers and Service Personnel in Britain (1939–45)*. London: Karia Press, 1985.

Singh, Kelvin. *Race and Class Struggles in a Colonial State: Trinidad 1917–1945*. Kingston: University of the West Indies Press, 1994.

Sint Jago, Junnes E. *Wuiven vanaf de Waranda: De interneringskampen op Bonaire en Curacao tijdens WO II*. Amsterdam: Gopher, 2007.

Smith, Jason Scott. *Building New Deal Liberalism: The Political Economy of Public Works, 1933–1956*.Cambridge: Cambridge University Press, 2006

Smith, Matthew J. *Liberty, Fraternity, Exile: Haiti and Jamaica after Emancipation*. Chapel Hill: University of North Carolina Press, 2014.

Somers, J.A. *Nederlands-Indië: Staatkundige ontwikkelingen binnen een koloniale relatie*. Zutphen, Netherlands: Walburg Pers, 2005.

Stanton, Miriam. *Escape from the Inferno of Europe*. London: M. Stanton, 1996.

Stentiford, Barry M. *The American Home Guard: The State Militia in the Twentieth Century*. College Station: Texas A&M University Press, 2002.

Thomas, Lorrin. *Puerto Rican Citizen: History and Political Identity in the Twentieth Century*. Chicago: University of Chicago Press, 2010.

Thomas, Martin. *Critical Perspectives on Empire: Violence and Colonial Order: Police, Workers and Protest in European Colonial Empires 1918–1940*. Cambridge: Cambridge University Press, 2012.

Timoléon, Jean-Charles. *Chronique du temps passé*. Basse-Terre, GP: OMCS, 1987.

van den Brand, Twan. *De Strafkolonie, een Nederlands concentratiekamp in Suriname 1942–1946*. Amsterdam: Uitgeverij Balans, 2006.

van der Horst, Liesbeth. *Wereldoorlog in de West: Suriname, de Nederlandse Antillen en Aruba 1940–1945*. Hilversum, Netherlands: Verloren, 2004.

Walkowitz, Judith. *Prostitution and Victorian Society: Women, Class, and the State*. Cambridge: Cambridge University Press, 1980.

Watson, Elvey. *The Carib Regiment of World War II*. New York: Vantage Press, 1964.

Wenger, O.C. *Caribbean Medical Center: The Organisation, Development and Activities of the Caribbean Medical Centre at Port of Spain, Trinidad, B.W.I. from 9 February 1943 to 1 March 1945*. Washington, DC: Caribbean Commission, 1946.

Whalen, Carmen Teresa, and Victor Vásquez-Hernández, eds. *The Puerto Rican Diaspora: Historical Perspectives*. Philadelphia: Temple University Press, 2005.

Wike, R.G. *British Empire Civil Censorship Devices, World War II: Trinidad and Tobago*. Perth: Chavril Press, 1993.

Williams, Eric. *From Columbus to Castro: The History of the Caribbean, 1492–1969*. New York: Vintage Books, 1984.

———. *History of the People of Trinidad and Tobago*. London: Andre Deutsch, 1962.

Williams, Gregor. *Unsung War Heroes of Saint Lucia: Honouring the Servicemen and Servicewomen of Saint Lucia*. Castries: Saint Lucia Ex-Service Legion, 2008.

Zabecki, David, ed. *World War II in Europe: An Encyclopaedia*. London: Garland-Taylor and Francis, 1999.

CHAPTERS

Alvarez Curbelo, Silvia. "The Color of War: Puerto Rican Soldiers and Discrimination during World War II". In *Beyond the Latino World War II Hero: The Social and Political Legacy of a Generation*, edited by Maggie Rivas-Rodríguez and Emilio Zamora, 110–24. Austin: University of Texas Press, 2009.

Captain, Esther, and Guno Jones. "The Netherlands: A Small Country with Imperial Ambitions". In *The Age of Empire: Overseas Empires in the Early Modern and Modern World*, edited by Robert Aldridge, 92–111. London: Thames and Hudson, 2007.

Fernández, Ronald. "Chapter 6: Prisoners of War". In *The Disenchanted Island: Puerto Rico and the United States in the Twentieth Century*, Ronald Fernández, 137–64. Westport, CT: Praeger, 1996.

Füllberg-Stolberg, Claus. "The Caribbean in the Second World War". In *UNESCO General History of the Caribbean*. Vol. 5: *The Caribbean in the Twentieth Century*, edited by Bridget Brereton, 82–140. Paris: UNESCO, 2004.

García Muñiz, Humberto. and Rebeca Campo. "French and American Imperial Accommodation in the Caribbean during World War II: The Experience of the Guyane and the Subaltern Roles of Puerto Rico". In *Colonial Crucible: Empire and the Making of the Modern American State*, edited by Alfred W. McCoy and Francisco A. Scarano, 441–52. Madison: University of Wisconsin Press, 2009.

Lindsay-Poland, John. "U.S. Military Bases in Latin America and the Caribbean". In *The Bases of Empire: The Global Struggle against U.S. Military Posts*, edited by Catherine Lutz, 71–95. New York: New York University Press, 2009.

Pengel, Pearl J. "Female Soldiers in Suriname 1942–1946". In *Engagement en distantie: Wetenschap in vele facetten, Liber Amicorum voor Prof. dr. Humphrey E. Lamur*, edited by Edwin Marshall, 33–42. Amsterdam: NiNsee, 2006.

Ramkeesoon, Gema. "Early Women's Organizations in Trinidad: 1920's to 1950's". In *Gender in Caribbean Development: Papers Presented at the Inaugural Seminar of the University of the West Indies*, edited by Patricia Mohammed and Catherine Shepherd, 353–56. Kingston: University of the West Indies, Women and Development Studies Project, 1988.

Roosevelt, Franklin D. "Fireside Chat (on German submarine attacks), Washington D.C., 11 September 1941". In *Franklin Delano Roosevelt: Great Speeches*, edited by John Grafton, 105–13. Mineola, NY: Dover, 1999.

Williams, Eric. "From Slavery to Chaguaramas: Paper Presented at a Meeting in Arima by the Premier, Dr Eric Williams, July 17, 1959". In *Major Party Documents*. Vol. 1, *People's National Movement*. Port of Spain: People's National Movement, 1966.

ARTICLES

Braithwaite, L.E. "America, Over the West Indies". *New Dawn* 1, no. 1 (1 November 1940): 10–11.

Chathuant, Dominique. "La Guadeloupe dans l'obédience de Vichy (1940–1943)". *Bulletin de la Société d'Histoire de la Guadeloupe* 91 (1992): 3–40.

Dooley, Edwin. "Wartime San Juan: The Forgotten American Home Front, 1941–1946". *Journal of Military History* 63, no. 4 (October 1999): 921–38.

Elisabeth, Léo. "Vichy aux Antilles et en Guyane, 1940–1943". *Outre-mers, Revue d'Histoire* 342 (2004):145–74.

Gigliotti, Simone. "'Acapulco in the Atlantic': Revisiting Sosúa, a Jewish Refugee Colony in the Caribbean". *Immigrants and Minorities* 24, 1 (2006): 22–50.

Jennings, Eric. "La dissidence aux Antilles, 1940–1943". *Vingtième Siècle, Revue d'histoire* 68 (October-December 2000): 55–71.

———. "Last Exit from Vichy France: The Martinique Escape Route and the Ambiguities of Emigration". *Journal of Modern History* 74, no. 2 (2002): 289–324.

McCollin, Debbie. "Friend or Foe: Venereal Diseases and the American Presence in Trinidad and Tobago during World War II". *History in Action* 1, no.1 (2010): 1–12.

Lansen, Oscar E. "Victims of Circumstance: Jewish Enemy Nationals in the Dutch West Indies 1938–1947". *Holocaust and Genocide Studies* 13, no. 3 (1999): 441–42.

Pantojas-García, Emilio. "End-of-the-Century Studies of Puerto Rico's Economy, Politics and Culture: What Lies Ahead?" *Latin American Research Review* 35, no. 3 (2000): 227–40.

———. "The Puerto Rican Paradox: Colonialism Revisited". *Latin American Research Review* 40, no. 3 (2005): 163–76.

Potworowski, Tomasz. "The Evacuation of Jewish Polish Citizens from Portugal to Jamaica 1941–1943". *Polin* 19 (2007): 155–82.

Ramsoedh, Hans. "Rumcola en Yankee-dollars". *OSO, Tijdschrift voor Surinaamse Taalkunde, Letterkunde, Cultuur en Geschiedenis* 14, no. 2 (1995): 135–47.

Saunders, Gail. "The 1942 Riot in Nassau: A Demand for Change?" *Journal of Caribbean History* 20, no. 2 (1985–1986): 117–46.

Teelucksingh, Jerome. "Political Ambitions and Contributions to Trade Unionism: Tubal Uriah 'Buzz' Butler during the 1930s and 1940s". *Caribbean Journal of Labour and Co-operative Studies* 1, no. 1 (October 2012): 1–15.

PAPERS AND DISSERTATIONS

Brereton, Bridget. "A Loyal Opposition? Trinidad's Left Wing Press and World War II". Paper presented at Staff Seminar Series 2015, Department of History, University of the West Indies, St Augustine, 10 April 2015.

Burrows, Geoff. "The New Deal in Puerto Rico: Public Works, Public Health and the Puerto Rico Reconstruction Administration, 1935–1955". PhD dissertation, CUNY Graduate Center, 2014.

Devaux, Robert. "History of the US Army Air Force Base Beane Field, St Lucia". Research paper, St Lucia Research Centre, 2000.

———. "History of the US Naval Air Station Reduit, St Lucia, 1939–1947". Research paper, St Lucia Research Centre, 2003.

———. "Military Face of Castries: The Free French". Research paper, St Lucia Research Centre, 1995.

———. "Recollections of the US Naval Base at Reduit". Research paper, St Lucia Research Centre, 1995.

Francis-Brown, Suzanne. "Gibraltar Camp 1940–1947: Isolation and Interaction in Colonial Jamaica". PhD dissertation, University of the West Indies, 2007.

Franqui-Rivera, Harry. "Fighting for the Nation: Military Service, Popular Political Mobilization and the Creation of Modern Puerto Rican National Identities: 1868–1952". PhD dissertation, University of Massachusetts Amherst, 2010.

Harmsen, Jolien. "Down the Line: Four Generations in a Caribbean Town, 1910–1998". PhD dissertation, Erasmus University, Rotterdam, 1999.

McCollin, Debbie. "The History of Health and Healthcare in Trinidad and Tobago 1938–1962". PhD dissertation, University of the West Indies, 2010.

Newman, Joanna. "Nearly the New World: Refugees and the British West Indies, 1933–1945". PhD dissertation, University of Southampton, 1998.

Pemberton, Rita. "The Evolution of Agricultural Policy in Trinidad and Tobago 1890–1945". PhD dissertation, University of the West Indies, St Augustine, 1997.

Saunders, Gail. "The Social History of the Bahamas, 1890–1953". PhD dissertation, University of Waterloo, 1985.

DOCUMENTS AND REPORTS

Bentley, Thomas. "Acquisition of Territory for US Air Base. Historical Report". Declassified Secret Report, United States Military, 5 May 1945.

Great Britain, *Report of the West India Royal Commission (1938–1939)*. London: His Majesty's Stationery Office, 1945.

Lada, John, ed. *Civil Affairs/Military Government Public Health Activities Preventive Medicine in World War II*. Vol. 8. Washington, DC: Office of the Surgeon General, Department of the Army, 1976.

Maxwell Air Force Base, Alabama. 24 August 1949 "Historical Report Beane Air Force Base, 1941–1949". Declassified Secret Report, Headquarters 5900th

Composite Wing Ramey Air Force Base, Puerto Rico. Microfilm roll A0030. Copy provided by Air Force Historical Research Agency.

Trinidad and Tobago. *Report of the Committee Appointed to Enquire into the Sugar Industry*. Council Paper No. 1 of 1944. Port of Spain: Government Printing Office, 1944.

Trinidad and Tobago. *Report of the Commission Appointed to Enquire into the Working of the Sugar Industry in Trinidad, 1948*. Port of Spain: Government Printing Office, 1948.

US House of Representatives. "Lend Lease Bill, dated January 10, 1941". HR 77A-D13, Record Group 233, National Archives.

INDEX

Afghanistan, 247
Africa, 7, 17, 58, 77, 125, 129, 133, 145, 162, 230, 242, 249, 252, 277, 279–81, 283–84, 294–96, 299, 392
agricultural production, 93, 132, 332, 335
Air Raid Precaution Organization (ARP), 363–64, 369
Air Raid Relief Centres, 371
Air Training Scheme, 358, 364
All Trinidad Sugar Estates and Factory Workers Trade Union, 19–21
Americans, vi, 6, 9,11,35, 44, 52, 94–95, 99, 115, 151, 153, 155–58, 163–64, 167–69, 171, 177–80, 184, 186, 193, 201, 205, 208–9, 211–14, 217, 226–27, 234, 241, 330, 346, 348
Amsterdam, 13, 85, 88–90, 261–62, 264, 269, 376, 382–87, 391
Anglo-American Destroyers for Bases Agreement, 6, 9, 21, 51, 55, 64, 93, 94, 154, 177–81, 182, 183, 185, 187, 190, 198, 205, 206, 210, 217
Anglo-American Caribbean Commission, 103, 219, 351, 356
Antigua: Antigua Distillery Limited, 210; Antigua Trades and Labour Union (ATLU), 211
Argentina, 49, 57, 111, 252
Army Nurses Corps, 52
Aruba, viii, 3, 5, 47, 48, 63, 77, 79, 82, 83, 84, 88, 89, 90, 207, 249, 253, 256, 269, 330, 336, 337, 381, 382, 386
Asia, 7, 17, 80, 250, 264
Australia, 249, 252, 322, 351
Austria, 192, 248, 251, 258, 259, 260, 261, 263, 271, 292
Auxiliary Military Pioneer Corps, 281
Auxiliary Territorial Services (ATS), 2, 215, 357, 360–62, 376, 377

Bahamas, 5, 51, 57, 66, 155, 206, 217, 249, 338, 352, 389
Balata Internment Camp, 128, 129
Barbados, 5, 152, 157, 163, 210, 212, 218, 249, 250, 261, 263, 265, 217, 322, 331–34, 336–38, 341, 345, 352–54, 360, 381, 383
Barbuda, 5, 215, 218–19, 352
bases: Beane Field, 163, 168, 169, 172, 175, 389; Coolidge, 10, 206, 208–9, 212, 213, 216; Crabs, 10, 206, 208–9, 216; Reduit, 9, 155–56, 158, 160–63, 165, 171–74, 389
bauxite, 5, 8, 48, 72, 76–78, 177, 207, 330
beet sugar, 207
Belgium, 78, 153, 251, 259, 260, 265
Benham Committee, 27, 29, 30, 32, 34
Bermuda, 51, 57, 155, 178, 206, 213, 219, 250, 279, 299, 300
Bermuda Conference, 250

391

black markets, 333
body politics, vi, 221, 222, 240
Bonaire, 4, 5, 13, 111, 253, 255–57, 266, 269, 386
Brazil, 46–47, 51, 57, 63, 77, 127, 130, 207, 252, 266
Brechin Castle, 23
British Guiana, 5, 34, 51, 57, 155, 178, 206–7, 249–50, 253, 255, 265, 269, 271, 288, 332, 338, 341, 343–46, 349, 352, 355, 385
British Honduras, 5, 57, 249–50, 268, 271, 281, 349, 352, 355
British Red Cross Society (BRCS), 358, 363, 366, 373
brothels, 305–6, 308–9, 311, 313, 316, 320, 323, 326

Camp Copieweg, 257
Canada, 7, 46, 57, 111–12, 133, 145, 154–56, 262, 277, 316, 371, 392
Canadian Women's Army Corps, 360
cane farmers, 22, 27, 36, 103
Caribbean Medical Centre (CMC), 13, 334, 348–49, 353–54, 386
Caribbean Regiment, 215, 277
Caribbean Sea Frontier, v, 39, 43, 46, 48, 50, 54, 56, 62
Caroni Limited, 24, 30, 33, 36
Casualty Clearing Stations, 338, 363, 364
Cayenne, 154
censorship, 97, 98, 134, 197, 232, 276, 359, 360, 370, 377, 386
Chile, 47, 57, 107, 265
Chinese Association, 366
Chinese Patriotic Relief Fund, 366
Colombia, 48–49, 57, 135, 247, 249, 254–55, 261, 263, 270
Colonial Defense Regulations, 95, 98, 195, 359

Colonial Development and Welfare Fund (CD&W), 343–47
common houses, 311
communicable diseases, 341, 350
concentration camp, 232, 257, 259, 260–61, 288
conscription, 3, 41, 78
Control of Medical Supplies Regulation, 334
convoy system, 7, 46, 333, 352
cost of living, 97, 113, 116, 141, 168, 335
Coterie of Social Workers, 374, 380
Cuba, vii, 3, 6–7, 13, 44, 46, 50, 57, 62, 111, 154, 199, 207, 249, 250, 252, 255, 256–58, 261–66, 269, 296, 333, 383–84
Curaçao, viii, 3–5, 13, 25, 35, 47–48, 63, 73–79, 82–88, 207, 249, 253–57, 266, 269, 279, 288–89, 336, 282, 286
Czechoslovakia, 143, 248, 254, 258, 262

Daljarrock, 365, 369, 378–79
Denmark, 111, 153, 259, 260
detainees, 279, 281–82, 298
diseases, ix, 11, 57, 164, 238, 307–8, 310, 313–15, 317–19, 321, 323, 325, 328–29, 331, 334, 338–41, 343, 345, 347–48, 350–51, 355, 388
displaced persons, 10, 98–99, 247, 258–59, 273, 296
Dominica, viii, ix, 5, 130, 133–35, 139, 141–43, 336, 345, 349, 352–53, 383
Dominican Republic, viii, 6, 47, 57, 127, 131, 249, 250, 252–53, 255, 256, 260, 263–64, 270, 333
Dutch Antilles, v, 8, 71–72, 74, 76–79, 82–85, 87
Dutch East Indies, 71–75, 78–79, 81, 89
Dutch Guiana, 250

Dutch Resistance Movement, 79

Ecuador, 57, 66
Egypt, 215, 319, 326
El Salvador, 57
Emergency Relief Appropriation Act, 54, 68
Emergency War Gardens, 103
emigration, 255, 260, 264, 267–68, 270, 336, 388
Encumbered Estates Act, 207
enemy aliens, 253, 257, 278–79, 281–83, 296, 298, 300, 359
England, 110, 134, 212, 286, 307, 358, 364, 367–68, 370, 372–73, 378
estates: Antigua Sugar Estate, 204, 208, 210–12; Betty's Hope, 210, 212, 218; Brown's, 210; Colebrook, 210; Harman's, 210; Hope's, 210; Lynch's, 210; Millar's, 209
Ethiopia, 192, 268
evacuees, viii, 273–74, 277, 286, 292, 294–95, 299, 300, 359
Evian Conference, 252

fascism, 5, 190–93, 202, 251, 258
Female Home Guard, 78
Fighting French, 130, 141, 144
Finland, 290
First Aid Posts, 38, 363
Florida, 4, 6, 46, 61, 206, 384
food: bill, 100–101, 116; imports, 40, 46, 100–101; issues, 95; prices, 101–2, 332, 333; production, viii, 92, 94, 101, 103–4, 106–8, 110–12, 116, 333, 368; resources, 100; shortages, viii, 93, 98–99, 111, 113, 132, 332–33; strategy, 94–95, 103–4, 107; supplies, 8, 100, 162, 331–32, 336, 340
Foraker Act, 223, 224

Fort Desaix, 154
Fort-de-France, 126–29, 131–32, 134, 137, 141–44, 148–50, 154, 161, 249, 266, 381
France, vii, 5, 9, 12, 125–34, 137–39, 141–50, 153–54, 157, 161, 121, 231, 233, 249, 250, 254–56, 258–59, 260, 262–64, 266, 268, 287, 331, 336, 366, 378, 381–82, 388
Free French Army, 336
Free French Fighting Force, 163
Free French Movement, 125, 133
Freemasons, 138
French Guiana, 142, 249, 250, 253, 265
funds: Aruba Relief, 82; Fighter, 358, 362, 371–75, 379; Grapefruit, 358; Navy, 358, 359; Seamen's, 358; Spitfire, 83, 358; Submarine, 83; Tobacco, 358; War Relief, 83

Gaullist, 133–34, 136, 139, 141–42, 145
Gendarmerie, 134, 139–40, 142, 148, 149, 381
German Jews, 142, 261, 270, 275, 281
German missionaries, 75
Germany, 6, 39, 47, 50, 58, 74, 110, 125, 129, 134, 143, 153–54, 157, 162, 178, 185, 191–92, 199, 206, 231, 248, 249, 251, 257–62, 264, 274, 280, 285, 343
Gibraltar Camp, 269, 274, 278, 284–91, 293, 294–97, 299, 300–301, 389
Girl Guides, 338, 358, 371, 376, 379
Girls Talent Club, 375
Great Depression, 40–44, 50, 53–54, 56–57, 60–61, 204, 207, 224–26, 228
Greece, 259
Grow More Food Campaign, 94, 102, 104, 106, 110, 116, 368

394   INDEX

Guadeloupe, viii, 2–3, 5, 13, 125–43, 146–50, 154, 381, 385, 388
Guantánamo Bay, 6, 46, 57
Guatemala, 57
Guyana. *See* British Guiana

Haiti, viii, 6, 57, 149, 249, 250, 253, 256, 333, 386
Hanover Street camp, 283, 285, 294
Hawaii, 36, 157, 265
health conditions, 11, 229, 329, 335
health service, 328, 337, 349, 351, 356
healthcare, 330, 342, 345, 347, 352, 353, 389
High Point Canfield, 209
Hillcote, 365
Hitlerism, 190–91
hoarding, 109, 114, 133
Holland, 84, 111, 259
home gardens, 331
Home Hospitality Programme, 374–75
Home Workers Service, 368
hooliganism, 99–100, 116
housing, 42, 53, 56, 156, 164–65, 169, 290, 292, 329, 335, 336
human experimentation, 222, 233, 240
Hungary, 254
hunger marches, 97

imperialism, v-vi, 7, 9, 57, 123, 176, 191, 193, 195, 202, 223, 242, 328, 391
Indonesia, 71–74, 79–81
infectious diseases, 329, 331, 340
inflation, 8, 61, 94
internee camps, 257
internment camps, 254–55, 274, 278, 280, 284, 286, 294, 298, 359. *See also* Gibraltar Camp
Iran, 247

Italy, 6, 63, 154, 157, 192, 206, 215, 248, 259

Jamaica Defence Regulations, 275–76
Japan, 6, 30, 47, 50, 74, 169, 206, 265
Jewish Ladies Association, 368
Jews, 138, 142, 251–53, 256–57, 259, 261, 264, 269, 270, 275, 278, 281, 287, 288, 291, 384
Jones Act, 41, 60, 223, 225, 226
Jones-Shafroth Act, 41

labour: riots, 20, 25, 118, 211; shortage, 20, 94
Ladies Shirt Guild, 358, 372
Land Acquisition Ordinance, 181–82, 187, 190
League of Surinamese War Veterans, 81
Lebanon, 247
Liebenau Camp, 285
lodging houses, 304, 305, 311, 320
Louisiana Purchase, 207

malaria, 68–69, 225, 329, 334, 344–45, 347–48, 355
Malaya, 50
malnourishment, 333
Malta, 274, 286
Manchuria, 192, 264, 268
Manifest Destiny, 176, 178
Martinique, viii, 5, 9, 125–46, 148–49, 153–54, 156, 158, 161–63, 173, 249, 153, 255, 257, 259, 264–66, 268, 344, 365, 378, 381, 388
Medical Centre, 13, 334, 348–49, 353–54, 386
medicine, 325, 327, 343, 344, 351, 354–55, 383, 389
Mexico, 46–47, 241, 249, 250, 254–56, 259, 263, 266, 268, 270, 383

Midwives Association, 359
Mill Reef Club, 214
Mona Family Camp, 278, 284, 294
Monroe Doctrine, 77, 127, 176, 178
Monuments of Gratitude, 85
Moyne Commission, 18, 28, 97, 309, 329, 343, 352
Mutual Aid Good Neighbours Association (MAGNA), 369–70

Nazism, 3, 126, 142, 190, 192, 202, 268, 275, 383
Negro Welfare Cultural and Social Association (NWCSA), 195, 197
Nelson's Island, 24, 32
neo-imperialism, 328
Netherlands, v, 3, 8, 13, 71–72, 74, 77–80, 82–85, 87–89, 126, 153, 250–51, 256, 259–61, 269, 282, 286–87, 391–92
Neutrality Acts, 51
New Deal, 42–45, 51, 55–56, 58–62, 67–68, 382, 384, 386, 389
Newfoundland, 51, 57, 127, 155, 178, 206, 330
Nicaragua, 57
Nigeria, 278–79, 285
Normandy, 231–32, 238
North Africa, 133, 162, 295
nurses, 52, 157, 337–38, 346–47, 349, 355, 357–59, 361, 364–65, 367, 377
nursing, 209, 338, 344, 358–59, 362–64, 376, 378

oil industry, 26, 77, 96, 191, 203, 336
Oilfield Workers Trade Union (OWTU), 19, 33, 191–92, 194
Operation Bootstrap, 61, 235, 384

Pacific, 12, 17, 21, 40, 47–49, 57, 125, 141, 157, 264–66, 330, 346
Palestine, 251–52
Panama, 4, 21, 48–49, 50, 53, 57, 63, 69, 154–55, 163, 207, 233–34, 243, 249, 254–55, 265, 330
Paraguay, 57
Parham's Harbor, 212
Pearl Harbor, 6, 36, 46, 47–51, 56, 63, 69, 90, 157, 228, 387
Peru, 57, 136
petroleum, 25, 177, 277
Philippines, 50
Poland, 153, 243, 248, 254, 257, 259–60, 271, 387
Portugal, 259, 263–64, 301, 388
Portuguese Association, 366
postal services, 357–58
poverty, 6, 18, 68, 84, 116, 170, 205, 207, 224, 226, 228, 237, 240, 242, 335
prisoners of war (POWs), 81, 274, 279–82, 288, 295, 296
profiteering, 93, 109, 110, 111, 114
prostitution, 11, 165, 205, 303–5, 307–9, 310–12, 315, 319–24, 386
Public Health Engineering Unit, 348
Puerto Rico Reconstruction Administration (PRRA), 42–44, 51, 53–56, 58–61, 67–68, 383, 389

ration cards, 107, 130, 367
rationing, 8, 94, 107, 109, 277, 284, 327, 333, 367
Robert-Greenslade Accord, 127
Rockefeller Foundation, 347–48, 350–51, 355
Romania, 254, 257–58, 266
Royal Air Force (RAF), 215, 277, 358, 371
Royal Naval Club, 358

sanitation, 42, 290, 327, 329–30, 335, 336, 344
schooner pool, 7, 103, 333
segregation, 52, 58, 65–66, 81, 167, 222, 229, 233, 285, 314
Sierra Leone, 279
social diseases, 331
Somalia, 247
South Africa, 252
South Caribbean Area, 360–61, 373
South Caribbean Forces, 336
South Women's Auxiliary Corps, 362
Spanish Civil War, 249, 253, 254, 255, 258
St James Barracks, 261, 360–61
St John's Deep Water Harbor, 214
St Lucia, 143, 159–60, 174, 349
Ste Madeleine Sugar Company, 24, 30, 33, 36
Sudan, 247
sugar: companies, 22, 23, 27, 32–33, 38, 152; estates, 19, 21, 23, 29, 35–36, 107, 204, 208, 210–12; factories, 204, 208, 210; prices, 29, 34, 38, 97; production, 17, 23, 24, 30–31; workers, 18–19, 22, 24, 28–30, 32, 33–34, 152, 211
Sugar Duties Equalization Act, 20, 207
Support to Dutch War Victims (SANOA), 82
Switzerland, 111, 251, 260, 263, 264
Syria, 247

Tate and Lyle, 24, 33
temperance bars, 311, 316
tourism, 9, 170, 213, 214, 217, 322
Trade Union Act of 1939, 211
trade unions, 9, 19–20, 38, 177, 190–99, 211, 320, 326
trade unionism, 38, 192, 193, 198, 388

Trinidad Goat Society, 109
Trinidad Junior War Workers, 364
Trinidad Light Infantry Volunteers, 358
Trinidad Royal Naval Volunteer Reserve, 358
Trinidad and Tobago, v-xi, 5, 8–9, 22, 25, 29, 31, 35–38, 57, 66, 92, 93, 95–97, 100–102, 104, 107, 116–18, 121, 163, 176, 178, 184, 191, 193, 194, 198, 200–202, 217, 249, 253, 255, 257, 259, 261–62, 266, 270, 328, 321, 347, 351–53, 355, 366, 377, 380, 381, 386, 388–92
Turkey, 247
typhoid, 165, 229, 340–41, 350

United Kingdom, 18, 35, 46, 51, 58, 118, 127–28, 143, 146, 174, 206, 218, 268, 275–76, 280, 297, 299, 352–56, 377
United Services Knitting Association (USKA), 373, 380
United States War Food Administration, 337
Up Park Camp, 394, 360
Up Park Military Camp, 353
Uruguay, 47, 49, 57, 63

venereal diseases, ix, 11, 315, 317–18, 323, 325, 328, 334, 338–39, 343, 351, 355, 388
Venezuela, 25, 46, 57, 77, 100, 112, 206–7, 249, 254–56, 261, 263, 265, 271, 337
veterans, 62, 80–81, 137, 215, 222, 224–25, 228, 230–31, 233, 235–39, 242
Vichy France, 9, 125, 127, 157, 249, 258, 268, 388
Vichy regime, 126, 239, 154, 162
Virgin Islands, 5, 249, 352

Voluntary Aid Detachments (VADs), 363

"war aphrodisiac", 306, 313
War Manpower Commission, 216, 337
West Africa, 277, 279, 280–81, 283, 284, 294, 299
Win the War Association, 358, 362, 372–74

Women's Army Auxiliary Corps, 230
Women's Camp, 276, 280, 283–84
Women's Emergency Corps (WEC), 357, 362
Women's Voluntary Services (WVS), 370
Woodford Lodge, 30, 36

CONTRIBUTORS

KAREN E. ECCLES is Faculty Liaison Librarian, Faculty of Humanities and Education, Alma Jordan Library, the University of the West Indies, St Augustine, Trinidad and Tobago.

DEBBIE McCOLLIN is Lecturer, Department of History, the University of the West Indies, St Augustine, Trinidad and Tobago. Her publications include the edited volume *In the Fires of Hope: Essays on the Modern History of Trinidad and Tobago, 1962–2012*.

DALEA BEAN is Lecturer and Graduate Coordinator, Regional Coordinating Office, Institute for Gender and Development Studies, the University of the West Indies, Mona, Jamaica.

BRIDGET BRERETON is Emerita Professor of History, the University of the West Indies, St Augustine, Trinidad and Tobago. Her many publications include *Race Relations in Colonial Trinidad, 1870–1900* and *A History of Modern Trinidad, 1783–1962*.

GEOFF BURROWS is an independent scholar of Latin American history. He focuses on the history of Puerto Rico and the legacy of US imperialism in the Hispanic Caribbean.

ESTHER CAPTAIN is a historian and head of the Knowledge Centre, Amsterdam, University of Applied Sciences, the Netherlands.

CHRISTIAN CWIK is Lecturer in European and Atlantic History, the University of the West Indies, St Augustine, Trinidad and Tobago.

ROBERT DEVAUX (d. 2013) was Director, St Lucia National Trust, and founder of the St Lucia Research Centre. His many publications include *St Lucia Historic Sites*; *A Century of Coaling in St Lucia*; *History and Analysis of Coastal Processes at Pigeon Island* and *They Called Us Brigands: The Saga of St Lucia's Freedom Fighters*. He is also co-author of *A History of St Lucia*.

GUY ELLIS is the former editor of the *Voice of St Lucia*, the island's leading newspaper, and author of *St Lucia* and *Saint Lucia: Helen of the West*.

LOVELL FRANCIS is Member of Parliament for Moruga/Tableland, Trinidad, and was appointed Minister of State in the Ministry of Education in Trinidad and Tobago in 2015.

SUZANNE FRANCIS-BROWN is Curator, Museum of the University of the West Indies, Mona, Jamaica. Her publications include *Mona: Past and Present: The History and Heritage of the Mona Campus, University of the West Indies* and *The Iron Bridge, Spanish Town, Jamaica*.

DANNELLE GUTARRA is Lecturer, Princeton Writing Program, Princeton University, New Jersey, United States.

JOLIEN HARMSEN is a Dutch historian based in St Lucia. Her publications include *Sugar, Slavery and Settlement: A Social History of Vieux Fort, St Lucia* and the novel *Rum Justice*. She is co-author of *A History of St Lucia*.

ERIC T. JENNINGS is Professor of History, University of Toronto, Canada. His books include *Free French Africa in World War II*; *Dalat and the Making and Undoing of French Indochina*; *Curing the Colonizers*; and *Vichy in the Tropics*.

GUNO JONES is a post-doc researcher, Faculty of Humanities, Institute for History, Leiden University, the Netherlands.

GELIEN MATTHEWS is Lecturer, Department of History, the University of the West Indies, St Augustine, Trinidad and Tobago. She is the author of *Caribbean Slave Revolts and the British Abolitionist Movement* and *History of the Church of the Nazarene in Trinidad and Tobago*.

VERENA MUTH is co-researcher in a project on flight and onward migration of Germans and Austrians to and from the Caribbean between 1933 and 1955 (University of Cologne, University of Graz, Future Fund of the Republic of Austria).

RITA PEMBERTON is an independent researcher and former Senior Lecturer, Department of History, the University of the West Indies, St Augustine, Trinidad and Tobago.

RONALD WILLIAMS teaches history, Caribbean studies and social studies at Trinity College, Moka, Maraval, Trinidad and Tobago.

www.ingramcontent.com/pod-product-compliance
Lightning Source LLC
Chambersburg PA
CBHW051243300426
44114CB00011B/866